APPLYING SOCIAL COGNITION TO CONSUMER-FOCUSED STRATEGY

Advertising and Consumer Psychology

A Series sponsored by the Society for Consumer Psychology

Aaker/Biel: *Brand Equity & Advertising: Advertising's Role in Building Strong Brands* (1993)

Clark/Brock/Stewart: *Attention, Attitude, and Affect in Response Advertising* (1994)

Englis: *Global and Multi-NationalAdvertising* (1994)

Goldberg/Fishbein/Middlestadt: *Social Marketing: Theoretical and Practical Perspectives* (1997)

Haugtvedt/Machleit/Yalch: *Online Consumer Psychology: Understanding and Influencing Consumer Behavior in the Virtual World* (2005)

Kahle/Chiagouris: *Values, Lifestyles, and Psychographics* (1997)

Kahle/Riley: *Sports Marketing and the Psychology of Marketing Communications* (2003)

Kardes/Herr/Nantel: *Applying Social Cognition to Consumer-Focused Strategy* (2005)

Mitchell: *Advertising Exposure, Memory, and Choice* (1993)

Schumann/Thorson: *Advertising and the World Wide Web* (1999)

Scott/Batra: *Persuasive Imagery: A Consumer Response Perspective* (2003)

Shrum: *The Psychology of Entertainment Media: Blurring the Lines Between Entertainment and Persuasion* (2004)

Thorson/Moore: *Integrated Communication: Synergy of Persuasive Voices* (1996)

Wells: *Measuring Advertising Effectiveness* (1997)

Williams/Lee/Haugtvedt: *Diversity in Advertising: Broadening the Scope of Research Directions* (2004)

APPLYING SOCIAL COGNITION TO CONSUMER-FOCUSED STRATEGY

Edited by

Frank R. Kardes
Uthversity of Cincinnati

Paul M. Herr
University of Colorado

Jacques Nantel
HEC Montreal

LEA LAWRENCE ERLBAUM ASSOCIATES, PUBLISHERS
2005   Mahwah, New Jersey   London

Lawrence Erlbaum Associates, Inc., Publishers
10 Industrial Avenue
Mahwah, New Jersey 07430
www.erlbaum.com

Cover design by Kathryn Houghtaling Lacey

Library of Congress Cataloging-in-Publication Data

Applying social cognition to consumer-focused strategy / edited by Frank R.
Kardes, Paul N. Herr, Jacques Nantel.
   p.   cm.
"Contains edited versions of papers presented at the 23rd annual Advertising
and Consumer Psychology Conference, which was held on May 21–23, 2004"—Pref.
Includes bibliographical references and index.
ISBN 0-8058-5520-3 (alk. paper)
   1. Consumer behavior.   2. Marketing—Psychological aspects.   3. Advertising—
Psychological aspects.   4. Cognition—Social aspects.   I. Kardes, Frank R.
II. Herr, Paul, 1956–   III. Nantel, Jacques.   IV. Conference on Advertising and
Consumer Psychology (23rd : 2004 : Montréal, Québec)
HF5415.32.A67   2005
658.8′342—dc22   2004065024
                                                                          CIP

Contents

Preface

The field of social cognition has made many innovative and important contributions to advertising and consumer psychology—including models of persuasion, the attitude–behavior relation, judgment and inference, cognitive representation, decision making, and many other important topics. This volume focuses on the most important recent developments at the interface of social cognition and marketing, and the contributors were encouraged to develop integrative theoretical frameworks with rich practical implications. Because most leading academic journals in psychology and in marketing discourage integrative theorizing and detailed discussion of the practical implications of one's research, this volume provides a unique outlet for this type of work. More specifically, the chapters in this volume offer a novel and thought-provoking perspective on consumer-focused strategy—or the effects of marketing stimuli and activities (e.g., promotion and advertising, branding strategies, product-line management, online and bricks-and-mortar retailing strategies) on an integrated system of consumer processes and responses (e.g., consumer information processing, judgment, inference, and decision making).

This volume contains edited versions of papers presented at the 23rd Annual Advertising and Consumer Psychology Conference, which was held on May 21–23, 2004, in Montreal, Canada. The conference was co-sponsored by the Society for Consumer Psychology, HEC Montreal, the RBC Financial Group Chair of E-Commerce (held by Jacques Nantel), and Allard Johnson Communications. The conference was co-chaired by Frank R. Kardes, Paul M. Herr, and Jacques Nantel, and we wish to thank our sponsors for their generous support. In our opinion, the papers presented at the conference were novel, important, and intellectually stimulating, and it is a pleasure to share these ideas with others through this edited volume.

The conference opened with an invited keynote address by Professor Robert S. Wyer, Jr., one of the founding fathers of the field of social cognition. Professor Wyer has held faculty positions in psychology and in marketing departments, and is, therefore, in a unique position to encourage and guide integrative theorizing that spans across the fields of psychology and marketing. He is the most prolific author in the history of the prestigious *Journal of Personality and Social Psychology* (50 articles), and is the recipient of the Ostrom Award and the Alexander von Humboldt Special Research Prize for Distinguished Scientists. The field of consumer psychology is also indebted to Professor Wyer for his distinguished service as the current Editor of our flagship journal, the *Journal of Consumer Psychology*. Professor Wyer's keynote address is presented in Chapter 1. This remarkable chapter develops a new theory of consumer information processing that integrates social cognition and behavioral decision research.

The book is organized in four subsections with an invited chapter leading each subsection. Wyer's chapter leads the first subsection on new perspectives on consumer information processing. This section also includes chapters by Posavac et al. on selective or one-sided information processing, and Silvera and Laufer on attribution theory.

The subsection on new perspectives on consumer information processing and research methods is led by a chapter by Machin and Fitzsimons on how asking questions in focus groups, surveys, and experiments leads consumers to create opinions that would not have occurred to them otherwise (i.e., in the absence of questioning). These opinions then take on a life of their own and influence other related judgments and responses. Chandrashekaran et al. advance a new approach for modeling uncertainty and a new framework for thinking about uncertainty. Tietje and Brunel summarize recent developments concerning the Implicit Association Test and their implications for branding strategy. March and Woodside develop a new approach for analyzing the effects of intention on behavior and for analyzing unplanned purchase behaviors.

Markman and Brendl's chapter on the devaluation effect, or the tendency to devalue objects unrelated to focal goals, leads the subsection on new perspectives on motivation and consumer information processing. This chapter and the following chapter by Chun and Kruglanski builds on Kruglanski's theory of goal systems. Kardes et al. show how implementation intentions can be used to increase new product consumption, and Florack et al. show how promotion versus prevention regulatory focus influences consumer preferences.

The final subsection focuses on consumer information processing and persuasion and is led by a remarkable chapter by Strahan, Spencer, and Zanna on how subliminal priming procedures enhance persuasion when primed goals match currently accessible goals. Dimofte and Yalch demonstrate that advertising can be effective even when consumers do not believe advertised claims. Mazzocco et al. review evidence demonstrating that advertising can be effective even when consumers are unable to remember critical details conveyed in advertised messages. Goodstein et al. show that negative comparative advertising can backfire initially but can have more desirable consequences later as time passes (similar to the sleeper effect). Yoon and Vargas show how counterfactual reasoning can alter the way consumers interpret prices, and Eighmey and Siu show how dual-process models, the theory of reasoned action, media priming, and consideration set processes shape decisions to join the military in the wake of September 11, 2001. Finally, Herr et al. provide a brief summary of the chapters presented in this volume and offer some suggestions for future research.

As the reader can infer from the complexity of the topics listed, this volume is intended for advanced graduate students, academics, and practitioners who embrace cutting-edge paradigms and methodologies in social-cognitive consumer research. Like the other volumes in the Lawrence Erlbaum Associates' series on Advertising and Consumer Psychology, this volume is unique because it targets highly knowledgeable readers and most publishers are unwilling to pursue this relatively small market segment. We thank Lawrence Erlbaum and Associates for their boldness and their willingness to serve this small but important segment.

Together, we believe these chapters significantly advance our understanding of consumer information processing and consumer-focused strategy. We hope that readers will build on this work in their own research or apply this work to their own marketing programs. *Nous espérons que le lecteur de ce recueil sera tout aussi stimulé et intéressé que nous l'avons nous-même été lors de la conférence.* We hope you find the chapters as interesting as we found them to be.

—*Frank R. Kardes*
—*Paul M. Herr*
—*Jacques Nantel*

I. NEW PERSPECTIVES ON CONSUMER INFORMATION PROCESSING

The Role of Information Processing in Single-Alternative and Multiple-Alternative Judgments and Decisions

Robert S. Wyer, Jr.
Hong Kong University of Science and Technology

Consumers make two types of decisions. On one hand, they decide if they want to make any purchase at all. For example, they may ponder whether to buy a new car, a color television, or go on a trip over the winter holidays. Or, they may encounter a particular piece of jewelry, an antique, or a new restaurant, and decide either to purchase it or try it out, or not. These *single-alternative* decisions are often mediated in part by the perception of whether the inherent desirability of the decision referent is sufficient to outweigh the cost or effort required to obtain it (cf. Dodds, Monroe, & Gruwal, 1991). A second, *multiple-alternative* decision is comparative. That is, people are confronted with several viable alternatives and must decide which of the options they prefer. These options can also be either general (e.g., whether to spend money on a new car or a vacation trip) or specific (e.g., whether to buy a Honda or a Toyota, or to vacation in either San Francisco or Hawaii).

The two types of decisions are obviously related. That is, a decision about which of several alternatives to buy is often preceded by a decision about whether to purchase anything at all. Furthermore, the set of alternatives from which one makes a selection is likely to be based on a prior determination that each alternative, if considered separately, is above some minimal threshold of acceptability (Kardes, Kalyanaram, Chandrashekaran, & Dornoff, 1993; Nedungadi, 1990). Finally, the causal relatedness of the two types of decisions may often be in the opposite direction. That is, a decision not to purchase anything can often result from an inability to decide which of a number of available alternatives is preferable (Dhar, 1997).

Despite their inherent relatedness, however, research in both psychology and consumer behavior has tended to focus on only one type of decision to the exclusion of the other. Research on single-alternative decisions (e.g., whether to engage in a particular course of action or to maintain the status quo) has its roots in the study of attitude formation and change (for reviews, see Albarracin, Johnson, & Zanna, in press; Eagly & Chaiken, 1993). This research is guided by the assumption that the effects of informational, situational, and individual difference variables on judgments and decisions are mediated by their impact on the cognitive activities that occur at several different stages of processing. These stages include:

1. The selective encoding and interpretation of stimulus information in terms of previously formed concepts and knowledge (for a review, see Higgins, 1996);
2. the representation and storage of stimulus information in memory (Srull & Wyer, 1989; Wyer & Radvansky, 1999);
3. the retrieval of some or all of this information and a construal of its positive and negative implications for the judgment to be made (McGuire, 1964; Petty & Cacioppo, 1986);
4. an integration of the implications of the information with those of other, previously acquired knowledge to compute a subjective evaluation of its referent (Anderson, 1981; Fishbein & Ajzen, 1975; Lichtenstein & Srull, 1985);
5. the transformation of a subjective inference into an overt judgment or behavioral decision (Adaval & Monroe, 2002; Fazio, 1990; Fishbein & Ajzen, 1975).

Based on these assumptions, information-processing researchers have typically attempted to identify the alternative processes that might occur at each stage of activity and to specify when these processes are likely to be applied. They then conceptualize the effects of informational, motivational, and situational variables in terms of their impact on processing at one or more of these stages. These conceptualizations provide the basis for a broader theoretical formulation that specifies when different stages of processing come into play and how they combine to influence a judgment or decision (McGuire, 1968, 1972; Wyer, 2004; Wyer & Srull, 1989).

Multiple-alternative decisions could also involve these processes. That is, individuals who are called upon to decide among several alternatives could compute an evaluation of each alternative separately and then compare these evaluations. An equally plausible possibility, however, is that individuals in these conditions compare the values of the alternatives along specific attribute dimensions and assess the relative desirability of these options on the basis of these dimension-by-dimension comparisons without evaluating the attractiveness of any particular option in isolation. Research based on this assumption has uncovered a number of factors that influence (a) the relative weight attached to different types of attributes (Kahneman & Tversky, 1979; Tversky & Kahneman, 1981, 1982); (b) the different computational strategies that might be applied (Dhar & Sherman, 1996; Houston, Sherman, & Baker, 1989; Shafir, Simonson, & Tversky, 1993; Tversky, 1972); and (c) the perception that the selection of one alternative is more justifiable than another (Shafir et al., 1993). These factors are typically assumed to exert their influence at the decision stage of processing, and the cognitive activities that occur at earlier stages are given little weight.

A question therefore arises as to whether an understanding of processing at other stages is really necessary. To the extent that differences in processing at earlier stages do not contribute appreciably to the prediction of consumer judgments and decisions, an understanding of this processing may be of little practical importance. I recall a conversation with Richard Shiffrin, one of the preeminent memory theorists of the past 50 years. He had recently developed an exceptionally powerful theory of recall and recognition that relied exclusively on retrieval processes with minimal assumptions about the mental representations that are formed of the information at the time it is first received and comprehended (cf. Gillund & Shiffrin, 1984; Raaijmakers & Shiffrin, 1981). In response to my skepticism that these initial representational processes were irrelevant to an understanding of memory, he appealed to parsimony. Specifically, he argued that it is always best to begin by developing a theory of the processes that occur in closest temporal proximity to the phenomenon being observed. If the theory is able to explain these phenomena without making assumptions about the cognitive activities that occur at earlier stages, a detailed consideration of these stages would add unnecessary complexity to the theory. If, on the other hand, important phenomena remain unexplained, one could then consider processing at earlier stages that, in combination with retrieval processes, might account for them.

A similar logic could apply in accounting for choice behavior. If the situational and informational influences on consumer decisions can be adequately explained in terms of processes that occur at the decision stage, there is surely no reason to encumber decision-making theory with assumptions about the cognitive activities that occur at earlier stages. It would certainly be nice if this were in fact the case. Unfortunately, however, it is not. In fact, Gilbert (2002) and others (e.g., Kardes, Posavac, & Cronley, 2004) postulated that later stages of processing only come into play in inference making when sufficient cognitive resources can be expended on these inferences and individuals are both willing and able to engage in this activity. When little cognitive effort is necessary to make a judgment, early stages of processing are more likely to have the predominant effect.

Indeed, several studies in our own laboratory, each in a different domain of inquiry, provide examples. Two series of studies exemplify the need to consider different stages of processing in accounting for multiple-alternative decisions. A third, on the role of affective reactions in consumer judgment, illustrates a similar need in accounting for single-alternative judgments and decisions, and a fourth on the role of mental accounting (Thaler, 1985, 1999) cuts across both types of decisions. After presenting these examples, we return to a more general consideration of their implications for the study of judgment and decision processes.

CONTEXT EFFECTS ON CONSUMER JUDGMENTS

One of the most intriguing phenomena to be uncovered in research on multiple-alternative decision making was first identified by Huber, Payne, and Puto (1982). Specifically, a choice alternative that is not itself a viable option can nevertheless influence people's relative preferences for the contenders. For example, suppose consumers are confronted with a choice between a target product (T) and a competitor product (C), whose ordinal values along two attribute dimensions are shown in the top half of Table 1.1. That is, T is superior to C along one dimension but is inferior to C along the other. If the dimensions are equally important, a decision between the two alternatives is obviously difficult. However, suppose third alternative, D, is added to the set. This alternative is clearly inferior to T but not to C. Huber et al. (1982) found that although D is not itself a viable option, adding it to the set increases the preference for T over C.

Alternative Explanations

Two general explanations have been given for this "decoy" effect. Simonson (1989) assumed that people seek justification for their decisions, and that if they cannot justify their choice on the basis of a direct comparison of the choice alternatives, they use other criteria. Thus, in our example, T is superior to D but C is

TABLE 1.1
Relative Values of Choice Alternatives and Stimulus
Materials Employed by Park and Kim (2005)

| | Choice Alternatives | | | |
	Target (T)	Competitor (C)	Standard Decoy (D)	Inferior Decoy (D_{inf})
Relative attractiveness				
Dimension 1	4	2	4	2
Dimension 2	2	4	1	1
Stimulus materials (restaurant)				
Walking distance (min)	13	25	13	25
Taste rating (1–10)	6.8	8.1	6.0	6.0

not. This could be used as justification for choosing T and, therefore, could increase preferences for it.

Theories of social and psychophysical judgment (cf. Ostrom & Upshaw, 1968; Parducci, 1965; for a recent application in the consumer domain, see Adaval & Monroe, 2002) suggested a quite different possibility. According to these conceptualizations, a context stimulus whose values along a dimension differ from those of the others can influence the subjective values that people assign to these alternatives. In the present example, two types of changes could occur. First, the low value of D along dimension 2 expands the range of values to which people are exposed along the dimension and, as a result, may lead T and C to be seen as subjectively more similar to one another (cf. Parducci, 1965). Consequently, their values along dimension 1, on which T is superior to C, should have relatively greater impact on their relative attractiveness. (If T and C were identical along dimension 2, their values along dimension 1 would of course be the sole basis for judgment.) Thus, if people base their decision on this criterion, their preference for T should increase relative to conditions in which D is not considered.

A second possibility, suggested by Pan and Lehmann (1993), has similar implications. That is, when two alternatives have similar or identical values along a dimension, they may be subjectively assigned to a common category. Once this category is formed, it may serve as an anchor, or comparative standard, for judging other options. As a result, the value of these options are judged as more dissimilar to the category value than they otherwise would. In our example, D has the same value as T along dimension 1. Therefore, adding it to the choice set could lead T and D to be placed in the same category along the dimension and used as a standard of comparison in evaluating C. As a result, C might be seen as more dissimilar to T along the dimension (i.e., as less favorable) than would otherwise be the case. This perception, in turn, could lead T to be judged as relatively more attractive than C and, therefore, could increase the likelihood of someone choosing it.

Wedell and Pettibone (1996) noted that the various effects of context on preferences described in the preceding paragraphs can potentially be reflected by its impact on components of the following equation:

$$P_T = \Sigma w_j(V_{T_j} - V_{C_j}) + J_T, \tag{1}$$

where V_{T_j} and V_{C_j} are values of T and C along dimension j, w_j is the weight attached to values along this dimension, and J_T is the amount of justification for choosing T over C independently of their relative values along the information dimensions.

In fact, Wedell and Pettibone (1996) appeared to find evidence for the contribution of both components of the equation. In one experimental session, they asked participants to judge the attractiveness of choice alternatives whose values along two attribute dimensions differed in a manner analogous to that described in

Table 1.1. Ratings of the alternatives along each dimension were also obtained. In a different session, participants indicated which alternative they preferred and the justifiability of choosing it. Introducing D influenced the relative attractiveness of T and C in the manner one would expect if it altered the values assigned to the alternatives along dimensions 1 and 2. However, it also increased preferences for T over C, and increased beliefs that the choice of T was more justified (J_T). Taken at face value, therefore, these data suggest that the effects of the decoy on preferences for T were a combined function of both shifts in the values assigned to the alternatives along the dimensions of judgment and the sufficient justification processes postulated by Shafir et al. (1993).

An Information-Processing Analysis

The conclusion that both shifts in attractiveness of the choice alternatives and sufficient justification simultaneously contributed to preference shifts identified by Wedell and Pettibone (1996) may nevertheless be misleading. In their studies, participants performed the attractiveness judgment task and the preference task in counterbalanced order, and the data were pooled over the two order conditions. It is therefore conceivable that attractiveness shifts and sufficient justification did not contribute simultaneously to any given individual's preference judgment. Rather, one factor alone might have influenced participants' choices in one order condition, and the other factor alone might have influenced preferences in the other condition.

An analysis of the phenomena from an information-processing perspective suggests that this is likely to be the case. Shifts in the values assigned to choice alternatives along each attribute dimension occur at the time the information is first received and comprehended. Moreover, these effects may occur without much awareness (Dhar & Simonson, 2003). In contrast, the judgment processes postulated by Shafir et al. (1993) occur more deliberatively at the decision stage of processing, when the relative values of the alternatives along each dimension are compared. In making these dimension-by-dimension comparisons, independent estimates of each choice alternative's attractiveness do not come into play at all.

In principle, these processes could contribute independently to preference decisions. In fact, however, this seems intuitively and theoretically unlikely. Chaiken (1987; see also Wyer, 2004) postulated that when people are confronted with a judgment or decision, they first consider the criterion that they can apply most quickly and easily and estimate their confidence that a judgment based on this criterion is valid. If their confidence is above some minimal threshold, they apply the criterion without further ado, ignoring other criteria that might also be considered. (For a similar assumption in analyzing the role of "satisficing" in decision making, see Simon, 1957.)

It seems reasonable to assume that in the conditions considered here, it is normally easier to perform a dimension-by-dimension comparison of the choice alternatives than it is to combine the values assigned to each alternative into an overall evaluation of it and then compare these evaluations. Therefore, when people have not been exposed to the alternatives they are considering before being called upon to make a decision, they are likely to use a sufficient-justification criterion as a basis for their choices. On the other hand, suppose people have had an occasion to evaluate each alternative separately before being asked to state a preference, and these evaluations are easily accessible in memory. Then, a comparison of these overall evaluations is undoubtedly the easiest criterion to use. To this extent, the effects of context stimuli should be mediated by their influence on processes suggested by social judgment formulations.

In the example we described earlier, the context stimulus (D) should theoretically have similar effects on preferences regardless of which criterion is used. However, this is not always the case. For example, suppose people in our earlier example are asked to choose between T, C, and a third alternative, D_{inf}, shown in the fourth column of the table. This alternative is clearly inferior to both T and C and, therefore, provides no justification for choosing one over the other. However, its value along dimension 2 expands the range of values to which participants are exposed along this dimension, and so exposure to the option should affect perceptions of T and C along the dimension in much the same way that D does. Furthermore, the value of D_{inf} along dimension 1 is similar to that of C. This may lead participants to place D_{inf} and C in the same category and to use the category's value as a standard in evaluating T, thus increasing perceptions of T as dissimilar (i.e., as more favorable). For either or both of these reasons, exposure to D_{inf} should increase the relative attractiveness of T, and should increase preferences for it when this decision criterion is applied.

Empirical Evidence

Park and Kim (2005) demonstrated these effects. College students received information about two restaurants, T and C, whose values along two dimensions (walking distance from campus and the tastiness of the food) varied as shown in the bottom half of Table 1.1. Some participants considered only these two restaurants. Others also received information about a third restaurant whose values along the dimension relative to those of T and C were either analogous to D in our earlier example or analogous to D_{inf}. In each case, participants in *attractiveness first* conditions estimated the attractiveness of each alternative separately before making preference judgments, whereas participants in *preference-first* conditions reported their preferences for the choice alternatives at the outset.

Attractiveness ratings of the alternatives under each condition are shown in the top section of Table 1.2. The introduction of a context stimulus increased the attractiveness of T relative to C. Furthermore, this was true regardless of which context stimulus (D or D_{inf}) was presented and regardless of the order in which judgments were made. This suggests that the computation of attractiveness was similar in both order conditions. This was not true of preference judgments, how-

TABLE 1.2
Preferences, Perceived Justifiability, and Ratings of the Choice Alternatives
(based on data from Park & Kim, 2005)

	Choice First			Rating First		
	Target (T)	Competitor (C)	Diff (T-C)	Target (T)	Competitor (C)	Diff (T-C)
Proportion of choices						
No decoy	.544 (31)$_a$	.456 (26)	.316 (18)$_a$	.684 (39)		
Standard decoy	.729 (43)$_b$	.271 (16)	.679 (38)$_b$	.321 (18)		
Inferior decoy	.542 (32)$_a$	.458 (27)	.586 (34)$_b$	.414 (24)		
Overall attractiveness						
No decoy	4.25	4.75	−0.50$_a$	3.98	5.00	−1.02$_a$
Standard decoy	5.22	4.98	0.24$_b$	5.23	4.91	0.32$_b$
Inferior decoy	5.32	5.34	−0.02$_b$	5.41	5.43	−0.02$_b$
Ratings along dimension 2 (taste)						
No decoy	3.40	5.61	−2.21$_a$	3.02	5.68	−2.67$_a$
Standard decoy	3.83	6.24	−2.41$_a$	3.73	6.39	−2.66$_a$
Inferior decoy	3.83	6.31	−2.47$_a$	3.62	6.43	−2.81$_a$
Ratings along dimension 1 (walking distance)						
No decoy	5.60	3.32	2.28$_a$	5.65	3.12	2.53$_a$
Standard decoy	5.32	2.78	2.54$_a$	5.93	2.29	3.64$_b$
Inferior decoy	5.93	2.19	3.75$_b$	6.28	2.16	4.12c

Note. Differences in each section with unlike subscripts differ at $p < .05$. The number of participants who chose each alternative is indicated in parentheses.

ever. As shown in the second section of Table 1.2, preferences that were reported at the outset were only affected by D, consistent with the assumption that these judgments were based on a sufficient-justification criterion. When they were reported after attractiveness judgments were made, however, preferences were influenced by D_{inf} as well.

This conclusion was further confirmed by supplementary mediation analyses. That is, when attractiveness ratings were made first, the relative attractiveness of T versus C was highly correlated with preferences. Moreover, the effect of context stimuli on preferences was reduced to nonsignificance when the relative attractiveness of the alternatives was controlled. When preference judgments were reported first, however, they were much less highly correlated with the relative attractiveness of the choice alternatives, and the effects of decoys on preference judgments remained significant when variance due to attractiveness was eliminated.

The effect of context on ratings of alternatives along each attribute dimension separately provided further clarification of the processes that mediated attractiveness ratings. These data are shown in the last two sections of Table 1.2. Contrary to expectations, context stimuli did not influence the values assigned to the choice alternatives along dimension 2, suggesting that in this study, participants' perceptions of the alternatives' similarity along this dimension were not affected by the range of values to which they were exposed. Rather, the effect of decoys on these perceptions was mediated by their effect on ratings of the choice alternatives along dimension 1. That is, presenting D, which had the same high value as T along this dimension (see Table 1.1), decreased the value assigned to C along this dimension. Presenting D_{inf}, which had the same low value as C, increased the value assigned to T along the dimensions. These shifts in values, which are consistent with the categorization effects postulated by Pan and Lehmann (1993), were the primary mediator of attractiveness judgments and, therefore, the preferences that were based on this attractiveness.

Further Considerations. The evidence that context effects can be mediated by processing at the comprehension stage rather than at the decision stage led Park and Kim (2005) to identify an effect of decoys that had not previously been reported. In this study, participants received information about two refrigerators (T and C). In some conditions, however, these alternatives were accompanied by a product in a different domain (i.e., a dishwasher) that varied along one of the dimensions that were common to T and C (price) but not the other. The relative values of the alternative along the dimensions to which information pertained are shown in the top of Table 1.3, and the stimulus values actually assigned along the dimensions are shown in the bottom half of the table. As this table indicates, the context stimulus provides no justification for choosing T over C. Nevertheless, it expands the range of prices to which participants were exposed and, therefore, could lead participants to perceive T and C as subjectively more similar in cost than they otherwise would. Therefore, it should decrease the effects of differences along this dimension on their relative attractiveness.

As expected, adding the dishwasher to the set of choice alternatives had no impact on participants' preferences when these preferences were reported at the outset. When participants had rated the attractiveness of each alternative separately before reporting their preferences, however, introducing the dishwasher increased the attractiveness of T relative to C and consequently increased the proportion of times that T was chosen.

Summary. The evidence that inducing people to make independent ratings of choice alternatives before reporting their preferences has an impact on these preferences is not very exciting in and of itself. However, it points out the need to consider different stages of processing in order to provide a complete account of context effects on preference judgments. There are many instances outside the laboratory in which consumers are likely to have to form overall evaluations of the alternatives they consider before making a decision. This is particularly true when people encounter products at different points in time, or when the information is conveyed in a way that makes direct dimension-by-dimension comparisons difficult (Houston et al., 1989).

Moreover, when people are not motivated a priori to make comparative judgments, they may not do so spontaneously (Wang & Wyer, 2002; see also Kardes,

TABLE 1.3
Relative Values of Choice Alternatives, Stimulus Materials, and Preferences
(based on data from Park & Kim, 2005, Experiment 2)

	Choice Alternatives		
	Target (T) (refrigerator)	Competitor (C) (refrigerator)	Decoy (D) (washer)
Relative attractiveness			
Dimension 1	4	2	—
Dimension 2	2	4	1
Dimension 3	—	—	4
Stimulus material			
Freezing time (min)	10	25	—
Running cost	$46	$40	$60
Artificial intelligence feature	—	—	available

	Proportion of Choices	
	Target	Competitor
Choice-only conditions		
No decoy	.341 (29)	.659 (56)
Decoy	.459 (39)	.541 (46)
Rating-first conditions		
No decoy	.477 (41)	.523 (45)
Expanded-range decoy	.651 (56)	.349 (30)

Note. The number of participants who chose each alternative is indicated in parentheses.

Sanbonmatsu, Cronley, & Houghton, 2002, for a similar conclusion). Even when people are motivated to make a choice, they may be relatively less inclined to resort to justification processes when they have an option of deferring their choice, as is typically the case outside the laboratory (see Dhar & Simonson, 2003, for a discussion of this possibility). In short, the effect observed by Park and Kim (2005) under the "rating first" condition might be more often the rule than the exception in actual purchase decisions. Thus, the evidence that context effects occur in conditions that are not predicted by the use of a sufficient-justification criterion may be of more general importance.

CULTURAL INFLUENCES ON DECISION MAKING

An understanding of the phenomena identified in a quite different area of inquiry also requires a consideration of different stages of processing. Research on the norms and values that distinguish Asian and Western cultures (Heine, Lehman,

Markus, & Kitayama, 1999; Hong & Chiu, 2001; Markus & Kitayama, 1991; Triandis, 1995) suggested that representatives of these cultures differ along a dimension of individualism–collectivism (Hofstede, 1980; Triandis, 1995). That is, European Americans typically value independence and individuality, whereas Asians have an other-directed orientation that is characterized by compromise and interdependence. However, although these different orientations may be characteristic of Western and Asian cultures in general, individual members of the cultures are often exposed to other norms and values as well. Consequently, culture-dominant norms may not always govern their behavior unless the norms are salient at the time a decision is made (cf. Hong, Morris, Chiu, & Benet-Martinez, 2000).

Normative Influences on Consumer Decisions

Indirect evidence that the effect of cultural norms depends on whether situational factors that increase their accessibility in memory was reported by Briley, Morris, and Simonson (2000). Asians and European Americans were asked to choose between three products whose values along a series of attribute dimensions varied favorableness in a manner analogous to the following:

	Alternative A	Alternative B	Alternative C
Dimension 1	+5	−5	+1
Dimension 2	+5	−5	−1
Dimension 3	−5	+5	+1
Dimension 4	−5	+5	−1

Thus, C, whose values along the dimensions fall between the values of A and B, represents a compromise choice. In fact, no cultural differences emerged in preferences when participants were simply asked to make choices without deliberating. In some conditions, however, participants were asked to give a reason for their choice. In this case, American participants increased their preferences for A and B, whereas Asians increased their preference for C.

Effects of Cultural Salience

Briley et al.'s (2000) data therefore suggested that stimulating participants to think more carefully about the reasons for their choices leads them to activate and use culture-related normative criteria as bases for their decisions. If this is so, however, a more direct manipulation of people's cultural identity might be expected to have comparable effects. A series of studies by Briley and Wyer (2002) investigated this possibility. To activate cultural norms and values, we used a procedure developed by Hong et al. (2000). That is, North American and Chinese participants were exposed to a series of pictures with instructions to indicate the period of history with which the referents were identified. The pictures conveyed symbols of either their own culture or a different one. (American symbols included the American flag, Marilyn Monroe, Abraham Lincoln, etc.; Chinese symbols included the Great Wall, the Chinese Dragon, a Chinese musical instrument, etc.) After completing this task, participants were exposed to the decision task constructed by Briley et al. (2000).

Based on the considerations raised earlier, it might seem reasonable to suppose that exposing Chinese to symbols of their own culture would increase their disposition to compromise, as reflected in their product choices, whereas exposing Americans to symbols of their own culture would decrease this tendency. However, this did not occur. Rather, both Americans and Chinese increased their disposition to choose the compromise alternative when symbols of their own culture were primed than when these symbols were not primed (.63 vs. .50), and this difference was similar regardless of their cultural background. Why should this be the case?

An Information-Processing Analysis

A possible answer to this question becomes apparent in analyzing the processes that underlie the task constructed by Briley et al. (2000). The use of compromise as a criterion for judgment presumably occurs at the time the alternatives are directly compared. However, processes at earlier stages could come into play as well. For example, the choice of C might not result from a desire to compromise per se. Rather, it could reflect the way each product's attributes are evaluated at an earlier stage of processing (cf. Simonson & Tversky, 1992, for an analysis of these evaluations). That is, suppose individuals compute an overall evaluation of each choice alternative separately on the basis of the attribute information and then compare these overall evaluations. Each evaluation could depend on both the subjective favorableness of the attribute descriptions and the weight attached to these descriptions when combining their implications to form a judgment of the choice alternatives as a whole. To this extent, people who attach relatively more importance to favorable attributes than to unfavorable ones should evaluate A and B more highly than C, whereas people who weight unfavorable attributes heavily should evaluate A and B less highly than C. In other words, the choice of C might not reflect a disposition to compromise that occurs at the time a choice is made. Rather, it may result from a tendency to weight negative features of the choice alternatives more heavily than positive features in the course of evaluating each of the choice alternatives separately, prior to making a choice. If this is so, and if making one's cultural identity salient increases the motivation to avoid negative decision consequences, this could account for the results that Briley and Wyer (2002) obtained.

In fact, this explanation is viable. Aaker and Lee (2001) found that inducing participants to imagine themselves as part of a group increased their attention to negative features of a hypothetical tennis match, as reflected in their memory for situational details. This suggests that thinking of oneself as a member of a group induces a *prevention focus* (Higgins, 1998), that is, a disposition to avoid negative decision outcomes. Once this disposition is activated, it could govern both interpersonal choice situations and intrapersonal ones. Briley and Wyer (2002) found direct support for this assumption. That is, inducing individuals to believe that they were participating in the experiment as members of a group increased their disposition to minimize negative outcomes to both themselves and others in a simulated resource-allocation situation, and to avoid the risk of postdecisional regret in an individual choice task. If making people aware of their cultural identity induces feelings of group membership, it could also induce a disposition to avoid undesirable decision consequences, as suggested by Simonson and Tversky (1992) and reflected in the situation constructed by Briley et al. (2000). That is, it could lead both Americans and Chinese to choose the "compromise" alternative (C), as Briley and Wyer (2002) found.

These considerations could also account for the cultural differences that Briley et al. (2000) identified when participants cultural identity was not explicitly called to their attention. In a comparison of parent–child interactions in Taiwan and North America, Miller, Fung, and Mintz (1996) found that Asian parents typically perceive their children's misbehavior as character deficiencies that need to be corrected, whereas American parents view their children's misdeeds as normal occurrences that, although serious, do not reflect on their children's status as admirable human beings. To this extent, Asian and North Americans may develop different normative dispositions to avoid negative consequences of their behavior that they apply spontaneously when decisions involving these outcomes are made. The question arises as to when cultural norms govern choice behavior, as in Briley et al.'s (2000) study, and when motivational conditions operate, as in Briley and Wyer's (2002) experiments. The answer to this question awaits further investigation. However, a consideration of different stages of processing is clearly necessary to come to grips with these phenomena and to develop a conceptualization that can account for the different effects that occur.

THE ROLE OF AFFECT IN CONSUMER JUDGMENT

As noted earlier, research on single-alternative decisions has more traditionally recognized the need to focus on different stages of processing. This recognition has been particularly evident in research on the impact of people's affective reactions on their responses to product information and their evaluations of the product being described. Theory and research outside the consumer domain has vacillated in terms of the emphasis it has placed on the different stages at which affect can play a role (for reviews, see Clore, Schwarz, & Conway, 1994; Wyer, Clore, & Isbell, 1999). However, the most widely accepted conceptualization of the impact of affective reactions on judgments and decisions was proposed by Schwarz and Clore (1983, 1988). They assumed that if people who are experiencing positive or negative affect at the time they are asked to evaluate a stimulus, they interpret these feelings as an indication of their reactions to the stimulus and use them as a basis for evaluating it. Therefore, they evaluate a stimulus more favorably if it elicits positive affect than if it elicits negative affect.

Moreover, people typically cannot distinguish clearly between the different sources of affect they are experiencing at any given time. As a consequence, a portion of the feelings they happen to be experiencing for irrelevant reasons (e.g., the mood they happen to be in) is often misattributed to the stimulus they are evaluating and, therefore, influences the judgments they make. Thus, for example, people report greater life satisfaction if they are asked on sunny days than if they are asked on rainy days (Schwarz & Clore, 1983); if they have just watched a funny movie rather than a depressing one (Adaval, 2001); or if the room they are in is clean and cheerful than if it is dirty and unkempt (Schwarz, Strack, Kommer, & Wagner, 1987). Perhaps the most intriguing demonstration of the informational influence of affect was provided by Strack, Martin, and Stepper (1988), who found that an unobtrusive manipulation of people's facial expressions while they judged cartoons (i.e., holding a felt-tip pen either between the teeth or between the lips) influenced the amusement they reported in response to the cartoons.

There are contingencies in the use of affect as information. For one thing, it must be considered applicable. Pham (1998; see also Adaval, 2001; Yeung & Wyer, 2004) found that although participants' mood has a positive impact on their evaluations of products that are typically evaluated on the basis of hedonic criteria (e.g., comfort, taste, etc.), it has little influence on judgments that are normally based on utilitarian considerations (material quality, workmanship, etc.). Nonetheless, the judgments that can be influenced by affective reactions are potentially quite diverse. For example, affect may be used as information that a situation one encounters is benign or potentially threatening and, therefore, may influence the attention paid to situational details (Schwarz, 1990). Alternatively, it may provide information about whether one has been successful in attaining a goal one is pursuing and may influence perseverance in goal-directed activity (Martin, Ward, Achee, & Wyer, 1993; see Wyer et al., 1999, for further implications of this possibility).

Influence of Affect at Other Stages of Processing

The use of affect as information is typically assumed to occur at the time a judgment or decision is made. The question is whether this assumption is sufficient to account for the impact of affect on judgments and decisions. Bower (1981) assumed that *affect* and *emotion* functioned as concepts in semantic memory that, once activated, function in much the same way as other concepts. Thus, affect can influence the interpretation of new information and the likelihood of encoding it into memory. Furthermore, it can cue the retrieval of information with which it has features in common (e.g., features that are similar in valence). To this extent, happy individuals might be more inclined than sad individuals to interpret ambiguous information more favorably (Forgas, Bower, & Krantz, 1984). Furthermore, people might selectively attend to information that is interpretable in terms of the concepts activated by their mood (Bower, Gilligan, & Monteiro, 1981; Forgas & Bower, 1987), and might selectively retrieve previously acquired knowledge that is congruent with these feelings (Bower, 1981).

Some research appeared to provide support for these hypotheses (for a summary, see Forgas, 1995). However, later studies raised questions about their validity. As I have argued elsewhere (Wyer, 2004; Wyer et al., 1999), the aforementioned effects are unlikely to be mediated by people's affective reactions per se. Rather, they reflect the impact of semantic concepts that are activated by the experimental procedures used to induce these reactions. Niedenthal and her colleagues (Niedenthal, Halberstadt, & Setterlund, 1997; Niedenthal & Setterlund, 1994) provided compelling evidence that when positive or negative emotions are induced in ways that do not explicitly refer to evaluatively toned semantic concepts (e.g., playing up-beat or dreary music), they activate concepts of the specific emotions being experienced but do not influence the accessibility of positively valenced and negatively valenced concepts in general. Moreover, Parrott and Sabini (1990) found that a similar mood induction technique led participants to recall past experiences that were evaluatively *in*consistent with their mood (e.g., they were more likely to recall a favorable past experience when they were experiencing negative affect than when they were experiencing positive affect). Thus, these and other results suggest that the impact of affect on information processing does not arise from its influence on the accessibility and use of similarly valenced concepts and knowledge in memory.

However, the conclusion that affective reactions only exert their influence on processing at the judgment and decision stage is premature. Several recent studies provide evidence that affect does influence the cognitive activity that people perform at early (i.e., prejudgment) states of processing. However, the nature of this influence differs from that assumed by Bower (1981) and others. Three studies provide examples.

Affect and Categorization

One of the most compelling demonstrations of the need to consider the impact of affect at early states of processing was conducted by Adaval (2003) in an investigation of the impact of brand name on product evaluations. Because a product's brand provides a general indication of its overall quality, it might often be used as a heuristic basis for judging a product when people are unmotivated or unable to conduct a more detailed analysis of the product's specific features (Maheswaran, Mackie, & Chaiken, 1992). Therefore, if people who experience positive affect are unmotivated to engage in extensive information processing (Schwarz & Clore, 1988), they may be particularly inclined to use brand as a basis for judgment. A study by Adaval (2003) appeared to support this conjecture. Participants who were induced to feel either happy or sad as a result of recalling a past experience were asked to evaluate products described by both (a) a favorable or unfavorable brand name and (b) a set of favorable or unfavorable specific attributes. Brand name had greater impact when participants were feeling happy than when they were not. On the surface, this finding seems quite consistent with the assumption that positive affect increases the use of brand as a heuristic, leading it to have more impact on judgments than it otherwise would.

In fact, however, this conclusion is incorrect. Using a parameter-estimation procedure developed by Zalinski and Anderson (1990), Adaval (2003) obtained separate estimates of both (a) the weight that participants attached to each piece of information in computing a judgment and (b) their perception of its evaluative implications. Analyses of these estimates showed that inducing positive affect had no impact on the weight attached to brand information. On the other hand, participants perceived the implications of brand to be more extreme when they were happy than when they were unhappy, independently of the weight they attached to it (i.e., they perceived the implications of favorable brands to be more favorable, and the implications of unfavorable brands to be more unfavorable).

Two factors in combination provide an explanation for why this is so. First, Bless et al. (1996) found that participants typically use broad, categorical criteria to interpret information when they are in a good mood. This could indicate that people pay more attention to categorical information (e.g., brand) in these conditions. However, this increased attention might occur at the time the information is first received and interpreted and not at the time of judgment. Tesser (1978) found that when people think more extensively about a stimulus that either predominately favorable or predominately unfavorable features, their evaluations of the stimulus become more polarized. One reason is that thought increases the number of stimulus-related features on which evaluations of the stimulus are based. If this is so, and if the attributes associated with a brand are evaluatively similar, factors that increase people's attention to brand at the time the information is presented should increase the extremity of their perceptions of its favorableness, as Adaval's (2003) findings indicate.

Further studies by Adaval confirmed implications of this interpretation. For example, if affect influences people's estimate of a brand's evaluative implications at the time they first encounter it, this estimate is likely to be stored in memory. Therefore, its effects may persist over time. To evaluate this possibility, Adaval (2003, Experiment 5) exposed happy and unhappy participants to a product described by either a favorable or an unfavorable brand name. Then, in a second session 24 hours later, participants were asked to recall this product and compare it to a new one whose brand name was normatively similar in favorableness. Suppose happy participants evaluate the brand more extremely in the first session, and recall these evaluations to use as a basis for judgment in the second session. Then, they should prefer the first product to the new one when the products' brand names are favorable, but should prefer the new product when the products' brand names are unfavorable. When participants experience negative affect in the first session, however, the extremity of the product's perceived implications should not be affected, and so their preference for the product in the second session should not be appreciably different from the new one.

This was in fact the case. When moderately favorable brand names were compared, participants were more likely to prefer the first product they had considered in the first session if they had experienced positive affect in this session (73%) than if they had experienced negative affect (23%). When the brands were moderately unfavorable, however, they were less likely to choose the first product if they had experienced positive affect at the time they encountered it than if they had experienced negative affect (0% vs. 36%).

Therefore, these studies suggest that the influence of affect on the impact of brand information does not result from its impact at the time of judgment. Rather, its influence occurs at an earlier stage of processing, when people construe the brand's evaluative implications. It would of course be incorrect to conclude that affect never has an impact on the weight attached to categorical information at the time of judgment (for evidence of these effects in other domains, see Bodenhausen, 1993; Isbell, 2004). However, the conclusion that its impact is always mediated by its influence on the weight attached to this information is equally inappropriate.

Affect Confirmation Processes

Adaval's (2003) studies concerned the impact of affect on reactions to brand name. In some cases, people's affective reactions can influence the impact of attribute information as well. An earlier series of studies by Adaval (2001) determined the nature of this influence. She argued that when the information about a product attribute elicits affect, people are likely to use this affect as a basis for construing the attribute's evaluative implications. However, there are two qualifications on this tendency. First, the attribute must be one that consumers typically evaluate on the basis of hedonic (affect-related) criteria (comfort, taste, etc.) rather than utilitarian considerations (durability, workmanship, warranty, etc.). Second, consumers must perceive their affective reactions to the attributes to be a reliable basis for judging it. This latter consideration comes into play in predicting the effect of extraneous affect. If the affect that consumers happen to be experiencing for objectively irrelevant reasons is similar to that elicited by the attribute, it may appear to confirm their reactions to the attribute. Consequently, they may weight the attribute heavily when combining its implications with those of other available information to form an overall product evaluation. However, suppose extraneous affect differs from that elicited by the attribute. Then, people may interpret these conflicting feelings as ambivalence about the attribute's implications and, therefore, may assign it less weight than they otherwise would.

Adaval confirmed this conclusion using procedures developed by Anderson (1971, 1981). She found that when an attribute was likely to be evaluated on the basis of affect-related criteria, the extraneous affect that participants experienced influenced the weight attached to it independently of its evaluative implications per se. When affect was not relevant to the evaluation to be made, however, extraneous affect had no impact on the weight attached to the attribute. Participants' weighting of the attribute information in this study presumably occurred at the integration stage, when participants combined its implications with those of other information available. To understand the reasons for this difference in weighting, however, one must consider the influence of processing at an earlier stage, when the implications of the attribute information are construed.

The Impact of Spontaneous Appraisals on Product Evaluations

A series of studies by Yeung (2003; Yeung & Wyer, 2004) showed a quite different way in which affect enters into prejudgment information processing. People often see a product in a store window, or encounter a picture of it in a magazine, before they receive specific information about its attributes. This experience may stimulate a spontaneous appraisal of the product's desirability that is accompanied by affective reactions (cf. Lazarus, 1982, 1991), and these reactions, in turn, may give rise to an initial evaluative impression of the product. Once this affect-based impression is formed, it may serve as a basis for later evaluations independently of any information that people receive subsequently, and independently of the criteria they might apply in the absence of this impression.

To investigate this possibility, Yeung asked participants to evaluate a product described by a set of specific attributes. Before receiving this information, they were induced to feel either happy or sad as a result of recalling an emotion-eliciting personal experience. Then, in one study, they evaluated a pair of running shoes on the basis of attribute descriptions with explicit instructions to use either hedonic criteria (e.g., comfort) or utilitarian criteria (e.g., durability). In a second study, the judgment criterion was not stated, but the product was one that was normally judged on the basis of either hedonic considerations (salad dressing) or utilitarian ones (a backpack). In these conditions, affect should exert its influence at the time of judgment, but only if it is relevant to the judgment to be made (Pham, 1998). That is, participants should evaluate hedonic products more favorably when they are feeling happy than when they are not, but should evaluate utilitarian products similarly regardless of the affect they were experiencing.

In other conditions, however, participants were shown an attractive picture of the product before they received specific information about its attributes. Moreover, this was done either before or after extraneous affect was induced. Yeung hypothesized that the picture would spontaneously elicit an affect-eliciting appraisal of the product and that participants would form an initial impression of the product on the basis of this appraisal. Therefore, if participants are experiencing affect for other reasons at the time they form this impression, it should influence this impression. This affect-based impression, in turn, should influence the judgments they report later, and this influence should occur regardless of the type of product being judged. On the other hand, suppose participants see a picture of the product at the outset. Then, they should form an initial impression based on the affect elicited by the picture alone, and the extraneous affect they experience subsequently should have no effect on this impression or the judgments that are based on it.

Results confirmed these hypotheses. Table 1.4 shows product evaluations in each experiment as a function of induced affect, the judgment criterion (hedonic vs. utilitarian), and picture conditions (no picture, picture–after affect, picture–before affect). As expected, extraneous affect under no-picture conditions had an impact on judgments when participants were induced to use a hedonic basis for judgment but not when they were stimulated to use a utilitarian criterion. When they had seen a picture of the product and were feeling either happy or sad at the time, these feelings had an impact on the impressions they formed on the basis of the picture, and consequently influenced their later product evaluations. When participants saw a picture of the product at the outset, however, they based their impression on the affect elicited by the picture alone, and the extraneous affect they experienced subsequently had no impact.

Summary

As Schwarz and Clore's (1983, 1988) conceptualization suggests, people often use the affect they are experiencing at the time they judge a product as an indication of their feelings about the product and, therefore, as a basis for evaluating it.

TABLE 1.4

Product Evaluations as a Function of Mood, Judgment Criterion, and Mood–Picture Order (based on data from Yeung & Wyer, 2004)

	Experiment 1		Experiment 2	
	Hedonic Criterion	Utilitarian Criterion	Hedonic Criterion	Utilitarian Criterion
No Picture				
Positive Mood	6.50	4.00	7.11	3.41
Negative Mood	4.00	4.13	4.67	3.78
Difference	2.50	−.13	2.44	−.37
Mood Induced Before Picture				
Positive Mood	5.25	5.25	6.38	4.88
Negative Mood	3.75	3.78	4.38	3.63
Difference	1.50	1.47	2.00	1.25
Mood Induced After Picture				
Positive Mood	3.46	3.89	3.18	4.11
Negative Mood	3.50	4.33	3.30	4.48
Difference	−.04	−.44	−.12	−.37

However, the impact of affect at the time of judgment cannot account for its influence. One must also consider the effects of affective reactions at earlier stages of processing, including the attention that is paid to information at the time it is received (Adaval, 2003), the construal of its evaluative implications (Adaval, 2001) and, in some cases, the impression of a product that is formed before any specific information about it is presented (Yeung & Wyer, 2004).

MENTAL ACCOUNTING PROCESSES

One of the most intriguing avenues of inquiry to emerge in consumer research was stimulated by Thaler's (1985) conceptualization of mental accounting (see Thaler, 1999, for a more recent review). This conceptualization assumes that people keep a mental account of the subjective costs and benefits of their transactions in a particular domain, and that their decisions are motivated by a desire to maximize the positive balance in this account or, at least, to keep themselves out of the red.

Several implications of a mental account metaphor derive from the assumption that people keep different *subaccounts*, each pertaining to a different life domain. As a result, the costs and benefits they experience in one domain may not compensate for the loss or gain they experience in other domains. To borrow examples from Thaler (1985), people imagine that they would bet more recklessly at poker if they are $50 ahead in the game than if they have just gained the same amount of money in the stock market, as the latter event is posted to a different account. For similar reasons, people imagine they would be happier if (a) they have won $20 in the lottery than if (b) they have won $100 in the lottery but find they must pay their landlord $80 to compensate for damages to their apartment.

The construction of subaccounts can occur for other reasons. Soman and Gourville (2001) provided an interesting example. That is, people who imagine having invested in a 4-day skiing pass costing $160 report greater willingness to give up a fourth day on the slopes than people who imagine prepurchasing four, single-day tickets costing $40 each. One interpretation of this finding assumes that people put the cost of the 4-day pass into a single account, and so the loss of a day's skiing does not put the account in the red. However, they put each of the four single-day passes in a different account. Thus, the loss of a day's skiing would have a severe effect on the balance of that day's account, increasing the desire to avoid this situation.

As these examples indicate, the primary focus of attention in this research has been on the factors that influence the reactions to different hypothetical-choice situations, based on descriptions of the costs and benefits associated with the alternatives. Predictions have been based in large part on *prospect theory* (Kahneman & Tversky, 1979), which defines the subjective utility associated with objective costs and benefits (defined in units of money, time, or effort, etc.). Because the utility function for positive outcomes differs from the function for negative ones, a number of interesting predictions can be generated. To give but one example, the theory predicts that people report being more willing to drive 20 minutes to save $5 on the purchase of a product that normally sells for $15 than to drive 20 minutes to save $5 on the purchase of a product that normally costs $125 (Tversky & Kahneman, 1981).

An Information-Processing Analysis

With few exceptions (cf. Gourville & Soman, 1998, Experiment 4; Soman & Gourville, 2001, Experiment 4), mental accounting phenomena have been investigated by stimulating participants to imagine either themselves or another in a particular choice situation and to predict which option they would choose (or, alternatively, to indicate how they would feel if a particular decision outcome occurred). These judgments are presumably guided by the subjective utility of the alternative outcomes that people compute on the basis of the information available and the manner in which it is conveyed. The results of this research provide insight into the nature of these computational processes. Possibly because of the restricted paradigm that has been used to examine these processes, however, the research has not called attention to processes that might occur at other stages. A consideration of the research within a broader theoretical perspective nevertheless raises additional questions about these processes and their implications.

1. Comprehension Processes

Many of the effects observed in mental accounting research can be conceptualized in terms of differences in the way the choice alternatives are "framed," based on the verbal descriptions that are given to them (Tversky & Kahneman, 1981). A classic example is provided by evidence that people react more favorably to a drug that will save the lives of 30% of the people who are afflicted with a disease than to a drug that is described as failing to save the lives of 70% of the victims. This is because the first option focuses on positive consequences whereas the second focuses attention on negative ones. Framing could come also into play in the studies cited previously. In Soman and Gourville's (2001) study, for example, the verbal descriptions of a multiple-day ski pass or four, single-day passes may stimulate people to frame the situations differently and to draw different conclusions as a result. Perhaps if participants in the multiple-pass condition were explicitly reminded that the cost of a multiple-pass ticket was equivalent to that of four, single-pass tickets, the effect of the verbal descriptions would be less. Other research can also be viewed as investigations of the way in which judgments are affected by the way choice alternatives are described (e.g., Kahneman & Miller, 1986).

The question is what cognitive processes underlie these framing phenomena. Considered from an information-processing perspective, the phenomena occur at the comprehension stage. Recent theories of comprehension (Wyer, 2004; see also Wyer, Adaval, & Colcombe, 2002; Wyer & Radvansky, 1999) assumed that in the course of comprehending a hypothetical sequence of events, people construct a mental simulation of the sequence, or *episode model*, based on their preexisting knowledge of events that are similar to the ones described (cf. Wyer & Radvansky, 1999). Then, once the representation is constructed, they may construe its implications with reference to a more general event representation, or *implicit theory*, about the causes and consequences of events similar to those described in the situation at hand (for more detailed discussions of the role of implicit theories in judgments and decisions, see Dweck, 1991; M. Ross, 1989; Wyer, 2004). The more closely the sequence described in the information matches that of the theory, the more plausible it is judged to be. These observations are consistent with previous studies of the role of mental simulations of events in judgments (Kahneman & Tversky, 1982; Ross, Lepper, Strack, & Steinmetz, 1977; Sherman, Skov, Hervitz, & Stock, 1981).

The use of a particular implicit theory to interpret and construe the implications of new information depends in part on the ease with which it comes to mind. This, in turn, can be influenced by the verbal description of the events to be comprehended, as suggested by the examples given earlier and by research on the cognitive dynamics of responses to opinion surveys (for summaries, see Schwarz, 1994; Strack, 1994). In an actual choice situation, however, the accessibility of a an implicit theory in memory is likely to be determined by features of the situational context in which the choice is made. To this extent, there is no a priori reason to suppose that a person who is actually confronted with a decision in situations of the sort constructed by Tversky and Kahneman (1981) and others will interpret the choice alternatives in a manner similar to the way they are described verbally in a hypothetical situation that people are told to imagine. For example, a person who purchases a multiple-day skiing pass might spontaneously interpret it as equivalent to four, single-day passes at the time of purchase rather than thinking of it as a "bundle." To this extent, the difference identified by Soman and Gourville on the basis of verbal descriptions of the choice situation might not occur (but see Soman & Gourville, 2001, Experiment 4, for some evidence on the generalizability of their findings to nonlaboratory situations).

The factors that influence the type of simulation that people construct at the time a decision is made are well worth investigating. The point of the present discussion is more general, however. To the extent the choice situations constructed in mental accounting research are comprehended and evaluated on the basis of episode models and implicit theories, it seems unlikely that people form judgments by performing an arithmetic computation of costs and benefits of the sort implied by the construct of a mental account.

2. Storage and Retrieval

To the extent that people form a mental account of the costs and benefits they receive in a given situation, the question arises as to how the account is represented and stored in memory, and the rules that govern its retrieval and use in making judgments. The processes are presumably similar to those that govern memory storage and retrieval more generally. In fact, however, few existing theories of memory can adequately capture the nature of a mental account as Thaler (1985, 1999) conceptualized it.

One conceptualization of memory that is somewhat congenial to the construct of a mental account was proposed by Wyer and Srull (1989) in the context of a more general theoretical formulation of information processing. According to this conceptualization, long-term memory is composed of a number of "referent bins," each containing information about the person, object, or event to which the bin refers. New information about a referent is transmitted to a bin in the order it is received, with the more recently acquired knowledge on top. Moreover, when a previously acquired unit of knowledge is recalled and thought about, a new representation of this knowledge is formed. Thus, the more often a piece of information is thought about, the more times it is represented in the bin. This becomes relevant in conceptualizing the likelihood of recalling the information later. When information about a referent is sought, a probabilistic top–down search of the bin is performed until information sufficient to attain one's objective has been retrieved. This means that the more recently and/or frequently a particular unit of knowledge is used, the more likely it is to be identified.

A mental account might be conceptualized as a specific type of referent bin. To this extent, however, several additional implications of the bin construct are worth noting.

1. The search of a bin for goal-relevant material is theoretically not exhaustive. Only a subset of information is identified that is considered sufficient for attaining the goal one is pursuing (for similar assumptions, see Chaiken, 1987; Higgins, 1996; Taylor & Fiske, 1978). Thus, for reasons noted earlier, knowledge that has been acquired and/or thought about most recently and frequently is most likely to be identified and used. In the present context, this suggests that the benefits and costs that have occurred most recently (or, alternatively, have been most recently or frequently thought about) are most likely to be used to compute an account balance.

2. The referent of a bin can be either specific or global. Moreover, the referents may be overlapping. For example, a person might have account bins pertaining to "real estate investments," to "stocks and bonds," and to "investments" more generally. To this extent, where a particular piece of information is stored depends on its relevance to one's goal at the time it is received and comprehended. Thus, if a person receives a property tax bill and thinks about it with reference to "real estate," the person might store it in a "real estate" bin and not a more general "investment" bin. Consequently, it might have little influence later on when the individual mentally computes the balance of his account on the basis of information stored in his more general "investment" bin.

As the previous example suggests, the bin construct can help to conceptualize the effects of different "subaccounts" postulated by Thaler (1985). On the other hand, it suggests that whether a particular cost or benefit is stored in a particular subaccount and, therefore, whether it affects decisions that are made later, depends on how the event is coded into memory at the time it is first received.

Retrieval-Based Conceptions of Memory. Although the bin construct is an obvious metaphor for conceptualizing the memory representation of a mental account, other conceptualizations are viable. Some memory theories (cf. Hintzman, 1986; Smith, 1990; Wyer & Radvansky, 1999) assumed that information has no particular organization in memory. Rather, each experience has its own memory trace and is stored independently of others. If previously acquired knowledge is required in order to attain a particular objective, a set of features (retrieval cues) is compiled that are relevant to this objective. The information items that contain these features are then retrieved, and a composite of other features that are common to these items is extracted and used as a basis for judgment. In the present context, this suggests that people do not spontaneously store the costs and benefits of a transaction in a single location, and that the "account" composed of these outcomes is not constructed until the decision is made, based on the subset of costs and benefits that come to mind most easily at the time.

This conceptualization is congenial to Gourville and Soman's (1998) analysis of the effects of cost depreciation on decisions. They found that although people who have paid money for the use of an athletic facility are motivated to justify its cost by using it. However, the strength of this motivation and the use of the facility are a function of the salience of the cost at the time the decision is made. For example, participants were more inclined to maintain their use of the facility over the course of a 1-year period if they paid for the activity in 1-month installments than if they had paid for it in a lump sum at the beginning of the year. Thus, although this finding is interesting, the necessity of postulating the existence of a mental account in order to account for it is unclear.

3. Effects of Prior Judgments on Subsequent Ones

Research in several areas indicates that once people have made a judgment and this judgment is stored in memory, the judgment is later recalled and used as a basis for later judgments and decisions independently of the information on which it was originally based (cf. Carlston, 1980; Higgins & Lurie, 1983; Sherman, Ahlm, Berman, & Lynn, 1978; Srull & Wyer, 1989). In the present context, this raises the possibility that when people receive new information about a cost or benefit derived from a choice, they do not compute an account "balance" by reviewing the specific outcomes they have received in the past. Rather, they simply retrieve a previously computed value of the balance and update it on the basis of the new information without reviewing the events that entered into its computation. This updated balance is then stored, thus being available for further updating when a new relevant outcome is encountered.

This possibility has intuitive appeal. Perhaps its most important implication is that judgments and decisions are based on the account balance alone, independently of the specific events that entered into its computation. However, it raises a question of how the account balance is actually incremented. On one hand, people might simply add or subtract an increment that is equal in magnitude to the subjective value of the new event. On the other hand, the implications of the new experience might be subjectively averaged with the preexisting account value (cf. Anderson, 1981). In the latter case, the new events would have a disproportional impact. Alternatively, the impact of a new experience might decrease as the number of other pieces that have preceded it increases. In this case, initial entrees into the account might have the greatest effect.

4. Summary

The considerations raised in the preceding pages do not invalidate the phenomena that have been identified in research performed within a mental accounting framework. On the other hand, they indicate that a consideration of this research within a broader conceptualization of information processing raises several additional questions about the reasons for the effects and the conditions in which they occur. That is, both contextual and informational factors may influence the interpretation of the events at the time they are encountered, and the sorts of implicit theories that are activated and used to construe the implications. Moreover, under conditions in which several different outcomes enter into a mental account, it may be necessary to specify the way the mental account is represented in memory and the storage and retrieval processes that govern its use.

Relationship Accounting: A Specific Application

A mental account is presumably constructed from a number of costs and benefits that occur over a period of time. The paradigm that has typically been employed in mental accounting research (in which participants are asked to compare verbally described situations and choice alternatives) does not capture the dynamic character of such an account. Indeed, the utility of the mental accounting construct in conceptualizing this research is not always apparent (but see Thaler, 1999). However, one area in which the utility of a mental accounting construct is of particular value surrounds the dynamics of giving and receiving favors. A conceptualization currently being developed by Candy Fong exemplifies this possibility. The conceptualization, which is part of Fong's dissertation research, is not fully developed at this writing. However, her formulation suggests that a mental accounting metaphor, although useful, is unlikely to be sufficient for explaining the phenomena that occur.

Fong assumes that people keep mental accounts of the favors they give and receive in their interaction with another person, and that when the favors they have received from a person outweigh the favors they have given (i.e., the account is imbalanced), they experience feelings of indebtedness. However, the receipt of a favor can also elicit feelings of appreciation, and that these feelings could also affect the motivation to reciprocate. Although feelings of indebtedness and feelings of appreciation can often co-occur in response to a favor, this is not always the case. Furthermore, the determinants and the effects of the two types of feelings can differ. For example, feelings of indebtedness arise when another's favor produces an imbalance in one's account. These feelings can therefore be eliminated by reciprocating the favor and, therefore, eliminating the imbalance that exists. In contrast, feelings of appreciation are positively valenced and their effects cannot easily be conceptualized within a mental-accounting framework. (For one thing, appreciation for another's gift is unlikely to be eliminated by giving a gift in return.) Several implications of this difference are worth noting.

1. Feelings of indebtedness (and, therefore, one's tendency to reciprocate) are contingent on one's past history of giving favors as well as receiving them. That is, they are unlikely to arise unless the combined value of favors received exceeds the combined value of favors given. In contrast, feelings of appreciation are a function of only the favors received, independently of past favors one has bestowed. Thus, they may stimulate reciprocity regardless of the number of favors given in the past.

2. Because feelings of indebtedness are unpleasant, people may attempt to eliminate them as soon as possible after they occur. That is, they are likely to reciprocate the favor soon after it is received. Furthermore, as implied by Thaler's (1985) conception of *subaccounts*, they may try to respond in kind. (Thus, people who are invited to a dinner party may extend a similar invitation to the host, but are less likely to buy the person a Christmas present.) On the other hand, negative feelings dissipate. Therefore, the likelihood of reciprocating an indebtedness-motivated favor decreases over time. In contrast, feelings of appreciation are positive and so there is little desire to reduce or eliminate this pleasant emotional state. Thus, there is less motivation to reciprocate the favor immediately. Moreover, feelings of appreciation may affect liking for the recipient, and this effect may persist after the feelings themselves have dissipated. Therefore, if liking stimulates favor doing, it may have an impact long after the appreciation-eliciting experience that gave rise to it occurred. Finally, this impact may be manifested in favors that differ in kind from those that elicited the feelings originally.

These and other hypotheses based on Fong's conceptualization are currently being tested. In the present context, however, the importance of her analysis lies in part in her recognition that although the mental accounting construct is a useful tool in conceptualizing the exchange of favors, it is unlikely to provide all of the answers.

FINAL REMARKS

Although the specific research discussed in this chapter is quite diverse, it converges on two general conclusions. First, research that has concentrated on a given stage of processing has uncovered a large number of interesting and important findings. At the same time, a consideration of the processing at this stage alone is insufficient to account for all of the phenomena that occur in the area being investigated. Thus, a conceptualization of the phenomena from a broader theoretical perspective is desirable.

Although the tendency to focus on a single stage of processing to the exclusion of other stages is evident in research on single-alternative decisions, it is more generally characteristic of research on multiple-alternative decisions. This research contributes to an understanding of information processing at a particular stage without denying the importance of processes that occur at other stages. As such, its implications are readily incorporated within a more general information-processing framework.

I personally believe that consumer research and theorizing is moving toward the development of a broad-based conceptualization of consumer judgment and decision making that can ultimately incorporate the effects of situational, informational, and individual difference variables at all stages of decision-related cognitive activity. The specific phenomena that capture the interests of individual investigators may differ, and few persons may themselves have an interest in developing the overall conceptualization within which their work will ultimately fall. (For a few recent attempts to develop a formulation of social information processing that has implications for consumer behavior as well, see Wyer, 2004; Wyer & Srull, 1989.) It would nevertheless be unfortunate if researchers do not keep this broader objective in mind.

There is always a danger that the inherent differences in research paradigms employed in research, and the conceptual approaches that dominate the use of these paradigms, are detrimental to the attainment of this objective rather than facilitative. In this regard, Simonson, Carmon, Dhar, Drolet, and Nowlis (2001) noted that empirical research in consumer behavior has seemed to fall within two "camps," characterized by information processing on one hand and behavior decision theory (BDT; see Einhorn & Hogarth, 1981; Slovic, Fischhoff, & Lichtenstein, 1977) on the other. Research in the latter area has been largely concerned with conditions in which individuals' judgments and decisions deviate from normative principles of rationality, as defined by classical economic theory (see Simon, 1978, for an alternative definition). This focus has often led to phenomenon-driven research rather than the sort of theory-driven research that characterizes information-processing investigations. As Simonson et al. (2001) noted, however, the methods employed in the two areas are often very similar. Moreover, there are many exceptions to any generalizations that might be drawn about differences between the areas. These considerations suggest that the two camps are, if anything, complementary, and not incompatible.

I share this view. Several distinctions between the two areas strike me as somewhat illusory. For example, behavior decision theorists are sometimes characterized as concerned with what phenomena occur, whereas information-processing proponents are concerned with why they occur. This distinction, however, may be rooted in differences of opinion as to what constitutes a sufficient explanation. Information-processing theorists prefer to explain a judgment or decision in terms of the sequence of cognitive activities that underlies its generation. Behavior decision researchers, on the other hand, are more inclined to explain phenomena in terms of their situational and informational determinants. Nevertheless, each type of explanation can be viewed as a set of "if–then" propositions (premises) that, in combination, generate an empirically verifiable conclusion. For a theory to be taken seriously, the validity of the premises as well as the conclusion must be established. However, this is true regardless of whether the premises are stated in terms of situational variables or cognitive ones. To this extent, one's satisfaction with each type of explanation may be largely a matter of taste. Perhaps a preference for explanations in terms of mental processes lies in the hope that different situational and informational variables stimulate similar mental processes and, therefore, have comparable effects on behavior. In contrast, explanations in terms of situational and informational features are necessarily context specific and, therefore, are likely to be of limited generalizability. However, there is undoubtedly a tradeoff between the generality of a theory's applicability and its ability to generate precise predictions in a particular situation. To this extent, the optimal level of generality at which one feels comfortable may be largely a matter of personal preference.

A second distinction surrounds the conceptual basis for the research questions that are asked. Behavioral decision research has been motivated in part by economic theories of choice. These theories are largely normative, specifying the rational choice strategy that should be applied in a given set of conditions. Behavioral decision research has attempted to identify the differences between the decisions that are defined as rational on the basis of normative criteria, and the decisions that people actually make. This research tradition is exemplified by Tversky and Kahneman's well-known studies of cognitive heuristics (for summaries, see Kahneman, Slovic, & Tversky, 1982; see also Nisbett & Ross, 1980) as well as consumer behavior.

There is little reason to suppose that normative models of choice bear much relationship to the processes in which people actually engage. To this end, the theories developed in information-processing research are descriptive rather than normative, being derived on the basis of empirically validated assumptions about the processes that underlie judgments and decisions. However, this certainly does not imply that the principles identified in behavior decision research should be ignored. To the contrary, these phenomena provide stimulants to the development of more general conceptualizations of the conditions in which these principles actually operate and the reasons for their application (cf. Chaiken, 1987; Menon, 1993; Norenzayan & Schwarz, 1999; Wyer, 2004; Wyer & Srull, 1989). Indeed, if it were not for research that has identified the existence of heuristic principles, and the phenomena uncovered by behavior decision researchers, there would be less for information-processing proponents to explain.

Perhaps the major difference between the two approaches lies in the personality and temperament of the investigators. That is, behavior decision researchers tend to be intrinsically interested in substantive phenomena as ends in themselves and do not normally consider these phenomena as arenas for theory testing (Simonson et al., 2001). This tendency should certainly not be discouraged. Many of the world's major scientific discoveries (most notably, radium and the transistor) emerged as a result of chance observations in the laboratory that occurred in the course of exploring ostensibly unrelated phenomena. As evidenced by the examples given in this chapter, a theoretical conceptualization of the phenomena may ultimately be necessary in order to move beyond this objective to a comprehensive understanding of the phenomena. Indeed, the imposition of a theoretical framework on observed phenomena can lead to the generation of predictions about new phenomena that might otherwise never be identified.

Whether the researchers who impose and evaluate these theories are the same individuals who generate the phenomena to which the theories pertain is actually irrelevant. We should nevertheless keep in mind that the development of a broad-based theory that can be used to explain and predict consumer behavior in a wide variety of situations is the ultimate objective of our discipline, and should see ourselves as implicit collaborators in the pursuit of this objective.

ACKNOWLEDGMENTS

The writing of this chapter and much of the research described were supported in part by grants RGC HKUST 6022/00H, HKUST 6053/01H, and HKUST 6192/04H from the Research Grants Council of the Hong Kong Special Administrative Region, China. Appreciation is extended to A. V. Muthukrishnan, Frank Kardes, and Itamar Simonson for comments on an earlier draft of the paper.

REFERENCES

Aaker, J. L., & Lee, A. Y. (2001). I seek pleasures, we avoid pains: The role of self-regulatory goals in information processing and persuasion. *Journal of Consumer Research, 27*, 33–49.
Adaval, R. (2001). Sometimes it just feels right: The differential weighting of affect-consistent and affect-inconsistent product information. *Journal of Consumer Research, 28*, 1–17.

Adaval, R. (2003). How good gets better and bad gets worse: Understanding the impact of affect on evaluations of known brands. *Journal of Consumer Research, 30,* 352–367.

Adaval, R., & Monroe, K. B. (2002). Automatic construction and use of contextual information for product and price evaluations. *Journal of Consumer Research, 28,* 572–588.

Albarracin, D., Johnson, B. J., & Zanna, M. (in press). *Handbook of attitudes and attitude change.* Mahwah, NJ: Lawrence Erlbaum Associates.

Anderson, N. H. (1971). Integration theory and attitude change. *Psychological Review, 78,* 171–206.

Anderson, N. H. (1981). *Foundations of information integration theory.* New York: Academic Press.

Bless, H., Clore, G. L., Schwarz, N., Golisano, V., Rabe, C., & Woelke, M. (1996). Mood and the use of scripts: Does being in a happy mood really lead to mindlessness? *Journal of Personality and Social Psychology, 71,* 665–679.

Bodenhausen, G. V. (1993). Emotions, arousal and stereotypic judgments: A heuristic model of affect and stereotyping. In D. M. Mackie & D. L. Hamilton (Eds.), *Affect, cognition and stereotyping: Interactive processes in group perception* (pp. 13–37). San Diego, CA: Academic Press.

Bower, G. H. (1981). Emotional mood and memory. *American Psychologist, 36,* 129–148.

Bower, G. H., Gilligan, S. J., & Monteiro, K. P. (1981). Selectivity of learning caused by affective states. *Journal of Experimental Psychology: General, 110,* 451–473.

Briley, D. A., Morris, M., & Simonson, I. (2000). Reasons as carriers of culture: Dynamic versus dispositional models of cultural influence on decision making. *Journal of Consumer Research, 27,* 157–178.

Briley, D. A., & Wyer, R. S. (2002). The effect of group membership salience on the avoidance of negative outcomes: Implications for social and consumer decisions. *Journal of Consumer Research, 29,* 400–415.

Carlston, D. E. (1980). Events, inferences and impression formation. In R. Hastie, T. Ostrom, E. Ebbesen, R. Wyer, D. Hamilton, & D. Carlston (Eds.), *Person memory: The cognitive basis of social perception* (pp. 89–119). Hillsdale, NJ: Lawrence Erlbaum Associates.

Chaiken, S. (1987). The heuristic model of persuasion. In M. P. Zanna, J. M. Olson, & C. P. Herman (Eds.), *Social influence: The Ontario Symposium* (Vol. 5, pp. 3–39). Hillsdale, NJ: Lawrence Erlbaum Associates.

Clore, G. L., Schwarz, N., & Conway, M. (1994). Affective causes and consequences of social information processing. In R. S. Wyer & T. K. Srull (Eds.), *Handbook of social cognition* (2nd ed., Vol. 1, pp. 323–417). Hillsdale, NJ: Lawrence Erlbaum Associates.

Dhar, R. (1997). Consumer preference for a no-choice option. *Journal of Consumer Research, 24,* 215–231.

Dhar, R., & Sherman, S. J. (1996). The effect of common and unique features in consumer choice. *Journal of Consumer Research, 23,* 193–203.

Dhar, R., & Simonson, I. (2003). The effect of forced choice on choice. *Journal of Marketing Research, 40,* 146–160.

Dodds, W. B., Monroe, K. B., & Gruwal, D. (1991). Effects of price, brand, and store information on buyers' product evaluations. *Journal of Marketing Research, 28,* 307–319.

Dweck, C. S. (1991). Self-theories and goals: Their role in motivation, personality and development. In R. Dienstbier (Ed.), *Nebraska Symposium on Motivation: Perspectives on motivation* (Vol. 38, pp. 199–235). Lincoln: University of Nebraska Press.

Eagly, A. H., & Chaiken, S. (1993). *The psychology of attitudes.* Fort Worth, TX: Harcourt Brace.

Einhorn, H. J., & Hogarth, R. M. (1981), Behavioral decision theory: Processes of judgment and choice. *Annual Review of Psychology, 32,* 53–88.

Fazio, R. H. (1990). Multiple processes by which attitudes guide behavior: The MODE model as an integrative framework. In M. P. Zanna (Ed.), *Advances in experimental social psychology* (Vol. 23, pp. 75–109). San Diego, CA: Academic Press.

Fishbein, M., & Ajzen, I. (1975). *Belief, attitude, intention, and behavior: An introduction to theory and research.* Reading, MA: Addison-Wesley.

Forgas, J. P. (1995). Mood and judgment: The affect infusion model (AIM). *Psychological Bulletin*, *117*, 39–66.

Forgas, J. P., & Bower, G. H. (1987). Mood effects on person perception judgments. *Journal of Personality and Social Psychology*, *53*, 53–60.

Forgas, J. P., Bower, G. H., & Krantz, S. (1984). The influence of mood on perceptions of social interactions. *Journal of Experimental Social Psychology*, *20*, 497–513.

Gilbert, D. T. (2002). Inferential correction. In T. Gilovich, D. Griffin, & D. Kahneman (Eds.), *Heuristics and biases: The psychology of intuitive judgment* (pp. 167–184). Cambridge, England: Cambridge University Press.

Gillund, G., & Shiffrin, R. M. (1984). A retrieval model for both recognition and recall. *Psychological Review*, *91*, 1–67.

Gourville, J. T., & Soman, D. (1998). Payment depreciation: The behavioral effects of temporally separating payments from consumption. *Journal of Consumer Research*, *25*, 160–174.

Heine, S. J., Lehman, D. R., Markus, H., & Kitayama, S. (1999). Is there a universal need for positive self-regard? *Psychological Review*, *106*, 766–794.

Higgins, E. T. (1996). Knowledge activation: Accessibility, applicability and salience. In E. T. Higgins & A. W. Kruglanski (Eds.), *Social psychology: Handbook of basic principles* (pp. 133–168). New York: Guilford.

Higgins, E. T. (1998). Promotion and prevention. Regulatory focus as a motivational principle. In M. P. Zanna (Ed.), *Advances in experimental social psychology* (Vol. 30, pp. 1–46). San Diego, CA: Academic Press.

Higgins, E. T., & Lurie, L. (1983). Context, categorization and recall: The "change-of-standard" effect. *Cognitive Psychology*, *15*, 525–547.

Hintzman, D. L. (1986). "Schema abstraction" in a multiple-trace model. *Psychological Review*, *93*, 411–428.

Hofstede, G. (1980). *Culture's consequences*. Newbury Park, CA: Sage.

Hong, Y. Y., & Chiu, C. Y. (2001). Toward a paradigm shift: From cross-cultural differences in social-cognitive mediation of cultural differences. *Social Cognition*, *19*, 181–196.

Hong, Y. Y., Morris, M., Chiu, C. Y., & Benet-Martinez, V. (2000). Multicultural minds: A dynamic constructivist approach to culture and cognition. *American Psychologist*, *55*, 709–720.

Houston, D. A., Sherman, S. J., & Baker, S. M. (1989). The influence of unique features and direction of comparison on preferences. *Journal of Experimental Social Psychology*, *25*, 121–141.

Huber, J., Payne, J. W., & Puto, C. (1982). Adding asymmetrically dominated alternatives: Violations of regularity and the similarity hypothesis. *Journal of Consumer Research*, *25*, 175–186.

Isbell, L. M. (2004). Not all happy people are lazy or stupid: Evidence of systematic processing in happy moods. *Journal of Experimental Social Psychology*.

Kahneman, D., & Miller, D. T. (1986). Norm theory: Comparing reality to its alternatives. *Psychological Review*, *93*, 136–153.

Kahneman, D., & Tversky, A. (1979). Prospect theory: An analysis of decision under risk. *Econometrica*, *47*, 263–291.

Kahneman, D., & Tversky, A. (1982). The simulation heuristic. In D. Kahneman, P. Slovic, & A. Tversky (Eds.), *Judgment under uncertainty: Heuristics and biases* (pp. 201–208). New York: Cambridge University Press.

Kahneman, D., Slovic, P., & Tversky, A. (Eds.). (1982). *Judgment under uncertainty: Heuristics and biases*. New York: Cambridge University Press.

Kardes, F. R., Kalyanaram, G., Chandrashekaran, M., & Dornoff, R. J. (1993). Brand retrieval, consideration set composition, consumer choice, and the pioneering advantage. *Journal of Consumer Research*, *15*, 225–233.

Kardes, F. R., Posavac, S. S., & Cronley, M. L. (2004). Consumer inference: A review of processes, bases, and judgment contexts. *Journal of Consumer Psychology*, *14*, 230–256.

Kardes, F. R., Sanbonmatsu, D. M., Cronley, M. L., & Houghton, D. C. (2002). Consideration set over evaluation: When impossibly favorable ratings of a set of brands are observed. *Journal of Consumer Psychology, 12*, 353–362.

Lazarus, R. S. (1982). Thoughts on the relations between emotion and cognition. *American Psychologist, 37*, 1019–1024.

Lazarus, R. S. (1991). *Emotion and adaptation.* New York: Oxford University Press.

Lichtenstein, M., & Srull, T. K. (1985). Conceptual and methodological issues in examining the relationship between consumer memory and judgment. In L. F. Alwitt & A. A. Mitchell (Eds.), *Psychological processes and advertising effects: Theory, research and application* (pp. XX–XX). Hillsdale, NJ: Lawrence Erlbaum Associates.

Maheswaran, D., Mackie, D. M., & Chaiken, S. (1992). Brand name as a heuristic cue: The effects of task importance and expectancy confirmation on consumer judgments. *Journal of Consumer Psychology, 1*, 317–336.

Markus, H., & Kitayama, S. (1991). Culture and the self: Implications for cognition, emotion and motivation. *Psychological Review, 98*, 224–253.

Martin, L. L., Ward, D. W., Achee, J. W., & Wyer, R. S. (1993). Mood as input: People have to interpret the motivational implications of their moods. *Journal of Personality and Social Psychology, 64*, 317–316.

McGuire, W. J. (1964). Inducing resistance to persuasion: Some contemporary approaches. In L. Berkowitz (Ed.), *Advances in experimental social psychology* (Vol. 1, pp. 191–229). New York: Academic Press.

McGuire, W. J. (1972). Attitude change: An information processing paradigm. In C. G. McClintock (Ed.), *Experimental social psychology* (pp. 108–141). New York: Holt, Rinehart & Winston.

Menon, G. (1993). The effects of accessibility of information in memory on judgments of behavioral frequencies. *Journal of Consumer Research, 20*, 431–440.

Miller, P. J., Fung, H., & Mintz, J. (1996). Self-construction through narrative practices: A Chinese and American comparison of early socialization. *Ethos, 24*, 237–280.

Nedungadi, P. (1990). Recall and consumer consideration sets: Influencing choice without altering brand evaluation. *Journal of Consumer Research, 15*, 169–184.

Niedenthal, P. M., Halberstadt, J. B., & Setterlund, M. B. (1997). Being happy and seeing "happy": Emotional state mediates visual word recognition. *Cognition and Emotion, 11*, 403–432.

Niedenthal, P. M., & Setterlund, M. B. (1994). Emotion congruence in perception. *Personality and Social Psychology Bulletin, 20*, 401–411.

Nisbett, R. E., & Ross, L. (1980). *Human inference: Strategies and shortcomings of social judgments.* Englewood Cliffs, NJ: Prentice-Hall.

Norenzayan, A., & Schwarz, N. (1999). Telling what they want to know: Participants tailor causal attributions to researchers' interests. *European Journal of Social Psychology, 29*, 1011–1020.

Ostrom, T. M., & Upshaw, H. S. (1968). Psychological perspective and attitude change. In A. G. Greenwald, T. C. Brock, & T. M. Ostrom (Eds.), *Psychological foundations of attitude* (pp. 217–242). New York: Academic Press.

Pan, Y., & Lehmann, D. R. (1993). The influence of new brand entry on subjective brand judgments. *Journal of Consumer Research, 20*, 76–86.

Parducci, A. (1965). Category judgment: A range–frequency model. *Psychological Review, 72*, 407–418.

Park, J. W., & Kim, J. K. (2005). The effects of decoys on preference shifts: The role of attractiveness and providing justification. *Journal of Consumer Psychology, 15*, 94–107.

Parrott, G., & Sabini, J. (1990). Mood and memory under natural conditions: Evidence for mood and incongruent recall. *Journal of Personality and Social Psychology, 59*, 321–336.

Petty, R. E., & Cacioppo, J. T. (1986). *Communication and persuasion: Central and peripheral routes to attitude change.* New York: Springer-Verlag.

Pham, M. T. (1998). Representativeness, relevance, and the use of feelings in decision making. *Journal of Consumer Research, 25*, 144–159.

Raaijmakers, J. G. W., & Shiffrin, R. M. (1981). Search of associative memory. *Psychological Review, 88*, 93–134.

Ross, L., Lepper, M. R., Strack, F., & Steinmetz, J. (1977). Social explanation and social expectation: Effects of real and hypothetical explanations on subjective likelihood. *Journal of Personality and Social Psychology, 35*, 817–829.

Ross, M. (1989). Relation of implicit theories to the construction of personal histories. *Psychological Review, 96*, 341–357.

Schwarz, N. (1990). Feelings as information: Informational and motivational functions of affective states. In R. M. Sorrentino & E. T. Higgins (Eds.), *Handbook of motivation and cognition: Foundations of social behavior* (Vol. 2, pp. 527–561). New York: Guilford.

Schwarz, N. (1994). Judgment in a social context: Biases, shortcomings, and the logic of conversation. In M. P. Zanna (Ed.), *Advances in experimental social psychology* (Vol. 24, pp. 123–162). San Diego, CA: Academic Press.

Schwarz, N., & Clore, G. L. (1983). Mood, misattribution, and judgments of well-being: Informative and directive functions of affective states. *Journal of Personality and Social Psychology, 45*, 513–523.

Schwarz, N., & Clore, G. L. (1988). How do I feel about it? Informative functions of affective states. In K. Fiedler & J. Forgas (Eds.), *Affect, cognition and social behavior* (pp. 44–62). Toronto. Hofgrefe International,

Schwarz, N., Strack, F., Kommer, D., & Wagner, D. (1987). Soccer, rooms, and the quality of your life: Mood effects on satisfaction with life in general and with specific life domains. *European Journal of Social Psychology, 17*, 69–79.

Shafir, E., Simonson, I., & Tversky, A. (1993). Reason-based choice. *Cognition, 49*, 11–36.

Sherman, S. J., Ahlm, K., Berman, L., & Lynn, S. (1978). Contrast effects and the relationship to subsequent behavior. *Journal of Experimental Social Psychology, 14*, 340–350.

Sherman, S. J., Skov, R. B., Hervitz, E. F., & Stock, C. B. (1981). The effects of explaining hypothetical future events: From possibility to probability to actuality and beyond. *Journal of Experimental Social Psychology, 17*, 142–158.

Simon, H. (1957). *Models of man: Social and rational.* New York: Wiley.

Simon, H. (1978). Rationality as a process and as product of thought. *American Economic Review, 68*, 1–16.

Simonson, I. (1989). Choice based on reasons: The case of attraction and compromise effects. *Journal of Consumer Research, 16*, 158–174.

Simonson, I., Carmon, Z., Dhar, R., Drolet, A., & Nowlis, S. M. (2001). Consumer research: In search of identity. *Annual Review of Psychology, 52*, 249–275.

Simonson, I., & Tversky, A. (1992). Choice in context: Tradeoff contrast and extremeness aversion. *Journal of Marketing Research, 29*, 281–295.

Slovic, P., Fischhoff, B., & Lichtenstein, S. (1977). Behavioral decision theory. *Annual Review of Psychology, 28*, 1–39.

Smith, E. R. (1990). Content and process specificity in the effects of prior experiences. In T. K. Srull & R. S. Wyer (Eds.), *Advances in social cognition* (Vol. 3, pp. 1–59). Hillsdale, NJ: Lawrence Erlbaum Associates,

Soman, D., & Gourville, J. T. (2001). Transaction decoupling: How price bundling affects the decision to consume. *Journal of Marketing Research, 38*, 30–44.

Srull, T. K., & Wyer, R. S. (1989). Person memory and judgment. *Psychological Review, 96*, 58–63.

Strack, F. (1994). Response processes in social judgment. In R. S. Wyer & T. K. Srull (Eds.), *Handbook of social cognition* (2nd ed., Vol. 1, pp. 287–322). Hillsdale, NJ: Lawrence Erlbaum Associates.

Strack, F., Martin, L. L., & Stepper, S. (1988). Inhibiting and facilitating conditions of the human smile: A nonobtrusive test of the facial feedback hypothesis. *Journal of Personality and Social Psychology, 54*, 768–777.

Taylor, S. E., & Fiske, S. T. (1978). Salience, attention and attribution: Top of the head phenomena. In L. Berkowitz (Ed.), *Advances in experimental social psychology* (Vol. 11, pp. 249–288). New York: Academic Press.

Tesser, A. (1978). Self-generated attitude change. In L. Berkowitz (Ed.), *Advances in experimental social psychology* (Vol. 11, pp. 289–338). New York: Academic Press.

Thaler, R. (1985). Mental accounting and consumer choice. *Marketing Science, 4*, 199–214.

Thaler, R. (1999). Mental accounting matters. *Journal of Behavioral Decision Making, 12*, 183–206.

Triandis, H. C. (1995). *Individualism and collectivism*. Boulder, CO: Westview.

Tversky, A. (1972). Elimination by aspects: A theory of choice. *Psychological Review, 79*, 281–299.

Tversky, A., & Kahneman, D. (1981). The framing of decisions and the rationality of choice. *Science, 211*, 453–458.

Tversky, A., & Kahneman, D. (1982). Causal schemas in judgments under uncertainty. In D. Kahneman, P. Slovic, & A. Tversky (Eds.), *Judgment under uncertainty: Heuristics and biases* (pp. 117–128). New York: Cambridge University Press.

Wang, J., & Wyer, R. S. (2002). Comparative judgment processes: The effects of task objectives and time delay on product evaluations. *Journal of Consumer Psychology, 12*, 327–340.

Wedell, D. H., & Pettibone, J. C. (1996). Using judgments to understand decoy effects in choice. *Organizational Behavior and Human Decision Processes, 67*, 326–344.

Wyer, R. S. (2004). *Social comprehension and judgment: The role of situation models, narratives and implicit theories*. Mahwah, NJ: Lawrence Erlbaum Associates.

Wyer, R. S., Adaval, R., & Colcombe, S. J. (2002). Narrative-based representations of social knowledge: Their construction and use in comprehension, memory and judgment. In M. P. Zanna (Ed.), *Advances in experimental social psychology* (Vol. 34, pp. 131–197). San Diego, CA: Academic Press.

Wyer, R. S., Clore, G. L., & Isbell, L. M. (1999). Affect and information processing. In M. P. Zanna (Ed.), *Advances in experimental social psychology* (Vol. 31, pp. 1–77). San Diego, CA: Academic Press.

Wyer, R. S., & Radvansky, G. A. (1999). The comprehension and validation of social information. *Psychological Review, 10*, 89–118.

Wyer, R. S., & Srull, T. K. (1989). *Memory and cognition in its social context*. Hillsdale, NJ: Lawrence Erlbaum Associates.

Yeung, C. W. M., & Wyer, R. S. (2004). Affect, appraisal, and consumer judgment. *Journal of Consumer Research, 31*, 412–424.

Yeung, W. M. (2003). *Affect, appraisal and consumer judgment*. Unpublished doctoral dissertation, Hong Kong University of Science and Technology.

Zalinski, J., & Anderson, N. H. (1990). Parameter estimation for averaging theory. In N. H. Anderson (Ed.), *Contributions to information integration theory* (Vol. 1, pp. 353–394). Hillsdale, NJ: Lawrence Erlbaum Associates.

CHAPTER TWO

Implications of Selective Processing for Marketing Managers

Steven S. Posavac
University of Rochester

Gavan J. Fitzsimons
Duke University

Frank R. Kardes
University of Cincinnati

David M. Sanbonmatsu
University of Utah

Recent research in selective processing theory has produced a myriad of important findings of interest to marketing managers. At a general level, two streams of selective processing research have emerged; the first considers how selective processing operates in consumer judgment and choice, the second focuses on how the judgments and decisions of managers may be influenced by selective processing. Our chapter begins with a discussion of selective processing theory, then summarizes the findings of studies that have focused on consumers. Following this discussion, we provide prescriptive advice for managers with respect to how consumers' tendency to process information selectively can be leveraged in brand promotion. Next, we present findings specific to how the quality of managers' evaluations of alternatives and choices can be adversely affected by their own proclivity for selective processing. Finally, we discuss how both managers and consumers can avoid making the inaccurate judgments and suboptimal decisions that often result when processing is selective.

SELECTIVE INFORMATION PROCESSING: MECHANICS AND CONSEQUENCES

Judgment is complicated. Whether one is acting in the role of consumer or the role of manager, each day presents numerous judgmental problems that demand solutions. Unfortunately, although our problems are usually readily apparent, the best solutions often are not. In most cases where a judgment must be rendered, there are multiple possible responses or solutions. If one's goal is to make the most accurate judgment, or choose the solution associated with the greatest expected value, every possible solution and all available evidence supporting and undermining each possibility must be considered. Importantly, maximizing judgmental accuracy requires a comparison of the evidence for each solution, and adoption of the solution with the most compelling evidence considered in aggregate.

Although perhaps unintuitive, it would be folly for a consumer to try to maximize the accuracy of each and every judgment. Consider a consumer in need of socks. To be confident of making the very best choice given idiosyncratic preferences, this consumer would need to (a) delineate all possible sock options, (b) enumerate all of the attributes and associated attribute values associated with each option, (c) decide on the relative importance of each attribute, and (d) create a summary judgment of what the best sock option is, which would then presumably inform a subsequent choice. This strategy would clearly require an enormous amount of time and effort. Although a consumer following it would be sure to be delighted with his or her socks, it is likely that negative consequences would also be experienced because energy that would otherwise be devoted to worthwhile activities such as spending time with one's family, or working, would instead be devoted to the calculus of optimal sock shopping.

Because individuals have neither unlimited time nor boundless energy, information processing is rarely as fully comparative as in the aforementioned example. Instead, often a much more selective information processing strategy is undertaken (Mussweiler, 2003). Sanbonmatsu, Posavac, Kardes, and Mantel (1998) forwarded the Selective Hypothesis Testing framework to understand how individuals typically deal with the necessity of making judgments under constraint.

A hypothesis in this framework refers to possible solutions or responses to a judgmental problem. The best or most accurate hypothesis can be determined only if all possible or plausible hypotheses are generated and pitted against each other in a series of evidentiary comparisons. Instead of this fully comparative strategy, individuals typically consider one focal hypothesis at a time. If evidence gathering in which an individual engages to test the hypothesis appears in an absolute sense to be compelling, the individual concludes that the focal hypothesis is correct. If evidence supporting the focal hypothesis is not easily marshaled, the hypothesis is rejected and another is entertained.

Unfortunately, bias enters into multiple stages of the hypothesis-testing process. Evidence is sought that, if present, would imply that the focal hypothesis is correct (Devine, Hirt, & Gehrke, 1990; Klayman & Ha, 1989). In contrast, evidence that would undermine the focal hypothesis, or support a competing hypothesis, is often neglected (Brenner, Koehler, & Tversky, 1996; Klayman & Ha, 1987; Van Wallendael & Hastie, 1990). In addition to these biases of evidence gathering, individuals also tend to interpret ambiguous evidence as being supportive of the focal hypothesis (Griffin & Ross, 1991), and aggregate available evidence in a manner that casts the focal hypothesis in a favorable light.

All of these processes tend to lead individuals to prematurely conclude that the focal hypothesis is best. Thus, factors that determine which hypothesis becomes focal (e.g., the salience and accessibility of hypotheses) have a tremendous influence on the outcome of judgment. Indeed, an initially considered hypothesis is at an advantage compared to other hypotheses because of individuals' proclivity to prematurely settle on focal hypotheses. The next section considers recent research that documents how consumers' judgments are influenced by selective processing, and the implications for their decisions.

SELECTIVE PROCESSING EFFECTS IN THE JUDGMENTS AND DECISIONS OF CONSUMERS

When consumers engage in careful deliberation about one focal brand to the exclusion of others, their evaluation of the focal brand may change. Evaluative judgments, like probabilistic judgments, require individuals to gather and interpret information. Thus, if individuals engage in selective processing of information about one brand and not others, their evaluation of the focal brand may become more extreme. Posavac, Sanbonmatsu, and Ho (2002) conducted a series of experiments to demonstrate how selective consideration of a focal brand can lead to changes in brand attitudes. In their first experiment, participants were randomly assigned to consider one of four charitable organizations with the use of a spinner board. After the focal charity was determined, participants were queried as to the importance of the activities of the focal charity, as well as general attitudes toward the charity. After this manipulation of selective focus, participants' relative attitudes toward all the charities were measured. Results demonstrated that participants were more favorable to the focal charity than would have been the case had the manipulation of focus not influenced attitudes. Thus, being prompted to carefully consider one but not other options causes the focal option to be evaluated more extremely. In addition to demonstrating the effects of selective consideration on attitudes, participants were also more likely to choose the focal charity than nonfocal charities to receive a donation, and were willing to pay more to the focal charity than to others. A subsequent experiment concerned with attitudes toward fast-food restaurants and charities demonstrated that when consumers selectively deliberate about a brand, the extremity of the attitude (e.g., the attitude itself) changes, not just its accessibility.

The final experiment of Posavac et al. (2002) explored a boundary condition of the positivity effects evidenced in the first two experiments, and delineated how selective deliberation about a focal brand can influence real choices involving money. This experiment was conducted in two sessions. In the first session, participants' attitudes toward four fast-food chains were measured. In a second session, participants were randomly assigned to selectively deliberate on the restaurant they liked best, second best, or least, or were assigned to a control condition in which they deliberated about a brand of soft drink. After deliberating, they were allowed to choose a coupon from one of the fast-food chains to take home. Although deliberating on a favorite brand is unlikely to affect market share in a simple-choice task (e.g., because the favorite is very likely to be chosen regardless of any manipulation), when participants selectively deliberated on the fast-food chain they had previously rated second best in the first experimental session, they were much more likely to choose it in the second session. Thus, in this condition, selective consideration affected choice by increasing the likelihood that the focal fast-food chain would be selected.

A very different pattern emerged when participants deliberated on the chain they had rated as least favorite in the first session—in this case the focal chain was not more likely to be chosen. Taken together, these results suggest that selective consideration is likely to increase choice likelihood of a brand that is liked, but is not a consumer's favorite brand. The favorite brand is unlikely to benefit from positivity effects due to ceiling effects, and attitudes toward brands that are not liked may be affected by selective consideration—but the resultant attitude may be more negative, and hence unlikely to affect choice.

Recent research has shown that much more subtle manipulations of selective processing can influence product judgments and choice. Posavac, Sanbonmatsu, Kardes, and Fitzsimons (2004) explore consumers' singular evaluations of brands, and how selective processing can influence these evaluations. Consumers commonly engage in singular brand evaluations. For example, when a consumer notices a brand on a grocer's endcap, he or she must form an absolute judgment of the worth of the brand to inform a decision of whether or not to purchase the brand. In such a situation, the evaluative process is likely to be singular because competing brands are not salient.

Experiment 1 of Posavac et al. (2004) was conducted to demonstrate that consumers' singular evaluations of brands are often overly favorable, and to delineate two important moderators of this effect. Participants were asked to rate one of four first-class hotel chains that are well known and well regarded. The focal chain was randomly determined for each participant. Ratings were made in one of four contexts; participants' cognitive capacity was either constrained or not constrained with a secondary task, and participants were either prompted or not prompted to consider alternatives to their focal chain while making their ratings. Results showed that in the default context in which cognitive capacity was not artificially constrained and consideration of alternatives was not explicitly prompted, participants expressed unrealistically favorable evaluations of the focal chain on a variety of measures (e.g., attitudes, choice intention), even though the determination of which chain was focal was randomly determined. However, if either cognitive capacity was constrained or consideration of alternatives was prompted, participants were much less likely to be influenced by context and report unwarranted enthusiasm for the focal chain.

The moderating variables delineated in the first experiment likely operated as they did because they decreased the likelihood that participants would engage in selective processing of the focal hotel chain. When cognitive load is high, consumers are unlikely to be able to devote sufficient resources to processing focal brand information for a positivity effect to occur. When the consideration of alternatives is prompted, processing is likely to become more comparative, thus again reducing the likelihood of overly favorable evaluations of the focal brand. Thus, because these variables moderated focal brand positivity bias, it appears that selective processing drove the effect.

Experiment 2 was conducted to bolster the implication of Experiment 1 that selective processing mediated focal brand positivity bias. In this experiment, participants again rated a focal hotel chain, and consideration of alternatives was either prompted or not prompted. After making the ratings, participants were asked to engage in a thought-listing task that was used to create an index of how selective versus comparative each participant's processing was (i.e., the number of thoughts in the listing about the focal chain divided by total number of thoughts). Results were consistent with Experiment 1; focal brand bias was more likely when consideration of alternatives was not prompted. More important, selective processing mediated this between condition effect, thus providing direct evidence of the role of selective processing in focal brand bias.

A third experiment reported by Posavac et al. (2004) was conducted with a sample of mature consumers by a mall intercept research firm retained by the authors. This experiment demonstrated focal brand positivity bias in a new category (*laundry detergents*), and showed that judgmental bias has implications for actual choice; consumers were more likely to choose a box of a randomly selected focal detergent to take home versus a nonfocal brand, unless consideration of alternatives was prompted when consumers rated the focal brand.

Recent work suggests that consumers' product knowledge may be an important moderator of whether singular brand evaluations will be overly favorable (Posavac, Kardes, Sanbonmatsu, & Fitzsimons, in press). Posavac et al. conducted a mall intercept study of evaluations of first-class hotels in which the finding of their earlier work that singular evaluations are often overly favorable was replicated. In addition to items measuring evaluations, they also measured consumers' expertise in two ways: (a) a self-report of knowledge of first-class hotels, and (b) consumers' stated likelihood of staying at a first-class hotel on their next out-of-town trip. Results revealed that the judgments of consumers who rated themselves as being either "very" or "extremely" knowledgeable about first-class hotels were much better calibrated than those who were "somewhat" or less knowledgeable. That is, experts made much more accurate singular evaluations that were less likely to be influenced by contextually induced selective processing than nonexperts. A similar data pattern emerged with respect to consumers' likelihood of staying at a first-class hotel on their next trip; those who were more likely to stay at a first-class hotel were much less likely to be overly favorable toward a focal hotel than consumers who were "somewhat" or less likely to stay at such a hotel.

The selective hypothesis testing processes Posavac et al. (2004) observed may explain the differences between evaluation of a single brand and joint evaluation of two brands (Hsee & Leclerc, 1998). In Hsee and Leclerc's experiments, two brands were each described by two attributes, and one brand was always superior on one attribute while inferior on the other. Both brands were either generally good or bad, based on the absolute values of the attributes. Participants were asked to evaluate either one brand, or evaluate both simultaneously. When a good brand was judged alone, judgments were more favorable than when both brands were judged simultaneously. In contrast, a bad brand was judged more unfavorably when judged alone versus when both brands were judged simultaneously. These results may be explained by selective processing. When a brand is judged in isolation, consumers likely consider attributes of the brand to the exclusion of attributes of other brands. Thus, a good brand will be judged to be excellent and a bad brand to be terrible because the benchmark provided by the other brand never becomes apparent. In contrast, when brands are judged at the same time, although one brand may be good, judgments may be only moderately favorable if a good competitor is also judged. In the same way, judgments of a bad brand may become more moderate if joint evaluation makes obvious that the alternatives are also unfavorable.

Selective processing has also been found to lead to distortion of product information when more than one brand is present in other contexts. When decision makers are encouraged to identify which of two brands is the leading brand after each of a series of attributes are examined, Russo, Meloy, and Medvec (1998) found that information that might otherwise be interpreted as neutral is found to be supportive of the brand leader. They find that this result is robust across situations where no prior brand preference existed and even when no choice was required. The magnitude of the "predecisional distortion" was found to be twice that typically observed in traditional postdecisional distortion due to dissonance reduction.

Similarly, Meyvis and Janiszewski (2002) found that selective processing can lead to a nonnormative dependence on irrelevant information in product judgments. In a typical study, they manipulated whether irrelevant information was present in a description of a singular product in a category and asked them to form judgments of the product. They found that participants held lower evaluations of products that had irrelevant information added to their descriptions relative to the same product description without the irrelevant information attached. Over a series of studies, they concluded that the mechanism driving this effect was selective processing. For example, decision makers asked to evaluate a toothpaste that fought cavities found support for their hypothesis that it was a good brand, while those asked to evaluate a toothpaste that fought cavities and came in a 6-ounce tube experienced this information as one supportive data point and one nonsupportive data point. The net result of this selective processing was that participants judged the former toothpaste as more attractive than the latter.

In addition to brand judgment and choice, selective processing also has been shown to have consequences for consumers' evaluations of gambling options, and their gambling choices. In a series of experiments investigating sports gambling judgments and decisions, Gibson, Sanbonmatsu, and Posavac (1997) found that when individuals selectively considered the likelihood that a given outcome would occur (e.g., that a given team would win an NCAA or NBA game, whether a team would cover a point spread in a given game), they typically overestimated the probability of the focal outcome. This overconfidence that a given outcome would occur translated into increased willingness to gamble generally, and specifically increased betting on the focal outcome. These results were mediated by selective processing; to the extent that an individual focused on reasons why a focal outcome might occur and ignored reasons supporting an alternate outcome, they were particularly likely to overestimate the likelihood of the focal outcome and gamble that it would occur.

Selective processing effects may be ubiquitous, including both judgments of consumer options and, more broadly, judgments of firms. Houghton and Kardes (1998) demonstrated that judgments of firm performance, specifically market share, may be erroneous as a result of selective processing. In their study, participants were given information about a focal company, and asked to estimate its market share as well as that of other companies. These market-share judgments appear to have been made selectively, as total market-share judgments across companies summed to well over 100% (an obvious impossibility). In the second part of the study, consumers were given additional information about the focal firm, and asked to estimate market share a second time. Of course, market share is a zero sum game, and if one firm gains or loses, remaining firms must lose or gain in correspondence. Houghton and Kardes (1998) found, though, that judgments of the focal firm were typically made independent of other firms. Thus, judgments of firm performance appear to have been made selectively according to some absolute assessment of firm worth instead of the normatively appropriate comparative strategy. This tendency was reduced when either participants were low in need for closure (Webster & Kruglanski, 1994), or there were a large number of nonfocal alternatives.

The findings reviewed so far demonstrate that selective processing can affect consumers' judgments and choices regarding specific objects or options. Recent research has shown that selective processing also can affect consumers' judgments of the sufficiency of consideration sets from which they choose (Kardes, Sanbonmatsu, Cronley, & Houghton, 2002). When presented with a randomly determined consideration set of 35mm cameras that was much smaller than the available number of options, consumers indicated a higher-than-possible probability that the set contained the best brand. Consistent with a selective processing explanation, this tendency was particularly severe for consumers who listed few brands in a subsequent task in which they were asked to generate as many camera brands as possible in 15 seconds. Thus, to the extent that consumers processed the given brands selectively and were less sensitive to consideration-set omissions, they were likely to overvalue the consideration set they were given.

The judgmental effects Kardes et al. (2002) report also had consequences for stated search behavior and choice intention; to the extent that consumers perceived that their consideration set contained the best brand, they indicated greater likelihood of buying one of the brands in the set, and less desire to search for information about other brands if they were in the market for a camera. Kardes et al. (2002) showed that these results are robust in different product categories, and when consideration sets are constructed from the offerings of big retailers as well as boutique shops. Results also suggest that consumers will be sensitive to the limitations of a given consideration set only when the absence of important brands is highly salient, and consumers are low in need for closure.

Sanbonmatsu, Kardes, Houghton, Ho, and Posavac (2003) demonstrated that consumers may be as insensitive to attributes that are missing from a product description as they are to brands that are not included in a consideration set. It is often the case that product descriptions, for example in advertisements, are incomplete and feature only the subset of attributes on which an advertised brand is highly competitive. In other cases, only attributes consistent with the desired brand positioning will be relayed. Because accurate brand judgment requires integration of all brand-relevant information, when information about a brand is missing, judgments should be moderate. Sanbonmatsu et al. (2003) showed, however, that consumers typically are insensitive to omissions of attribute information. Instead, when consumers receive information about some attributes of a brand, they typically perceive the attributes that are presented as the most important to consider when making a decision from the category to which the brand belongs. This overweighing of presented attributes, in turn, leads to overly extreme judgments of the favorableness of the brand. These tendencies are attenuated only when (a) consumers possess high knowledge about the relevant category; (b) a comparison brand described by more attribute information than the target brand is present, thus highlighting that some attribute information about the target brand is missing; and/or (c) consumers consider their judgmental criteria before being exposed to brand information, thus limiting the impact of context on their judgments.

Although selective processing can affect perceptions of the importance of attributes, it can also affect consumers' perceptions of the relation between attributes of a product. Kardes, Cronley, Kellaris, and Posavac (2004) demonstrate that selective processing is an important contributor to consumers' tendency to overestimate the correlation between the price and quality of products. Consumers typically believe that the price of a product is predictive of its quality. This perception acts as a select hypothesis when consumers process information about the attributes of brands. Specifically, when a consumer is trying to form an inference about the strength of the price–quality correlation in a particular category, he or she is likely to focus on cases that confirm expectations; that is, instances where a high price is associated with a high quality brand, and instances of a low-priced, poor-quality brand.

Kardes et al. (2004) conducted a series of experiments aimed at understanding moderators of the strength of consumers' price–quality perceptions when they encounter brand information. Similar to Posavac et al. (2004), Kardes et al. reasoned that if selective processing was a contributor to price–quality relation overestimation, variables that increased the likelihood of selective processing would commensurately increase consumers' perceptions of how strongly predictive prices are of quality in different categories. Kardes et al. (2004) replicated the finding that consumers typically dramatically overestimate the price–quality relationship. However, they also demonstrated that this overestimation was less severe when concern about closure is low, if information load is low, and information about brands' prices and quality is presented randomly versus rank-ordered by price. These moderators influenced participants' estimations of the price–quality relation because they influenced the likelihood of selective processing. Specifically, selective processing is less likely when concern about closure is low. Moreover, when brand price and quality information is random versus presented in rank order, it is more difficult to selectively consider cases confirmatory of the initial hypothesis (i.e., that price predicts quality). Similarly, selective processing is less likely when there are a small number of cases because consumers are more likely to encounter belief-inconsistent cases because they are unlikely to screen cases that do not conform to expectations (as they would if there were many cases).

A second project on the role of selective processing in consumers' estimates of the relation between price and quality provides direct empirical evidence that selective processing underlies consumers' formation of price–quality inferences (Cronley, Posavac, Meyer, Kardes, & Kellaris, in press). Additionally, this paper shows in a real-choice setting that when context induces high need for closure and accordingly the perception of a strong correlation between price and quality, consumers will buy more expensive products.

HOW MANAGERS CAN LEVERAGE CONSUMERS' PROCLIVITY TO PROCESS INFORMATION SELECTIVELY

One important conclusion of the research just summarized is that good brands are often evaluated more favorably than they should be when judgments are singular. Brands that are moderately good may be particularly likely to be overvalued when judged singularly. This finding has implications for the promotion of both superior brands, and brands that are good but are not the best brand in a given choice category. Generally, taken together, the selective processing literature highlights the importance of being considered early in the consumer's decision process. Consistent with these studies are sales data documenting the remarkably consistent ability of end-cap displays to increase market share; likely a result of consumers' selective processing tendencies.

Positivity effects in singular-brand judgment are particularly likely in product categories that are novel to the consumer or are purchased infrequently. In each of these cases, consideration sets are not likely to be preformed, and the order in which a consumer considers brands in the category is not set. Many infrequently purchased goods are likely to fall prey to brand-positivity effects as products in these categories are more likely to be sold in a way that facilitates singular comparison. For example, automobiles are often sold through exclusive dealerships where the brand the consumer is considering is the only brand available for evaluation. Similarly, high-end kitchen supply stores often carry only one brand of stove, refrigerator, and dishwasher, while customers in the market for a riding lawnmower typically find only one brand available for evaluation at any given store.

The brand-positivity effect is good news for marketers of brands in such product categories that are good but not great. Marketers often assume that increasing the positivity with which consumers evaluate a brand requires revision of the brand. However, the research discussed suggests the simpler intervention of facilitating the consideration of the brand early in the decision process. If a good but not great brand is evaluated first, the positivity of consumers' evaluations of the brand, as well as purchase likelihood, may increase. Practically, this suggests a shift in emphasis in a moderately good brand's promotional campaign from, for example, a benefits-focused campaign to a campaign that attempts to build brand awareness, or potentially away from an advertising based campaign towards a campaign that induces trial (e.g., free samples, etc.).

Being evaluated early in the choice process will also be important for marketers of superior brands. In this case, being evaluated first is important because it would preclude the possibility of consumers evaluating and coming to prefer a competing good that may be relatively inferior, but nevertheless acceptable. Although marketers of a superior brand may not directly benefit from the brand-positivity effect if their brand is evaluated singularly (i.e., inflated evaluations and purchase likelihood), being evaluated first may prevent a relatively inferior competitor from gaining from the effect. While a shift in promotional emphasis away from a benefit emphasis and toward awareness building may fly in the face of conventional wisdom for a leading/superior brand, the strategic value of preempting any potential brand-positivity effect for inferior brands may justify such an approach.

Positivity biases in favor of a focal brand may be particularly likely when less than the total available number of brands are salient at the time of decision making. This situation arises, for example, when a choice is memory based (i.e., options are not specified in the decision context, e.g., choosing a restaurant for lunch based on remembered options), or a limited number of options are presented in a stimulus-based choice (e.g., a grocer's shelf typically omits many brands). Research has shown that consumers often consider many fewer than the total number of possible options when making decisions (Nedungadi, 1990; Posavac, San-bonmatsu, & Fazio, 1997; Posavac, Herzenstein, & Sanbonmatsu, 2003). As noted earlier, selective processing often results in consumers being satisfied, even enthusiastic, about a consideration set from which myriad good options are missing (Kardes et al., 2002). These processes again suggest that marketers must strive for high awareness of their brands. Indeed, even if a firm markets a great product, consumers will blissfully ignore it if is not readily incorporated into their consideration set.

The tendency for consumers to engage in selective processing also has relevance for media planning. Consistent with the position of expert media planners (Ephron, 1998), we suggest that it will be extremely important for advertisements to reach consumers in close temporal proximity to their decisions so that brand awareness will be high. Thus, continuous scheduling may typically be necessary for advertising to have a meaningful impact on brand choice.

Although marketers typically will want to encourage selective consideration of their brands, in some cases a strategy that encourages comparative evaluation will be best. If a target brand and its competitors are mediocre, or a target brand has a liability on an attribute that is common to category alternatives, comparative evaluation will ensure that the focal brand is not disparaged more than it should be given its standing among competitors. Comparative advertising may be an apt option for a marketer faced with such a situation.

Consumers' selective processing tendencies suggest an opportunity for managers to affect brand choice by manipulating consumers' perceptions of the strength of the relationship between brand price and quality. If a manager wants to move low-end items (e.g., a store brand, or an overstocked, low-priced brand), he or she should create a choice context in which need for closure is low and it is difficult for consumers to selectively attend to high price/high quality and low price/low quality products. For example, a retailer could arrange store shelves such that product arrangement is independent of price and brand quality. Similarly, the order of items presented by a catalog publisher should be nonsystematic with respect to price and quality. In either case, consumers are likely to perceive a relatively low association between price and quality, and thus are likely to choose lower-end products because they will not be worried that doing so will mean a commensurate loss of quality.

A marketer desiring to sell relatively more high-end products should do the reverse. Specifically high need for closure should be facilitated, and products should be presented ordered according to quality. In this case, consumers would likely examine less price–quality data points, and those considered would be more likely to suggest a high price–quality relationship. Consumers' perceptions of a strong price–quality relationship, in turn, would likely translate to choice of higher-priced products because they perceive that spending more would be needed to ensure a quality purchase.

SELECTIVE PROCESSING IN THE JUDGMENTS
AND DECISIONS OF MANAGERS

Recent research in managerial decision making has shown that the singular judgments of managers may show focal object positivity bias similar to that evidenced in studies of consumer judgment. For example, Sanbonmatsu, Posavac, and Stasny (1997) conducted a series of experiments to understand how selective processing may influence evaluations of job candidates. In one experiment, participants were given descriptions of four equally positive job candidates, and were asked to evaluate the likelihood that one randomly selected candidate would receive the job. Although there were no differences in judgments across the candidates, the focal candidate was routinely perceived to be more likely to be hired than nonfocal candidates on a variety of measures. Thus, singular evaluations of job candidates can result in unwarranted enthusiasm about a focal candidate. Subsequent experiments reported by Sanbonmatsu et al. (1997) delineated the role of selective processing in positivity bias in job-candidate judgments by showing that more information about the focal candidate was recalled than for nonfocal candidates, and that selectivity in information processing predicted judgment favorableness; participants were more favorable toward the focal candidate to the extent that they were more selective in considering attributes about the focal candidate versus nonfocal candidates.

Sanbonmatsu et al. (1997) also made the important point that singular evaluations are not necessarily overly positive, but instead are likely to be overly extreme. Their third experiment featured judgments of a focal job candidate randomly selected from a set of candidates who were each described by equally valenced, negative information. Generally, participants perceived the focal candidate as being overly unfavorable. This trend emerged because participants tended to selectively consider attributes of the focal candidate to the exclusion of nonfocal candidates, and thus became convinced that the focal candidate was particularly bad.

Managers' judgments and choices regarding marketing strategy may be similarly suspect to bias interjected by their tendency to process information selectively. Posavac, Kardes, and Brakus (2004) conducted an experiment with a sample of individuals with a mean of 6 years of work experience to show how decisions regarding new-product development may be adversely affected when processing is singular versus comparative. In their study, participants were asked to imagine that they were managing a computer company, and were going to launch one of four recently conceived prototypes, which varied with respect to attributes but were each equally favorable in aggregate. Each participant was randomly assigned to evaluate one of these prototypes. Their results demonstrated that participants were overly favorable to the focal prototype, even though it was determined randomly. Specifically, participants indicated greater likelihood that the focal prototype was the best, and that a greater percentage of executive board members would support the focal prototype versus a nonfocal prototype, than if the manipulation of which prototype was focal had no effect on judgment. Moreover, participants' expressed unwarranted enthusiasm for the focal prototype on a Likert measure, and were more likely to choose the focal prototype for launch than if the manipulation of focus had no effect. Analyses demonstrated that selective processing mediated these results; participants were overly favorable toward the focal prototype to the extent that they selectively considered information about the focal prototype to the exclusion of information about nonfocal prototypes.

In a second experiment, Posavac et al. (2004) considered more general brand strategy. Specifically, a similar sample was presented with a managerial situation in which sales of a company's paint were stagnant, and management decided to intervene to increase sales. Four strategies were described (e.g., increased ad spending, investment in research and development), and participants were asked to evaluate one of these strategies with dependent variables similar to the first experiment. A similar pattern of results obtained, as participants were overly enthusiastic that the focal strategy was best, simply as a result of it being focal. As with the first experiment, selective processing drove the effects; to the extent that participants selectively considered the focal strategy to the exclusion of the competing strategies, they were likely to be overly influenced by context and become overly favorable toward the focal strategy. Clearly, a manager who becomes convinced that a prototype or strategy is best simply because it has become focal risks making poor judgments and decisions, and moreover is a liability to his or her firm.

AVOIDING ERRONEOUS SINGULAR JUDGMENTS AND SUBOPTIMAL DECISIONS

The research discussed in this chapter reveals an important shortcoming that often characterizes both consumers' and managers' judgments. An initially considered object, whether it be a brand or an attribute, a person, a possible outcome, or a company, is likely to be judged as being of more worth or value than it should be simply because the object has become focal. As discussed earlier, there is clear upside for managers who understand how consumers are often influenced by selective hypothesis testing processes when they make judgments and decisions. Moreover, a manager who recognizes the liabilities engendered by his or her own selective processing tendencies may be able to make better decisions untainted by irrelevant situational factors that randomly highlight particular courses of action.

To avoid being unduly influenced by selective hypothesis testing processes, it is important for managers to understand how options typically become salient, and to question whether the determinants of whether an option has become salient have any relation to the expected value of choosing the option. In some cases, particularly good options are likely to become salient. For example, the suggestions of a bright subordinate whose incentives are well aligned with the firm's interests are fertile ground for quality hypotheses. In contrast, sometimes relatively poor hypotheses will come to the foreground. For example, a subordinate acting in self-interest, or seeking to curry favor, is likely to suggest courses of action that are inferior from the firm's perspective. If the latter state of affairs is likely there is particularly high risk of a bad decision if the manager processes the focal course of action selectively.

As the research reviewed in this chapter delineates, the processes underlying overly favorable singular evaluations are similar whether the judgment is of a consumer product or a managerial strategy; selectively focusing on an option that has become salient typically leads to unwarranted favorableness toward it. Thus, it is crucial for managers to engage in comparative processing so that irrelevant contextual factors that influence which options become focal do not have undue influence on their judgments and decisions. By first generating a list of possibilities (e.g., managerial actions, causal theories about a marketplace phenomenon), then considering the relative merits and liabilities of each possibility, managers will be able to make judgments free from the bias typically engendered by selective processing in singular evaluation. A potentially useful implementation facilitative of comparative processing may be to assign each member of an organizational committee to argue for a different possibility. Thus, the evidence for and worth of multiple possibilities are sure to be considered, as will evidence against and liabilities of those possibilities.

REFERENCES

Brenner, L. A., Koehler, D. J., & Tversky, A. (1996). On the evaluation of one-sided evidence. *Journal of Behavioral Decision Making, 9*, 59–70.

Cronley, M. L., Posavac, S. S., Meyer, T., Kardes, F. R., & Kellaris, J. J. (in press). A selective hypothesis testing perspective on price–quality inference and inference-based choice. *Journal of Consumer Psychology*.

Devine, P. G., Hirt, E. R., & Gehrke, E. M. (1990). Diagnostic and confirmation strategies in trait hypothesis testing. *Journal of Personality and Social Psychology, 44*, 952–963.

Ephron, E. (1998). The new recency planning. *Mediaweek, 8*, 14–15.

Gibson, B. D., Sanbonmatsu, D. M., & Posavac, S. S. (1997). The effects of selective hypothesis testing on gambling. *Journal of Experimental Psychology: Applied, 3*, 126–142.

Griffin, D. W., & Ross, L. (1991). Subjective construal, social influence, and human misunderstanding. In M. P. Zanna (Ed.), *Advances in experimental social psychology* (Vol. 24, pp. 319–359). New York: Academic Press.

Houghton, D. C., & Kardes, F. R. (1998). Market share overestimation and the noncomplementarity effect. *Marketing Letters, 9*(3), 313–320.

Hsee, C. K., & Leclerc, F. (1998). Will products look more attractive when presented separately or together? *Journal of Consumer Research, 25*, 175–186.

Kardes, F. R., Cronley, M. L., Kellaris, J. J., & Posavac, S. S. (2004). The role of selective information processing in price–quality inference. *Journal of Consumer Research, 31*, 368–374.

Kardes, F. R., Sanbonmatsu, D. M., Cronley, M. L., & Houghton, D. C. (2002). Consideration set overvaluation: When impossibly favorable ratings of a set of brands are observed. *Journal of Consumer Psychology, 12*(4), 353–361.

Klayman, J., & Ha, Y.-W. (1987). Confirmation, disconfirmation, and information in hypothesis testing. *Psychological Review, 94*, 211–228.

Klayman, J., & Ha, Y.-W. (1989). Hypothesis testing in rule discovery: Strategy, structure, and content. *Journal of Experimental Psychology: Learning, Memory, & Cognition, 15*, 596–604.

Meyvis, T., & Janiszewski, C. (2002). Consumers' beliefs about product benefits: The effect of obviously irrelevant product information. *Journal of Consumer Research, 28*, 618–635.

Mussweiler, T. (2003). Comparison processes in social judgment: Mechanisms and consequences. *Psychological Review, 110*, 472–489.

Nedungadi, P. (1990). Recall and consumer consideration sets: Influencing choice without altering brand evaluations. *Journal of Consumer Research, 17*, 263–276.

Posavac, S. S., Herzenstein, M., & Sanbonmatsu, D. M. (2003). The role of decision importance and the salience of alternatives in determining the consistency between consumers' attitudes and decisions. *Marketing Letters, 14*, 47–57.

Posavac, S. S., Kardes, F. R., & Brakus, J. J. (2004). *When focus induces tunnel vision in marketing management decision making.* Working paper, University of Rochester.

Posavac, S. S., Kardes, F. R., Sanbonmatsu, D. M., & Fitzsimons, G. J. (in press). Blissful insularity: When brands are judged in isolation from competitors. *Marketing Letters.*

Posavac, S. S., Sanbonmatsu, D. M., & Fazio, R. H. (1997). Considering the best choice: Effects of the salience and accessibility of alternatives on attitude–decision consistency. *Journal of Personality and Social Psychology, 72*, 253–261.

Posavac, S. S., Sanbonmatsu, D. M., & Ho, E. A. (2002). The effects of the selective consideration of alternatives on consumer choice and attitude–decision consistency. *Journal of Consumer Psychology, 12*(3), 203–213.

Posavac, S. S., Sanbonmatsu, D. M., Kardes, F. R., & Fitzsimons, G. J. (2004). The brand positivity effect: When evaluation confers preference. *Journal of Consumer Research, 31*, 643–651.

Russo, J. E., Meloy, M. G., & Medvec, V. (1998). Predecisional distortion of product information. *Journal of Marketing Research, 35*, 438–452.

Sanbonmatsu, D. M., Kardes, F. R., Houghton, D. C., Ho, E. A., & Posavac, S. S. (2003). Overestimating the importance of the given information in multiattribute consumer judgment. *Journal of Consumer Psychology, 13*(3), 289–300.

Sanbonmatsu, D. M., Posavac, S. S., Kardes, F. R., & Mantel, S. P. (1998). Selective hypothesis testing. *Psychonomic Bulletin & Review, 5*, 197–220.

Sanbonmatsu, D. M., Posavac, S. S., & Stasny, R. (1997). The subjective beliefs underlying probability overestimation. *Journal of Experimental Social Psychology, 33*, 276–295.

Van Wallendael, L. R., & Hastie, R. (1990). Tracing the footsteps of Sherlock Holmes: Cognitive representations of hypothesis testing. *Memory and Cognition, 18*, 240–250.

Webster, D. M., & Kruglanski, A. W. (1994). Individual differences in need for cognitive closure. *Journal of Personality and Social Psychology, 67*, 1049–1062.

CHAPTER THREE

Recent Developments in Attribution Research and Their Implications for Consumer Judgments and Behavior

David H. Silvera
The University of Tromsø, Norway

Daniel Laufer
University of Cincinnati

Classical attribution theory is concerned with causal judgments, in addition to the antecedents and consequences of such judgments. Recently, important developments in attribution research have broadened the scope of this domain as well as identifying several factors that influence attributions. The purpose of the present chapter is to summarize these developments and to examine their implications for consumer behavior researchers. This chapter is divided into three sections: (a) a review of the foundations of attribution theory, (b) an examination of recent theoretical developments in the study of attributions, and (c) a discussion of potential applications of attribution theory and these recent developments for consumer behavior research.

THE FOUNDATIONS OF ATTRIBUTION THEORY

Attributional Antecedents

Heider's (1958) theory of "naïve psychology" is widely viewed as the starting point for modern attribution theory and research. In particular, this theory offers two contributions that continue to influence attribution research. First, Heider distinguished between personal (dispositional) causation in which the behavior of some individual is the primary cause of an outcome, and environmental (situational) causation, in which some type of external influence is the primary cause of an outcome. Heider's second contribution is his proposition that behavior "has

53

such salient properties it tends to engulf the total field rather than be confined to its proper position as a local stimulus whose interpretation requires the additional data of a surrounding field—the situation in social perception" (1958, p. 54). With this proposition, Heider correctly predicted that observers would tend to prefer dispositional over situational causal explanations, although the claim that salience would be the cause of this effect has been the subject of theoretical debate (Gilbert & Malone, 1995).

Although Heider's (1958) work provided some core ideas that have played a central role in subsequent attribution research, two later theories clarified these ideas to render them more easily tested empirically and to enable the development of attribution theory as a mainstream topic in social psychology. The first of these theories is Kelley's (1967) *Covariation Theory*, which describes the types of information observers should consider when trying to determine causality. Let us consider an event: Our friend Jack recommends a local restaurant called Prima Vista. There are a number of possible explanations for Jack's recommendation, ranging from the possibility that Jack recommends every restaurant he tries to the possibility that Prima Vista is in fact an excellent restaurant. Kelley suggests that we should resolve this attributional ambiguity using three types of information: (a) Do other people also recommend Prima Vista? (*consensus* information); (b) Is Prima Vista the only restaurant Jack recommends? (*distinctiveness* information); and (c) Does Jack repeatedly recommend Prima Vista? (*consistency* information). Covariation Theory describes how we can combine these three types of information to form a judgment about the true cause of Jack's recommendation (e.g., high consensus, high distinctiveness, and high consistency—"yes" to all three questions—implies that Jack's recommendation is caused by the fact that Prima Vista is a good restaurant).

It should be noted that Kelley's (1967) Covariation Theory has the classic attributional focus on causality—what *caused* Jack's recommendation of Prima Vista? The second major elaboration of Heider's (1958) early work in attribution theory, Jones and Davis' (1965) *Correspondent Inference Theory*, does not share this focus. Instead, the goal of Correspondent Inference Theory is to use an observed behavior to identify the characteristics of the person performing that behavior (the "actor"). Specifically, the objective of Correspondent Inference Theory is to identify circumstances under which it is justifiable to make correspondent inferences about the actor, where a correspondent inference is described as "a straightforward extrapolation from the behavior observed: The behavior is seen as corresponding to or reflecting an underlying disposition of the actor . . . for example, to call a person hostile after observing a hostile act would be to draw a correspondent inference" (Jones, 1990, pp. 46–47). Correspondent Inference Theory identifies three pieces of information as particularly important for making correspondent inferences. First, correspondent inferences are most appropriate when the actor has *free choice* as to whether he or she performs the observed behavior. Second, behaviors are only diagnostic to the extent that they are *unexpected—*

when an individual behaves in a way that is completely expected (e.g., looking frightened while being mugged at gunpoint), the behavior does not necessarily reveal anything about the individual's personal characteristics (Jones, Davis, & Gergen, 1961). Finally, behaviors that result in a *single clear effect* are more diagnostic of the actor's goals in performing the behavior and thus serve as a stronger basis for correspondent inferences.

Attributional Consequents

The preceding theories have treated attributions as end-states, focusing on the kind of information that is or should be used to make attributional judgments. Given the goal of developing a theoretical understanding of social judgments, this is probably a desirable approach. However, this approach does have some limitations from the perspective of a practitioner who is more interested in outcomes than in "what goes on inside people's heads." From this perspective, theories concerned with attributional antecedents share two important limitations: (a) they all focus primarily on attributional locus (e.g., disposition vs. situation), and thus overlook potentially important distinctions between attributions to the same source (e.g., ability vs. effort); and (b) because these theories treat attributions as an end-state, they do not consider the impact of attributions on subsequent cognitive and affective reactions by the observer.

Probably the best known and most frequently used model addressing these limitations was developed by Weiner (1985, 1986). In addition to the *locus* (dispositional vs. situational) dimension, Weiner (1985, 1986) proposed a framework that includes *controllability* and *stability* as additional attributional dimensions. For example, effort is controllable but not necessarily stable, whereas ability tends to be stable but not controllable. Weiner's theory also focuses on the implications of different types of attribution for subsequent reactions related to an event. For example, when negative outcomes are perceived as the result of controllable causes, actors tend to be viewed with anger and tend to subsequently be punished or neglected.

Weiner's (1985, 1986) classification framework has proven useful in predicting important outcomes in a wide variety of applied domains. Given the focus on attributional consequents, Weiner's theory has numerous straightforward applications to marketing and consumer behavior. However, it should also be noted that Weiner's theory contributes relatively little in terms of understanding the nature of the process by which attributions are made. Furthermore, there is relatively little communication between researchers who emphasize a basic social cognition approach focused on attributional antecedents and researchers who emphasize an applied approach focused on attributional consequents. Perhaps the greatest challenge facing consumer behavior researchers interested in attribution is to find a way to integrate these two different theoretical perspectives in order to find practical applications for theoretically oriented attribution research.

RECENT DEVELOPMENTS IN ATTRIBUTION RESEARCH

Early theories examining antecedents of attributions were normative in nature—they provided prescriptions concerning what information should be used and how this information should be used in order to arrive at a valid and accurate attribution. As one might imagine, however, if observers actually made attributions in the normative manner described by these theories, attribution would be a dead topic by now. Luckily for attribution researchers, people deviate from the normative prescriptions of early attribution theories in a variety of ways. Perhaps the most notable of these is the tendency for observers to prefer dispositional explanations for behavior even when the observed data are more consistent with situational explanations. This tendency, referred to as the *fundamental attribution error* (L. Ross, 1977) or *correspondence bias* (Gilbert & Jones, 1986), has proven to be an extremely robust phenomenon (Quattrone, 1982). Moreover, the inability of the research community to agree upon a single "best" explanation of correspondence bias (Gilbert & Malone, 1995) has stimulated a substantial amount of research on this topic. This research has focused on the following perspectives concerning attributions: (a) identifying the cognitive steps involved in the process of attribution with the goal of identifying potential sources of error in each step; (b) identifying individual differences in observers that might increase or reduce attributional bias; (c) identifying motivational factors that might influence attributional bias; and (d) examining cultural differences that might influence attributional bias. In addition, recent research suggests that there might be important differences between causal attributions (cf. Kelley's, 1967, Covariation Theory) and dispositional inferences (cf. Jones & Davis', 1965, Correspondent Inference Theory). The present section examines each of these developments.

The Process of Attribution

A great deal of research has focused on breaking the attributional process into a number of stages or subprocesses. Perhaps the first of these "process models" was proposed by Quattrone (1982), who suggested that observers use an *anchoring and adjustment* heuristic (cf. Tversky & Kahneman, 1974) when they make attributions—they use the observed behavior to establish an anchor, or starting point, for their assessment of the actor's disposition, then adjust this anchor for information about external (e.g., situational) constraints that might have influenced the behavior. Insufficient adjustment, as is often observed in numerical tasks performed in judgment and decision-making research, would result in correspondence bias. Several models of the attributional process have subsequently been developed (e.g., Gilbert, Pelham, & Krull, 1988; Trope, 1986), but perhaps the most complete model was proposed by Gilbert and Malone (1995). This model describes attributions as involving four stages: situation perception, behavioral expectation, behavior perception, and attribution. According to Gilbert and Malone, information-processing difficulties in each of these stages can result in correspondence bias.

Situation Perception.   In order to make an accurate attribution, the observer must first recognize the situation in which the actor is behaving. Unfortunately, situations are not always easy to recognize because they often have no physical manifestation (Gilbert & Malone, 1995)—peer expectations, audience pressure, and fear of terrorists might all influence our behavior in various ways, but none of these situational forces are readily available to an external observer. When the causal influence of the situation is overlooked or ignored, observers tend to make biased dispositional attributions. For example, in the well-known experiment by L. Ross, Amabile, and Steinmetz (1977), participants were randomly assigned to play either the role of contestant or quizmaster in a mock game show. Quiz-masters were asked to generate a set of questions from their own general knowledge and contestants were asked to try to answer those questions. Because almost everyone knows things that most other people do not know, this situation was de-signed to favor the quizmaster, and indeed contestants failed to answer most of the questions. Presumably, the poor performance of contestants was due to the difficulty of answering questions from somebody else's store of personal knowledge; nevertheless, observers of this mock game show concluded that quizmasters were significantly smarter than contestants. In other words, because observers were unable to "see" the situational constraint imposed by task difficulty, they made overly dispositional attributions concerning the game show participants.

Behavioral Expectation.   In addition to recognizing what the situation is, an accurate observer must also understand how that situation is likely to influence behavior. Observers who lack such understanding are likely to have erroneous ex-pectations for how a person would normally behave and thus misjudge the attributional implications of how the actor actually does behave. For example, ob-servers generally underestimate the percentage of participants who will deliver the maximum shock level in Milgram's (1963) classic obedience paradigm (Bier-brauer, 1979). For those who are familiar with Milgram's research (in which 65% of participants administered the maximum shock), participants who administer high levels of shock appear to be behaving normally, whereas participants who re-fuse to administer shocks are noteworthy for their disobedience. Conversely, indi-viduals who have inaccurate expectations about what is typical behavior in this situation will have quite the reverse reaction: Participants who administer high levels of shock will be seen as cruel and sadistic, whereas participants who refuse to give high levels of shock will be viewed as typical. These differences highlight the fact that correct identification of what behaviors should normally be expected in a given situation is crucial to forming an accurate and valid attribution.

Behavior Perception. Considering that the previous two stages of the attributional process resulted in errors when observers were unaware of situational constraint information, one might conclude that a realistic understanding of the situation protects observers against correspondence bias. Paradoxically, it is exactly such an understanding that can cause errors when an observer is trying to interpret the behavior itself. Observers' knowledge of the situation can result in correspondent expectations for behavior in that situation, which can in turn bias interpretations of the actor's actual behavior through a process called *perceptual assimilation* (Trope, 1986; Trope & Alfieri, 1997).

Knowledge that a situational force (e.g., a hostile audience) is likely to induce a particular behavior (e.g., a nervous speech) induces an observer to expect that behavior. The observer's expectations are then likely to influence his interpretation of the behavior, frequently resulting in perceptions that the behavior corresponds more closely with his expectations (and with the situational constraints) than it actually does. In the example of a nervous speech, this perceptual assimilation process would result in a perception that the speech was more nervous than it actually was, and subsequently in an unduly dispositional inference that the speaker was more nervous than he actually was. This type of effect has also been demonstrated experimentally, as research indicates that when observers expect a particular type of behavior, and when the behavior is sufficiently ambiguous to permit perceptual assimilation effects, people are more likely to perceive the behavior as corresponding with the situation and thus to make stronger dispositional attributions about the actor (e.g., Trope, Cohen, & Maoz, 1988).

Attribution. Even when observers correctly identify both the situation and the behavior, it is still possible for them to exhibit correspondence bias if they do not properly integrate these pieces of information. As noted, Quattrone (1982) proposed that observers tend to anchor on dispositional explanations, then insufficiently adjust that anchor based on situational information. A more elaborate explanation of this effect is provided by the *Sequential Operations Model* of attribution developed by Gilbert and his colleagues (Gilbert et al., 1988).

This model suggests that people draw dispositional inferences based on the results of a three-stage process. In the first stage, called *categorization*, observers identify the actor's behavior (e.g., Jane is acting excited). In the second stage, called *characterization*, observers directly transfer their interpretation of the behavior into a correspondent dispositional inference (e.g., Jane is an excitable type of person). In the third stage, called *correction*, observers adjust their inference based on situational information (e.g., Jane just won the state lottery, which would make most people excited. Thus, Jane might not be such an excitable person after all). Importantly, Gilbert and his colleagues proposed that the three stages of the attributional process differ in terms of the cognitive demands they place on observers: The first two stages are relatively effortless and automatic, whereas the correction stage is substantially more cognitively demanding. Thus, when observers lack motivation, mental energy, or cognitive skills, they are able to categorize the behavior and characterize the individual has having traits that correspond to that behavior, but they are often unable to correct for moderating situational factors and thus exhibit correspondence bias. A substantial body of research has supported this model by demonstrating that observers who lack either cognitive resources (Gilbert et al., 1988) or motivation (Webster, 1993) show increased correspondence bias.

Individual Differences in Attribution

The Sequential Operations Model implies not only that certain circumstances (e.g., when observers are required to perform multiple mental tasks simultaneously) might increase correspondence bias, but also that certain types of people might be particularly prone to correspondence bias. Indeed, as Gilbert et al. (1988) pointed out, some observers seem to make attributional errors even under optimal judgment conditions, whereas others seem to make relatively accurate attributions even when the deck is stacked against them. This line of reasoning has resulted in a substantial amount of research examining the impact of individual difference factors on attributions. This research has focused primarily on the final two stages of the attribution process, in which observers interpret or perceive the behavior, and integrate situational and behavioral information.

Individual Differences Related to Motivation. According to Blumberg and Silvera (1998), individual differences related to motivation should influence behavioral perception. Despite the fact that identifying behavior has been described as a relatively effortless process (Gilbert et al., 1988), this has typically only been demonstrated in highly controlled situations in which limited information is provided to participants. Most notably, participants typically have no prior experience evaluating the actor and no prior expectations concerning the actor's behavior. When multiple behavioral identification cues are available (e.g., an expectancy as well as the behavior itself), it seems reasonable to expect that unmotivated individuals will choose the simplest cue available to identify the behavior. Under circumstances when the situational context is clear and easily processed (e.g., a familiar situation or an unambiguous sentence like "the experimenter told the author to write a pro-Castro essay") but the behavior is ambiguous or complex (e.g., a two-sided argument presented in a long essay), unmotivated observers might infer the behavior from the situation via perceptual-assimilation processes and thus show correspondence bias (Trope, 1986). Consistent with this analysis, Blumberg and Silvera (1998) found that behavior perceptions of observers who were dispositionally low in the motivation to engage in attributional processing were more strongly influenced by behavioral expectancies based on situational information than by the behavior itself.

More typically, however, research examining individual differences related to motivation suggests that motivational differences have the greatest impact on the correction stage of the Sequential Operations Model. For example, high *need for cognition* is associated with deeper analytic processing, whereas high *need for cognitive closure* motivates people to quickly terminate analytic processing. Thus, individuals who are low in need for cognition and high in need for cognitive closure tend to engage in less correction of their initial dispositional judgments and to show high levels of correspondence bias (D'Agostino & Fincher-Kiefer, 1992; Webster, 1993).

Individual Differences in Cognitive Ability.   Research has also investigated the role of cognitive skills in the attributional process. Specifically, the correction phase of the attributional process requires the integration of multiple pieces of information (e.g., behavioral and situational) and thus places demands on the observer that might be beyond the capacity of certain individuals. This is consistent with the fact that young adults (15 to 20 years of age) tend to use a more integrative, interactionist view of behavior than older children (9 to 10 years of age; Blumberg & Silvera, 1998) and the fact that young adults' predictions of future behavior tend to be based more on situational information than the rigid dispositional predictions made by older children (e.g., Newman, 1991). These cognitive changes are consistent with a Piagetian developmental framework (Rotenberg, 1982). Piaget's (1952) theory of cognitive development postulates that the cognitive abilities of individuals in concrete operations (roughly 7 to 11 years of age) are quite different from those of individuals who have attained formal operations (12+ years of age). Most importantly, concrete operational individuals can evaluate only single factors when solving a problem, and as such may have a dualistic view of reality: either one thing or another caused an effect, but rarely both (Inhelder & Piaget, 1958). In contrast, formal operational individuals can consider how multiple factors interact and influence one another. These more cognitively advanced individuals can form numerous mental hypotheses and use systematic deductive reasoning to solve problems. Referring back to the research on age differences in attribution, most young adults with a more integrative view of behavior would presumably be in the formal operations stage, whereas older children who rely on simple, rigid explanations for behavior would primarily be in the concrete operations stage. This analysis suggests that formal operational processing is necessary for the formation of valid attributions, and Blumberg and Silvera (1998) found that observers who had not yet achieved formal operations engaged in less attributional correction and showed more correspondence bias than their formal operational counterparts.

Individual Differences in Attributional Style.   In addition to attributional differences in motivation and ability to think carefully about attributional questions, certain individuals appear to prefer certain types of causal explanation. Individual difference measures related to this type of preference generally refer to a person's tendency to explain causality based on internal (dispositional) versus external (situational) determinants. Early measures of this tendency such as *locus of control* and *attributional style* were designed specifically with causal attributions in mind—*internals* were defined as people who believe in substantial personal control over outcomes, whereas *externals* were defined as people who believe that outcomes are more situationally determined. Unsurprisingly, internally oriented observers are more inclined to make dispositional attributions than their externally oriented counterparts.

A related psychological construct that appears to influence attributions is an individual's *Implicit Theory of Personality* (Dweck, Hong, & Chiu, 1993). Dweck and her colleagues have identified individuals with two types of implicit theory: (a) *entity theorists*, who tend to view personality as a permanent, static trait that has very little potential for change and development; and (b) *incremental theorists*, who see personality as a dynamic variable with substantial potential for change and development (Dweck, Chiu, & Hong, 1995). Research has shown that entity theorists are more likely to make spontaneous trait inferences than incremental theorists (Hong, 1994), that entity theorists are more prone to demonstrate correspondence bias than incremental theorists (Dweck, Hong, & Chiu, 1993; Dweck et al., 1995), and that entity theorists tend to correct their initial dispositional inferences less than incremental theorists (Silvera, Moe, & Iversen, 2000).

Recent research has also focused on a broader psychological construct called *idiocentrism*, which identifies individuals as either individualist, believing primarily in the power and rights of the individual over society or as *collectivist*, believing that the society as a whole is most important and the individuals within it are secondary. *Individualism* has been defined by various researchers as a focus on rights above duties, a concern for oneself and immediate family above the society as a whole, an emphasis on personal autonomy and self-fulfillment, a tendency to base personal identity on accomplishments, and an emphasis on personal responsibility and freedom of choice (Hofstede, 1980; Waterman, 1984). All of these definitions conceptualize the person (e.g., personal goals, personal uniqueness) as central and societal forces as peripheral (Markus & Kitayama, 1991; Triandis, 1995). High levels of idiocentrism, then, indicate that reasoning (and attributions) are likely to be oriented toward the person rather than the situation because of the central, causal role played by the decontextualized self (Choi, Nisbett, & Norenzayan, 1999; Newman, 1993). In contrast, low levels of idiocentrism should be associated with a tendency to view situational constraints and the behavioral context as especially powerful determinants of behavior (Miller, 1984; Morris & Peng, 1994). Consistent with this reasoning, a recent meta-analysis concluded that higher levels of idiocentrism were associated with increases in the tendency to make dispositional attributions (Oyserman, Coon, & Kemmelmeier, 2002).

Motivational Effects on Attributions

Although motivations have long been a part of attributional theory (e.g., Heider, 1958), there has been a great deal of theoretical debate about their importance. Some researchers have even claimed that all evidence for motivated reasoning could be reinterpreted based on purely cognitive, nonmotivational processes (e.g., Nisbett & Ross, 1980). Nevertheless, the consensus at this point appears to be that motivations do play a role in determining the cognitive processes and information that is used to interpret causality (Kunda, 1990). These motivations generally fall into two categories: the motive for accuracy, and the motivation to reach a particular (directional) conclusion (Kruglanski, 1980; Kunda, 1990).

Motivation for Accuracy. When observers are assigned the goal of making accurate attributions, for example by being told that they would have to justify their attributions to others, they are less likely to either show correspondence bias or to make unjustified dispositional attributions (e.g., Tetlock, 1985). Although this suggests that the motivation for accuracy results in more accurate and unbiased attributions, Kunda (1990) argued that accuracy goals only reduce bias when observers (a) have access to superior "deep processing" strategies for analyzing attributional information, (b) realize that these strategies are better than their superficial strategies, and (c) are capable of accessing these strategies. Accuracy goals cause observers to apply strategies and information that they view as most appropriate and can also lead them to consider more evidence and evaluate more alternative hypotheses (e.g., Kruglanski, 1980). It is frequently the case that this results in more accurate attributions; however, accuracy goals can also increase bias when the observer has false beliefs that invalid information-processing strategies are the most valid way to analyze attributional data.

Directional Motivation. Research suggests that motivations and desires are an important determinant of our initial expectations. For example, people are more likely to spontaneously report past self-relevant events that are consistent with their currently desired self-concepts, attitudes, or beliefs (Ross, McFarland, & Fletcher, 1981; Sanitioso, Kunda, & Fong, 1990), and people generate memories and endorse self-descriptive traits more quickly when those memories and traits are consistent with their desired self-concepts (Sanitioso, Kunda, & Fong, 1990). This is a potential problem for attributions because initial expectations have a substantial impact on social judgments—observers tend to exhibit a phenomenon called *confirmation bias*, which refers to a tendency to seek out information that confirms their prior expectations in preference to information that disconfirms their expectations (see Klayman & Ha, 1987, for a review). Thus, when observers have access to a combination of hypothesis-confirming and hypothesis-disconfirming evidence, they are likely to place more weight on the confirming evidence and arrive at a conclusion that is consistent with their original expectations (e.g., Snyder & Swann, 1978). Furthermore, research indicates that confirmatory information is often processed spontaneously, whereas disconfirming information might only be considered when people are explicitly instructed to do so (Koriat, Lichtenstein, & Fischhoff, 1980).

Thus, it appears that directional goals can influence reasoning much like accuracy goals by influencing the information that is considered while making a judgment (Kruglanski, 1980). Furthermore, Pyszczynski and Greenberg (1987) argued that motivations influence not only our selection of information but also the hypotheses we test and the rules we use to test them. Kunda (1990) went so far as to describe the judgment process as "a biased search through memory for relevant beliefs and rules" (p. 483), concluding that motivations serve as initiators for a string of cognitive processes leading to the conclusions desired by the observer. In short, directional goals induce people to use information-processing strategies and select information that increases their likelihood of reaching a desired conclusion.

Need for Control. One particular type of motivation that has been frequently studied in attribution research is the need for control. The importance of feeling personal control over one's life is well documented (e.g., Langer & Rodin, 1976; Seligman & Maier, 1967; Hiroto, 1974), and the need for control also impacts attributions. In particular, *belief in a just world* and the *defensive attribution hypothesis* derive from this need.

Belief in a just world can be illustrated by an experiment performed by Lerner and Simmons (1966). In this experiment, participants were told that they were participating in a study about the perception of emotions. One participant, actually a confederate, was apparently randomly selected to take a memory test while the other subjects watched. Each time this confederate made a mistake on the test, she was ostensibly given a painful electric shock. One might expect that participants in this study would feel sympathetic toward the confederate—but for the luck of random selection, the other participants could easily have been in the position of having to endure the shocks themselves. Rather than sympathy, however, participants showed a strong tendency to ridicule and criticize the test taker. Lerner (1980) argued that the tendency to criticize victims in this way derives from a deep-seated belief in a just world, a belief that people get what they deserve in life. According to Lerner, people need to view the world as a place where outcomes are always fair—where hard work will always be rewarded and bad behavior will always be punished. To believe otherwise is to believe that random chance has a powerful influence over our lives and to admit that we do not have the control that we feel we need to have. Thus, it is frequently assumed that poor people are lazy (Furnham & Gunter, 1984), rape victims are careless (Carli & Leonard, 1990), battered wives provoke their abusive husbands (Summers & Feldman, 1984), and people infected with AIDS are immoral (Hunter & Ross, 1991). Furthermore, research suggests that belief in a just world is motivationally based, deriving from a desire to avoid believing that negative outcomes can happen by sheer chance.

The defensive attribution hypothesis posits that observers are especially likely to blame the perpetrator of an accident when (a) a negative outcome is especially severe or undesirable; and (b) they feel similar to the victim, such that the negative outcome could just as easily have happened to them. Consistent with the first of these conditions, two meta-analyses (Burger, 1981; Robbennolt, 2000) reported significant positive associations between severity of negative outcomes and measures of responsibility and blame for those outcomes. The second condition reflects the fact that observers are more likely to make defensive attributions when they feel personally vulnerable to harm occurring to them.

> As the consequences of an action become more severe, they become more unpleasant, and the notion that they might be accidental becomes less tolerable: The fear that the same thing might involve the self becomes a realistic possibility. Seeing the actions as avoidable and blaming a person for their occurrence makes the actions more predictable and hence avoidable by the self. (Fiske & Taylor, 1991, p. 85)

Culture and Attributions

Another important factor that influences attributions is culture. A great deal of research indicates that there are substantial cross-cultural differences in attributions, and that these differences derive at least in part from differences in culturally based conceptions of the self and others in terms of *individualism* and *collectivism* (Markus & Kitayama, 1991; Miller, 1984). Individualistic cultures, such as those of the United States, England, and Australia, have been defined in a variety of ways: (a) Hofstede (1980) conceptualized individualism as a focus on rights above duties, on personal autonomy, on deriving personal identity from accomplishments, and on oneself and one's immediate family over society as a whole; (b) Waterman (1984) emphasized individualism's focus on freedom of choice and personal responsibility; and (c) Schwartz (1990) described individualistic societies as contractual in nature, focusing on negotiated social relations and obligations and achieving increased status. Collectively, these definitions characterize individualism as focusing on the person in terms of goals, achievements, and control, while minimizing the importance of social and societal effects (e.g., Markus & Kitayama, 1991; Oyserman et al., 2002; Triandis, 1995). In contrast, people in collectivist cultures such as most East Asian and Latin American countries tend to emphasize the importance of society as a whole and to view the individual primarily as a part of the collective (Krull, 2001).

The consequences of these worldviews are that individualists tend to believe that the decontextualized individual, rather than the situation or social context, is the primary source of causality (e.g., Choi et al., 1999; Newman, 1993). In contrast, collectivists are more likely to view the situation, social context, and societally defined roles as primary sources of causality. Consistent with these propositions, several researchers have found attributional differences between observers in individualistic and collectivistic societies. For example, a study by Miller (1984) compared the attributions of people in various age groups from India and the United States. Young children showed no cultural differences in attributions; as age increased, however, American participants had an increasing tendency to make dispositional (but not situational) attributions, whereas Indian participants made increasingly strong situational (but not dispositional) attributions.

Attributions Versus Inferences

As noted earlier, Kelley's (1967) Covariation Theory is primarily concerned with judgments of causality, whereas Jones and Davis' (1965) Correspondent Inference Theory focuses on inferences about the characteristics of the actor. For many years, attribution researchers treated these two types of judgment as synonymous and described errors in both types of judgment as the *fundamental attribution error*. However, recent research argues that causal judgments differ from trait inferences in several important ways and that errors in these two types of judgment have different consequences and different antecedents (Hilton, Smith, & Kim, 1995; Krull, 2001). Based on this distinction, Krull recommended the use of the term *dispositionalism* to describe a general preference for dispositional over situational causal explanations, and the term *correspondence bias* (cf. Gilbert & Jones, 1986) to describe the tendency for observers to infer that dispositions correspond to behavior.

Although this might seem like a trivial distinction, there is substantial evidence that inferences and causal attributions are in fact different types of judgment. First, causal attributions and correspondent inferences appear to be made through different mechanisms (e.g., Bassili, 1989; Erickson & Krull, 1999; Hamilton, 1988; Hilton et al., 1995; Johnson, Jemmott, & Pettigrew, 1984). For example, Bassili (1989) found very little trait activation in participants who were instructed to make causal judgments relative to a target individual, even when the causal judgments indicated a dispositional attribution. Furthermore, Johnson et al. (1984) demonstrated that knowledge that a behavior was caused by situational forces did not eliminate correspondence bias, thereby concluding that trait inferences and causal attributions are largely independent.

Research also suggests that trait inferences are often relatively quick and effortless (see Uleman, Newman, & Moskowitz, 1996, for a review), whereas causal attributions are typically slower and more deliberate judgments (Smith & Miller, 1983). Importantly, this rules out the possibility that perceivers first allocate causality (e.g., Janet is endorsing Pepsi™ for dispositional reasons), then use that causal information to generate inferences (e.g., Janet likes Pepsi); instead, it suggests that inferences occur spontaneously but that causal judgments are only made when needed (e.g., when an experimenter asks for them; Hamilton, 1988).

Finally, as noted, research suggests that dispositionalism is particularly prevalent in individualist cultures. However, a growing body of research indicates that correspondence bias is universal across cultures, regardless of the country's level of individualism or collectivism (e.g., Krull et al., 1999). For example, Krull et al. found that participants from the United States and Taiwan showed equal and significant amounts of correspondence bias using both the attitude-attribution (Jones & Harris, 1967) and the quizmaster (L. Ross et al., 1977) paradigms.

RESEARCH DIRECTIONS AND APPLICATIONS OF ATTRIBUTION THEORY

The final section of this chapter presents some potential applications of attribution theory, as well as recent developments in attribution research, to consumer behavior contexts. A substantial amount of research in marketing has examined attributions, including work involving consumer reactions to negative word of mouth (Laczniak, DeCarlo, & Ramaswami, 2001); consumer reactions to service delays (Taylor, 1994) and failures (Maxham & Netemeyer, 2002); consumer evaluations of different sources of product information (Gershoff, Broniarczyk, & West, 2001); the impact of attributions on salesperson performance (Dixon, 2001); and consumer attributions about pricing (Lichtenstein & Bearden, 1989); price promotions (Raghubir & Corfman, 1999) and price increases (Campbell, 1999). However, the focus of this section is not to provide a summary of existing consumer research but to suggest some research directions for which attributional and inferential judgments might provide new and valuable insights into marketing-related phenomena. To that end, this section focuses on three research areas: (a) potential applications of the defensive attribution hypothesis to product failures and product harm crises; (b) potential implications of research on trait inferences for consumer behavior in general and for endorsement advertisements in particular; and (c) a brief examination of potential gaps in our understanding of attributions based on differences in focal issues for theoretical versus applied attribution researchers.

Attributions About Product Failures and Product Harm Crises

One area in which causal attributions are likely to have important implications is the domain of product-harm crises. Research suggests that blame attributions to a company for a product failure or product-harm crisis can have severe consequences, including anger toward the company, negative word-of-mouth behavior (Folkes, 1988), and a reduced likelihood of purchasing the company's products (Siomkos & Kurzbard, 1994). Despite the importance of this topic, few studies have examined how consumers arrive at blame attributions (Folkes, 1988; Weiner, 2000).

The defensive attribution hypothesis appears to be a natural framework for examining blame attributions in relation to product failures and product-harm crises, proposing that (a) when an incident results in a more severe outcome, more blame will be attributed to a potentially responsible party, and (b) this tendency toward defensive blame attributions will be particularly prevalent when consumers feel vulnerable to harm occurring to them. Product failures provide an excellent opportunity to evaluate the defensive attribution hypothesis because of their natural variations in severity. Some product failures might involve only mild inconvenience to the consumer due to minor product defects, whereas product-harm crises can be sufficiently serious as to result in severe injuries and even death. For example, recent high-profile, product-harm crises involving Tylenol™, Coca-Cola™, and Firestone™ tires involved direct physical harm to consumers.

Outcome Severity. Despite the potential relevance of the defensive attribution hypothesis for predicting consumer behavior, very little research has investigated this issue. Moreover, in one of the few studies examining the defensive attribution hypothesis in a marketing context, Su and Tippins (1998) found exactly the opposite of what the defensive attribution hypothesis would predict: More blame was assessed to the manufacturer for a minor product failure than for a major product failure. Although this result appears to cast doubt on the applicability of the defensive attribution hypothesis, these researchers proposed that their results might have occurred due to methodological weaknesses in their study; in particular, the operationalization of severity is problematic because these researchers did not use any genuinely severe problems (the "major" problem was a deep scratch in a shoe), and the problems they used concerned the appearance of the product rather than affecting performance or resulting in any kind of physical harm to consumers of the product. The severity construct in the defensive attribution hypothesis literature is typically operationalized by varying the degree of physical harm caused in an accident rather than by reducing consumption utility due to product failure (see Burger, 1981; Robbennolt, 2000), and a true test of the defensive attribution hypothesis in consumer contexts should probably use a similar operationalization of severity.

Another interesting area to explore is examining severity in relation to Weiner's (1985, 1986) attribution framework, which suggested that negative and unexpected outcomes increase causal search (Weiner, 1986). It seems clear that increased severity makes a product-harm crisis both more negative and more unexpected, and therefore that severity should increase causal search. What is less clear is how increased severity of an outcome impacts the results of the causal search by the observer. More specifically, the relationship between the severity of an event and resulting attributions along the three basic causal dimensions outlined in Weiner's model (locus, stability, and controllability) remains unclear. For example, do more severe product-harm crises result in more blame to the company as compared with consumers? Do observers perceive company causes as more stable in nature when an event is more severe? Do observers perceive companies to have more control over possible causes when the outcome is more severe? The defensive attribution literature does not address these questions, particularly with regard to stability and controllability. As such, future research should investigate these issues in order to increase our understanding of the role of severity in consumer attributions associated with product failures and product-harm crises.

Personal Vulnerability. A recent study by Laufer and Gillespie (2004) examined the impact of personal vulnerability on blame attributions related to a product-harm crisis. Based on previous work suggesting that certain biological and sociological factors lead women to feel more personally vulnerable to negative outcomes than men (Campbell, 1999; Harris & Miller, 2000; Stets & Strauss, 1990), these researchers examined gender differences in blame attributions concerning an ambiguous product-harm crisis in which blame could reasonably be ascribed either to the company or to consumers of the product. Consistent with the experimental hypotheses, female participants were more likely than male participants to blame the company for the product-harm crisis.

Future research should continue to investigate the role of personal vulnerability in blame attributions, both in terms of directly measuring perceived vulnerability and its relation to blame attributions and examining other demographic or individual difference variables that are associated with increased personal vulnerability. For example, one might expect that older consumers, due to their diminished physical capabilities and perceived loss of personal control (e.g., Langer & Rodin, 1976), might also feel increased personal vulnerability in association with a product-harm crisis and thereby blame the company more than younger consumers. Another important factor in assessing personal vulnerability is the perceived similarity between the victim and the observer. If the observer does not view him or herself as similar to the victim, the situation is less likely to be perceived as threatening. Personal similarity has been examined in a number of ways in the defensive attribution hypothesis literature, including similarity between observers and victims in age, values (Shaver, 1970) and gender (Shaw & McMartin, 1977). The results of these studies generally support a moderating role of personal similarity in the relationship between the severity of an outcome and blame, although at this time there appears to be no research examining the impact of personal similarity on blame attributions in consumer contexts.

Trait Inferences in Consumer Research

The defensive attribution hypothesis focuses on causal attributions rather than trait inferences, which is consistent with most marketing research related to attribution theory. In fact, Folkes (1988) went so far as to say that "correspondent inference theory has not had much influence on attribution research" (p. 549). Although we are inclined to agree with Folkes that Correspondent Inference Theory has had relatively little impact on consumer research, we believe this is an unfortunate trend that is overdue for a reversal for a number of reasons. First, a great deal of the social psychological research that purports to study attributions, including almost all of the work using the classic attitude-attribution paradigm in which observers infer an author's dispositional attitude based on reading an essay written under either choice or no choice conditions, actually studies trait inferences (Krull, 2001). As such, a great deal of the attributional knowledge we try to apply to marketing contexts is in fact inferential knowledge. Secondly, dispositional inferences (and not causal attributions) are most commonly the dependent measure that is truly of interest in marketing. For example, marketers are more likely to be interested in whether consumers think Corn Flakes *taste good* (trait inference) than whether consumers think that their recent favorable experience at breakfast was *caused* by the positive attributes of the Corn Flakes they ate (causal attribution).

In addition, there remains some theoretical work to be done in analyzing dispositional inferences by consumers. Social psychological research in this area typically examines inferences related to simple situations involving a single person (the actor), a single behavior, and direct questions asking research participants (observers) to make inferences about the actor. Each of these conditions is potentially problematic in generalizing to consumer inferences. First, consumer inferences will frequently be about companies or products rather than about people. Although it might be the case that inferences about people readily generalize to other types of "actor," it is also possible that our cognitive system is either hard-wired or socially learns to view individuals as "where the action is," such that inferences about other types of entity follow different rules. Secondly, consumer inferences are more likely to relate to multiple events due to a high likelihood of repeated exposure to products. For example, I might infer that my car is reliable based on the fact that it has worked properly each of the last 500 times I drove it or that my DVD player is unreliable based on the fact that it broke down after only 6 months of operation. This is substantially different than the single-observation inferences that are made in most social psychological laboratories, and none of the classical attribution theories make predictions or prescriptions for inferences across multiple observations.

Finally, the vast majority of consumer inferences are likely to be made spontaneously rather than based on direct questions by a researcher. Consequently, the question of whether consumers make inferences spontaneously is extremely important for consumer researchers. Fortunately, this topic has received substantial attention in recent years (see Uleman et al., 1996, for a review), and there is reasonably strong evidence that trait inferences can be made spontaneously (Krull, 2001). Nevertheless, the boundary conditions of spontaneous inferences for consumer-related information remain to be examined, and this could be an important issue for future research.

Trait Inferences About Product Endorsers.   One question related to trait inferences that is particularly relevant to consumer research is the question of whether (and when) consumers infer that product endorsers have positive attitudes toward the products they endorse. A recent estimate indicates that approximately 25% of American commercials use celebrity endorsers (Shimp, 2000), and that this practice can result in more favorable advertisement ratings and product evaluations (Dean & Biswas, 2001) as well as having a substantial positive impact on financial returns for the companies that use them (Erdogan, 2001). However, the utility of celebrity endorsers appears to be limited by certain constraints. For example, endorser effectiveness is reduced when there is a bad "fit" between the endorser and the product (Till & Shimp, 1998) or when the celebrity endorses several products (Tripp, Jensen, & Carlson, 1994). It is worth noting that both of these constraints are analogous to issues that have been examined in the social psychological literature. Bad fit is likely to be viewed as unexpected behavior, which according to Jones and Davis (1965) leads observers to think more carefully about their inferences rather than mindlessly assuming the endorser actually likes the product; endorsing several products creates the likelihood that the celebrity has an ulterior motive to cash in the value of their name recognition, and such ulterior motives have been shown to reduce an observer's tendency to make correspondent inferences (e.g., Fein, 1996).

Despite the relevance of attribution theory to the domain of endorser advertisements, previous research on endorsers has seldom adopted this perspective. Instead, previous research examining the effectiveness of celebrity endorsements has focused primarily on personal attributes of the celebrity that enhance his or her persuasiveness (see Erdogan, 1999, for a review). For example, a number of researchers have used models in which source credibility, typically viewed as a function of trustworthiness and expertise, is the primary factor determining how influential the endorser will be (e.g., Ohanian, 1991). Other researchers have emphasized the importance of source attractiveness in determining liking for the endorser and thereby increasing endorsement effectiveness in general (e.g., H. H. Friedman & L. Friedman, 1979), or in situations where attractiveness is relevant to the product domain (e.g., Kamins, 1990).

Unfortunately, measures of global celebrity characteristics like credibility and trustworthiness are likely to be problematic to the extent that the effectiveness of a celebrity endorser varies as a function of the product type, the current popularity of the celebrity, and perhaps even societal conditions at the time and place where the advertisement is shown. As such, it could be fruitful to abandon the use of measures of the celebrity endorser's global characteristics in favor of directly measuring the degree to which individuals evaluate the celebrity as liking the endorsed product after viewing the advertisement. In other words, we propose that the correspondent inferences about celebrity endorsers in the context of the specific advertisement are likely to be the most reliable way to predict endorser effectiveness, and that such an approach has the added benefit of enabling researchers to make use of the social psychological literature related to trait inferences.

Two lines of recent research have examined correspondent inferences about endorsers, focusing on two propositions. The first of these propositions is that correspondent inferences should predict consumers' attitudes toward and intentions to purchase the advertised product. This proposition must be supported in order for correspondent inferences to be a useful tool for consumer researchers, and that seems to be the case. Cronley, Kardes, Goddard, and Houghton (1999) found that correspondent inferences about an endorser were positively associated with participants' attitudes toward the advertisement, the product, and the endorser. Silvera and his colleagues replicated this result, in addition to demonstrating that correspondent inferences about endorsers are positively related to purchase intentions for the advertised product (Sørum, Grape, & Silvera, 2003; Silvera, Grape, & Sørum, 2004; Silvera & Austad, in press).

The second proposition is that consumers will tend to exhibit correspondence bias in evaluating an endorser's motives for recommending a product by viewing the endorser as liking the advertised product better than the typical person who is not endorsing the product. This proposition has received mixed support. Cronley et al. (1999) found evidence for correspondence bias using an advertisement that included several arguments for the product and used the celebrity's name repeatedly, but not in a more typical advertisement that included only a picture and a single presentation of the celebrity's name. Silvera and his colleagues (Sørum et al., 2003; Silvera et al., 2004; Silvera & Austad, 2004) found no evidence for correspondence bias using simple advertisements involving several different endorsers and product types, and in many cases these researchers found a reversal of correspondence bias such that endorsers were viewed as liking the advertised product less than the typical individual. A number of differences with regard to methodology and participant populations can potentially explain the different results from these two lines of research; nevertheless, these differences testify to the complexity of the correspondent inference process in relation to endorser advertisements and thus indicate a need for further research in this area. The authors of these research programs have suggested a number of potential moderators for correspondent inferences about endorsers, including cultural factors, individual differences in consumers, and characteristics of both the advertisement and the product. Future research should develop a coherent model to integrate these factors.

Building a More Comprehensive Theoretical Model of Attributions

As a final note, we would like to call the reader's attention to some gaps in our current understanding of attributions and their implications for consumer research. Consider the model shown in Fig. 3.1, which combines Gilbert and Malone's (1995) analysis of the causes of correspondence bias with Weiner's

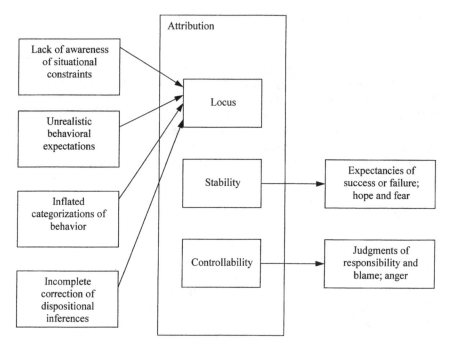

FIG. 3.1.   Antecedents and consequences of attributions.

(2000) analysis of the implications of different types of attribution for consumer behavioral outcomes.

Although there are a few exceptions to this general trend, the purpose of this diagram is to make it clear that (a) researchers interested in the antecedents of attributions have focused primarily on determinants of locus—when do we infer dispositional versus situational causality, but (b) researchers interested in the consequences of attributions have been relatively more likely to focus on the implications of stable versus unstable and controllable versus uncontrollable attributions. Moreover, Weiner (2000) recommended an intensification of the search for important applications of the stability and controllability dimensions. Although such a search might lead to important results, we would like to suggest two other directions for future research that might be of particular interest to consumer researchers.

First, we view it as desirable to establish a chain of mental and behavioral events from exposure to a stimulus, through attributions, to important outcomes such as purchase intentions and behavior. To achieve this goal, it is necessary to obtain a better understanding of the antecedents of the stability and controllability dimensions of attributions and to examine the processes by which observers rate these dimensions. Secondly, it is important to go beyond the "main effect" stage of attributional analysis and to examine how the different attributional dimensions interact to predict outcome variables. In particular, the interaction of the locus dimension with the other two dimensions should be more thoroughly investigated. A better integration of the locus dimension with research examining attributional consequences will enable consumer behavior researchers both to incorporate the vast body of social psychological research examining antecedents of attributional locus judgments and to form a more integrated picture of how attributions as a whole impact important variables in consumer psychology.

REFERENCES

Bassili, J. N. (1989). Traits as action categories versus traits as person attributes in social cognition. In J. N. Bassili (Ed.), On-line cognition in person perception (pp. 61–89). Hillsdale, NJ: Lawrence Erlbaum Associates.

Bierbrauer, G. (1979). Why did he do it? Attribution of obedience and the phenomenon of dispositional bias. European Journal of Social Psychology, 9, 67–84.

Blumberg, S. J., & Silvera, D. H. (1998). An individual differences perspective on the motivational and cognitive requirements for attribution. Social Cognition, 16, 253–266.

Burger, J. M. (1981). Motivational biases in the attribution of responsibility for an accident. A meta-analysis of the defensive-attribution hypothesis. Psychological Bulletin, 90, 496–512.

Campbell, M. C. (1999). Perceptions of price unfairness: Antecedents and consequences. Journal of Marketing Research, 36, 187–199.

Carli, L. L., & Leonard, J. B. (1990). The effect of hindsight on victim derogation. Journal of Social and Clinical Psychology, 9, 331–343.

Choi, I., Nisbett, R. E., & Norenzayan, A. (1999). Causal attribution across cultures: Variation and universality. Psychological Bulletin, 125, 47–63.

Cronley, M. L., Kardes, F. R., Goddard, P., & Houghton, D. C. (1999). Endorsing products for money: The role of the correspondence bias in celebrity advertising. Advances in Consumer Research, 26, 627–631.

D'Agostino, P. R., & Fincher-Kiefer, R. (1992). Need for cognition and the correspondence bias. Social Cognition, 10, 151–163.

Dean, D. H., & Biswas, A. (2001). Third-party organization endorsement of products: An advertising cue affecting consumer prepurchase evaluation of goods and services. Journal of Advertising, 30, 41–57.

Dixon, A. L. (2001). Successful and unsuccessful sales calls: Measuring salesperson attributions and behavioral intentions. Journal of Marketing, 65, 64–78.

Dweck, C. S., Chiu, C., & Hong, Y. (1995). Implicit theories and their role in judgments and reactions: A world from two perspectives. Psychological Inquiry, 6, 267–285.

Dweck, C. S., Hong, Y., & Chiu, C. (1993). Implicit theories: Individual differences in the likelihood and meaning of dispositional inference. Personality and Social Psychology Bulletin, 19, 644–656.

Erdogan, B. Z. (1999). Celebrity endorsement: A literature review. Journal of Marketing Management, 15, 291–324.

Erdogan, B. Z. (2001). Selecting celebrity endorsers: The practitioner's perspective. Journal of Advertising Research, 41, 39–48.

Erickson, D. J., & Krull, D. S. (1999). Distinguishing judgments about what from judgments about why: Effects of behavior extremity on correspondent inferences and causal attributions. Basic and Applied Social Psychology, 21, 1–11.

Fein, S. (1996). Effects of suspicion on attributional thinking and the correspondence bias. Journal of Personality and Social Psychology, 70, 1164–1184.

Fiske, S. T., & Taylor, S. E. (1991). *Social cognition* (2nd ed.). New York: McGraw-Hill.

Folkes, V. S. (1988). Recent attribution research in consumer behavior: A review and new directions. *Journal of Consumer Research, 14*, 548–565.

Friedman, H. H., & Friedman, L. (1979). Endorsers effectiveness by product type. *Journal of Advertising Research, 19*, 63–71.

Furnham, A., & Gunter, B. (1984). Just world beliefs and attitudes towards the poor. *British Journal of Social Psychology, 23*, 265–269.

Gershoff, A. D., Broniarczyk, S. M., & West, P. M. (2001). Recommendation or evaluation? Task sensitivity in information source selection. *Journal of Consumer Research, 28*, 418–438.

Gilbert, D. T., & Jones, E. E. (1986). Perceiver-induced constraint: Interpretations of self-generated reality. *Journal of Personality and Social Psychology, 50*, 269–280.

Gilbert, D. T., & Malone, P. S. (1995). The correspondence bias. *Psychological Bulletin, 117*, 21–38.

Gilbert, D. T., Pelham, B. W., & Krull, D. S. (1988). Inference and interaction: When person perceivers meets persons perceived. *Journal of Personality and Social Psychology, 54*, 733–740.

Hamilton, D. L. (1988). Causal attribution viewed from an information processing perspective. In D. Bar-Tal & A. W. Kruglanski (Eds.), *The social psychology of knowledge* (pp. 359–385). New York: Cambridge University Press.

Harris, M. B., & Miller, K. C. (2000). Gender and perceptions of danger. *Sex Roles, 43*, 843–863.

Heider, F. (1958). *The psychology of interpersonal relations*. New York: Wiley.

Hilton, D. J., Smith, R. H., & Kim, S. H. (1995). Processes of causal explanation and dispositional attribution. *Journal of Personality and Social Psychology, 68*, 377–387.

Hiroto, D. S. (1974). Locus of control and learned helplessness. *Journal of Experimental Psychology, 102*, 187–193.

Hofstede, G. (1980). *Culture's consequences: International differences in work-related values*. Beverly Hills, CA: Sage.

Hong, Y. (1994). *Predicting trait versus process inferences: The role of implicit theories.* Unpublished doctoral dissertation, Columbia University, New York.

Hunter, C. E., & Ross, M. W. (1991). Determinants of health-care workers' attitudes toward people with AIDS. *Journal of Applied Social Psychology, 21*, 947–956.

Inhelder, B., & Piaget, J. (1958). *The growth of logical thinking from childhood to adolescence*. New York: Basic Books.

Johnson, J. T., Jemmott, J. B., III, & Pettigrew, T. F. (1984). Causal attribution and dispositional inference: Evidence of inconsistent judgments. *Journal of Experimental Social Psychology, 20*, 567–585.

Jones, E. E. (1990). *Interpersonal perception*. New York: Macmillan.

Jones, E. E., & Davis, K. E. (1965). From acts to dispositions: The attribution process in person perception. In L. Berkowitz (Ed.), *Advances in experimental social psychology* (Vol. 2, pp. 219–266). New York: Academic Press.

Jones, E. E., Davis, K. E., & Gergen, K. J. (1961). Role playing variations and their informational value for person perception. *Journal of Abnormal and Social Psychology, 63*, 302–310.

Jones, E. E., & Harris, V. A. (1967). The attribution of attitudes. *Journal of Experimental Social Psychology, 3*, 1–24.

Kamins, M. A. (1990). An investigation into the "match-up" hypothesis in celebrity advertising: When beauty may only be skin deep. *Journal of Advertising, 19*(1), 4–13.

Kelley, H. H. (1967). Attribution theory in social psychology. In D. Levine (Ed.), *Nebraska Symposium on Motivation* (Vol. 15, pp. 192–238). Lincoln: University of Nebraska Press.

Klayman, J., & Ha, Y.-W. (1987). Confirmation, disconfirmation, and information in hypothesis testing. *Psychological Review, 94*, 211–228.

Koriat, A., Lichtenstein, S., & Fischhoff, B. (1980). Reasons for confidence. *Journal of Experimental Psychology: Human Learning and Memory, 6*, 107–118.

Kruglanski, A. W. (1980). Lay epistemology process and contents. *Psychological Review, 87*, 70–87.

Krull, D. S. (2001). On partitioning the fundamental attribution error: Dispositionalism and the corre-spondence bias. In G. B. Moskowitz (Ed.), *Cognitive social psychology: The Princeton Sympo-sium on the Legacy and Future of Social Cognition* (pp. 211–227). Mahwah, NJ: Lawrence Erlbaum Associates.

Krull, D. S., Loy, M. H.-M., Lin, J., Wang, C.-F., Chen, S., & Zhao, X. (1999). The fundamental attri-bution error: Correspondence bias in independent and interdependent cultures. *Personality and So-cial Psychology Bulletin, 25,* 1208–1219.

Kunda, Z. (1990). The case for motivated reasoning. *Psychological Bulletin, 208,* 480–498.

Laczniak, R. N., DeCarlo, T. E., & Ramaswami, S. N. (2001). Consumers' responses to negative word-of-mouth communication: An attribution theory perspective. *Journal of Consumer Psychol-ogy, 11,* 57–73.

Langer, E. J., & Rodin, J. (1976). The effects of choice and enhanced personal responsibility for the aged: A field experiment. *Journal of Personality and Social Psychology, 34,* 191–198.

Laufer, D., & Gillespie, K. (2004). Differences in consumer attributions of blame between men and women: The role of perceived vulnerability and empathic concern. *Psychology & Marketing, 21,* 141–157.

Lerner, M. J. (1980). *The belief in a just world: A fundamental delusion.* New York: Plenum.

Lerner, M. J., & Simmons, C. H. (1966). Observers' reaction to the "innocent victim" Compassion or rejection? *Journal of Personality and Social Psychology, 4,* 203–210.

Lichtenstein, D. R., & Bearden, W. O. (1989). Contextual influences on perceptions of merchant-supplied reference prices. *Journal of Consumer Research, 16,* 55–66.

Markus, H. R., & Kitayama, S. (1991). Culture and the self: Implications for cognition, emotion, and motivation. *Psychological Review, 98,* 224–253.

Maxham, J. G., & Netemeyer, R. G. (2002). A longitudinal study of complaining customers' evalua-tions of multiple service failures and recovery efforts. *Journal of Marketing, 66,* 57–71.

Milgram, S. (1963). Behavioral study of obedience. *Journal of Abnormal and Social Psychology, 67,* 371–378.

Miller, J. G. (1984). Culture and the development of everyday social explanation. *Journal of Personal-ity and Social Psychology, 46,* 961–978.

Morris, M. W., & Peng, K. (1994). Culture and cause: American and Chinese attributions for social and physical events. *Journal of Personality and Social Psychology, 67,* 949–971.

Newman, L. S. (1991). Why are traits inferred spontaneously? A developmental approach. *Social Cognition, 9,* 221–253.

Newman, L. S. (1993). How individualists interpret behavior: Idiocentrism and spontaneous trait in-ference. *Social Cognition, 11,* 243–269.

Nisbett, R. E., & Ross, L. (1980). *Human inference: Strategies and shortcomings of social judgment.* Englewood Cliffs, NJ: Prentice-Hall.

Ohanian, R. (1991). The impact of celebrity spokesperson's perceived image on consumers' intention to purchase. *Journal of Advertising Research, 31,* 46–52.

Oyserman, D., Coon, H. M., & Kemmelmeier, M. (2002). Rethinking individualism and collectivism: Evaluation of theoretical assumptions and meta-analyses. *Psychological Bulletin, 128,* 3–72.

Piaget, J. (1952). *The origins of intelligence in children.* New York: Harcourt Brace.

Pyszczynski, T., & Greenberg, J. (1987). Toward an integration of cognitive and motivational per-spectives on social inference: A biased hypothesis-testing model. In L. Berkowitz (Ed.), *Advances in experimental social psychology* (Vol. 20, pp. 297–340). New York: Academic Press.

Quattrone, G. A. (1982). Overattribution and unit formation: When behavior engulfs the person. *Jour-nal of Personality and Social Psychology, 42,* 593–607.

Raghubir, P., & Corfman, K. (1999). When do price promotions affect pretrial brand evaluations? *Journal of Marketing Research, 36,* 211–222.

Robbennolt, J. K. (2000). Outcome severity and judgments of responsibility: A meta-analytic review. *Journal of Applied Social Psychology, 30,* 2575–2609.

Ross, L. (1977). The intuitive psychologist and his shortcomings. In L. Berkowitz (Ed.), *Advances in experimental social psychology* (Vol. 10, pp. 173–220). San Diego, CA: Academic Press.

Ross, L., Amabile, T. M., & Steinmetz, J. L. (1977). Social roles, social control, and biases in social-perception processes. *Journal of Personality and Social Psychology, 35,* 485–494.

Ross, M., McFarland, C., & Fletcher, G. J. O. (1981). The effect of attitude on recall of past histories. *Journal of Personality and Social Psychology, 10,* 627–634.

Rotenberg, K. J. (1982). Development of character constancy of self and other. *Child Development, 53,* 505–515.

Sanitioso, R., Kunda, Z., & Fong, G. T. (1990). Motivated recruitment of autobiographical memory. *Journal of Personality and Social Psychology, 59,* 229–241.

Schwartz, S. H. (1990). Individualism–collectivism: Critique and proposed refinements. *Journal of Cross-Cultural Psychology, 21,* 139–157.

Seligman, M. E. P., & Maier, S. F. (1967). Failure to escape traumatic shock. *Journal of Experimental Psychology, 74,* 1–9.

Shaver, K. G. (1970). Defensive attribution: Effects on severity and relevance on the responsibility assigned for an accident. *Journal of Personality and Social Psychology, 14,* 101–113.

Shaw, J. I., & McMartin, J. A. (1977). Personal and situational determinants of attribution of responsibility for an accident. *Human Relations, 30,* 95–107.

Shimp, T. A. (2000). *Advertising, promotion: Supplemental aspects of integrated marketing communications* (5th ed.). Fort Worth, TX: Dryden Press.

Silvera, D. H., & Austad, B. (2004). Factors predicting the effectiveness of celebrity endorsement advertisements. *European Journal of Marketing, 38,* 1509–1526.

Silvera, D. H., Grape, K. M., & Sørum, K. A. (2004). *Correspondent inferences and their impact on endorser effectiveness in the United States and Norway.* Unpublished manuscript.

Silvera, D. H., Moe, S.-K., & Iversen, P. (2000). The association between implicit theories of personality and the attributional process. *Scandinavian Journal of Psychology, 41,* 107–111.

Siomkos, G. J., & Kurzbard, G. (1994). The hidden crisis in product-harm crisis management. *European Journal of Marketing, 28,* 30–41.

Smith, E. R., & Miller, F. D. (1983). Mediation among attributional inferences and comprehension processes: Initial findings and a general method. *Journal of Personality and Social Psychology, 44,* 492–505.

Snyder, M., & Swann, W. B. (1978). Hypothesis-testing processes in social interaction. *Journal of Personality and Social Psychology, 36,* 1202–1212.

Sørum, K. A., Grape, K. M., & Silvera, D. (2003). Do dispositional attributions regarding peer endorsers influence product evaluations? *Scandinavian Journal of Psychology, 44,* 39–46.

Stets, J. E., & Strauss, M. A. (1990). Gender differences in reporting marital violence and its medical and psychological consequences. In M. A. Strauss & R. J. Gelles (Eds.), *Physical violence in American families* (pp. 151–180). London: Transaction.

Su, W., & Tippins, M. J. (1998). Consumer attributions of product failure to channel members and self: The impact of situational cues. In T. K. Srull (Ed.), *Advances in consumer research* (Vol. 25, pp. 139–145). Provo, UT: Association for Consumer Research.

Summers, G., & Feldman, N. S. (1984). Blaming the victim versus blaming the perpetrator: An attributional analysis of spouse abuse. *Journal of Social and Clinical Psychology, 2,* 339–347.

Taylor, S. (1994). Waiting for service: The relationship between delays and evaluations of service. *Journal of Marketing, 58,* 56–69.

Tetlock, P. E. (1985). Accountability: A social check on the fundamental attribution error. *Social Psychology Quarterly, 48,* 227–236.

Till, B. D., & Shimp, T. A. (1998). Endorsers in advertising: The case of negative celebrity information. *Journal of Advertising, 27,* 67–82.

Triandis, H. C. (1995). *Individualism and collectivism.* Boulder, CO: Westview Press.

Tripp, C., Jensen, T. D., & Carlson, L. (1994). The effects of multiple product endorsements by celebrities on consumers' attitudes and intentions. *Journal of Consumer Research, 20,* 535–547.

Trope, Y. (1986). Identification and inferential processes in dispositional attribution. *Psychological Review*, *93*, 239–257.

Trope, Y., & Alfieri, T. (1997). Effortfulness and flexibility of dispositional judgment processes. *Journal of Personality and Social Psychology*, *73*, 662–674.

Trope, Y., Cohen, O., & Maoz, T. (1988). The perceptual and inferential effects of situational inducements on dispositional attributions. *Journal of Personality and Social Psychology*, *55*, 165–177.

Tversky, A., & Kahneman, D. (1974). Judgments under uncertainty: Heuristics and biases. *Science*, *185*, 1124–1131.

Uleman, J. S., Newman, L. S., & Moskowitz, G. B. (1996). People as flexible interpreters: Evidence and issues from spontaneous trait inference. In M. P. Zanna (Ed.), *Advances in experimental social psychology* (Vol. 28, pp. 211–279). San Diego, CA: Academic Press.

Waterman, A. S. (1984). *The psychology of individualism*. New York: Praeger.

Webster, D. M. (1993). Motivated augmentation and reduction of the overattribution bias. *Journal of Personality and Social Psychology*, *65*, 261–271.

Weiner, B. (1985). "Spontaneous" causal thinking. *Psychological Bulletin*, *97*, 74–84.

Weiner, B. (1986). *An attributional theory of motivation and emotion*. New York: Springer-Verlag.

Weiner, B. (2000). Attributional thoughts about consumer behavior. *Journal of Consumer Research*, *27*, 382–387.

II. NEW PERSPECTIVES ON CONSUMER INFORMATION PROCESSING AND RESEARCH METHODS

CHAPTER FOUR

Marketing by Mistake: The Unintended Consequences of Consumer Research

Jane E. Machin
University of Pennsylvania

Gavan J. Fitzsimons
Duke University

Imagine for a moment that you are a market-research professional interested in understanding women's attitudes toward home pregnancy tests. You want to understand current usage patterns and determine which features are most important. As a first step, you decide to conduct focus groups. You recruit six women through telephone interviews and invite them to attend a discussion on pregnancy-related matters. As an ethical researcher, you inform the women accurately in advance what the discussion will be about and they freely sign consent forms. You explain that anything they say will be confidential and assure them of their anonymity. You also make clear that nothing will be sold to them during the course of the research and make clear that they are free to leave at any time. During the discussion, you ask them to imagine what they would do if they believed they might be pregnant. If they mention a home pregnancy test, you ask them to explain the reasoning behind that choice. You then introduce your brand and ask them to rate their feelings for it. At the end of the session, you feel pleased. You feel you have effectively met your research objectives while protecting the rights and interests of the respondent in the process. This chapter argues that while you were well intentioned, it is quite likely that you inadvertently failed to follow the basic research dictum, "Do no harm."

The fundamental goal of consumer researchers, both in academic and applied settings, is to enrich our understanding of consumer behavior. We attempt to gain this understanding by using a variety of research techniques. These approaches range from large-scale, quantitative studies, such as habits-and-attitudes surveys, to traditional laboratory experiments, to qualitative research, such as focus groups or one-on-one interviews. In general, consumer researchers assume it is possible to practice these techniques in isolation—that is, without contaminating either the data or the subject. However, much recent research in social cognition has demonstrated that it is possible to influence beliefs, attitudes, goals and behavior through unconscious processes. This has important consequences for consumer researchers. It suggests that the research process itself has the potential to inadvertently influence the consumer's responses and behavior. In the opening vignette, there are several occasions when the research process could have unintentionally influenced the respondents. For example, anticipating the discussion might have led them to unconsciously alter the attitudes they planned to express in the group. Or, imagining they suspected pregnancy for the sake of the study, might lead the subjects to later believe they actually experienced this event. Alternatively, asking the respondents to list reasons for their attitude might have unintentionally disrupted the link between their stated attitude toward a pregnancy test brand and their intention to purchase it. Exposure to the subject matter may have also inadvertently initiated pursuit of a goal to become pregnant that the participant is not aware of. Note that not only could these nonconscious processes affect participant responses during the focus group, but, perhaps more importantly, their participation in the study could affect their subsequent "real-life" behavior.

The fact that research can influence participants unintentionally is acknowledged with varying degrees within the field of consumer research. At times, it is effectively ignored. In industry, for example, marketing decisions such as sales forecasts, new product launches, and advertising designs are based on research results with little consideration for the potential influence of the research process on that data. At other times, the ability to influence research participants outside their awareness is purposely employed. For example, political campaigners may ask leading survey questions to introduce damaging knowledge about the opposition (*push polls*; see Fitzsimons & Shiv, 2001) whereas unscrupulous marketers may attempt to sell products under the guise of market research (*sugging*), an activity that not only violates marketing research ethical codes, but is illegal (Bowers, 1995). In academia, supraliminal and subliminal priming techniques are used as a means of more elegantly testing research hypotheses. Many other research approaches may overlook or underestimate the potentially contaminating effect of the research process on the participant. Given the difficulty associated with undoing or reversing many types of biases in decision making (e.g., Arkes, 1991) the inadvertent introduction of such biases on behavior raises numerous cautionary flags.

In this chapter we interpret a growing body of work on nonconscious processes and apply it to the field of consumer research. Our goal is to encourage a broader recognition of the implications of research on nonconscious processes for all consumer researchers. We begin by providing a brief overview of the central role played by automatic attitudes and behavior in everyday life. The substance of the chapter highlights numerous research streams, emphasizing the relevance to consumer researchers. We have grouped the research streams into three broad categories, depending on the type of inadvertent influence on consumer responses: *exposure*, *measurement*, and *introspection*. Some overlap no doubt exists between the three categories and some theories will no doubt have been omitted. The goal of this chapter is not to provide a comprehensive literature review, but to stimulate thought about how routine consumer research might have consequences that are not typically considered. Finally, we conclude with a brief discussion of the ethical and public-policy issues raised by inadvertently influencing respondents through the consumer-research process.

AUTOMATIC OR NONCONSCIOUS ATTITUDES AND BEHAVIOR

Historically, consumer research has had a purely cognitive focus and Bargh (2002) noted that this approach remains popular, particularly in areas such as decision making. A cognitive focus also dominates popular behavior prediction theories, such as Social Cognitive Theory (Bandura, 1997), the Theory of Reasoned Action (Ajzen & Fishbein, 1980), and the Integrated Model of Behavior Change (Fishbein & Yzer, 2001). However, the increasing popularity of dual-process models (see Petty, Wegener, & Fabrigar, 1997; Wood, 2000, for reviews) such as the elaboration likelihood model (ELM; Petty, Cacioppo, & Schumann, 1983) and the heuristic-systematic model (HSM; Chaiken, 1980) suggests that many researchers accept the possibility that nonsystematic processing may guide behavior, at least under certain conditions. These dual-mode processing theories propose that when the respondent lacks the motivation, opportunity, or ability, a peripheral, automatic processing mode will kick in, using heuristic cues such as spokesperson attractiveness. The past 10 years has seen an increase in research examining automatic processes in social domains covering perception (Carlston & Skowronski, 1994), emotion (Berridge & Winkielman, 2003), goal pursuit (Chartrand & Bargh, 1996, 2002), attitude formation (Fazio, Sanbonmatsu, Powell, & Kardes, 1986), and numerous other domains (see Bargh & Chartrand, 1999, for a review). This research stream suggests that a person's conscious attentional capacity is limited and so, to function effectively, most psychological life must occur automatically, without conscious awareness. Baumeister, Bratslavsky, Muraven, and Tice (1998) concluded that the conscious self only plays a role about 5% of the time. This allows for the possibility of influencing attitudes, beliefs, and behavior outside of conscious awareness. The fact that this can happen raises important ethical questions. The remainder of the chapter focuses on the literature that finds these nonconscious effects on attitudes, beliefs, goals, and behavior. As noted earlier, these effects are grouped into three broad categories, based on their type. Within each section, we highlight the implications of the work for consumer researchers, illustrating potential concerns with real-world examples.

Exposure Inadvertently Influences Responses

A growing body of work suggests that the initial information subjects are exposed to can direct their subsequent responses, without their awareness. It is not hard to imagine how this is relevant to consumer research. Exposure to a stimulus presented in the early stages of a survey, experiment, or focus group can unintentionally and unconsciously influence the attitudes, beliefs, or behavior examined in later sections of the research. This effect has been shown to hold for a variety of different types of stimuli. Reviewed in this chapter is exposure to questions and numbers as well as pictorial and textual primes. Exposure to stimuli can inadvertently influence responses in two ways: It can bias responses to objects encountered after the stimuli, or it can affect responses to the stimuli itself. The former will be discussed first.

In their discussion of self-generated validity, Feldman and Lynch (1988) suggested that a subject's responses to early questions can automatically influence his or her answers to subsequent questions, if the earlier response is accessible and perceived to be more diagnostic than other available information. This influence of early judgments on later judgments is suggested to be most evident when the early judgment is diagnostic of the later judgment. To update the example that Feldman and Lynch used, a subject's answer to the question "Is Enron trustworthy?" might be more diagnostic for the question "Is big business trustworthy?" than the answer to big business would be for Enron. The relevance to consumer research is obvious, because the initial information is something that almost all research uses—a question. Much has been written about the implications of this process for research validity and Feldman and Lynch themselves suggest that these effects have important consequences for the respondent as well. The process of asking questions biases beliefs, attitudes, intentions, and behavior. Even if the measured constructs do not originally exist in a subject's long-term memory, the belief, attitude, or intention can be created by the measurement itself, and these responses can direct answers to other questions that follow in the survey, or influence their beliefs and behavior after the research is completed. Through the very questions we ask, we unintentionally affect attitudes, beliefs, and intentions. Interestingly, the question can be purely hypothetical and still unintentionally bias behavior. For example, in a simulated election, Fitzsimons and Shiv (2001) showed that when asked the suppositional question, "If you learned that Bob Clark had been convicted of fraud in 1988 on a charge stemming from several illegal donations accepted and subsequently misrepresented during his successful campaign for state treasurer, would your opinion of him increase or decrease?" the percentage of respondents choosing Bob Clark decreased from 79% to 25%. If they cognitively elaborated on the question (because they expected to justify their decision), the number of people choosing Candidate A decreased even further. In a second study, Fitzsimons and Shiv (2001) also showed that asking hypothetical questions can influence actual behavior. The percentage of respondents who chose cake over fruit salad increased substantially if the respondents had been asked a hypothetical question 1 hour earlier about the benefits of eating baked goods. When respondents were confronted with the possibility that the hypothetical question may have guided their later behavior, they steadfastly denied any connection. Once again, this has important ethical implications. An unscrupulous market researcher could, for example, disparage a competitor's product by asking suppositional questions with negative information, much as political campaigners do in so-called push polls (Traugott & Kang, 2000). The longevity of the effect depends on how exactly the effect takes place. As Fitzsimons and Shiv (2001) noted, this is an area that requires more research, but if hypothetical questions actually alter preferences, they could also alter behavior later in time. This could have negative consequences for the consumer—for example, if he or she were asked a hypothetical question about positive consequences of using drugs or smoking.

Exposure to a question is not the only stimulus that can bias subsequent responses. Exposure to a number can also be used unconsciously by the consumer to answer subsequent questions, a process known as *anchoring*. In a classic study, Tversky and Kahneman (1974) showed that when people guessed whether the percentage of African countries in the United Nations was more or less than a number from a "wheel of fortune spin," estimates were significantly higher if they began with a high spin than if they began with a low spin. This effect has been shown in a variety of contexts and occurs even when the prior information is completely uninformative. For example, in a series of studies, Wilson, Houston, Etling, and Brekke (1996) showed that completely arbitrary numbers can anchor people's judgments, even when there is no logical reason to consider the numbers as answers to subsequent questions, an effect that is moderated by attention and knowledge. Of importance to this review is that Wilson et al. (1996) found the process occurred unintentionally and unconsciously; warning people about the effects did not eliminate them. To relate this to the consumer-research context, imagine the marketer trying to understand purchase interest for a new product. A study is conducted, where consumers are asked what price they would pay for the new product. As part of the same survey, however, they initially were required to write their home address. It is possible for that initial task to provide an arbitrary anchor value that unintentionally influences their answer to the pricing question. Not only is the research validity now questionable, but we have accidentally affected the attitude of the respondent. Much as a careless park visitor, we have left our trace on the environment, that is, the consumer.

Exposure to a prime can also inadvertently influence responses to subsequently encountered material. *Priming* occurs when attention to some stimulus increases the saliency of a category, attitude, identity or goal, which in turn increases the likelihood it will be used when judging a subsequently encountered stimulus. Primes can be delivered subliminally, where the affected person is unaware of the prime, or supraliminally, where he or she is aware of the prime but not of the potential influence. Primes have been shown to have unintentional effects in a variety of areas, including racial attitudes (Fazio, Jackson, Dunton, & Williams, 1995), conformity to social pressure (Epley & Gilovich, 1999), goals (Chartrand & Bargh, 1996), memory (Dijksterhuis, Aarts, Bargh, & van Knippenberg, 2000), mood (Berridge & Winkielman, 2003), and behavior (Dovidio, Gaertner, & Kawakami, 2002; Wilson, Lindsey, & Schooler, 2000). A common priming technique is to expose the respondent to images or words on a computer screen below the threshold of awareness (typically less than 30 ms). Strahan, Spencer, and Zanna (2002), for example, used this technique to subliminally prime thirst. They found this automatically activated a desire to quench thirst and, if respondents were indeed thirsty, increased the amount that people drank. An alternative priming technique is to give respondents a series of scrambled words, such as "he what gain did summer," from which they have to form a four-word sentence. The words used in the sentence have been shown to prime a particular mood or a goal (Srull & Wyer, 1979). In the example given the word "gain" is the prime. Research has shown that such primes can nonconsciously activate a goal to succeed, leading the person to take steps to fulfill that goal. Individuals can succeed or fail at nonconsciously pursued goals and this has downstream consequences for moods and beyond. Chartrand (2004) showed that failure at a nonconscious goal can depress mood, whereas success can improve it. The consequences of altering someone's mood are far-reaching. A rich literature shows that mood can affect both attitude and behavior (see Luomala & Laaksonen, 2000, for a review). For example, mood can influence estimates of risk (Gasper & Clore, 1998; Johnson & Tversky, 1983; Lerner & Keltner, 2001), product ratings (Srull, 1983), preferences (Winkielman, Zajonc, & Schwarz, 1997), purchase intention (Deshpande, Hoyer, & Donthu, 1986), and task performance (Chartrand, 2004). Mood can also be primed unconsciously. Winkielman, Berridge, and Wilbarger (2005) primed mood with happy, neutral, or angry faces, and although subjects' ratings of mood did not change, the amount of a drink poured and consumed, as well as ratings of the drink, did. Overall, this literature suggests that the environment, specifically the research context, can guide attitudes, beliefs, and behavior without conscious awareness. For example, during advertising research, it would not be unusual for participants to encounter images of happy people. This could unintentionally prime their mood, or set a goal in motion, impacting their behavior when they leave the research environment.

Exposing someone to a particular social identity can also unconsciously change attitudes and behavior. The identity can be one the respondent holds about others or about themselves. As an example of the former, Bargh, Chen, and Burrows (1996) found that young participants unconsciously primed with elderly related material subsequently behaved more in line with the stereotype than participants who were not primed—that is, they walked more slowly down the hallway after leaving the experiment. Regarding the self-identity, Shih, Pittinsky, and Ambady (1999) examined Asian American women's performance on a math test.

When their female identity was implicitly primed, the women performed significantly worse than when their Asian identity was primed, in line with popular cultural stereotypes. Social identity theory helps to explain the latter result. Social identity refers to the degree to which an individual identifies with a particular social group or role (Reed, 2002; Tajfel & Turner, 1979). Everybody has multiple social identities that together make up a global self. Some identities are more salient than others and particular identities become more salient at different times. Identity salience—when an individual spontaneously and often unconsciously categorizes him or herself by some identity-orientated criteria—can happen for a variety of reasons. *Distinctiveness theory* (McGuire, 1984) predicts that a person's distinctive traits will become more salient when compared to the traits of everyone else in a given social context. Being in a numeric minority is one situation when the unique trait will become more salient. For example, a woman will become most aware of her gender identity in a room of men. Grier and Deshpande (2001) argued that other socioeconomic factors, such as the group's social status and economic power, will also influence whether a consumer feels distinctive in a particular situation. Importantly, the process is again unconscious—people are not aware that they are responding in a manner influenced by a particular identity. This research suggests that if an earlier question or stimulus raises respondents' awareness of a particular, socially distinctive identity, their subsequent responses will reflect this identity. For example, Forehand, Deshpande, and Reed (2002) showed that attitudes towards in-group advertising improved when the participants' in-group, socially distinctive identity was made salient through a nonconscious prime. This result is particularly worrying if the salient identity is perceived negatively by the respondent, as it could cause emotional discomfort. For example, Levy (1996) primed elderly people with either a negative or positive stereotype of the elderly, respectively impairing or improving performance on a memory task. It is not a big leap to see how numerically and socially distinctive identities could be made salient in the course of marketing research—a single African American focus group participant is likely to be very aware of his ethnic identity, for example. The effect could not only bias the responses expressed in the research, but could endure afterward, affecting poststudy emotions and behavior.

As noted earlier, exposure to a stimulus not only influences subsequently encountered material, it can also influence attitudes toward the stimulus itself. Two related streams of research—the *mere-exposure effect* and the *truth effect*—suggest that simply exposing respondents to stimuli can alter their assessment of the attitude object itself. Mere exposure describes the process by which simple repetition leads to improved assessments of an object. The truth effect refers to the fact that simply exposing respondents to information can increase the perceived truth value of that information. Zajonc (1968) first reported the fact that repeated exposure to a stimulus can improve affective evaluations of it. In a meta-analysis of the mere-exposure effect, Bornstein (1989) found over 200 published experiments that replicated this effect with a variety of attitude objects. Replicating earlier work (Hasher, Goldstein, & Toppino, 1977; Schwartz, 1982) on the truth effect, Hawkins and Hoch (1992) showed that people will rate an ambiguous trivia statement, such as "Buffered aspirin tends to work more slowly than unbuffered aspirin" (Hawkins & Hoch, 1992, p. 217), as more true if they have been exposed to it before. They found this basic effect increased when involvement was low and suggest that familiarity ("It rings a bell") is the key mediator of the effect. Hawkins and Hoch (1992), and later Hawkins, Hoch, and Meyers-Levy (2001), suggested that the truth effect differs from the mere-exposure effect in that recognition appears to be necessary for the former, but inhibitive for the latter. Indeed, Bornstein and D'Agostino (1992) showed that subliminal priming produces significantly larger mere-exposure effects, but when the respondent is aware that they have been exposed to stimuli they are about to rate, they can correct their initial evaluation. Nonetheless, these two research streams have important implications for consumer researchers; whether a respondent is aware of being exposed to a stimulus or not, the process of being exposed can alter their rating of the statement, or the degree to which they believe the statement. These results were found in experimental conditions, without the clutter, perhaps, of applied market research. Nonetheless, they do suggest that seemingly innocuous statements used in focus groups or other experiments will be liked more and will be more likely to be accepted as true by respondents who subsequently encounter them. Once again, the researcher has altered the environment they entered.

Measurement Inadvertently Influences Consumer Response

A second broad category of unintentional influences on participants' attitudes, beliefs, and behavior stems from *measuring* their intentions. An increasing number of studies find that simply measuring someone's intention to perform a behavior influences the likelihood that they will then perform that behavior. This "mere-measurement" effect holds true across a variety of behaviors, including volunteering (Sherman, 1980), voting (Greenwald, Carnot, Beach, & Young, 1987), name generation (Spangenberg & Greenwald, 1999), and automobile shopping (Morwitz, Johnson, & Schmittlein, 1993). For example, Morwitz et al. (1993) found that respondents asked about their intent to purchase an automobile in the next 6 months increased their purchase rates of actual automobiles by almost 40% versus a control group not asked the intent question. There is also evidence that the effect is fairly durable. In a field experiment, Dholakia and Morwitz (2002) showed that measuring satisfaction not only affects the one-time purchase of financial services, but also leads to improved relational behaviors, such as customer profitability and defection, over an extended period of time. An important aspect of the hypothesized process is that the intention measure increases the accessibility of attitudes about the behavior, which leads to increased or decreased choice depending on the valence of the attitude (Fitzsimons & Morwitz, 1996; Morwitz &

Fitzsimons, 2004). Williams, Fitzsimons, and Block (2004) suggested that this occurs because intention questions slip beneath the respondent's natural defense mechanisms, preventing normal coping tactics from kicking in (Friestad & Wright, 1994). The unintended hazards of measuring intentions are fairly wide-ranging. Of perhaps greatest concern are respondents asked about likelihood to engage in risky or unhealthy behaviors (e.g., drug use, unsafe sex) by researchers doing marketing or public-policy research. Although the respondents may have an explicit negative attitude toward engaging in the risky behavior, they may also hold an implicit positive attitude toward engaging in the risky behavior. If the implicit positive attitude dominates in situations of temptation, having been asked an earlier intention question could well have the effect of liberating the respondent to engage in the risky behavior.

Introspection Inadvertently Influences Consumer Response

A common task in much consumer research is to ask the respondent to think about or list their reasons for a particular preference. This seemingly simple task has been shown to accidentally affect behavior. Wilson, Dunn, Bybee, Hyman, and Rotondo (1984) and Wilson, Hodges, and LaFleur (1995) showed that analyzing the reasons behind an expressed object attitude can decrease attitude–behavior consistency, an effect known as *disruption*. In their studies, people who expressed a positive attitude toward an object were less likely to choose that object at a later time if they had analyzed their reasons for liking it, compared to a control group who had not analyzed their reasons. Sengupta and Fitzsimons (2000) suggested that the extent to which disruption will occur depends on moderating factors such as whether there is a delay between the attitude and behavior measurement and the timing of the reasons analysis. Specifically, they find that analyzing reasons before taking an attitude measurement will decrease the attitude–behavior link, when behavior is measured after a delay, the situation most likely in commercial marketing research contexts. Not only does this mean that analyzing reasons can have counterproductive effects from the marketer's perspective, it means, once again, researchers are altering the environment they enter.

Another kind of introspection has also been shown to influence attitudes. Schlosser and Shavitt (2002) demonstrated that when people anticipate participating in a group discussion they mentally rehearse—introspect—about what they will say, focusing on less important, but more easily explainable or available information, and this can alter the attitude they express in the discussion in accordance with the valence of the information. When outside the group context, however, they will base their attitude on all information, including that which is not readily explainable, which may differ from the attitude they have expressed. This has obvious implications not only for focus groups, but perhaps for all research situations where the respondent is expected to justify his or her attitude and hence rehearses what to say. Once again, the process of conducting research has resulted in an unintended consequence for the subject.

Introspection can also reverse some of the already mentioned identity prime effects. Reflecting on others' expectations about a particular salient identity can unconsciously change their behavior. For example, looking at the performance of Chinese women on math tests, Cheryan and Bodenhausen (2000) showed that priming the positive stereotype (Chinese) can actually lead to poorer math results if awareness of other people's expectations is simultaneously raised. Imagination can also be considered a form of introspection, and this too can alter beliefs. Thomas and Loftus (2002) showed that after repeated imagination of both bizarre acts (such as "kiss the magnifying glass") and familiar acts (such as "flip the coin"), people later believe they have actually performed the act. Once again, this has important ethical considerations for consumer researchers. Moderators in focus groups often ask respondents to imagine themselves in a particular situation. Thomas and Loftus' results suggest that this could lead people to believe those situations actually took place. Finally, literature in the debiasing field has relevance in this section, in particular, the hindsight bias. This occurs when people "tend to view what has happened as having been inevitable" (Fischhoff, 1982, p. 428). To counteract this bias, respondents are usually encouraged to think of reasons why the event may have turned out otherwise. Sanna, Schwarz, and Stocker (2001) showed however that this strategy can backfire. They found that when participants attempt to list many thoughts, the hindsight bias actually increases. The authors hypothesized that because respondents find the introspection task difficult, they believe that the actual outcome was indeed the most likely. Importantly, for this chapter, although participants were aware that the thoughts-listing task was difficult, they were not conscious of the influence of the task on their attitude formation.

A related line of research by Schwartz and colleagues (Schwartz et al., 1991; Schwartz & Vaughn, 2000) found that when participants are asked to generate either a small number or a large number of reasons either for or against an issue, they use the ease with which they can generate the reasons as an input to their subsequent attitude. For example, a participant asked to generate a large number of behaviors consistent with a particular personality trait judges him- or herself as being lower on that trait than does a participant asked to generate a small number. (Ease of retrieval is low for the large number but high for the small number, leading participants to change their self-perceptions; Schwartz et al., 1991.) In a consumer domain, Menon and Raghubir (2003) demonstrated similar effects with brands as targets, and concluded that the application of the ease-of-retrieval cue to brand attitudes occurs outside of conscious awareness. In applied market research, it is common to ask respondents to make lists—of behaviors or brand names, for example. The aforementioned literature suggests that the ease with which they can generate such lists will influence their attitude, bringing into question the validity of the research results.

CONCLUSIONS

Altering the attitudes, beliefs, and behaviors of consumers without their awareness raises significant ethical issues that have not been satisfactorily discussed to date. Kimmel and Smith (2001) pointed out that marketing, when compared to the fields of psychology and sociology, has a limited history of addressing ethically sensitive practices, especially from the perspective of the consumer. Early literature on marketing-research ethics focused on the rights of the client to accurate information or the responsibilities of the researcher to undertake research without fraud, fabrication, falsification, prevarication, plagiarism, or profiteering (Holbrook, 1994). Literature from the perspective of the respondent has tended to focus on issues such as his or her rights to privacy, informed consent, or freedom to withdraw (see Giacobbe & Segal, 2000, for review). There has been some research on the ethical issues associated with deliberate trading-off of ethical beliefs and other attributes (Irwin, 1999) or with deliberate transgressions, such as selling under the guise of marketing research (Bowers, 1995) or intentionally deceptive practices (Kimmel & Smith, 2001). To date, however, little attention has been paid to the impact of the numerous unintentional effects of marketing research from the perspective of the subject.

The research conducted in the opening vignette of this chapter follows the guidelines suggested by the American Marketing Association and the Marketing Research Association. It does not expose the participant to serious mental or physical risk and does not knowingly deceive or inflict harm. We believe this is insufficient. Changing someone's behavioral responses without their knowledge violates certain rights, including those listed by Holbrook (1994) as autonomy, dignity, candor, and informed consent. We propose a code of marketing research conduct that mimics the National Park Service's "Leave no trace" principles, one of which invites the visitor to enjoy the environment, but to leave it as it was found. Applying this code to marketing research implies that we should seek to understand the respondent's mental and emotional state, but try to leave it unchanged. To be sure, this is no easy matter. We have laid out examples in this chapter that demonstrate that almost all consumer research—applied and academic—risks these unintentional hazards for the respondent and, as many of the effects occur outside of conscious awareness, it may be impossible to avoid them. In some cases, a rigorous debriefing after the research may suffice to "undo" any accidental effects, although the robustness of some of the effects would seem to preclude this. In other cases, it may be possible to use alternative research techniques in order to avoid the effects in the first place. Clearly, this is an area where further research is necessary. By raising awareness of the risks, however, we aim to encourage the researcher to at least be aware of the consequences of their work.

REFERENCES

Ajzen, I., & Fishbein, M. (1980). *Understanding attitudes and predicting social behavior.* Englewood Cliffs, NJ: Prentice-Hall.

Arkes, H. R. (1991). Costs and benefits of judgment errors: Implications for debiasing. *Psychological Bulletin, 110*(3), 486–498.

Bandura, A. (1997). *Self-efficacy: The exercise of control.* New York: Freeman & Co.

Bargh, J. A. (2002). Losing consciousness: Automatic influences on consumer judgment, behavior and motivation. *Journal of Consumer Research, 29,* 280–285.

Bargh, J. A., & Chartrand, T. L. (1999). The unbearable automaticity of being. *American Psychologist, 54,* 462–479.

Bargh, J. A., Chen, M., & Burrows, L. (1996). Automaticity of social behavior: Direct effects of trait construct and stereotype activation on action. *Journal of Personality and Social Psychology, 71,* 230–244.

Baumeister, R. F., Bratslavsky, E., Muraven, M., & Tice, D. M. (1998). Ego depletion: Is the active self a limited resource? *Journal of Personality and Social Psychology, 74,* 1252–1265.

Berridge, K. C., & Winkielman, P. (2003). What is an unconscious emotion? (The case for unconscious "liking"). *Cognition & Emotion, 17*(2), 181–211.

Bornstein, R. F. (1989). Exposure and affect: Overview and meta-analysis of research, 1968–1987. *Psychological Bulletin, 106,* 265–289.

Bornstein, R. F., & D'Agostino, P. R. (1992). Stimulus recognition and the mere exposure effect. *Journal of Personality and Social Psychology, 63*(4), 545–552.

Bowers, D. K. (1995). Sugging banned, at last. *Marketing Research, 7*(4), 40.

Carlston, D. E., & Skowronski, J. J. (1994). Savings in the relearning of trait information as evidence for spontaneous inference generation. *Journal of Personality and Social Psychology, 66,* 840–856.

Chaiken, S. (1980). Heuristic versus systematic information processing and the use of source versus message cues in persuasion. *Journal of Personality and Social Psychology, 39*(5), 753–766.

Chartrand, T. L. (2004). *Mystery moods and perplexing performance: The consequences of succeeding or failing at a nonconscious goal.* Manuscript submitted for publication, Duke University.

Chartrand, T. L., & Bargh, J. A. (1996). Automatic activation of impression formation and memorization goals: Nonconscious goal priming reproduces effects of explicit task instructions. *Journal of Personality and Social Psychology, 71,* 464–478.

Chartrand, T. L., & Bargh, J. A. (2002). Nonconscious motivations: Their activation, operation, and consequences. In A. Tesser, D. Stapel, & J. Wood (Eds.), *Self and motivation: Emerging psychological perspectives* (pp. 13–41). Washington, DC: American Psychological Association.

Cheryan, S., & Bodenhausen, G. V. (2000). When positive stereotypes threaten intellectual performance: The psychological hazards of "model minority" status. *Psychological Science, 11,* 399–402.

Deshpande, R., Hoyer, W. D., & Donthu, N. (1986). The intensity of ethnic affiliation: A study of the sociology of Hispanic consumption. *Journal of Consumer Research, 13,* 214–220.

Dholakia, U. M., & Morwitz, V. G. (2002). The scope and persistence of mere-measurement effects: Evidence from a field study of customer satisfaction measurement. *Journal of Consumer Research, 29,* 159–167.

Dijksterhuis, A., Aarts, H., Bargh, J. A., & van Knippenberg, A. (2000). On the relation between associative strength and automatic behavior. *Journal of Experimental Social Psychology, 36,* 531–544.

Dovidio, J. F., Kawakami, K., & Gaertner, S. L. (2002). Implicit and explicit prejudice and interracial interactions. *Journal of Personality and Social Psychology, 82*, 62–68.

Epley, N., & Gilovich, T. (1999). Just going along: Nonconscious priming and conformity to social pressure. *Journal of Experimental Social Psychology, 35*, 578–589.

Fazio, R. H., Jackson, J. R., Dunton, B. C., & Williams, C. J. (1995). Variability in automatic activation as an unobtrusive measure of racial attitudes: A bona fide pipeline? *Journal of Personality and Social Psychology, 69*, 1013–1027.

Fazio, R. H., Sanbonmatsu, D. M., Powell, M. C., & Kardes, F. R. (1986). On the automatic activation of attitudes. *Journal of Personality and Social Psychology, 50*, 229–238.

Feldman, J. M., & Lynch, J. G., Jr. (1988). Self-generated validity and other effects of measurement on belief, attitude, intention, and behavior. *Journal of Applied Psychology, 73*, 421–435.

Fischhoff, B. (1982). Debiasing. In D. Kahneman, P. Slovic, & A. Tversky (Eds.), *Judgment under uncertainty: Heuristic and biases* (pp. 422–444). New York: Cambridge University Press.

Fishbein, M., & Yzer, M. C. (2003). Using theory to design effective health behavior interventions. *Communication Theory, 2003*(13), 164–183.

Fitzsimons, G. J., & Morwitz, V. (1996). The effect of measuring intent on brand level purchase behavior. *Journal of Consumer Research, 23*, 1–11.

Fitzsimons, G. J., & Shiv, B. (2001). Nonconscious and contaminative effects of hypothetical questions on subsequent decision making. *Journal of Consumer Research, 28*, 224–238.

Forehand, M., Deshpande, R., & Reed, A., II. (2002). Identity salience and the influence of differential activation of the social self schema on advertising response. *Journal of Applied Psychology, 87*(6), 1086–1099.

Friestad, M., & Wright, P. (1994). The persuasion knowledge model: How people cope with persuasion attempts. *Journal of Consumer Research, 21*, 1–31.

Gasper, K., & Clore, G. L. (1998). The persistent use of negative affect by anxious individuals to estimate risk. *Journal of Personality and Social Psychology, 74*(5), 1350–1363.

Giacobbe, R., & Segal, M. (2000). A comparative analysis of ethical perceptions in marketing research: U.S.A. vs. Canada. *Journal of Business Ethics, 27*, 229–245.

Greenwald, A. G., Carnot, C. G., Beach, R., & Young, B. (1987). Increasing voting behavior by asking people if they expect to vote. *Journal of Applied Psychology, 72*, 315–318.

Grier, S. A., & Deshpande, R. (2001). Social dimensions of consumer distinctiveness: The influence of social status on group identity and advertising persuasion. *Journal of Marketing Research, 38*, 216–224.

Hasher, L., Goldstein, D., & Toppino, T. (1977). Frequency and the conference of referential validity. *Journal of Verbal Learning and Verbal Behavior, 16*(1), 107–112.

Hawkins, S. A., & Hoch, S. J. (1992). Low-involvement learning: Memory without evaluation. *Journal of Consumer Research, 19*(2), 212–225.

Hawkins, S. A., Hoch, S. J., & Meyers-Levy, J. (2001). Low-involvement learning: Repetition and coherence in familiarity and belief. *Journal of Consumer Psychology, 11*(1), 1–11.

Holbrook, M. B. (1994). Ethics in consumer research: An overview and prospectus. *Advances in Consumer Research, 21*, 566–571.

Irwin, J. R. (1999). Introduction to the special issue on ethical trade-offs in consumer decision making. *Journal of Consumer Psychology, 8*(3), 211–214.

Johnson, E. J., & Tversky, A. (1983). Affect, generalization and the perception of risk. *Journal of Personality and Social Psychology, 45*(1), 20–31.

Kimmel, A. J., & Smith, C. N. (2001). Deception in marketing research: Ethical, methodological, and disciplinary implications. *Psychology & Marketing, 18*, 663–689.

Lerner, J. S., & Keltner, D. (2001). Fear, anger and risk. *Journal of Personality and Social Psychology, 81*(1), 146–159.

Levy, B. (1996). Improving memory in old age through implicit self-stereotyping. *Journal of Personality and Social Psychology, 71*, 1092–1107.

Luomala, H. T., & Laaksonen, M. (2000). Contributions from mood research. *Psychology and Marketing, 17*, 195–233.

McGuire, W. (1984). Search for the self: Going beyond self-esteem and the reactive self. In R. A. Sucker, J. Aronoff, & A. I. Rabin (Eds.), *Personality and the prediction of behavior* (pp. 73–120). New York: Academic Press.

Menon, G., & Raghubir, P. (2003). Ease-of-retrieval as an automatic input in judgments: A mere-accessibility framework? *Journal of Consumer Research, 30*, 230–243.

Morwitz, V. G., & Fitzsimons, G. J. (2004). The mere-measurement effect: Why does measuring intentions change actual purchase behavior? *Journal of Consumer Psychology, 14*(1,2), 64–74.

Morwitz, V. G., Johnson, E., & Schmittlein, D. (1993). Does measuring intent change behavior? *Journal of Consumer Research, 20*, 46–61.

Petty, R. E., Cacioppo, J. T., & Schumann, D. (1983). Central and peripheral routes to advertising effectiveness: The moderating role of involvement. *Journal of Consumer Research, 10*, 135–146.

Petty, R. E., Wegener, D. T., & Fabrigar, L. R. (1997). Attitudes and attitude change. *Annual Review of Psychology, 48*, 609–647.

Reed, A., II. (2002). Social identity as a useful perspective for self-concept-based consumer research. *Psychology and Marketing, 19*, 235–266.

Sanna, L. J., Schwarz, N., & Stocker, S. L. (2001). When debiasing backfires: Accessible content and accessibility experiences in debiasing hindsight. *Journal of Experimental Psychology: Learning, Memory and Cognition, 28*(3), 497–502.

Schlosser, A. E., & Shavitt, S. (2002). Anticipating discussion about a product: Rehearsing what to say can affect your judgments. *Journal of Consumer Research, 29*, 101–115.

Schwartz, M. (1982). Repetition and rated truth value of statements. *American Journal of Psychology, 95*, 393–407.

Schwarz, N., Bless, H., Strack, F., Klumpp, G., Rittenauer-Schatka, H., & Simons, A. (1991). Ease of retrieval as information: Another look at the availability heuristic. *Journal of Personality and Social Psychology, 61*, 195–202.

Schwarz, N., & Vaughn, L. A. (2000). The availability heuristic revisited: Ease of recall and content of recall as distinct sources of information. In T. Gilovich, D. Griffin, & D. Kahneman (Eds.), *Heuristics and biases: The psychology of intuitive judgment* (pp. 103–119). Cambridge, England: Cambridge University Press.

Sengupta, J., & Fitzsimons, G. J. (2000). The effects of analyzing reasons for brand preferences: Disruption or reinforcement. *Journal of Marketing Research, 37*(3), 318–330.

Sherman, S. J. (1980). On the self-erasing nature of errors of prediction. *Journal of Personality and Social Psychology, 39*, 211–221.

Shih, M., Pittinsky, T. L., & Ambady, N. (1999). Stereotype susceptibility: Identity salience and shifts in quantitative performance. *Psychological Science, 10*(1), 80–83.

Spangenberg, E. R., & Greenwald, A. G. (1999). Social influence by requesting self-prophecy. *Journal of Consumer Psychology, 8*(1), 61–89.

Srull, T. K. (1983). The impact of effective reactions in advertising on the representation of product information in memory. In R. Bagozzi & A. Tybout (Eds.), *Advances in consumer research* (Vol. 10, pp. 520–525). Ann Arbor, MI: Association for Consumer Research.

Srull, T. K., & Wyer, R. S. (1979). The role of category accessibility in the interpretation of information about persons: Some determinants and implications. *Journal of Personality and Social Psychology, 37*, 1660–1672.

Strahan, E. J., Spencer, S. J., & Zanna, M. P. (2002). Subliminal priming and persuasion: Striking while the iron is hot. *Journal of Experimental Social Psychology, 38*, 556–568.

Tajfel, H., & Turner, J. (1979). An integrative theory of intergroup conflict. In W. H. Austin & S. Worchel (Eds.), *The social psychology of intergroup relations* (pp. 33–47). Monterey, CA: Brooks/Cole.

Thomas, A. K., & Loftus, E. F. (2002). Creating bizarre false memories through imagination. *Memory & Cognition, 30*(3), 423–431.

Traugott, M. W., & Kang, M.-E. (2000). Push polls as negative persuasive strategies. In P. J. Lavrakas & M. W. Traugott (Eds.), *Election polls, the news media, and democracy* (pp. 281–300). New York: Seven Bridges Press.

Tversky, A., & Kahneman, D. (1974). Judgment under uncertainty: Heuristics and biases. *Science, 185*, 1124–1131.

Williams, P., Fitzsimons, G. J., & Block, L. G. (2004). When consumers don't recognize 'benign' intentions questions as persuasion attempts. *Journal of Consumer Research, 31*, 540–551.

Wilson, T. D., Dunn, D. S., Bybee, J. A., Hyman, D. B., & Rotondo, J. A. (1984). Effects of analyzing reasons on attitude-behavior consistency. *Journal of Personality and Social Psychology, 47*, 5–16.

Wilson, T. D., Hodges, S. D., & LaFleur, S. J. (1995). Effects of introspecting about reasons: Inferring attitudes from accessible thoughts. *Journal of Personality and Social Psychology, 69*, 16–28.

Wilson, T. D., Houston, C. E., Etling, K. M., & Brekke, N. (1996). A new look at anchoring effects: Basic anchoring and its antecedents. *Journal of Experimental Psychology: General, 125*(4), 387–402.

Wilson, T. D., Lindsey, S., & Schooler, T. (2000). A model of dual attitudes *Psychological Review, 107*, 101–126.

Winkielman, P., Berridge, K. C., & Wilbarger, J. (2005). Unconscious affective reactions to masked happy versus angry faces influence consumption behavior and judgments of value. *Personality and Social Psychology Bulletin, 1*, 121–135.

Winkielman, P., Zajonc, R. B., & Schwarz, N. (1997). Subliminal affective priming resists attributional interventions. *Cognition and Emotion, 11*, 433–465.

Wood, W. (2000). Attitude change: Persuasion and social influence. *Annual Review of Psychology, 51*, 539–570.

Zajonc, R. B. (1968). Attitudinal effects of mere exposure. *Journal of Personality and Social Psychology* (Monograph Supplement, Part 2), 1–27.

CHAPTER FIVE

Knowledge in Error: Decoding Consumer Judgments With the JUMP Model

Murali Chandrashekaran
Kristin Rotte
University of New South Wales

Rajdeep Grewal
Pennsylvania State University

> *Although we believe a great many things, we hold some of our beliefs with greater conviction than others.*
>
> —Koehler (1994, p. 461)

Social scientists work with judgments. Any approach to modeling the antecedents and/or consequences of judgments begins by defining an overt response to a task situation. Possible judgment responses could be an attitude toward a focal object or act, evaluation of the attributes of a product, choice between two or more alternatives, evaluation of a course of action, statement of intention to perform a task, evaluation of a brand, or rank-ordering of a set of alternatives. In all cases, the overt or "manifest" judgment is presumed to capture an unobserved or "latent" construct (e.g., an attitude is an unobservable construct but we work with an overt attitude judgment measured via a scale).

As Koehler's sentiment illustrates, it is perhaps banal to contend that all judgments are associated with uncertainty. The degree of uncertainty, of course, varies by individual, by situation, and by time. For the most part, however, researchers across the various social sciences focus on decision-making dynamics fostered solely by variations in judgment *magnitude* (also termed *judgment extremity* in the literature). Because it is associated with a lack of "conviction," uncertainty in a judgment has a direct bearing on the subsequent utilization of the judgment. Consider two individuals who express identical magnitudes of judgments, but differ in the degree of certainty with which they profess their judgments. Conventional analyses focusing only on the magnitude of judgments will treat these two individuals as identical in terms of both the antecedents and consequences of their judgments. As a result, incomplete process explanations of decision making will obtain.

Despite the ubiquitous nature of uncertainty in judgment and decision making, systematic inquiry into the nature and causes of judgment uncertainty is rare. This state of affairs, however, appears to be changing. Over the last few years, researchers have increasingly sought to understand the origins and dynamics of judgment uncertainty (e.g., Gigerenzer, Hoffrage, & Kleinbölting, 1991; Juslin & Olsson, 1997; Wallsten & González-Vallejo, 1994). Largely couched in terms of judgment accuracy, however, these attempts describe deviations in subjective judgments from an objective truth, paying little attention to the factors that may actually drive uncertainty in judgments. In contrast, we are motivated by Erev, Wallsten, and Budescu's (1994) call: "It is time for basic judgment research to orient away from questions of judgment accuracy . . . how do overt estimates depend on covert judgment and error, how such judgment arises, what factors affect it, and the extent and locus of errors. . . . To date we do not know the answer" (p. 526).

This chapter centers on a model whose central thesis builds on the simple assertion that all judgments are fuzzy to some extent, that is, overt judgment embodies two dimensions—the judgment magnitude and the judgment uncertainty. Specifically, we focus on the Judgment Uncertainty and Magnitude Parameters (JUMP) model (Chandrashekaran, McNeilly, Russ, & Marinova, 2000), which is designed to take an overt judgment and *simultaneously* model the magnitude and uncertainty inherent in the overt judgment.[1] The value of the JUMP model for consumer research stems from the fact that simultaneously modeling the magnitude and uncertainty inherent in overt judgments will provide greater and more valid insights into the process by which consumer judgments are formed, utilized, and altered. Moreover, from a substantive viewpoint, because some independent variables may impact the magnitude of a consumer judgment but not the uncertainty, and vice versa, it is of interest to estimate the impact of independent variables on judgment magnitude as well as on uncertainty. Furthermore, because some variables may drive both dimensions, richer conceptual insights will obtain if we tease out the impact of theoretically important variables on judgment uncertainty from that on judgment magnitude.

To be sure, the judgment uncertainty that is estimated by the JUMP model bears similarity to indices of the "strength" with which judgments are held (e.g.,

---

[1]It is important to place the present discussion in the vast body of judgment and decision-making research. Indeed, one area of human behavior that has certainly fascinated social scientists for centuries is decision making under uncertainty. Fueled by important contributions from the time of Bernoulli (1738/1967), a staggering amount of literature on specifying, modeling, and estimating probabilistic choice systems has been built in the social sciences (e.g., Keeney & Raiffa, 1976; Tversky & Kahneman, 1981; von Nuemann & Morgenstern, 1944). This stream of research, however, centers on how individuals make judgments under uncertainty, not on the antecedents of uncertainty. We thus do not deal in this chapter with this body of research.

stated confidence/conviction or attitude accessibility measured via a response latency task). It is, however, unlike any other index of judgment strength in five important ways: (a) it does not require another explicit measure of judgment strength; (b) it is an integral component of the covert process at the individual level, and is one dimension of the overt response; (c) it is a function of independent variables, and can be gleaned from one measure of the overt judgment; (d) unlike measures of confidence or response latency, it is unconfounded with judgment extremity (as indexed by the deviation of a scalar value from the neutral point on the scale); and (e) unlike response latency measures, it is independent of the valence of the overt judgment. We subsequently elaborate on these points.

The remainder of this chapter is organized as follows. In the next section, we provide a conceptual background that motivates the JUMP model. Anchored by the threads of thought emerging from over 50 years ago that flirt with the simultaneity of judgment magnitude and uncertainty, we contend that the social sciences, in general, have, perhaps to the detriment of deep understanding, unquestioningly and uncritically adopted, from the physical sciences, a *true score–observed score* paradigm in modeling overt judgments. These approaches have tended to treat "error" largely as a nuisance, or have focused almost entirely on addressing measurement error in theory testing. We however maintain, and strongly demonstrate, that there is knowledge in error—what has been characterized as *measurement error* thus far confounds judgment uncertainty and true measurement error. Following the conceptual background, we discuss the JUMP model structure and its estimation. Subsequently, we turn to an empirical assessment of the model by focusing on consumer brand evaluation, *judgment formation*. We employ data from an experiment that establishes the viability of the JUMP model to uniquely and simultaneously identify judgment magnitude and uncertainty parameters of important consumer judgments. We then summarize findings from reanalysis of existing data to engage the issue of consumer judgment *utilization*—how do uncertainty laden consumer judgments impact subsequent decision making? Specifically, we focus on consumer trust judgment magnitude and trust uncertainty following a failed service encounter and a recovery attempt by the service provider. Suggesting that trust uncertainty sheds light on customer vulnerability, we then provide evidence that trust uncertainty estimated by the JUMP model has a strong influence on the subsequent provision of positive word-of-mouth and customer loyalty. In concluding the chapter, we discuss the implications of the JUMP model for measurement theory and theory testing.

THEORETICAL BACKGROUND: MOTIVATING THE JUMP MODEL

In this section, we first journey back to the 1940s to revisit the ideas espoused by Brunswik (1943, 1952), that were eventually formalized in the social judgment theory (e.g., Hammond, Stewart, Brehmer, & Steinman, 1975), and by Lazarsfeld

(1954; see also Lazarsfeld & Dudman, 1951), that subsequently spawned latent class analysis (e.g., DeSarbo & Wedel, 1994). We also discuss the ideas by Woodruff (1972a, 1972b) and Wyer (1973) that unfortunately do not appear to have generated as much attention as we believe they should have. These totally divergent streams of thought had two aspects in common: (a) they all hinted at the simultaneity of judgment magnitude and uncertainty, that is, the simultaneity in what we believe and how convicted we are in those beliefs; and (b) none of them sought to explicitly parameterize both judgment magnitude and judgment uncertainty, and, consequently, were not able to quantify and test the impact of theoretically derived variables on the two dimensions of judgments. Following this conceptual background, we describe the quantitative structure underlying the dominant current approach to modeling judgments.

Conceptual Foundations

Brunswik and Probabilistic Functionalism.   In a series of brilliant papers, Brunswik (1943, 1952, 1955b) introduced the notion of *probabilistic functionalism*, to suggest that the aim of psychology is to comprehend the functional relationship between an organism and its environment. An important underpinning of this view is the distinction between *distal criteria* and *proximal cues*. Distal criteria refer to sources of information (e.g., events, objects, people) external to the organism with which the organism must cope. Distal criteria present themselves to individuals as proximal cues, which are then subsequently processed within the individual to generate some functional response. Brunswik theorized that proximal cues (a) are only probabilistically related to distal criteria, and (b) would likely evidence overlap with each other because different distal criteria could present as similar proximal cues. Thus, a decision-making environment presents cues that are entangled and overlapping. In this scenario, Brunswik suggested that the primary behavioral focus of psychology was the simultaneous investigation of the way in which distal criteria presented themselves as proximal cues and the internal processing of these less-than-perfect indicators of the environment. Two sources of uncertainty, therefore, are relevant in the Brunswikian perspective: (a) the uncertainty in the decision-making environment, and (b) uncertainty within the organism regarding which cues are to be used and how.

Brunswik's ideas stood in sharp contrast to the widely accepted experimental design paradigm, which called for factorial designs in which environmental variables could be orthogonalized such that causality could be unambiguously imputed to the design variables. He suggested that using controlled experimental designs was precisely the wrong way to study individual decision making, and noted that in the experimental paradigm, generalizability was limited to individuals, rather than contexts outside the scope of the focal investigation. Scholars in marketing have also grappled with these themes; for instance, couched under a discussion of "external validity," consumer psychologists (e.g., Calder, Phillips, &

Tybout, 1982; Lynch, 1982) engaged the merits and weaknesses of experimental designs that focus on the "representative" individual (see also Hutchinson, Kamakura, & Lynch, 2000). Despite early resistance (see Brunswik, 1955a), psychologists eventually formalized Brunswik's notions in the Social Judgment Theory (e.g., Hammond et al., 1975), and a large body of literature attests to the persuasive nature of Brunswik's views, especially in the study of judgment and decision making (see Brehmer & Joyce, 1988; see also Cooksey, 1996, for an excellent review of social judgment theory research). And almost 50 years after Brunswik's initial ideas, social psychologists who have followed an experimental paradigm appear to agree with Brunswik. For instance, Ross and Nisbett (1991) lamented that despite the several decades of research directed at understanding human behavior, it is unlikely that we will ever be able to predict well what an individual, even someone well known to us, would do when placed in a novel situation.

Two implications of the Brunswikian perspective are relevant for our discussion. First, because experimental designs depict the "average" individual under atypical conditions, empirical generalizations from controlled experiments score high on the precision criterion but not on that of scope (see Barwise, 1995, for a discussion of these aspects of empirical generalizations). Indeed, this issue of the "flaw of averages" appears to be increasingly gaining the attention of consumer psychologists who claim that even in the tightest of between-subjects experiments, findings regarding interactions have the potential to be erroneous (see Hutchinson et al., 2000, for some examples and illustrations). The preoccupation of social scientists with the average (or the mean) is also excellently highlighted by Louviere (2001), who noted that researchers tend to formulate and test hypotheses about "means of behavioral response distributions," while "the variance of behavioral responses (i.e., response variability) is rarely viewed as a behavioral phenomenon" (p. 506).

Second, if individuals are immersed in an environment characterized by varying degrees of uncertainty and they are unsure about which cues to use and how (i.e., decision task ambiguity), their overt judgments will inevitably be laden with uncertainty (Hammond, 1996; Koehler, 1994). This component of Brunswik's notions remains unexplored. Furthermore, even in the tightest of experimental designs, because a given experimental stimulus is interpreted differently by different subjects (as evidenced by significant variation often observed in scores on manipulation checks), we contend that the interpreted design variable (i.e., the proximal cue) has the potential to influence the magnitude of judgments and the associated uncertainty. Specifically, this judgmental uncertainty has its roots in the utilization of inferences, data, and incomplete knowledge about the states of nature, and needs to be contrasted with random perturbations of the response organism as in sensory tasks (Juslin & Olsson, 1997, refer to the latter as Thurstonian sources of uncertainty). Interestingly, this line of reasoning can be traced to Hammond et al. (1975), who, drawing on the proximal–distal distinction, highlighted the *zone of ambiguity*, which represents a region of entangled probabilistic relationships between given cues and inferred conditions, but never sought to link these concepts to contemporaneous judgmental uncertainty. The JUMP model enables us to bring this murky concept of Brunswikian uncertainty into sharper focus, as well as respond to Louviere's call for research aimed at treating the variance of behavioral responses as an important behavioral phenomenon.

Lazarsfeld and Latent Structure Analysis.   If the Brunswikian perspective recognized the distinction between "what is" on one hand and "what is observed and responded to" on the other hand, latent structure analysis makes this distinction far more explicit. The literature on latent class analysis fathered by Lazarsfeld (1954; see also Lazarsfeld & Dudman, 1951) relies heavily on the "manifest–latent" distinction. Three aspects characterize *latent structure analysis*. First, it is a measurement model, intended to identify a latent structure from a number of manifest items. Second, there is no inherent relationship between the distribution on the latent and the manifest—that is, the type of measurement of a manifest item and the trait (or construct) being measured are independent entities. For instance, we might measure "consumer preferences" using Likert scales, constant-sum scales, or polychotomous choice scales. The distribution of scores on the manifest dimension need not bear a relationship to the distribution of the underlying consumer preferences. Third, the relationship between the manifest items and the latent construct is probabilistic. The root of this probabilistic relationship stems from a degree of randomness in human behavior, taken on any given level of explanation. Importantly, this randomness is not simply because of an error of measurement; rather, it is inherent in human behavior. This last characteristic implies that for any given variable, there are a number of possible latent positions a respondent might occupy, and for any given latent position, there is a probability that a person holding that position will show a given manifest position.

   The distinction between "measurement error" and the probabilistic nature of the latent–manifest relationship is an important one. Scholars in the social sciences have typically invoked the notions of "true" scores and "observed" scores to capture differences between the latent and manifest. In turn, the concept of *reliability* has been employed to quantify the relationship between true and observed scores. The genesis of this perspective can be traced to the period when the normal distribution was often referred to as the *normal curve of error*. For instance, errors of observation made by astronomers observing the position of a fixed star were described well by a normal distribution. Here, the notion of reliability makes sense. This perspective was carried over to test psychology (see Nunnally & Bernstein, 1994), and subsequently to other social sciences, including marketing and consumer behavior. However, we often observe that the reliability of tests, or the relationships between variables, often differs for different groups of subjects (see DeSarbo & Wedel, 1994; Titterington, Smith, & Makov, 1985). And because the trait (or construct) being measured is itself unobserved, and is inferred from the measure, the comparability to a fixed star is tenuous, at best, and the concept of *error* becomes fuzzy.

Consequently, Lazarsfeld coined the phrase *latent probabilities* to refer to the link between the latent position and the manifest judgment. To support their rejection of the term *reliability* to refer to this link, latent structure analysts point to the fact that much of the random change in items stems from behavioral considerations rather than a consequence of the measure used. Foreshadowing the notions of irreducible uncertainty and inevitable error, espoused by Hammond (1996), Wiggins (1973), for instance, draws on the idea of function fluctuation from test psychology to note that (a) even in data that are perfectly reliable (in the measurement theory sense), strong random behavior emerges; (b) this random factor behaves mathematically like an error of measurement but is "demonstrably not such" (p. 26); and (c) measurement error is confounded with latent probabilities, and "mathematically, they are inseparable" (p. 9). With the JUMP model, however, these entities are indeed separable, and that once these are separated out, novel insights into judgment analysis can be secured.

Beginning with Lazarsfeld's view that this probabilistic link between the latent and manifest cannot be merely labeled measurement error, scholars across a variety of disciplines including statistics (e.g., Titterington et al., 1985), marketing (e.g., DeSarbo & Wedel, 1994), and consumer behavior (e.g., Hutchinson et al., 2000) have employed latent structure analysis to test relationships among variables. Operationally, however, the probabilistic link between the latent and manifest has been reduced to a recognition that (a) there are a finite number of homogenous classes in the population, and (b) there is a probability that any one individual belongs to any one latent class.

Despite the early recognition that human judgments are inherently uncertain, latent structure analysts went on to ignore one important manifestation of the covert uncertainty in overt judgments. The JUMP model draws on the concepts underlying latent structure analysis to recognize that an individual's overt judgment is a probabilistic realization from a distribution of latent positions. In turn, the model recognizes that the variance of the distribution is a function of the inherent judgment uncertainty. When the uncertainty is low, the distribution is tight, and the probability that a stated judgment captures the latent judgment is very high. On the other hand, when the uncertainty is high, the distribution is wide, and the probability that a stated judgment captures the latent judgment is low. And in both cases, the measurement error could be the same. This is also consistent with the widely accepted characterization, within psychological research on individual decision making, of uncertainty as the second-order probability distribution where greater the dispersion of the second-order distribution, the greater is the uncertainty (e.g., Abelson & Levi, 1985).

Woodruff, Wyer, and the Information Theoretic Perspective. A third line of thinking that provides a conceptual foundation for the JUMP model has its roots in an information theoretic perspective. Bearing great similarity in thought, Woodruff (1972a, 1972b) and Wyer (1973) independently presented arguments that sought to establish the simultaneity of object evaluation and evaluation uncertainty.

Woodruff (1972a, 1972b) was preoccupied with the impact of brand information on consumer opinions and the attendant uncertainty. Largely *methodological* in approach, Woodruff's (1972b) work was built on the recognition that when a consumer provides a scale rating on a brand-attribute, he may, in addition to stating an evaluation of the brand-attribute, be forming a "probability distribution over all the scale gradations he considers possibly applicable . . ." (p. 260). Tantalizingly similar in spirit to the notion of latent probabilities espoused by latent structure analysts, Woodruff was perhaps the first consumer behavior researcher to recognize the simultaneity of evaluation and uncertainty. His approach to quantify the evaluation and the attendant uncertainty, however, was perhaps a bit cumbersome, especially when a large number of objects need to be evaluated. For each evaluation object, each subject was required to first complete a standard multipoint evaluation scale (referred to as Scale I). Then, for each evaluation object, each subject was confronted with another scale (referred to as Scale II) on which he was required to (a) designate a range of values which could possibly be accurate evaluations of the object, and (b) allocate points to every value within this range so that the relative number of points for each scale value represented that subject's relative likelihood of the accuracy of that judgment. In turn, the dispersion of each distribution measured the uncertainty about Scale I responses. Woodruff's (1972a) research provides insights that might be obtained from simultaneously focusing on evaluations and uncertainty inherent in the evaluations—a given variable may influence both consumer opinions and uncertainty, but in different ways.

If Woodruff's approach was largely methodological, Wyer (1973) sought to establish a *theoretical* link between the category rating of an object and the associated uncertainty. In contrast to an averaging model of belief integration, Wyer suggested that individuals proceeded through a *concept identification* process to form attitudes. In a process similar to one advocated by latent structure analysts and one that is captured by Woodruff's Scale II, Wyer (1973) conjectured that individuals use information to "circumscribe the categories to which the object can belong, and the object is then assigned to the most representative of these categories" (p. 466).

Building on Woodruff (1972a) and Wyer (1973), Gatignon (1984) adopted a similar information theoretic perspective to examine the effects of advertising copy on consumer attitude and purchase intentions. Four similarities to Woodruff characterize Gatignon's work: (a) an explicit recognition that advertising copy may influence the uncertainty inherent in consumer opinions as well as the underlying ratings of attributes of products featured in the ad; (b) equating variance of the distribution of scores to uncertainty; (c) observing changes in the variance and equating it to changes in uncertainty; and (d) a largely methodological focus, in the sense that the author was not interested in explicitly testing or quantifying the impact of variables on attitudes/opinions and the uncertainty surrounding those attitudes/opinions. Despite the promise of these attempts, researchers in marketing and other social sciences have tended to focus largely on the magnitude of judgments and not on the uncertainty inherent in these judgments.[2]

Conventional Approach to Modeling Judgments

A conventional modeling of the judgment formation process proceeds by developing conjectures regarding the possible effect of some independent variables on the dependent variable ($RESP_i$). To simplify discussion, we focus on an overt judgment (e.g., evaluation of a target object) elicited via an interval scale, and define $RESP_i$ as the observed response of an individual i from a sample of size N. The set of conjectures regarding the effect of the independent variables is commonly viewed as a "theory." The validity of the theory is assessed by estimating a regression model, as follows (because ANOVA models can be represented as a dummy variable or effects-coded regression models [see Greene, 1997], all the models in this chapter are presented as regression models):

$$RESP_i = \alpha + \mu_i + \varepsilon_i, \tag{1a}$$

$$var(\varepsilon_i) = \sigma^2 \tag{1b}$$

$$\mu_i = \mathbf{X_i}\boldsymbol{\beta} \tag{1c}$$

where $\mathbf{X_i} = [x_{1i}, x_{2i}, \ldots, x_{pi}]$ denotes a row-vector of p variables hypothesized to impact the judgment, α denotes an intercept term, $\boldsymbol{\beta} = [\beta_1, \beta_2, \ldots, \beta_p]$ denotes a column-vector of corresponding impacts, and ε_i is the error term.

Estimation and Testing. Theory testing in this framework focuses on testing hypotheses regarding $\boldsymbol{\beta}$. Naturally, this depends on the nature of RESP. While statisticians and econometricians have developed approaches for dealing with various types of data (continuous, dichotomous choice, multichotomous choice, rank-ordered, and so on), social scientists are perhaps most familiar with measuring $RESP_i$ on interval scales (e.g., Likert scale). Here, the most common approach is to utilize a regression framework. The implicit assumption of course is that ε_i is normally distributed and that $var(\varepsilon_i) = \sigma^2$, that is, the classic homoscedasticity as-

---

[2]We hasten to recognize, however, that researchers routinely elicit confidence judgments immediately following attitude/evaluation judgments. These measures of confidence are then seen as providing insights into the certainty surrounding the attitude/evaluation judgments. We subsequently comment on this practice, and reason that this approach is unlikely to provide much diagnostic information because of measurement-induced confounding.

sumption that all individuals have the same error variance. In essence, the model structure is captured by the following two equations:

$$e(RESP_i) = \alpha + \mu_i = \alpha + \mathbf{X_i\beta} \tag{2a}$$

$$var(RESP_i) = var(\varepsilon_i) = \sigma^2 \tag{2b}$$

where e(.) and var(.) denote the expectation and variance operators, respectively. In turn, estimation proceeds by estimating an ordinary least squares (OLS) model. Similar estimates obtain by employing a maximum-likelihood approach (Greene, 1997). The statistics used to test the theorizing (e.g., overall model fit, impact of the independent variables) are well known; therefore, we will not discuss them.

THE JUMP MODEL—FROM COVERT JUDGMENT TO OVERT RESPONSE

The JUMP model starts with the recognition that when an individual is exposed to a task situation, a covert analysis ensues (Chandrashekaran et al., 2000). The resulting judgment is reported as an overt response, RESP, that contains information on two conceptually related, yet distinct, dimensions. First, *judgment magnitude* (JM) deals with the position of the judgment along a subjective continuum. Second, *judgment uncertainty* (JU) sheds light on the covert analysis and can be viewed in terms of the degree of certainty or strength with which the judgment is held. Importantly, the two dimensions of judgment are inevitably, but not intractably, linked and are embodied in the same overt response. The psychological essence of judgment uncertainty (JU) lies in the heterogeneity in the covert analysis across and within individuals. Within the JUMP model, the origins of judgment uncertainty are Brunswikian in nature—utilization of inferences, data, and incomplete knowledge about the states of nature. Within a given decision context, consumers are likely to differ in the levels of knowledge about the states of nature. Likewise, across decision contexts, a given consumer will possess different levels of information and knowledge. Thus, when a consumer in a given decision context expresses an overt judgment, it inevitably reflects a degree of incertitude. And consistent with a latent structure perspective, the JUMP model recognizes that the variance of the distribution is a function of the inherent judgment uncertainty. When the uncertainty is low (high), the distribution is tight (wide), and the probability that a stated judgment represents the latent judgment well is high (low).

Any number of factors may influence the judgment uncertainty. Indeed, like any other human phenomenon, judgment uncertainty is likely to be a function of situational and person factors (Lewin, 1951). Task-related factors such as information volume, information diagnosticity, information elaboration (e.g., Abelson,

1988), information accessibility (Fazio, 1990; Kellogg, 1931; Volkmann, 1934), decision ambiguity (e.g., Gross, Holtz, & Miller, 1995), and time pressure may influence judgmental uncertainty. Likewise, individual attributes such as need for certainty (Sorrentino & Short, 1986), need for closure (Kruglanski, Webster, & Klem, 1993), dogmatism (Palmer & Kalin, 1991), need for cognition (Cacioppo & Petty, 1982), cultural differences (Hofstede, 1991), and even depression (Coyne, 1976) have been suggested as potential antecedents to judgmental uncertainty. It is important to note, however, that this fundamental uncertainty is not associated with the measuring instrument or random perturbations of the response organism as in sensory tasks. This line of reasoning is similar to that employed by latent structure analysts and Wyer (1973) to articulate the theoretical link between subjective uncertainty in an attitude and the beliefs that were employed to arrive at the attitude. We return to this distinction later and suggest that conventional treatments of measurement error have confounded judgment uncertainty with error resulting from the nature of the measuring instrument.

Model Structure

Given *one measure of the overt response*, the JUMP model begins with the same basic structure of the conventional approach, and systematically incorporates uncertainty in a manner that preserves the conceptual foundations of the judgment uncertainty dimension. We focus in this discussion only on continuous data, and begin with the following structure:

$$\text{RESP}_i = \alpha + \text{JM}_i + \varepsilon_i \tag{3a}$$

$$\text{var}(\varepsilon_i) = \sigma^2 + \text{JU}_i + \kappa_i \tag{3b}$$

where σ^2 denotes the measurement- and model-error variance and κ_i captures sources of error variance not accounted for by JU. Note that as the strength of the judgment increases, the variance of the distribution of RESP decreases. When $\text{JU}_i = 0$, that is, the judgment is held with low uncertainty and high strength, the variance of the distribution of RESP will be smaller than when $\text{JU}_i > 0$. In turn, as JU_i increases, the variance of RESP will steadily increase.

It is important to note that JU is not equal to the variance of the overt judgment—it is simply one component of the total variance. Model misspecification and measurement error that are traditionally captured by an error variance are very much part of the model, i.e., as σ^2. Likewise, κ_i includes sources of error variance not explained by JU. By ignoring judgment uncertainty, extant research has assumed that the entire variance in stated judgment is captured by σ^2. We, however, are recognizing that a part of what has been hitherto labeled as *model error variance* may be due, in part, to the inherent uncertainty in revealed judgment, and can therefore be identified if parameterized as a function of independent variables. Thus, in the JUMP model, judgment uncertainty manifests itself in the potential variability in the overt response. Unlike Woodruff (1972a) and Gatignon (1984), who equate variability to uncertainty, within the JUMP model, potential variability in responses does not at once suggest the presence of uncertainty. Even in the rare condition when JU = 0, the overt response still exhibits potential variability, that is, var(RESP$_i$) = σ^2 (here, of course, the conventional analysis applies).

JM and JU are now expressed as follows:

$$JM_i = X_i\beta \tag{4a}$$

$$JU_i = Z_i\gamma \tag{4b}$$

where $X_i = [x_{1i}, x_{2i}, \ldots, x_{pi}]$ and $Z_i = [z_{1i}, z_{2i}, \ldots, z_{ki}]$ denote row-vectors of variables hypothesized to impact judgment magnitude and uncertainty, respectively, and $\beta = [\beta_1, \beta_2, \ldots, \beta_p]$ and $\gamma = [\gamma_1, \gamma_2, \ldots, \gamma_k]$ denote column-vectors of the impacts of X_i and Z_i, respectively. The specific elements of X_i and Z_i will come from theory and the specific substantive setting of the particular research study.

It is also important to recognize that X and Z are influencing *different aspects of the distribution of* the overt response. First, X, the vector of antecedents of judgment magnitude, is influencing the mean (or the first moment) of the RESP distribution (note from Equation 3a that e(RESP$_i$) = α + JM$_i$). In turn, Z, the vector of antecedents of judgment uncertainty, is affecting the variance (or the second moment) of that distribution (note from Equations 3b and 4b that e[var(RESP$_i$)] = JU$_i$ + σ^2). Because the first and second moments of the normal distribution are uncorrelated (Greene, 1997), X and Z vectors can witness overlap and the estimation of the parameters will not be affected. Consequently, we can tease out the impact of variables on judgment magnitude from their impact on judgment uncertainty. In addition, stemming from the fact that X and Z are focusing on orthogonal components of a latent distribution, the uncertainty estimation will not be influenced by the omission of relevant variables in the magnitude specification. Note that variable omission in the magnitude specification does not automatically increase judgment uncertainty—it will however increase σ^2, and the JUMP model makes an explicit distinction between σ^2 and judgment uncertainty.

The parameters of interest can be estimated in a straightforward manner using iterated feasible generalized least squares (Amemiya, 1985). Note that because each individual customer has a unique variance term, Equations 3a through 4b constitute a heteroscedastic regression model. The approach, therefore, is decompositional, where one measure of a stated judgment is decomposed into a mean and variance component, and the effects of their antecedents are simultaneously estimated within the regression model. The Appendix presents a detailed discussion of the estimation and identification of the parameters.

The JUMP Model in Perspective

Relationship to Emerging Thought in Psychology. The JUMP model is similar in spirit to Wallsten and González-Vallejo's (1994) stochastic model of judgment and response (SJM) where the central objective is to distinguish covert degree of confidence from overt responding. It is, however, different in both structure and objectives. In terms of model structure, the JUMP model centers on the overt response, and models the magnitude and certainty in one framework. In contrast, the SJM assumes that an overt (true/false) response follows from a covert degree of confidence. In terms of model objectives, the SJM was designed to study judgments about the truth of statements in real-world domains. The JUMP model does not address the issue of judgment accuracy. Rather, it is a general framework within which researchers can simultaneously test the antecedents of magnitude and uncertainty of expressed judgments.

That JM and JU are simultaneously produced and are dimensions of an underlying process is consistent with the Brunswikian perspective embodied in the probabilistic mental model (PMM) presented by Gigerenzer et al. (1991). Developed to understand confidence assessments in choice tasks, the PMM recognizes that choice and confidence are simultaneously produced from one underlying process, and that "they need not be generated in a temporal sequence choice followed by confidence" (Gigerenzer et al., 1991, p. 509). The seemingly temporal sequence is enforced by researchers when they ask respondents to report their judgments on scales and follow this up with a confidence scale. In the context of the JUMP model, the magnitude dimension is the first moment of an underlying distribution of potential responses and the uncertainty dimension is contained within the second moment of the underlying distribution. The JUMP model recognizes that variables may impact the two moments of any judgment differently. Moreover, because the first and second moments of a normal distribution are uncorrelated, any improvement in explaining uncertainty does not automatically improve the fit of the magnitude dimension. Thus, in the JUMP model framework, we may well witness a situation wherein we do a good job of explaining the uncertainty dimension but not the magnitude (and vice versa); that is, the results eventually depend on the quality of the theory regarding the variables that drive the two dimensions of judgments.

Estimating Uncertainty Versus Measuring Judgment Strength. An important aspect of the JUMP model is that it takes one measure of an overt judgment and decomposes it into magnitude and uncertainty dimensions. Thus, uncertainty is estimated within the model, and not explicitly measured as a separate construct. More generally, however, the judgment uncertainty estimated within the JUMP model bears similarity to indices of judgment strength. In this sense, we position the JUMP model alongside prior work that has focused on attitude strength. Numerous strength-related dimensions have been proposed in the literature—attitude accessibility, confidence in one's own attitude, the manner of attitude formation, or affective–cognitive consistency (see Fazio, Powell, & Williams, 1989, for a discussion). We, however, depart from prior empirical work that either measures judgment strength or confidence as a separate construct, infers judgment strength based on observed changes in judgment magnitude (e.g., Haugtvedt, 1994), or measures accessibility driven judgment strength via response latency.

Research has documented that attempts to measure judgment confidence often produce a significant correlation between judgment extremity and judgment confidence—individuals stating extreme judgments are more likely to state high confidence levels as well (e.g., Bassili, 1996; Gross et al., 1995). We suggest that this is due to measurement-induced confounding. First, there is an implicit assumption that there is a temporal sequence in the production of a judgment and the associated confidence. Indeed, as Gigerenzer et al. (1991) indicated, this is reflected in the practice of first measuring a judgment and then following this up with a confidence scale. This practice prompts a naive reasoning within respondents—if their responses are extreme, this must imply (to the respondents) greater confidence. On the other hand, if the respondents offer moderate judgments, they believe that they must not be very confident.

The issue of confounding judgment extremity and measures of confidence is important because researchers also engage in naive reasoning—they often think that the potential variation associated with responses in the middle of a scale is greater than that associated with responses at the ends of a scale. This (erroneous) logic would lead one to conclude that extreme (moderate) judgments are strongly (weakly) held. Although random perturbations in observed responses may well produce variation across individuals (that reinforces this logic), the JUMP model focuses on the variation that is produced by uncertainty within each individual. The JUMP model overcomes measurement-induced confounding by creating a framework in which individuals are allowed to be absolutely certain in professing moderate judgments or highly uncertain in holding extreme judgments. We explicitly test this assertion by examining the correlation between judgment uncertainty estimated by the model and the extremity of the stated judgment. And despite the fact that judgment uncertainty is specified in terms of same variables that also drive judgment magnitude, we find that the judgment uncertainty estimated by the JUMP model is not confounded with the extremity of the stated judgment. Thus, while shedding light on the *simultaneous* production of judgment magnitude and uncertainty, the JUMP model provides an uncontaminated measure of the covertly held uncertainty.

Recent research offers another perspective that points to the need to estimate judgment uncertainty rather than measure respondent confidence. Recognizing that accurate assessment of variability is necessary to estimate confidence, Kareev, Arnon, and Horwitz-Zeliger (2002) reported findings from a series of experiments that strongly indicate that individuals are poor at detecting variability. Specifically, Kareev et al. (2002) found that individuals perceive the world as less variable and more regular than it really is. Therefore, when individuals are asked to report confidence associated with revealed judgments, it is likely that these confidence estimates are biased upward. Moreover, individuals are likely to differ in the degree to which they fall prey to an illusion of control (Langer, 1975). Thus, significant heterogeneity is likely to accompany the bias in individual confidence judgments. As a result, sophisticated methodological procedures for assessing variability and individual uncertainty are needed.

Research has also consistently demonstrated that attitude accessibility measured via response latency evidences significant correlation with the valence of the response (e.g., "yes" responses take reliably longer than "no" responses; see Smith & Miller, 1983), and with attitude extremity (e.g., Bassili, 1996; Fazio et al., 1989). This implies that more favorable and more unfavorable attitudes are associated with greater accessibility than neutral attitudes—the resultant confounding between accessibility and extremity is likely to produce erroneous conclusions regarding the subsequent activation and use of such attitudes. Indeed, in contrast to Fazio, Sanbonmatsu, Powell, and Kardes (1986) who conjectured that highly accessible attitudes will be automatically activated on the mention of the object, and therefore drive subsequent behavior to a greater extent, Bargh, Chaiken, Govender, and Pratto (1992) found that "most evaluations stored in memory, for social and nonsocial objects alike, become activated automatically on the mere presence or mention of the object in the environment" (p. 893; but see Fazio, 1993, for a rejoinder). In turn, Bargh et al. (1992) "call into question the assumption that the variety of variables that researchers have identified as indicators of attitude strength are reducible to a single construct that is best conceptualized in terms of the associative connection between the attitude object and a single evaluation" (p. 908). While that dialogue is beyond the scope of this chapter, we are certainly not denigrating the use of response latency to shed light on attitude strength or on information-processing issues. Instead, we are attempting, with the JUMP model, to develop an index of judgment strength that (a) is not confounded with judgment extremity, (b) does not require an additional measurement exercise, and (c) enables the researcher to uncover theoretically relevant drivers of judgment uncertainty.

Statistical Issues.   In the JUMP model, uncertainty in judgments is manifested in the variability in observed responses. Thus, highly uncertain and weakly held judgments are associated with larger variability about the mean than strongly and certainly held judgments. This view therefore extends the perspective of classical test theory where variation in observed responses is seen as measurement error, and the large variation in observed responses is associated with poor reliability. Specifically, the JUMP model is built on the recognition that a perfectly reliable measure may still produce large variation on account of inherent judgmental uncertainty (see discussion surrounding Equation 4b).

The failure of conventional analyses to recognize judgmental uncertainty is tantamount to ignoring a violation of the homoscedasticity assumption. Immediate consequences include a loss of power, bias in the estimate of standard errors, and an overall threat to statistical conclusion validity. Conventional analyses are therefore likely to reach erroneous conclusions regarding the impact of each of the independent variables on the judgment magnitude itself. Furthermore, although subsequent utilization of judgments is strongly linked to the uncertainty dimension, conventional analyses are not in a position to explain why some judgments are utilized and others are not, despite similarity in their magnitudes.

We also note that in the conventional view, advances in theory generation are a direct function of our ability to better specify $\mathbf{X}$. Indeed, in the conventional analysis, the goal of theory-building is to predict and estimate the effects of more complex $\mathbf{X}$s (for instance, a four-way interaction suggests a more complex theory than four main effects). The focus, therefore, is only on the magnitude dimension of the overt response—the analysis parameterizes only the average or the mean of the behavioral response, while ignoring the contemporaneous dimension of judgment uncertainty that resides in the variance of the overt response. Consequently, we receive an incomplete view of the judgment-formation process. In contrast, the JUMP model explicitly incorporates judgment uncertainty into the analysis; we are therefore likely to obtain richer insights into judgmental dynamics. Furthermore, by explicitly parameterizing the variance in judgmental responses as a function of judgmental uncertainty, the JUMP model is responsive to Louviere's (2001) call for research to focus on the mean and variance in behavioral responses.

Third, because the JUMP model is aimed at the psychological foundations of uncertainty, it should be independent of variations that emerge due to the measuring instrument. Thus, the JUMP model estimates should not be subject to floor and/or ceiling effects; we empirically verify this assertion.

Finally, although the JUMP model was originally presented in the context of interval-scaled data, the logic governing the specification and estimation of the JUMP model can be employed to model various kinds of judgments, including dichotomous choice, multichotomous choice, and ranking of objects. In this chapter, however, we seek to establish the viability and validity of the basic JUMP model in decomposing routinely measured consumer judgments (e.g., brand evaluation and consumer trust).

Estimation of the JUMP Model

The general structure of the JUMP model is captured by Equations 3a through 4b. Estimation of the JUMP model implies estimating three sets of parameters—$\boldsymbol{\beta} = [\beta_1, \beta_2, \ldots, \beta_p]$, $\boldsymbol{\gamma} = [\gamma_1, \gamma_2, \ldots, \gamma_k]$, and σ^2. The Appendix presents the steps involved in the estimation of the JUMP model and discusses identification. As derived in the Appendix, the JUMP model estimates $\hat{\boldsymbol{\beta}}$ and $\hat{\boldsymbol{\gamma}}$ possess the desirable properties of asymptotic normality, unbiasedness, consistency, and efficiency. At the convergence estimates, the likelihood function values for the judgment uncertainty and magnitude dimensions, are given by:

$$L_{JU} = \prod_i s_\psi^{-1} \phi[\hat{e}_i^2 - W_i \hat{\eta} / s_\psi | \hat{e}_i^2 > 0] \tag{5a}$$

$$L_{JM} = \prod_i (W_i \hat{\eta})^{-0.5} \phi[(\hat{e}_i) / (W_i \hat{\eta})]^{0.5} \tag{5b}$$

where $\hat{e}_i = RESP_i - \hat{\alpha} - X\hat{\beta}$, $W_i = [1, Z_i]$, $\hat{\eta} = [\hat{\sigma}^2, \hat{\gamma}]$, and ϕ [.] denotes the standard normal probability density function.

Testing Within the JUMP Model

Testing within the JUMP model revolves around the contribution of hypothesized variables in our understanding of judgment dynamics. To meaningfully address the issue of contribution, we first define ω_X and ω_Z as "effect sizes" of X (the hypothesized drivers of judgment magnitude) and Z (the hypothesized drivers of judgment uncertainty). Consistent with maximum-likelihood testing, these are computed, in log-likelihood units, as follows:

$$\omega_X = (ln\ L_{JM}) - (ln\ L_{JM} | \beta = 0) \tag{6a}$$

$$\omega_Z = (ln\ L_{JU}) - (ln\ L_{JU} | \delta = 0) \tag{6b}$$

where L_{JM} and L_{JU} are expressed in Equations 5a and 5b, respectively. Three important questions can now be addressed in the JUMP model framework.

Question 1: Is the Overall JUMP Model Significant? As in an overall "model-fit" test, we are interested in assessing the extent to which the variables included in the analysis explain judgment magnitude and judgment uncertainty. This is a test of the null hypothesis H_0: $\beta = \delta = 0$, with $p + k$ degrees of freedom. Consistent with standard likelihood-ratio testing, we employ the following test statistic:

$$2[(ln\ L_{JU} - ln\ L_{JU} | \delta = 0) + (ln\ L_{JM} - ln\ L_{JM} | \beta = \delta = 0)]$$
$$= 2[\omega_Z + ln\ L_{JM} - ln\ L_{JM} | \beta = \delta = 0] \sim \chi^2_{p+k}. \tag{7}$$

Question 2: Is There a Significant Contribution of X? This is test of the overall judgment magnitude specification, that is, a test of the null hypothesis H_0: $\beta = 0$. This test involves p degrees of freedom, and employs the following test statistic:

$$2\omega_X \sim \chi^2_p. \tag{8}$$

Question 3: Is There a Significant Contribution of Z?   This question can be addressed in two ways because **Z** contributes through two distinct mechanisms—in identifying the conceptual underpinnings of judgment uncertainty and in delivering efficiency gains in the estimation of the drivers of judgment magnitude. We consider each in turn.

(a) First, in its conceptual contribution, the significance of **Z** is assessed by a test of the null hypothesis H_0: $\delta = 0$. This test involves k degrees of freedom, and employs the following test statistic:

$$2\omega_Z \sim \chi^2_k. \tag{9}$$

(b) Second, incorporating **Z** into the analysis (by explicitly modeling judgment uncertainty) allows the researcher to obtain efficient estimates for the drivers of judgment magnitude. Thus, as **Z** does an increasingly better job of explaining judgment uncertainty, we get an increasingly powerful test of H_0: $\beta = 0$. Essentially, this test involves comparing the log-likelihoods of a judgment magnitude model with and without incorporating judgment uncertainty. Conceptually this is identical to comparing the performance of the judgment magnitude specification under the JUMP model estimation and the conventional OLS estimation. The test involves k degrees of freedom and the appropriate test statistic is given by:

$$2[ln\ L_{JM} - ln\ L_{JM}|\delta = 0] \sim \chi^2_k. \tag{10}$$

STUDY I—IMPACT OF INFORMATION ON BRAND EXTENSION EVALUATION

Problem Setting and Motivation

In today's economy, firms are increasingly capitalizing on powerful brands in one product category to introduce products in different product categories. These new products are referred to as brand extensions because they utilize existing brand names. As firms continue to attempt to take strategic advantage of existing brand name awareness and image to enter new markets, brand extensions continue to gain popularity as a market-entry strategy. Understanding how consumers form evaluations of these brand extensions therefore is a critical aspect of consumer-focused strategy. In this study, we illustrate the value of the JUMP model in this endeavor.

How do individuals form judgments when exposed to a new object? This question has spawned immense research employing a variety of theoretical and empirical perspectives. At a fundamental level, classical information-processing researchers have examined the role of beliefs and inferences that surface on exposure to the focal object. The expectation is simple—positive beliefs are expected to produce positive evaluations, whereas negative beliefs precipitate negative evaluations. Captured broadly by the information-integration perspective and consistent with attitude research (e.g., Eagly & Chaiken, 1993), an individual's preferences are thus modeled as a function of the number of positive and negative beliefs that are generated for each alternative. Focus on the number of beliefs as a predictor of judgments is also justified by research on cognitive responses to persuasion (Petty, 1981), frequency effects on judgment, and on set-size effects (Anderson, 1981).

For the most part, however, extant research has focused on judgment magnitude. And although information theorists recognize that the amount of information influences the confidence with which judgments are held (see Anderson, 1981), the two dimensions of judgments have been explored independently of one another. Motivated by the JUMP model underpinnings, we explore the role of newly generated positive and negative information in simultaneously shaping judgment magnitude and judgment uncertainty. Letting $EVAL_i$ denote the observed evaluation of the focal object for the ith individual, we follow the JUMP model framework (see Equations 3a through 4c) to specify the following:

$$EVAL_i = \alpha + EM_i + \varepsilon_i \qquad (11a)$$

$$var(\varepsilon_i) = \sigma^2 + EU_i + \kappa_i \qquad (11b)$$

$$EM_i = \mathbf{X_i\beta} \qquad (11c)$$

$$EU_i = \mathbf{Z_i\gamma} \qquad (11d)$$

where EM_i and EU_i denote, respectively, the evaluation magnitude and uncertainty for the ith consumer; $\mathbf{X_i} = [x_{1i}, x_{2i}, \ldots, x_{pi}]$ and $\mathbf{Z_i} = [z_{1i}, z_{2i}, \ldots, z_{ki}]$ denote row-vectors of variables hypothesized to impact EM and EU, respectively, and $\boldsymbol{\beta} = [\beta_1, \beta_2, \ldots, \beta_p]$ and $\boldsymbol{\gamma} = [\gamma_1, \gamma_2, \ldots, \gamma_k]$ denote column-vectors of the impacts of $\mathbf{X_i}$ and $\mathbf{Z_i}$, respectively.

Specifying Evaluation Magnitude (EM)

At a most fundamental level, insights into evaluation magnitude can be obtained by identifying beliefs that emerge while processing information about the brand extension. Evaluation magnitude should therefore be a function of the positive and negative, inferences (beliefs) that a consumer generates on exposure to the brand extension. At same time, a judgment updating perspective would suggest that the impact of newly generated information will be contingent on prior experience and attitudes toward the parent brand. Indeed, the brand equity literature (e.g., Keller, 2002) would suggest that prior positive (favorable) attitudes will (a) enhance (make larger) the positive impact of newly generated positive information; and (b) mitigate (make smaller) the negative impact of newly generated negative information.[3]

We therefore specify this dimension for each consumer as follows:

$$EM_i = \mathbf{X_i\beta} = \beta_1 INF_{iP} + \beta_2 INF_{iN} + \beta_3 PATT_i$$
$$+ \beta_4 INF_{iP}*PATT_i + \beta_5 INF_{iN}*PATT_i \qquad (12)$$

where INF denotes the number of extension-specific beliefs, the subscripts "P" and "N" refer to positive and negative inferences, respectively; PATT denotes the prior attitude toward the parent brand; and β_1 through β_5 identify the relative impact of the five effects. In terms of these parameters, we expect that $\beta_1 > 0$, $\beta_2 < 0$, $\beta_3 > 0$, $\beta_4 > 0$, and $\beta_5 > 0$.

Specifying Evaluation Uncertainty (EU)

We once again draw on the information-processing literature to articulate the impact of inferences and prior attitude on evaluation uncertainty. Specifically, we conjecture that positive inferences will lower uncertainty and expect positive prior attitude to further enhance this effect. In turn, we expect that negative information will lower uncertainty among individuals who have a negative prior attitude toward the parent brand—consistency of newly generated inferences and prior attitude promotes more certainty in evaluations. On the other hand, we expect negative information to increase uncertainty for consumers who have positive prior attitude toward the parent brand. Finally, we expect consumers with favorable prior attitudes to evidence lower uncertainty. Accordingly, we specify the following structure to capture brand evaluation uncertainty:

$$EU_i = \mathbf{Z_i\gamma} = \gamma_1 INF_{iP} + \gamma_2 INF_{iN} + \gamma_3 PATT_i$$
$$+ \gamma_4 INF_{iP}*PATT_i + \gamma_5 INF_{iN}*PATT_i \qquad (13)$$

In terms of the model parameters, we expect $\gamma_1 < 0$, $\gamma_2 < 0$, $\gamma_3 < 0$, $\gamma_4 < 0$, and $\gamma_5 > 0$.

---

[3]We recognize that more elaborate conceptual frameworks can be specified. For instance, we may model the effect of prior attitudes and the similarity of the extension category to the parent category. Our purpose in this study, however, is to illustrate the JUMP model dynamics in one setting, and explore the impact of amount of positive and negative information on evaluation judgment magnitude and uncertainty. Moreover, the extant brand extension research (e.g., Broniarczyk & Alba, 1994) indicates that the brand evaluation process may be best captured by an inference process in which newly generated inferences about the extension per se are the crucial determinants of brand extension evaluation. Likewise, we work under the assumption that all beliefs that are generated in a concurrent protocol are equally salient.

The Study

We sought to simulate a decision context that would (a) allow us to demonstrate the ability of the JUMP model to estimate the drivers of variation in judgment magnitude and uncertainty across individuals, and (b) permit an examination of the impact of newly generated beliefs on judgment formation. Set in the context of brand extensions, this study employs a between-subjects design to explore individual judgment formation for four new products (see Shocker, Srivastava, & Ruekert, 1994, for an overview of the brand-extension research stream). Utilizing brands and categories that have been the focus of previous brand-extension studies, we selected *yogurt* and *hotels* as the original product categories (Dannon and Yoplait; Hilton and Sheraton were the parent brands). Yogurt extended into puddings and salad dressings, and hotels extended into restaurants and credit cards.

One hundred and six undergraduate business students at a large midwestern university took part in the study and were given course credit for their participation. Ten subjects did not provide complete data and were excluded from the analyses. Subsequent analyses were therefore performed with a sample size of 96. Subjects were randomly assigned to one of the eight product type (yogurt/hotels)–extension category (puddings/salad dressings or restaurants/credit cards)–brand (Dannon/Yoplait or Hilton/Sheraton) combinations. They first read a description of a hypothetical brand extension, which included features common to actual competitors (as suggested by a pretest) in the extension market. Exhibit 1 presented descriptions of each of the extension products. Upon reading this description, subjects were provided space to write down their thoughts as they formed their evaluation of the extension. Subjects then indicated their evaluation of the extension on two 7-point scales anchored at *strongly unfavorable* and *strongly favorable*, and *very good* and *very bad*.

To code beliefs, the concurrent written protocols were broken into units expressing a single thought (Cacioppo & Petty, 1981) or, approximately, a "proposition" (Kintsch, Kozminsky, Stroby, McKoon, & Keenan, 1975). We focused on beliefs generated about the focal object, and classified these into two groups: extension-specific inferences (e.g., *no annual fee is good*) and brand-image sentiments (e.g., *Hilton is classy*). Within these groups, the sentiment (negative vs. positive) of the beliefs was marked. Beliefs were coded independently by two judges, one who was aware of the experimental conditions and the other blind to the conditions of the experiment. Intercoder reliability was 87%. Furthermore, 20% of the questionnaires were independently coded by a third judge who was aware of the conditions of the experiment; the intercoder reliability among the three coders was 84%. Prior attitude (PATT) was measured as the difference between the number of positive and negative brand-image related thoughts. Consistent with the notion of subjective attitudinal ambivalence (e.g., Priester & Petty, 2001), more positive (negative) than negative (positive) brand-image related thoughts imply positive (negative) prior attitude, whereas an equal number of pos-

EXHIBIT I.   BRAND EXTENSION DESCRIPTIONS

Restaurants: The brand manager of SHERATON (HILTON) Hotels is currently reviewing a proposal for opening a restaurant chain nationwide. The new restaurant, SHERATON'S (HILTON'S) will have a festive, casual, saloon-type atmosphere catering to people of all ages. Patrons will be offered a full menu selection—at inexpensive prices—ranging from sandwiches and burgers to various ethnic specialties (e.g., Mexican fajitas).

Credit cards: The brand manager of SHERATON (HILTON) Hotels is currently reviewing a proposal to offer a new credit card. This credit card, the SHERATON (HILTON) CARD, will be widely accepted worldwide and will charge no annual fee. In addition, this credit card will have a finance charge that is competitive with the interest rates of current credit cards. Finally, customers will be provided a service, via a toll-free number, 24 hours a day (for example, customers can report lost or stolen cards at any time).

Pudding: The brand manager of DANNON™ (YOPLAIT™) yogurt is currently reviewing a proposal for producing a new line of pudding. The pudding, DANNON (YOPLAIT) PUDDING, will come in a variety of flavors such as vanilla and chocolate. Consumers will be able to find prepackaged individual portions—sold in groups of six—in the dairy case. In addition, the pudding will be sold in a dry, instant form so that consumers can make the pudding themselves by just adding milk.

Salad dressing: The brand manager of DANNON (YOPLAIT) yogurt is currently reviewing a proposal for producing a new line of salad dressing. The salad dressing, DANNON (YOPLAIT) SALAD DRESSING, will come in a variety of flavors such as Ranch, Italian, and Thousand Island. DANNON (YOPLAIT) also plans to introduce a "LITE" line of these dressings which will have fewer calories, less fat but the same full flavoring as the regular line of dressings.

itive and negative brand-image related thoughts would indicate relative neutrality of prior attitude (PATT values ranged from –2 to +3).

Results

Three different models were estimated. The first model (M_H) simultaneously considered evaluation magnitude and uncertainty, the second model (M_R) dealt only with evaluation magnitude, and the third model (M_0) was the null model that modeled neither evaluation magnitude nor uncertainty. Consistent with the JUMP model testing, the following questions were addressed.

1. Is the overall JUMP model significant? A likelihood-ratio test (see Equation 7) reveals that model M_H outperforms the null model M_0 ($\chi^2_{10} = 104.2$, $p < .0001$).

2. Is there a significant contribution of **X**? A likelihood-ratio test (Equation 8) indicates that there is significant contribution of the drivers of evaluation magnitude ($\chi^2_5 = 41.16$, $p < .0001$). Furthermore, the interaction between extension-specific inferences and prior attitude explains 26% of the variance in stated evaluations.

3. Is there a significant contribution of **Z**? A likelihood-ratio test (Equation 9) strongly supports the contribution of the hypothesized antecedents of evaluation uncertainty ($\chi^2_5 = 64.62$, $p < .0001$).

4. Does including the uncertainty dimension significantly improve model fit? Once again, a likelihood-ratio test demonstrates that the proposed two-dimensional conceptualizations of evaluation judgments (model M_H) significantly outperform a model (M_R) that considers only judgment magnitude while ignoring the uncertainty dimension ($\chi^2_5 = 12.8$, $p < .05$).

The results of estimating the parameters of model M1 are presented in Table 5.1, which also presents the results from the conventional analysis that ignores evaluation uncertainty.

TABLE 5.1
Study 1—Estimation Results

Evaluation Dimension	Independent Variable	Parameter	JUMP Model Estimates (standard error)	OLS Model Estimates (standard error)
Evaluation Magnitude	INF_P	β_1	.508*** (.080)	.514*** (.127)
	INF_N	β_2	−.284** (.117)	−.239 (.202)
	PATT	β_3	.403** (.169)	.447** (.172)
	INF_P*PATT	β_4	.704* (.364)	.731* (.369)
	INF_N*PATT	β_5	.284* (.131)	−.048 (.241)
Evaluation Uncertainty	INF_P	γ_1	−.358** (.175)	—[a]
	INF_N	γ_2	−1.307*** (.279)	—
	PATT	γ_3	−.147 (.237)	—
	INF_P*PATT	γ_4	.077 (.511)	—
	INF_N*PATT	γ_5	1.519*** (.333)	—

[a]A dash (—) indicates that the conventional OLS model does not explicitly model judgment uncertainty.
*$p < .05$. **$p < .01$. ***$p < .0001$.

Evaluation Magnitude.   Observe in Table 5.1 that the JUMP model, as expected, reveals that EM increases as INF_P increases ($b_1 = .51, p < .0001$). In turn, as INF_N increases, EM decreases ($b_2 = -.28, p < .02$). Next, note that favorable prior attitudes are associated with more favorable evaluations of the extension ($b_3 = .404, p < .02$). The two interaction terms are also significant—favorable prior attitudes enhance the impact of positive extension-specific inferences ($b_4 = .704, p < .05$) and reduces (makes less negative) the impact of negative inferences ($b_5 = .285, p < .02$).

Examining the results from the conventional analysis that ignores evaluation uncertainty reveals the power of the JUMP model. Ignoring uncertainty produces a model in which negative information has nonsignificant effects—note that the coefficients for INF_N and the INF_N*PATT interaction are nonsignificant. Why does this happen? As discussed earlier, ignoring uncertainty is statistically tantamount to ignoring heteroscedasticity. As a result, the conventional analysis suffers from inefficiency and a lack of statistical power to detect significant effects. Observing the standard errors reveals the consequences of low statistical power—the standard errors of the parameter estimates in the JUMP model are consistently smaller than those from the conventional analysis that ignores evaluation uncertainty. As a result, we are able to detect effects of negative information in the JUMP model but not in the less powerful conventional analysis.

Evaluation Uncertainty.   Observe in Table 5.1 that the results generally support our theorizing. First, positive inferences lower uncertainty ($-.358, p < .05$); the INF_P*PATT interaction however is nonsignificant. Second, INF_N has a significant main effect and interacts with PATT to influence uncertainty (coefficients are $-1.31, p < .0001$ and $1.52, p < .0001$, respectively). Third, although PATT had a direct impact on the magnitude of evaluations, it does not appear to have a direct impact on evaluation uncertainty.

Owing to the significant interaction with PATT, we examined the direct effect of INF_N at various levels of PATT by computing and testing $\gamma_2 + \gamma_5 PATT$. Results revealed that for individuals with unfavorable prior attitudes (PATT = -2), the net effect of INF_N was negative and highly significant ($-4.35, p < .0001$)—negative inferences lower evaluation uncertainty when prior attitudes are also unfavorable. In turn, for individuals with favorable prior attitudes (PATT = 3), the net effect of INF_N was positive and significant ($3.22, p < .0001$)—negative inferences increase uncertainty when prior attitudes are favorable (we examined the relationship between INF_N and PATT to see if individuals with unfavorable prior attitudes toward the parent brand generated more negative inferences about the brand extension—the relationship was nonsignificant multiple correlation = $.013, p = .28$).

Figure 5.1 depicts the net impact of INF_N at various levels of PATT on both evaluation certainty and evaluation magnitude. Note that as prior attitude becomes more unfavorable, the impact of negative inferences becomes more nega-

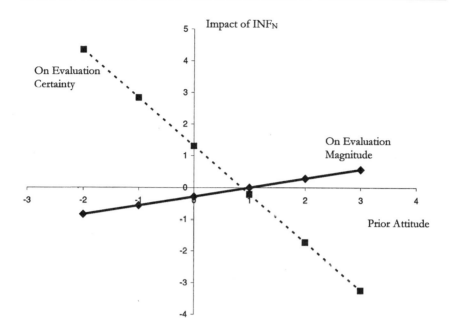

FIG. 5.1.   Impact of negative inferences on evaluation magnitude and evaluation certainty. *Note:* The impact of INF_N on evaluation magnitude was computed as $\hat{\beta}_2 + \hat{\beta}_5 PATT$ (see equation 12) and the impact of INF_N on evaluation certainty was computed as $\hat{\gamma}_2 + \hat{\gamma}_5 PATT$ (see equation 13).

tive. At the same time, however, the impact of negative beliefs is to increase the certainty with which these negative evaluations are professed. On the other hand, although favorable prior attitudes mitigates (makes less negative) the impact of negative inferences, these less negative evaluations are fraught with more uncertainty. This pattern of effects clearly reveals (a) the damaging impact of negative inferences, and (b) that managers cannot rely on prior favorable attitudes to bail them out—although customers appear to "forgive" the brand when it comes to evaluation magnitude, this evaluation is associated with more uncertainty. Clearly, this uncertainty has implications for subsequent behavior, for example, choice and patronage. We engage the impact of judgment uncertainty on subsequent consumer judgments in the next study.

Properties of the Evaluation Uncertainty Estimated by the JUMP Model

At the outset of this research, we claimed that unlike other indicants of attitude strength (e.g., stated confidence), the JUMP model overcame measurement-induced confounding of judgment uncertainty and judgment extremity (this aspect of the JUMP model was not considered by Chandrashekaran et al., 2000, in their empirical work). To test this claim, we examined the correlation between evaluation extremity (measured by $E_{ext} = |EVAL - 4|$) and the estimated uncertainty given by $\hat{E}_U = \mathbf{Z}\hat{\gamma}$ (corresponding to Equation 13). The results indicate that the evaluation uncertainty estimated by the model is not confounded with the extremity of the stated evaluation—the multiple correlation (R^2) between E_{ext} and $\hat{E}_U$ was .006 ($p = .45$). We also examined the relationship between the estimated uncertainty ($\hat{E}_U$) and the evaluation magnitude given by $\hat{E}_M = \mathbf{X}\hat{\beta}$ (corresponding to Equation 12). The multiple correlation (R^2) between $\hat{E}_M$ and $\hat{E}_U$ was .01 ($p = .22$).

Robustness of the JUMP Model Estimates to Floor/Ceiling Effects. We also claimed that the JUMP model estimates produced by the iterative procedure should be vastly similar to those produced by an estimation procedure that explicitly corrects for the anchored nature of scales. To assess this claim, we estimated the JUMP model by specifying, in steps 1 and 5 of the iterative procedure, regression models that explicitly corrected for censoring at both ends of the response scale (i.e., "double-censored" regression models; see Greene, 1997, for specification of likelihood function). The results were very similar in terms of the pattern of the estimates and theoretical conclusions reached.

Discussion

Our purpose in this study was to illustrate the JUMP model dynamics in a consumer behavior setting, and explore the impact of amount of positive and negative information on evaluation formation. The findings from the JUMP model estimation reveal that newly generated information interacted with prior attitude in shaping both judgment magnitude and judgment uncertainty. These insights would not have been forthcoming in a model that ignored judgment uncertainty. Indeed, in the context we examined, if we had failed to model uncertainty, we would have (a) concluded that negative beliefs do not assume importance in the judgment-formation process, and (b) failed to find that judgment uncertainty is shaped by the inferences generated by the consumer and moderated by prior brand attitude.

**STUDY 2: CONSUMER TRUST AND SERVICE FAILURES—
REANALYSIS OF DATA FROM TAX ET AL. (1998)**

In Study 1 we employed the JUMP model to study consumer judgment formation. In Study 2, we engage the issue of consumer judgment *utilization*—how do uncertainty-laden consumer judgments impact subsequent decision making? To do this, we summarize key findings from Rotte, Chandrashekaran, Grewal, and Tax

(2004). These authors employed the JUMP model to study consumer trust within a frequently occurring situation—consumer complaining following a failed service encounter. Uncertainty associated with stated judgments (e.g., trust) is especially crucial following service failures. Because service failures bring to the surface risks to consumers, they increase uncertainties and misgivings that can destabilize the trust on which the relationship is built, and can result in consumers becoming vulnerable to defection. Despite significant advances in the services literature, it has been only in the past few years that we have witnessed systematic research on consumer evaluations of complaint handling following service failures (e.g., Maxham & Netemeyer, 2002; Smith, Bolton, & Wagner, 1999; Tax, Brown, & Chandrashekaran, 1998). Examining key consumer judgments following critical service encounters affords us an opportunity to examine how these encounters contribute to solidifying or eroding buyer–seller relationships.

The central thesis in Rotte et al. (2004) was that decomposing stated trust judgments bears the potential to illuminate the paradox of defection despite trust— why do some customers display low levels of loyalty despite professing high levels of trust? The primary motivation for their research stemmed from the fact that extant research has focused only on the magnitude of consumer sentiments (e.g., the extent/degree to which a consumer trusts a service provider). As a result, we have not secured insights into how these judgments either crystallize into strongly held sentiments, producing "secure" and loyal consumers, or become increasingly fragile, producing vulnerable consumers who might profess favorable sentiments that may in fact be weakly held and laden with uncertainty.

Study and Results

Rotte et al. (2004) reanalyzed the data from Tax et al. (1998) to understand the dynamics of trust following service encounters. The following models were specified:

$$\text{TRUST}_i = \alpha + \text{TM}_i + \varepsilon_i \tag{14a}$$

$$\text{var}(\varepsilon_i) = \sigma^2 + \text{TU}_i + \kappa_i \tag{14b}$$

$$\text{TM}_i = f(\text{SAT, PEXP, SAT*PEXP}) \tag{14c}$$

$$\text{TU}_i = g(\text{SAT, PEXP, SAT*PEXP}) \tag{14d}$$

$$\text{LOYALTY} = h(\text{TRUST, TU, TRUST*TU}) \tag{14e}$$

where TRUST, TM_i, and TU_i denote, respectively, the stated trust, latent trust magnitude, and latent trust uncertainty for the ith consumer; SAT denotes the satisfaction following the complaint handling and PEXP captures the valence of the prior experience with the service provider. Loyalty was measured in terms of psychological loyalty and focused on commitment and propensity to give positive word-of-mouth (please see Tax et al., 1998, for details of the study and measures). Equation 14e conjectures that the translation of stated trust to loyalty will depend on the uncertainty inherent in the stated trust. Rotte et al. (2004) anticipated that the interaction will be negative—uncertainty in judgments will inhibit the subsequent utilization of that judgment.

Key Findings.   In a significant JUMP model, Rotte et al. (2004) found that consumers with prior positive experiences "forgive" a service provider for poor complaint handling (and state higher levels of trust than consumers with prior negative experiences), but they hold their trust with the highest levels of uncertainty. Recall a similar pattern of effects in Study 1 concerning brand evaluations.

In turn, this uncertainty underlies consumer vulnerability. Specifically, it was found that the level of uncertainty surrounding stated trust assumes a central role in the translation of trust to loyalty. When TU = 0, the net impact of trust on positive word-of-mouth (PWOM) was estimated to be 1.1 ($p < .0001$), and is no different (statistically) from a value of 1.0. Thus, when the stated trust is held with very little uncertainty, a unit-increase in trust generates an equal increase in PWOM. However, as TU increases, the net effect of stated trust on PWOM steadily decreases, and at the highest levels of TU, the net effect is estimated to be .53 ($p < .0001$)—an almost 50% reduction from when TU = 0. Importantly, the net effect of .53 is significantly less than 1.0 ($p < .0001$). The corresponding values for commitment were 1.06 and .61 (a 40% reduction in the translation of stated trust to loyalty from when TU = 0). Thus, an individual who circles a value of "5" on the trust scale but holds this trust with very high uncertainty will be likely to switch service providers if the opportunity provided itself, that is behave like an individual who circles a value of "3" on the trust scale but who holds this trust with low uncertainty.

These decreases in the translation of stated trust clearly reveal that consumers with high levels of trust uncertainty are vulnerable relative to those who hold their trust with more certainty. Thus, for these individuals, their statements of trust appear to be a significantly less resolute indicator of future behavior. This is particularly insightful because the magnitude of trust does not appear to diminish substantially following one service failure, but one service failure surely increases uncertainty in that trust. In turn, the uncertainty comes to systematically influence and hurt important relationship variables such as word-of-mouth and loyalty. These findings illuminate the psychological mechanisms that govern post service-failure consumer judgments, and contribute to a better understanding of consumer vulnerability and the paradox of defection despite trust.

DISCUSSION AND CONCLUSION

Motivated by over 60 years of psychological and methodological thought, the JUMP model recognizes that all judgments are fuzzy to some extent and involve some uncertainty. Conceptualizing overt judgments and behavior as the realization of covert processes that inevitably involve uncertainty, the JUMP model allows an independent variable to shape both judgment uncertainty and magnitude. Given one measure of the overt response, the model statistically separates out, simultaneously, the drivers of judgment magnitude from those of judgment uncertainty. Following a discussion of the estimation procedure and testing within the JUMP model, we presented an application of the JUMP model in a consumer brand-evaluation context. Numerous model comparisons were performed to assess the feasibility of estimating theoretically meaningful and valid effects with the JUMP model. We were most concerned with the ability of the JUMP model to identify drivers of consumer judgmental uncertainty that have theoretical grounding. Espousing the view that measurement of confidence is plagued with measurement-induced confounding, we demonstrated the ability of the JUMP model to (a) identify theoretically meaningful antecedents of judgment uncertainty that have significant impact on subsequent behavior, and (b) estimate individual judgment uncertainty that is unconfounded with the extremity of the overt judgment. We are thus confident in proposing the JUMP model as a powerful vehicle to better understand consumer judgments.

Implications

Information Effects on Attitude Uncertainty. In Study 1, we engaged the basic question of how information characteristics influence attitude uncertainty in addition to attitude magnitude. Set against a backdrop of a vast literature base focusing on the impact of information on the magnitude of attitudes, and given one measure of an attitude, we sought to *simultaneously* assess the impact of these variables on attitude magnitude and uncertainty. Following rigorous model comparisons, we supported, at a fundamental level, the extant view that information volume influences attitude uncertainty. This provides basic support for the ability of the JUMP model to identify drivers of judgment uncertainty. However, we uncovered two interesting moderators of this effect. First, the valence of information influences the impact of information volume—negative information increased uncertainty, whereas positive information reduced it. Next, we found that prior attitudes moderated the impact of information volume and valence. Information consistent with prior attitudes lowered uncertainty.

Several interesting questions, however, emerge. For instance, how do these effects depend on individual traits, such as need for cognitive closure (NFCC; e.g., Kruglanski et al., 1993) or uncertainty orientation (e.g., Sorrentino & Short, 1986)? Kruglanski et al. (1993) contended that NFCC will manifest via preference for order, structure, and decisiveness. Thus, it is likely that NFCC will influence the impact of information on attitude uncertainty. Likewise, Sorrentino and Short (1986) noted that individuals who are higher in uncertainty orientation will be open to new information and actively seek to incorporate such information in decision making. Are such individuals likely to hold their attitudes with greater certainty? These are all worthy questions that can be addressed via the JUMP model. Importantly, a researcher does not need to collect new data to address these questions—one measure of attitude is sufficient to examine drivers of both attitude magnitude and uncertainty. Consequently, the JUMP model can be employed to reanalyze existing attitude data, gathered over the last 60 years involving a range of situational and personality variables, from which novel insights into attitude uncertainty are certain to emerge.

Consumer Trust. The JUMP model enabled us to support the notion that consumer vulnerability emerges from covert uncertainty surrounding stated trust. Particularly troubling, from a practitioner's viewpoint, are the dynamics of those consumers who have had prior positive experiences. Such individuals may profess that they still trust a service provider following a service failure and a poor service recovery, but unbeknown to the service provider, and perhaps to themselves, they hold this trust with greater uncertainty—such a trust is rather fragile. As a result, practitioners may not be able to depend on customers' statements of trust/satisfaction to gauge their future behavior.

More insights can be gleaned, of course, by focusing on the uncertainty in other customer judgments (e.g., satisfaction). We believe that there is great value in monitoring consumer judgmental uncertainty over time because of its profound impact on consumer behavior. Although the perspective that there is valuable information in the variance surrounding observed phenomena is rather well established in the finance literature where the value of an option is dependent on the interplay of the returns and the contemporaneous volatility (captured by the variance term), marketers and consumer-behavior scholars have been slow to adopt the view that the variation in observed responses is an important behavioral phenomenon in its own right (see Louviere, 2001). A key message in this chapter is that although individual consumer behavior surely depends upon beliefs, it also strongly depends on the conviction with which those beliefs are held. Simultaneously investigating the magnitude and uncertainty of stated consumer judgments is likely to shed more light on the drivers of consumer vulnerability and the *why* of consumer behavior. Again, researchers need not go out and collect new data; reanalysis of existing data, with the aid of the JUMP model, is likely to shed more light on the drivers of customer vulnerability and customer behavior.

Implications for Measurement Theory

At the outset of this research, we highlighted that the JUMP model focuses on a fundamental uncertainty that is not associated with the measuring instrument. And we suggested that conventional treatments of measurement error have confounded judgment uncertainty with uncertainty resulting from the nature of the measurement instrument. We now turn to the implications of this assertion.

The most widely used measure of scale reliability is Cronbach's α. Consistent with classical test theory notions, α is defined within the following framework (Nunnally & Bernstein, 1994). Each individual i, $i = 1, 2, \ldots, N$, provides responses (RESP) on k scale items that measure a construct. Then, given $RESP_{ij} = \mu_i + \varepsilon_{ij}$, where $\varepsilon_{ij} \sim N(0, \sigma^2_j)$, and $j = 1, 2, \ldots, k$ denotes the scale item, the coefficient α is computed as follows:

$$\alpha = \frac{k}{k-1}\left(1 - \frac{\sum_j \sigma^2_j}{\sigma^2_{RESP}}\right). \tag{15}$$

Capturing the extent to which information is lost due to measurement error, the just-mentioned expression has been referred to as "one of the most important deductions from the domain-sampling theory of measurement error" (Nunnally & Bernstein, 1994, p. 234). It is readily apparent that this measure fails to incorporate the fundamental source of uncertainty that the JUMP model has uncovered. Furthermore, consistent with traditional models of judgment, the assumption is that individuals are identical in terms of this measurement error as well (i.e., the *homoscedasticity assumption*).

Within the JUMP model framework, we explicitly recognized that individuals are heterogeneous with regard to judgmental uncertainty. Thus, we derived that $\sigma^2_j = JU_i + \theta^2_j$, where θ^2_j is the true measurement error and JU_i is the judgment uncertainty. Substituting this in Equation 15, we can observe that the estimate of Cronbach's α is confounding the two sources of uncertainty—uncertainty in capturing the construct (θ^2_j), and individual-level judgmental uncertainty (i.e., uncertainty in that which we seek to measure, given by JU_i). We can therefore recognize that α is estimating the following quantity:

$$\alpha = \frac{k}{k-1}\left(1 - \frac{k * JU_i + \sum_j \theta^2_j}{\sigma^2_{RESP}}\right), \tag{16}$$

whereas the true measure of the information recovered despite measurement error is given by:

$$C = \frac{k}{k-1}\left(1 - \frac{\sum_j \theta_j^2}{\sigma_{RESP}^2}\right). \qquad (17)$$

It is easy to demonstrate that α underestimates the performance of a scale relative to the C index. Furthermore, the extent to which Cronbach's α underestimates true reliability, C index, increases with judgment uncertainty. Thus, because JU has not been considered, it is likely that many researchers have been led to reject scales that in reality may have possessed desirable psychometric properties. The notion underlying the C index, however, is consistent with a thesis that recognizing that there is knowledge in error, and attempting to uncover and harness that knowledge is the essence of scholarly progress.

Conclusion

The JUMP model engages a pervasive and fundamental aspect of judgments—all judgments are fuzzy to some extent. Importantly, simultaneously modeling the central tendency of judgments along with the uncertainty inherent in the judgment provides greater insights into how judgments are formed, how they are utilized, and how they are altered. The results demonstrate the capability of the JUMP model to separate out the antecedents of judgment magnitude from those of judgment uncertainty. Importantly, all the effects we uncovered follow from theoretical expectations. Furthermore, because the JUMP model allows the same variables to have different effects on the two dimensions of judgments, it enables us to better understand why some judgments are utilized and others are not, despite their similarity in magnitudes. Profound in its implications for measurement theory, the JUMP model is simple and easy to estimate. Almost all areas of social science that attempt to understand judgmental dynamics can benefit from employing the JUMP model. We hope that the JUMP model is received as a vehicle that will lead to a greater understanding of judgments.

APPENDIX.   ESTIMATION AND IDENTIFICATION ISSUES IN THE JUMP MODEL

The JUMP model can be generally expressed as:

$$\text{RESP}_i = \mathbf{X_i\beta} + \varepsilon_i \text{ and } \text{var}(\varepsilon_i) = \sigma^2 + \mathbf{Z_i\gamma} + \kappa_i \qquad (A1)$$

The estimation of β and γ proceeds in the following iterative process:

Step 1. Estimate a OLS regression model with RESP as the dependent variable and X as the vector of independent variables. Let b be the estimate of β and $s(b)$ be the standard error of b. Although b is an unbiased and consistent estimate of β, it is inefficient and $s(b)$ is biased (Greene, 1997; Jobson & Fuller, 1980). The inefficiency stems from the fact that although the residuals, $e = RESP - Xb$, will have the same limiting distribution as that of ε, the estimation ignores the heteroscedasticity in ε (note that $E(\text{var}(\varepsilon_i)) = Z_i\gamma + \sigma^2 \neq \text{constant} \ \forall \ i$).

Step 2. Compute $e_i^2 = (RESP_i - X_ib)^2$. Note that

$$e_i = RESP_i - X_ib = RESP_i - X_i\beta - X_i(b - \beta) = \varepsilon_i - X_i(b - \beta) \quad (A2)$$

$$e_i^2 = \varepsilon_i^2 + [X_i(b - \beta)]^2 - 2\varepsilon_{iXi}(b - \beta) \quad (A3)$$

Now, because $E(\varepsilon_i^2) = \text{var}(\varepsilon_i)$, and because the latter two terms in Equation (A4) will be asymptotically negligible, we can write substitute from A2 to express A3 as follows:

$$e_i^2 = W_i\delta + \kappa_i \quad (A4)$$

where $W_i = [Z_i, 1]$ and $\delta = [\gamma, \sigma^2]$.

Step 3. Estimate Equation A4 via OLS regression. Let d_1 be the estimate of δ and $s(d_1)$ be the standard error of d_1. Although Equation A4 resembles a classical regression model, three properties of κ are relevant in small samples: (i) it has a non-zero mean, (ii) it is correlated across observations because each ψ has been constructed from the same estimate of β, and (iii) it is heteroscedastic. Amemiya (1985), however, showed that the first and second issues are absent in large samples—κ_i has a zero mean and is nonautocorrelated. We can therefore expect the d_1 $= [\hat{\gamma}, \hat{\sigma}^2]$ to be a consistent estimator of $\delta = [\gamma, \sigma^2]$. This estimation, therefore, allows us to quantify the extent to which Z explains variance in the second moment of the RESP distribution. In turn, we can correct for the heteroscedastic nature of κ_i because we know that $E(\text{var}(e_i^2)) = 2(W_i\delta)^2$; see Amemiya, 1985).

Step 4. Compute $\omega_U = 0.5(W_id)^{-2}$. Estimate Equation A4 using weighted least squares with ω_U as the weight, *given the condition that the predicted dependent variable from the regression is nonnegative*. Specifying this condition is important to preserve the conceptual underpinnings of the model that predicted variances cannot be negative. Let d_2 be the estimate of δ and $s(d_2)$ be the standard error of d_2. Importantly, d_2 has the desirable property of asymptotic normality and consistency (see Amemiya, 1977, for a rigorous proof; see Goldfeld & Quandt, 1972, for simulation results on the small sample properties).

Step 5. Compute $\omega_L = [E(W_id_2| W_id_2 > 0)]^{-1}$ and estimate a weighted regression model with RESP as the dependent variable, X as the vector of independent variables, and ω_L as the weight. Let $\mathbf{b}_2$ be the estimate of β and $s(\mathbf{b}_2)$ be the standard error of $\mathbf{b}_2$.

Step 6. Compute $\Delta_b = |s(\mathbf{b}_2) - s(\mathbf{b})|$ and $\Delta_d = |s(\mathbf{d}_2) - s(\mathbf{d}_1)|$ and let φ be a very small number (say 0.0001). If $\Delta_b > \varphi$, replace $\mathbf{b}$ with $\mathbf{b}_2$, go back to step 2 and proceed, and if $\Delta_b \leq \varphi$, examine Δ_d. In turn, if $\Delta_d > \varphi$, replace $\mathbf{d}_1$ with $\mathbf{d}_2$, go back to step 4 and proceed, and if $\Delta_d \leq \varphi$, stop. The convergence estimates of $\mathbf{b}_2$ and $\mathbf{d}_2$ $= [\hat{\gamma}, \hat{\sigma}^2]$ possess the desirable properties of asymptotic normality, unbiasedness, consistency, and efficiency.

REFERENCES

Abelson, R. P. (1988). Conviction. *American Psychologist, 43*, 267–275.

Abelson, R. P., & Levi, A. (1985). Decision making and decision theory. In G. Lindzey & E. Aronson (Eds.), *The handbook of social psychology* (pp. 231–309). New York: Random House.

Amemiya, T. (1985). *Advanced econometrics*. Cambridge, MA: Harvard University Press.

Anderson, N. H. (1981). *Foundations of information integration theory*. New York: Academic Press.

Bargh, J. A., Chaiken, S., Govender, R., & Pratto, F. (1992). The generality of the automatic activation effect. *Journal of Personality and Social Psychology, 62*, 893–912.

Barwise, P. (1995). Good empirical generalizations. *Marketing Science, 14*, G29–G35.

Bassili, J. N. (1996). Meta-judgmental versus operative indexes of psychological attributes: The case of measures of attitude strength. *Journal of Personality and Social Psychology, 71*, 637–653.

Bernoulli, D. (1967). *Exposition of a new theory on the measurement of risk*. Farnsborough Hants, England: Gregg Press. (Original work published 1738)

Brehmer, B., & Joyce, C. R. B. (1988). *Human judgment: The SJT view*. Amsterdam: North Holland, Elsevier.

Broniarczyk, S. M., & Alba, J. W. (1994). The importance of the brand in brand extension. *Journal of Marketing Research, 31*, 214–228.

Brunswik, E. (1943). Organismic achievement and environmental probability. *Psychological Review, 50*, 255–272.

Brunswik, E. (1952). *The conceptual framework of psychology*. Chicago: University of Chicago Press.

Brunswik, E. (1955a). In defense of probabilistic functionalism: A reply. *Psychological Review, 62*, 236–242.

Brunswik, E. (1955b). Representative design and probabilistic theory in a functional psychology. *Psychological Review, 62*, 193–217.

Cacioppo, J. T., & Petty, R. E. (1982). The need for cognition. *Journal of Personality and Social Psychology, 42*, 116–131.

Calder, B. J., Phillips, L. W., & Tybout, A. M. (1982). Beyond external validity. *Journal of Consumer Research, 9*, 240–244.

Chandrashekaran, M., McNeilly, K., Russ, F. A., & Marinova, D. (2000). From uncertain intentions to actual behavior: A threshold model of whether and when salespeople quit. *Journal of Marketing Research, 37*, 463–479.

Cooksey, R. W. (1996). *Judgment analysis: Theory, methods, and applications*. New York: Academic Press.

Coyne, J. C. (1976). Toward an interactional description of depression. *Psychiatry, 39*, 28–40.

DeSarbo, W., & Wedel, M. (1994). A review of recent developments in latent class regression models. In R. P. Bagozzi (Ed.), *Handbook of marketing research* (pp. 352–388). New York: Blackwell.

Eagly, A., & Chaiken, S. (1993). *The psychology of attitudes*. New York: Harcourt Brace Jovanovich.

Erev, I., Wallsten, T. S., & Budescu, D. V. (1994). Simultaneous over- and underconfidence: The role of error in judgment processes. *Psychological Review, 101*, 519–527.

Fazio, R. H. (1990). A practical guide to the use of response latency in social psychological research. In C. Hendrick & M. S. Clark (Eds.), *Research methods in personality and social psychology* (pp. 74–97). Newbury Park, CA: Sage.

Fazio, R. H., Powell, M. C., & Williams, C. J. (1989). The role of attitude accessibility in the attitude-to-behavior process. *Journal of Consumer Research, 16*, 280–288.

Fazio, R. H., Sanbonmatsu, D. M., Powell, M. C., & Kardes, F. R. (1986). On the automatic activation of attitudes. *Journal of Personality and Social Psychology, 50*, 229–238.

Gatignon, H. A. (1984). Toward a methodology for measuring advertising copy effects. *Marketing Science, 3*, 308–326.

Gigerenzer, G., Hoffrage, U., & Kleinbölting, H. (1991). Probabilistic mental models: A Brunswikian theory of confidence. *Psychological Review, 98*, 506–528.

Goldfeld, S. M., & Quandt, R. E. (1972). *Nonlinear methods in econometrics.* Amsterdam: North-Holland.

Greene, W. H. (1997). *Econometric analysis.* New York: Macmillan.

Gross, S. R., Holtz, R., & Miller, N. (1995). Attitude certainty. In R. E. Petty & J. A. Krosnick (Eds.), *Attitude strength: Antecedents and consequences.* Hillsdale, NJ: Lawrence Erlbaum Associates.

Hammond, K. R. (1996). *Human judgment and social policy. Irreducible uncertainty, inevitable error, unavoidable justice.* New York: Oxford University Press.

Hammond, K. R., Stewart, T. R., Brehmer, B., & Steinman, D. O. (1975). Social judgment theory. In M. Kaplan & S. Schwartz (Eds.), *Human judgment and decision process* (pp. 271–312). New York: Academic Press.

Haugtvedt, C. P. (1994). Advertising repetition and variation strategies: Implications for understanding attitude strength. *Journal of Consumer Research, 21*, 176–189.

Hofstede, G. (1991). *Cultures and organizations: Software of the mind.* London: McGraw-Hill.

Hutchinson, J. W., Kamakura, W. A., & Lynch, J. G., Jr. (2000). Unobserved heterogeneity as an alternative explanation for 'reversal' effects in behavioral research. *Journal of Consumer Research, 27*, 323–344.

Jobson, J. D., & Fuller, W. A. (1980). Least squares estimation when the covariance matrix and parameter vector are functionally related. *Journal of the American Statistical Association, 75*, 176–181.

Juslin, P., & Olsson, H. (1997). Thurstonian and Brunswikian origins of uncertainty in judgment: A sampling model of confidence in sensory discrimination. *Psychological Review, 104*, 344–366.

Kareev, Y., Arnon, S., & Horwitz-Zeliger, R. (2002). On the misperception of variability. *Journal of Experimental Psychology: General, 131*, 287–297.

Keeney, R. L., & Raiffa, H. (1976). *Decisions with multiple objectives: Preferences and value trade-offs.* New York: Wiley.

Keller, K. L. (2002). *Branding and brand equity.* Cambridge, MA: Marketing Science Institute.

Kellogg, W. N. (1931). Time of judgment in psychometric measures. *American Journal of Psychology, 43*, 65–86.

Kintsch, W., Kozminsky, E., Stroby, W. J., McKoon, G., & Keenan, J. M. (1975). Comprehension and recall of text as a function of content variables. *Journal of Verbal Learning and Verbal Behavior, 14*, 196–214.

Koehler, D. J. (1994). Hypothesis generation and confidence in judgment. *Journal of Experimental Psychology, 20*, 461–469.

Kruglanski, A. W., Webster, D. M., & Klem, A. (1993). Motivated resistance and openness to persuasion in the presence or absence of prior information. *Journal of Personality and Social Psychology, 65*, 861–876.

Langer, E. J. (1975). The illusion of control. *Journal of Personality and Social Psychology, 32*, 311–328.

Lazarsfeld, P. F. (1954). A conceptual introduction to latent structure analysis. In P. F. Lazarsfeld (Ed.), *Mathematical thinking in the social sciences* (pp. 2–46). Glencoe: The Free Press.

Lazarsfeld, P. F., & Dudman, J. (1951). Mathematical developments in latent structure analysis. In P. F. Lazarsfeld (Ed.), *The use of mathematical models in measurement of attitudes* (pp. 4–23). Santa Monica, CA: The Rand Corporation.

Lewin, K. (1951). *Field theory in social sciences*. New York: Harper & Row.

Louviere, J. (2001). What if consumer experiments impact variances as well as means? Response variability as a behavioral phenomenon. *Journal of Consumer Research, 28*, 506–511.

Lynch, J. G., Jr. (1982). On the external validity of experiments in consumer research. *Journal of Consumer Research, 9*, 225–239.

Maxham, J. G., III, & Netemeyer, R. G. (2002). A longitudinal study of complaining customers' evaluations of multiple service failures and recovery efforts. *Journal of Marketing, 66*, 57–73.

Nunnally, J. C., & Bernstein, I. H. (1994). *Psychometric theory*. New York: McGraw-Hill.

Palmer, D. L., & Kalin, R. (1991). Predictive validity of the dogmatic rejection scale. *Personality and Social Psychology Bulletin, 17*, 212–218.

Petty, R. E. (1981). The role of cognitive responses in attitude change processes. In R. C. Petty, T. M. Ostrom, & T. C. Brock (Eds.), *Cognitive responses in persuasion* (pp. 81–124). Hillsdale, NJ: Lawrence Erlbaum Associates.

Priester, J. R., & Petty, R. E. (2001). Extending the bases of subjective attitudinal ambivalence: Interpersonal and intrapersonal antecedents of evaluative tension. *Journal of Personality and Social Psychology, 80*, 19–34.

Ross, L., & Nisbett, R. (1991). *The person and the situation: Perspectives of social psychology*. New York: McGraw-Hill.

Rotte, K. N., Chandrashekaran, M., Grewal, R., & Tax, S. S. (2004). *Covert uncertainty to overt responses: Consumer trust and loyalty following service failures* (Working Paper No. 2004-1R). Australian Graduate School of Management, University of New South Wales, Sydney, Australia.

Shocker, A. D., Srivastava, R. K., & Ruekert, R. W. (1994). Challenges and opportunities facing brand management: An introduction to the special issue. *Journal of Marketing Research, 31*, 149–158.

Smith, A. K., Bolton, R. N., & Wagner, J. (1999). A model of customer satisfaction with service encounters involving failure and recovery. *Journal of Marketing Research, 36*, 356–372.

Smith, E. R., & Miller, F. D. (1983). Mediation among attributional inferences and comprehension processes: Initial findings and a general method. *Journal of Personality and Social Psychology, 44*, 492–505.

Sorrentino, R. M., & Short, J. C. (1986). Uncertainty orientation, motivation and cognition. In R. M. Sorrentino & E. T. Higgens (Eds.), *The handbook of motivation and cognition: Foundations of social behavior* (pp. 379–403). New York: Guilford Press.

Tax, S. S., Brown, S. W., & Chandrashekaran, M. (1998). Customer evaluations of service recovery experiences: Implications for relationship marketing. *Journal of Marketing, 66*, 60–76.

Titterington, D. M., Smith, A. F. M., & Makov, U. E. (1985). *Statistical analysis of finite mixture distributions*. New York: Wiley.

Tversky, A., & Kahneman, D. (1981). The framing of decisions and the psychology of choice. *Science, 211*, 453–458.

Volkmann, J. (1934). The relation of time of judgment to the certainty of judgment. *Psychological Bulletin, 31*, 672–673.

von Nuemann, J., & Morgenstern, O. (1944). *Theory of games and economic behavior*. Princeton, NJ: Princeton University Press.

Wallsten, T. S., & González-Vallejo, C. (1994). Statement verification: A stochastic model of judgment and response. *Psychological Review, 101*, 490–504.

Wiggins, L. M. (1973). *Panel analysis: Latent probability models for attitude and behavior processes*. San Francisco: Jossey-Bass.

Woodruff, R. B. (1972a). Brand information sources, opinion change, and uncertainty. *Journal of Marketing Research, 9*, 414–418.

Woodruff, R. B. (1972b). Measurement of consumers' prior brand information. *Journal of Marketing Research, 9*, 258–263.

Wyer, R. S., Jr. (1973). Category rating as 'subjective expected values': Implications for attitude formation and change. *Psychological Review, 80*, 446–467.

CHAPTER SIX

Toward a Unified Implicit Brand Theory

Brian C. Tietje
Cal Poly State University

Frédéric F. Brunel
Boston University

There has been much research into the psychology of branding, and this has generated numerous advances in our understanding of the fundamental social psychological constructs that govern consumers' brand perceptions, cognitions, and relationships. This proliferation of brand research has accumulated abundant empirical evidence and produced numerous consumer psychology theories around key brand constructs, including brand evaluations, brand awareness, brand image, brand equity, brand personality, brand relationships, brand associations, brand extensions, brand community, and brand alliances. Although there is little or no debate on the merits of these various constructs and theories, it is our contention that this somewhat diffused knowledge is ripe for greater integration between the concepts along with a better articulation of their interconnections within a general framework or theory.

We are well aware that "grand unifying attempts" at developing one model or theory of consumer behavior were the hallmark of early consumer psychology research, and we believe that there would be much naïveté in fully revisiting these attempts. However, we also believe that recent developments in social cognition research, and implicit social cognition in particular, provide us with the means to articulate formally a more unified brand theory that can integrate many of the constructs we identified earlier.

Our research aims for theoretical integration at two levels. First, we seek to develop a framework that pulls together the numerous brand-related constructs that have emerged in the marketing literature. Second, we incorporate chief constructs from social cognition into branding theory (e.g., attitudes, stereotypes, self-esteem, and self-concept) in order to explain and predict consumer response and prescribe brand strategy. Third, we chiefly focus our effort on implicit brand cognitions (i.e., beliefs that consumers are either unaware of, or unwilling to share). Our goal is to introduce and articulate the key principles of a unified theory of implicit brand cognitions, and we recognize that at this stage, there are many issues that will warrant further empirical enquiries. However, we hope that the development of this framework will set forth future research to fully support the unified brand theory. To this end, we propose testable implications of the theory and discuss measures of consumer social knowledge structure (at both the explicit and implicit level) to identify the structures, dynamics and influence of the implicit consumer social knowledge structure.

We begin this chapter by summarizing the key elements of the unified theory of implicit social cognition (Greenwald et al., 2002) and the Implicit Association Test (IAT; Greenwald, McGhee, & Schwartz, 1998), which provides valid measurements for testing the principles of the unified theory. Then, we expand the concepts of the *unified theory of implicit social cognition* to the consumer branding literature to demonstrate how numerous brand-related concepts can be defined and operationalized within a single framework. We present testable propositions based on a unified implicit brand theory, and explain how the IAT can be used to test them. Finally, we suggest novel insights that can be drawn from a unified implicit brand theory, and how these insights might enable us to reexamine fundamental approaches to consumer behavior, including theories of persuasion and behavioral modification.

THE UNIFIED THEORY OF IMPLICIT ATTITUDES, STEREOTYPES, SELF-ESTEEM, AND SELF-CONCEPT

Overview

The unified theory of implicit attitudes, stereotypes, self-esteem, and self-concept (Greenwald et al., 2002) provides a theoretical framework that integrates key constructs in social psychology, defines them in the context of associations between concepts, explains how they are formed, predicts their interrelationships, and has been empirically validated at the implicit level using the IAT. This theory stems from (a) the current increased attention to implicit cognition, (b) the availability of valid implicit measurements (e.g., the IAT), and (c) the foundations offered by consistency theories from the 1950s (e.g., congruity theory, cognitive dissonance, and balance theory; Greenwald et al., 2002). The major elements of this theory are presented here to precede its extension to a branding context.

Constructs

The unified theory of implicit social cognition is based on an associative network model and is described using familiar terms including *concept, association strength*, and *concept activation*. It follows that a person's associative social knowledge structure can be represented through a network of concepts and nodes, where each of the social constructs is conceptualized as a set of associations between concepts in the knowledge structure. Concept is a primitive term from social psychology that refers to persons, groups, or attributes (including the positive and negative valence attribute concepts). In a typical social knowledge structure, the concept of *self* is at the center and is connected to other social concepts (Greenwald et al., 2002). In the unified theory, positive and negative valences are special classes of attribute concepts. The inclusion of valence attribute concepts enables the operationalization of evaluative constructs such as attitudes and self-esteem. Association strength describes the relationship between two concepts and the degree to which the activation of one concept activates another. Concept activation is a temporary state that is induced when one concept is closely associated with another concept that has been activated (Collins & Loftus, 1975). These relationships are visually represented using node and link diagrams that have been used in various theoretical approaches such as associative memory models (Anderson & Bower, 1973; Collins & Loftus, 1975; Wyer & Srull, 1989). Further, following Heider's (1958) balance theory, the unified theory is based on a series of principles, one of them being balance congruity (see Greenwald et al., 2002). As such, the knowledge structure aims toward balance across first order shared links. Figure 6.1 depicts a hypothetical social knowledge structure (SKS) that includes attitudes, stereotypes, self-esteem, and self-concept, and illustrates their interrelationship.

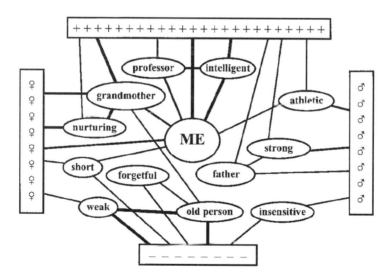

FIG. 6.1. Hypothetical social knowledge structure for a computer consumer, adapted from Greenwald et al. (2002). The concept of self is at the center; the attribute, person, and group concepts are represented in the ovals. The positive and negative attribute valence concepts (two especially important attribute concepts) are represented by the + and – sign rectangles. The thickness of the links between concepts represents the strength of the automatic association between concepts.

The unified theory defines four of the most important constructs in social psychology as associations between distinctive types of concepts. In this type of structural representation, *attitude* is defined as the association between a social object or social group concept and a valence attribute concept. For example, the association between "old person" and the negative valence concept in Fig. 6.1 depicts a negative attitude toward the elderly. Thus, measuring the strength of the automatic association of a social concept with a valence attribute can provide a measure of one's automatic attitude toward the concept. This theoretical approach is consistent with the associative network view of memory (Anderson & Bower, 1973; Collins & Loftus, 1975) and the description of an attitude as the association between an attitude-object and a valence concept (Fazio, 1995; Fazio, Chen, McDonel, & Sherman, 1982). *Stereotype* is defined as the association between a social group concept and one or more nonvalence attribute concepts, as illustrated by the association between "old person" and "weak" in Fig. 6.1. *Self-esteem* is the association between the concept of *self* and a *valence attribute* concept, and *self-concept* is the association between the concept of self and one or more nonvalence attribute concepts, such as the link between "me" and "professor," "intelligent," and "athletic" in Fig. 6.1.

Assumptions, Definitions and Principles

In addition to these terms and definitions, unified theory also relies on some fundamental assumptions that have been well-established in the psychological literature. First, a person's social knowledge can be represented visually using an associative knowledge structure. Second, self is the central concept in the associative knowledge structure. Finally, because the theory defines self-esteem as the association between self and a valence attribute concept, and because self-esteem is known to be positive in normal populations, the associative knowledge structure presumes an association between the self node and a positive valence node. These three assumptions—an associative knowledge structure, centrality of self, and self-positivity—provide structural rules for the construction of a social knowledge structure.

Not only can the unified theory of implicit attitudes, stereotypes, self-esteem, and self-concept define and depict static constructs, it can also be used to explain and predict formation and changes in a person's SKS, including the relationships between attitudes, stereotypes, self-esteem and self-concept. These dynamic links among social psychology's major affective and cognitive constructs are described using three definitions and principles.

The first definition states that when two nodes are each linked to the same third node, they are said to have a shared first-order link (e.g., "nurturing" and "me" are both linked to "grandmother" in the example in Fig. 6.1). The first principle follows from this definition. According to the balance-congruity principle, when two unlinked or weakly linked nodes share a first-order link, the association between these nodes will strengthen. For example, the link between "me" and "nurturing" should form and strengthen when the links between "grandmother" and "me" and between "grandmother" and "nurturing" are activated.

The obvious implication of the balance-congruity principle is that links could eventually form between every concept within a person's social knowledge structure. This implication is problematic in cases where a concept might become linked with concepts that seem to conflict, such as *positive* and *negative valence*. Such an untenable outcome is addressed by the second principle of unified theory—imbalance-dissonance. Definition 2 states that when two nodes share fewer associations than would be expected by chance, they are described as bipolar opposed. In Fig. 6.1, positive and negative valence share fewer associations than would be expected by chance, as do the *male* and *female attribute* concepts. According to the imbalance-dissonance principle, the network resists forming links that would cause a single node to have a shared first order link with nodes that are bipolar-opposed. For example, in Fig. 6.1, both "me" and "male" have a shared first-order link with "athletic." According to the balance-congruity principle, activation of this shared first-order link should strengthen the link between "me" and "male." The imbalance-dissonance principle resists this linkage, however, in order to avoid a linkage between "me" and both "male" and "female," because the latter two concepts are bipolar-opposed.

A conflict can emerge between the balance-congruity and imbalance-dissonance principles. According to definition 3, when repeated influences cause a concept to develop a link with both of two bipolar-opposed concepts, the concept is known to be "pressured." As a result the third principle of unified theory proposes that a pressured concept will split into subconcepts, each of which will be linked to one of the bipolar-opposed nodes. For example, if the "grandmother" node in Fig. 6.1 was continually pressured to link both to the positive and negative valence nodes, "grandmother" would split into two subconcepts—one linked to the positive and the other linked to the negative valence nodes.

Empirical Testing

The principles and predictions just stated can be empirically tested. Figure 6.2 summarizes the balanced identity design based on unified theory that illustrates these predictions. The balanced identity design has two fundamental characteristics. First, self is included as the central concept in the social knowledge structure, as explained in the "centrality of self" assumption of unified theory. Second, the valence of associations within the design exhibit a consistency that is derived from Heider's (1958) balance theory. For example, if we assume that a person possesses positive self-esteem (i.e., a positive association between self and the positive valence attribute concept), then the group–self and group–attribute association should both be either negative or positive in order for the triad of associa-

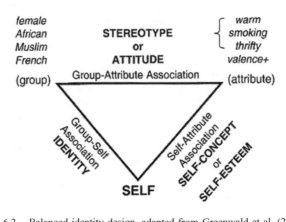

FIG. 6.2.   Balanced identity design, adapted from Greenwald et al. (2002).

tions to have consistency. These characteristics imply several empirical predictions (Greenwald et al., 2002).

First, any one of the measures of the associations in the triad should be a multiplicative function of the other two measures of association. For example, Fig. 6.1 depicts a triadic relationship between the concepts *me*, *grandmother*, and the positive valence concept. If the measure of the group–self association (grandmother and me in Fig. 6.1; also see Fig. 6.2) is the criterion variable C and measures of the other two associations (me and positive valence; grandmother and positive valence) are the predictors (A and B), a two-step hierarchical regression analysis is used to test that the group–self association (C) is a multiplicative function of self-esteem (A) and attitude toward the group (B). The two models to be estimated are the following:

$$\text{Step 1: } C = b0 + b1(A*B) + e$$

$$\text{Step 2: } C = b0 + b1(A*B) + b2(A) + b3(B) + e$$

In order to support the balanced identity design, five criteria are to be met (Greenwald et al., 2002):

1. significant R-squared in step 1,
2. b1 is significant and positive in step 1,
3. b1 is significant and positive in step 2,
4. the R-squared change in step 2 (as compared to step 1) is not significant, and
5. b2 and b3 are insignificant in step 2.

If the pattern of results matches these five conditions, then it can be concluded that the variance in C is a function primarily of the interaction between A and B.

The balanced identity design also implies another pattern in the measures of association between concepts (Greenwald et al., 2002). When any measure of association in the design is polarized toward its upper end, the zero-order correlation between the other two measures should be positive. Conversely, if any measure of association in the design is polarized toward its lower end, correlation between the other two measures should be negative. Finally, if the variable's distribution is distributed across its entire potential range, the correlation between the other measures should not differ from zero. For example, if the association between "intelligent" and the *positive valence* concept in Fig. 6.1 is extremely high, the zero-order correlation between the "me-intelligent" and "me-positive" measures should be positive.

Empirical Support

Greenwald et al. (2002) used both explicit and implicit measures (IAT) to test their predictions. Empirical results with IAT measures were consistent with the predictions, whereas results from explicit measures were not. The IAT (Greenwald et al., 1998) has become the most well-known implicit measure in psychology (Fazio & Olson, 2003a), and has been recently introduced into the marketing literature (Brunel, Tietje, & Greenwald, 2004; Maison, Greenwald, & Bruin, 2004). The IAT is assumed to measure association strengths, without regard to whether the respondent is or is not aware of the strengths of the associations being assessed (Forehand & Perkins, 2004; Greenwald et al., 2002). Although the IAT can measure associations that operate outside conscious awareness, it can obviously assess conscious associations as well. In this respect, it can be seen as an unobtrusive measure. However this is not the main *raison d'être* for this measure. The IAT measures automatic associations that are less susceptible to impression management than explicit measures. Therefore, it is well suited for research that seeks to distinguish associations that are within a person's conscious awareness and control, and those that are not. Also, it should be noted that the IAT might not be a very efficient measure if one is interested in concepts that can be measured explicitly. There is little justification for the use of a complex procedure if a similar outcome can be obtained through a questionnaire. The IAT will be especially useful in situations in which it can predict variations in consumer behavior beyond those explained by parallel explicit measures.

Given that the IAT has already been widely used in social psychology research in a relatively short period of time, new discoveries about the methodology are constantly emerging. Fazio and Olson (2003b), for example, developed a "personalized" IAT that purportedly reduces the IAT's susceptibility to associations that are in one's memory, but that do not contribute to one's evaluation of an object. These associations, termed *extrapersonal* by the authors, may be driven by societal standards, for example, but are not an actual component of a person's own social knowledge structure. These types of modifications to the IAT, along with various improvements to the scoring algorithm (Greenwald, Nosek, & Banaji, 2003), further solidify its usefulness and precision as a measurement method for implicit cognition.

In the presentation of the unified theory, Greenwald et al. (2002) reported on several empirical results that are consistent with predictions based on the balanced identity design. Implicit measures of female-self, female-positive, and self-positive associations (i.e., implicit gender identity, gender attitude, and self-esteem, respectively) among women were related to one another in terms of zero-order correlation and interaction terms in multiple regression that would be expected by the balance identity design. However, explicit measures of gender identity, gender attitude, and self-esteem among the same participants did not exhibit a pattern consistent with these predictions, leading the researchers to conclude that "the IAT provides better access to associative knowledge than does self-report" (Greenwald et al., 2002, p. 27).

In the next section, the unified theory of implicit attitudes, stereotypes, self-esteem, and self-concept is applied to implicit consumer brand cognitions. The unified theory of implicit consumer brand cognitions integrates many of the constructs that have emerged in the branding literature into a single framework. The balanced identity design is also applied to branding to yield predictable hypotheses that can be tested, in part, using the IAT.

APPLYING UNIFIED THEORY AND THE IAT TO IMPLICIT CONSUMER BRAND COGNITIONS

Consumer Social Knowledge Structure

According to unified theory, concepts include *persons*, *groups*, *attributes*, and *valence attributes*. Besides the types of concepts discussed thus far, the unified brand theory also includes concepts such as *brands*, *companies*, and *product categories*. The idea that a semantic network can include concepts other than nouns or adjectives is consistent with prior research in cognitive memory (Ashcraft, 1994). Figure 6.3 depicts a hypothetical consumer social knowledge structure that incorporates the concepts of *consumer self* (the person at the center), *attributes*, *valence attributes*, and *social objects* (such as brands or products). The nodes depict concepts, and the thickness of the lines symbolizes the strength of the automatic association between the concepts. This structure specifically applies to brand-related knowledge. In it, we can define and depict many brand related concepts such as *brand attitudes*, *brand beliefs*, *image and/or personality*, *brand identification or relationship*, *brand-endorsement*, and *brand alliances*.

Although a schematic representation has been used in previous branding research to illustrate brand-related associations (see, for example, Aaker, 1991;

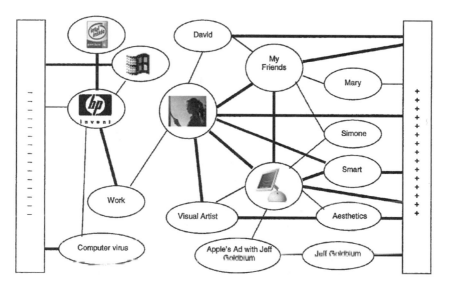

FIG. 6.3.   Hypothetical consumer social knowledge structure.

Samu, Krishnan, & Smith, 1999), its use in unified brand theory provides several important advances. First, prior node and link diagrams did not include valence attribute concepts, thus precluding the depiction of evaluative constructs such as brand attitude. Second, an application of the balanced identity design in a branding context implies testable hypotheses, whereas prior representations of a consumer social knowledge structure were not necessarily intended to convey testable, empirical patterns among specific types of measures.

Main Constructs

An extensive collection of terms and constructs has emerged in the branding literature, and unified brand theory distills them into several constructs that can be defined as associations between concepts—brand attitude, brand belief, brand personality, brand stereotypes, brand alliances, brand awareness, brand accessibility, brand identification, and brand community. Brand attitude, also referred to as attitude towards the brand and brand evaluation in the literature, has been defined as "consumers' learned tendencies to evaluate brands in a consistently favorable or unfavorable way" (Assael, 1992, p. 196), or "consumers' overall evaluations of a brand" (Keller, 1993, p. 4). The unified brand theory defines a brand attitude as the association between a brand concept and a valence attribute concept. For example, it is possible to infer that the consumer in Fig. 6.3 has a favorable attitude toward Apple™ Computers based on the positive associations with this brand concept (direct and indirect positive valence associations). Recent work has demonstrated the validity of this conceptualization. Brunel et al. (2004) showed that explicit and implicit measures of attitudes are correlated when consumers have access to their brand attitudes and lack the motivation to disguise them in explicit measures. Also, Maison et al. (2004) showed that using the IAT to measure brand attitudes along with traditional explicit measures allows explaining incremental portions of the variance in purchase and consumption behavior. The representation of attitudes within a consumer social knowledge structure is consistent with prior theoretical approaches such as expectancy-value (Ajzen & Fishbein, 1980; Fishbein & Ajzen, 1975). According to this model, attitudes are a multiplicative function of the beliefs held about a brand (i.e., associations between a brand and attribute concepts), and evaluative judgment of those beliefs. This evaluative judgment is depicted in the consumer social knowledge structure as an association between an attribute concept and a valence attribute concept. According to the balance-congruity principle, if both a brand concept and the positive valence concept have a shared first-order link with an attribute, activation of this shared link will strengthen the association between the brand concept and positive valence. This process explains one way in which a positive brand attitude is formed and/or strengthened.

Unified brand theory's definition of a brand belief is the association between a brand concept and one or more (nonvalence) attribute concepts. Numerous types of attribute concepts can become associated with a brand. Associations between brand and attribute concepts have been described in the literature with terms such as *brand attributes, brand associations* (Aaker, 1991; Janiszewski & Van Osselaer, 2000; Samu et al., 1999; Van Osselaer & Janiszewski, 2001), *brand perceptions,* and *brand image. Brand beliefs* also incorporate *brand personality.* Brand personality is defined by Aaker (1997) as "the set of human characteristics associated with a brand" (p. 347). In terms of unified brand theory, brand personality is the association between a brand concept and one or more (nonvalence) attribute concepts that are commonly associated with people (person-related). Thus, brand personality is considered a special type of brand belief. Based on the structure in Fig. 6.3, for example, the consumer's image of HP™ (Hewlett-Packard) computers and Microsoft™ involves work and computer viruses. The association between work and HP is strong but the association with viruses is weaker, suggesting that one has been reinforced over time and the other might be more transient or weaker. From a brand personality perspective, it can be inferred that Apple is perceived as friendly and aesthetic in this example.

One of the most common brand-related stereotypes in consumer research relates to the use of country of origin as a heuristic cue (Hong & Wyer, 1989; Kardes, 1994; LeClerc, Schmitt, & Dube, 1994; Maheswaran, 1994; Peterson & Jolibert, 1995). In the customary country-of-origin research model, information pertaining to a brand's geographic origin mediates subjective evaluations of the brand's attractiveness and performance capabilities. For example, a person's knowledge that a brand of automobile was manufactured in Japan (creating an association between the brand and a *social group* concept), may lead the person to associate the brand with concepts commonly associated with Japan, such as *efficiency, miniaturization,* and *precision engineering.* Inhabitants of a particular geographic region comprise only one type of social group concept. Other social group concepts may include *ethnicity, sexual orientation,* and *political* and *religious affiliation.* Associations that are formed between brands and these social group concepts can have a demonstrative impact on a consumer social knowledge structure.

Co-branding, brand alliances (Park, Jun, & Shocker, 1996; Simonin & Ruth, 1998), ingredient branding, and other strategies are depicted by unified brand theory as an association between two or more brand concepts. Because multiple brands are often associated with one another either intentionally or unintentionally, it is important that unified brand theory accommodate multiple brand relationships within its theoretical and schematic framework. In Fig. 6.3, we see that this consumer associates two other brands to HP computers: Microsoft and Intel™. This could be the result of the "Intel inside" campaign and also of the pairing of Microsoft Windows with almost every personal computer (PC) sold.

Categorization schemes are prevalent in branding concepts, and brands are commonly associated with the categories to which they belong. *Brand awareness*—an important construct in marketing strategy—refers to the strength of the association between a brand and product category, and is sometimes called *brand strength, brand recognition, brand recall, brand familiarity,* and *brand typicality* (Keller, 1993; Loken & Ward, 1990; Samu et al., 1999). A related but distinctive term is *brand accessibility,* defined by Samu et al. (1999) as "the speed with which the brand node can be accessed when the product node is activated" (p. 61). Both of these concepts can be defined and operationalized by unified brand theory. Brand awareness is defined in unified brand theory as the association between a brand concept and a product category concept. Brand accessibility is the retrieval speed of this association, and can be tested using response latency measures such as those used in the IAT.

Brand identification is defined in unified brand theory as the association between a brand concept and self. This construct is related to terms such as brand loyalty (a behavioral manifestation of brand identity), brand relationships (Fournier, 1998), consumer–company identification (Bhattacharya & Sen, 2003), material possession attachment (S. S. Kleine, R. E. Kleine, & Allen, 1995) and the extended self (Belk, 1988) in consumer research. Self-referencing research demonstrates the facilitating role of self as a knowledge and memory structure (Burnkrant & Unnava, 1995; Sujan, Bettman, & Baumgartner, 1993). When brand information is closely associated with self, consumers process the information more deeply, remember it better, and evaluate it more favorably. These outcomes are readily accounted for in unified brand theory. Activating the association between a brand and self strengthens the shared first-order links between the brand and concepts that are closely associated with self, including *personality traits, past experiences, close friends, one's favorite color or sports personality.* The formation of multiple associations between a brand and numerous self-related concepts not only facilitates memory and recall (Burnkrant & Unnava, 1995; Sujan et al., 1993), but also enhances the brand's positivity because it is associated with self. In the example in Fig. 6.3, the *Apple* concept is directly linked to the concept of *self* and this association is strong, therefore we can conclude that there is a strong brand identification (or brand relationship), and that Apple is probably part of the extended self for this consumer. The opposite could be true for the competing brand, HP, which is unrelated to self and has an association with negative valence. Brunel et al. (2004) tested a similar set of relationships and showed that for Apple users, there was a strong implicit brand–self identification/ relationship whereas for PC (Windows™-based machines) users there was no brand–self identification, confirming that some brands are central to one's identity and others are not, and that these effects can be automatic.

Brand community (McAlexander, Schouten, & Koenig, 2002; Muniz & O'Guinn, 2001) is another concept from consumer research that is accommodated within a consumer social knowledge structure. The association between social group concepts, self, and the brand capture the social and brand identification dimensions of brand community. In our example we see that Apple computer is connected to a set of social relationships (friends, Simone), and therefore it could be inferred that for this hypothetical consumer, this brand is meaningful in part due to the community of users that surround it.

Just as the social knowledge structure and the balanced identity design from unified theory include *self* as the central concept (Greenwald et al., 2002), unified brand theory is also centered on the self-concept. One might suggest that the brand concept should be central in a consumer context, but in this research, we argue that self remains the central concept, and a brand obtains its meaning, relevance, and valence primarily through its integration into a person's self-concept. In the next section, the balanced identity design is used to generate predictions that can be applied and tested in a branding context.

EMPIRICAL TESTING OF UNIFIED IMPLICIT BRAND THEORY

The empirical properties of the balanced identity design, applied to the context of the consumer social knowledge structure, yield several testable predictions. We discuss two of these. Our first proposition is that brand attitude is a multiplicative function of brand–self identification and self-esteem. The implications of this proposition are noteworthy. We are proposing that as a component of a consumer's knowledge structure, the brand is also part of a consumer's self-concept.

Thus, one route to enhancing brand attitude is to strengthen a person's relationship with a brand, which we have termed brand identification. This suggestion is certainly not novel; it reflects the significance that has been placed on relationship marketing in contemporary practice and academic research. The contribution of the unified theory approach, however, is that it explains why relationships are an important component of brand attitudes, and it provides a research model for measuring the strength of these relationships at both the implicit and explicit level.

The suggestion that brand attitudes are a function of self-esteem is an idea that we believe is novel to consumer research. Furthermore, it implies a more direct connection between the major constructs in social psychology and branding. Because self-esteem is an individual difference variable and is most likely measurable but not malleable, we would expect that favorable brand attitudes can be achieved by establishing strong brand identification among consumers with relatively favorable self-esteem.

To test this proposition, we would use the IAT and explicit instruments to measure associations A, B, and C depicted in Fig. 6.2. Then, we would conduct the two-step hierarchical regression analysis that was discussed earlier, where the first equation is $C = b0 + b1(A \cdot B) + e$, and the second equation is $C = b0 + b1(A \cdot B) + b2(A) + b3(B) + e$. A data pattern consistent with our proposition would meet the following five criteria: (1) significant R-squared in equation 1, (2) $b1 > 0$ in equation 1, (3) $b1 > 0$ in equation 2, (4) the increment in R-squared in the second equation is not significant, and (5) $b2 = b3 = 0$. Furthermore, if any of the three measures of association in the design is polarized toward its upper end, the zero-order correlation between the other two measures should be positive. Conversely, if any of the measures of association in the design is polarized toward its lower end, correlation between the other two measures should be negative. For example, if brand–self identification is toward its upper end, we would expect that the zero-order correlation between self-esteem and brand attitude would be positive.

Our second proposition is as follows: Brand personality should be a multiplicative function of the strengths of brand–self identification and self-personality. This is consistent with research that suggest that consumers are more influenced by products or agents that display personality characteristics similar to their own (Moon, 2002) or that, in general, individuals are more responsive to others that share similar personality traits (Blankenship, Hnat, Hess, & Brown, 1984). This proposition could be tested using the balanced identity approach discussed earlier.

It should be noted that this algebraic representation can be applied to other constructs in the consumer social knowledge structure, and therefore multiple propositions linking consumer brand cognitions can be developed using the balanced identity design. Furthermore, if empirical results indicate that one association within a triad is a multiplicative function of the other two associations, the other two associations can also be tested as a multiplicative function of their counterparts in the triad. Such findings can provide insights about the interdependence of numerous constructs within a consumer social knowledge structure, and can demonstrate how brands become inextricably imbedded within a consumer's self-concept.

CAN OTHER PHENOMENA IN CONSUMER PSYCHOLOGY BE EXPLAINED BY THE UNIFIED THEORY?

Beyond its capability to integrate, explain, and predict the properties and interrelationships between branding concepts, the unified theory approach might also provide additional insights about other significant domains in consumer psychology. We discuss two of these: classical conditioning and affect transfer processes exhibited by attitude toward the ad and mere possession.

In one of the seminal demonstrations of classical conditioning in a marketing context, Gorn (1982) designed an experimental manipulation that, in effect, created an association between the unconditioned stimulus of likable or dislikable music and the conditioned stimulus of a beige or blue pen. The unconditioned response was choice preference for one pen versus another. Repeatedly pairing either likable or dislikable music with a particular color of pen eventually influenced the participants' pen preference. Another example used by both Mc-Sweeney and Bierley (1984) and Nord and Peter (1980) is that by pairing the voice of a famous sportscaster (the unconditioned stimulus) to advertisements for products (the conditioned stimulus), the excitement (unconditioned response) evoked by the voices becomes associated with the advertised product. Can the unified theory and its balanced identity design account for these effects? We think so. In the colored pen example (Gorn, 1982), consider the triadic relationship between a blue pen, likable music, and the positive valence attribute concept. By preselecting "likable" music, the link between the music and positive valence is established. Playing the likable music while displaying slides of the blue pen activated their association with one another. According to the balance-congruity principle, because the blue pen and the positive valence concept share a first-order link to the likable music, a positive attitude toward the blue pen will develop, thus leading to a preference for blue versus beige. Similarly, because the advertised product and the emotional concept of *excitement* share a first-order link with the spokesperson's voice in the Nord and Peter (1980) example, the balance-congruity principle would predict that the association between the advertised product and excitement will be strengthened.

If classical conditioning effects can be explained by the unified theory, the question remains whether this theoretical approach affords new insights. At the minimum, the balanced identity design and the empirical testing approach available through the IAT permit greater understanding of how classical conditioning might actually work, and its limiting conditions. For example, research findings to date suggest that classical conditioning obtains stronger effects under forward conditioning, when the conditioned stimulus precedes the unconditioned stimulus

(Hoyer & MacInnis, 1997). Using the IAT to measure the strength of implicit associations between the unconditioned and conditioned stimulus and unconditioned response would allow greater understanding of when, how, and how much the linking process occurs between concepts. Furthermore, the unified theory approach can help frame classical conditioning within the context of social psychology's fundamental constructs of self-esteem, attitudes, stereotypes, and self-concept. Classical conditioning has traditionally been viewed as a means of behavioral modification, whether that be pecking a mirror or selecting a brand, primarily without cognitive mediation. The unified theory approach to classical conditioning suggests that the behavioral outcomes are mediated by cognitive processes, but the cognitions may occur primarily at the implicit level, of which the IAT affords measurement, and explicit measures do not.

The other consumer psychological domain that offers a potential for renewed discovery through the lens of the unified theory is affect transfer, a process demonstrated through attitude toward the ad (MacKenzie & Lutz, 1996; MacKenzie, Lutz, & Belch, 1986; Mitchell, 1986; Mitchell & Olson, 1981) and mere possession effects (Beggan, 1992; Sen & Johnson, 1997). Both of these effects are presumed to occur through an affect-transfer process, whereby the positive affect of one concept is transferred to another. The unified theory approach can be used to explain these effects, and the balanced identity design and IAT can be used to test their underlying processes and limiting conditions. In the case of attitude toward the ad, the triadic consistency of the links between the ad, the advertised brand or product, and the positive valence concept can be tested at both the implicit and explicit level. Research to date suggests that the attitude-toward-the-ad effect occurs primarily when cognitive processing and attention is very low (Hoyer & MacInnis, 1997), suggesting that the triadic consistency will be more likely to occur at the implicit, but not the explicit level. Such a proposition can be directly tested, yielding greater understanding of the relationship between attitudes toward several social objects or concepts that are a component of a single implicit consumer-knowledge structure. Also it should be noted that in a context of socially sensitive issues like the race of a spokesperson in an ad, it has been shown that the IAT can detect differences in attitudes toward the ad that explicit measures do not reveal (Brunel et al., 2004).

The mere possession effect (Beggan, 1992; Sen & Johnson, 1997) can also be explained through a unified theory approach. By assigning ownership of an object (e.g., a certain brand, color, or type of product) to someone, the experimenter has activated the link between the object and the participant. The self-positive link is already assumed to be established, so the object and the positive-valence concept have a shared first-order link with the participant, thus causing the link between the object and the positive-valence concept (i.e., the attitude toward the brand, color, or type of product) to be strengthened. Again, this effect could be tested using the balanced-identity design and the IAT. If results indicate that the triadic consistency is obtained at the implicit, but not explicit, level, this would suggest that affect transfer effects do not exclude cognitive mediation, they simply involve implicit cognitive mediation.

CONCLUSION AND FUTURE DIRECTIONS

The unified theory of implicit social cognition (Greenwald et al., 2002) provides a theoretical framework that integrates all of social psychology's major constructs, including attitudes, stereotypes, self-esteem, and self-concept. These constructs, significant in their own right, offer even greater insights when they are integrated. Furthermore, the empirical model operationalized by the balanced identity design and IAT provides a basis for empirically testing the interrelationships and dynamics of these constructs within a social knowledge structure.

The unified theory of implicit consumer brand cognitions offers similar contributions to research in consumer psychology and branding. Numerous constructs relating to branding have been identified in the literature, and the exploration of their unique contributions to our understanding of consumer–brand relationships and cognitions has begun. The unified theory approach allows greater integration of these constructs within a theoretical framework and also provides a functional articulation of the relationship between constructs, along with a testing methodology (the two-step process and its five validation conditions) and measurement instruments (the IAT). The relationship between core-branding constructs such as brand attitudes and brand personality, for example, can now be formally understood. Furthermore, the dynamics that lead to the formation of favorable brand attitudes through brand relationships can be articulated and empirically tested.

Beyond its capability to integrate a broad range of brand-related constructs, the unified theory, along with the balanced design and IAT, provides a research approach to explore consumer-brand cognitions at the implicit level. Theories of behavioral modification and persuasion that were previously considered devoid of cognitive mediation may now be further understood in light of implicit cognitive processes that can be measured using the IAT. We have offered only an introductory glance at the potential of the unified theory approach to consumer psychology and branding. We anticipate further discoveries that extend our ideas and advance our understanding of the complex web of cognitions that comprise the consumer psyche.

REFERENCES

Aaker, D. A. (1991). *Managing brand equity: Capitalizing on the value of a brand name.* New York: The Free Press.
Aaker, J. L. (1997). Dimensions of brand personality. *Journal of Marketing Research, 34,* 347–356.
Ajzen, I., & Fishbein, M. (1980). *Understanding attitudes and predicting social behavior.* Englewood Cliffs, NJ: Prentice-Hall.

Anderson, J. R., & Bower, G. H. (1973). *Human associative memory.* Washington, DC: Winston.

Ashcraft, M. H. (1994). *Human memory and cognition* (2nd ed.). New York: HarperCollins.

Assael, H. (1992). *Consumer behavior and marketing action* (4th ed.). Boston: PWS-Kent.

Beggan, J. K. (1992). On the social nature of nonsocial perception: The mere-possession effect. *Journal of Personality and Social Psychology, 62,* 229–237.

Belk, R. W. (1988). Possessions and the extended self. *Journal of Consumer Research, 15,* 139–168.

Bhattacharya, C. B., & Sen, S. (2003). Consumer–company identification: A framework for understanding consumers' relationships with companies. *Journal of Marketing, 67,* 76–88.

Blankenship, V. E., Hnat, S. M., Hess, T. G., & Brown, D. R. (1984). Reciprocal interaction and similarity of personality attributes. *Journal of Social and Personal Relationships, 1,* 415–432.

Brunel, F., Tietje, B. C., & Greenwald, A. G. (2004). Is the Implicit Association Test a valid and valuable measure of implicit consumer social cognition? *Journal of Consumer Psychology, 14*(4), 385–404.

Burnkrant, R. E., & Unnava, H. R. (1995). Effects of self-referencing on persuasion. *Journal of Consumer Research, 22,* 17–25.

Collins, A. M., & Loftus, E. F. (1975). A spreading-activation theory of semantic processing. *Psychological Review, 82,* 407–428.

Fazio, R. H. (1995). Attitudes as object–evaluation associations: Determinants, consequences, and correlates of attitude accessibility. In R. E. Petty & J. A. Krosnick (Eds.), *Attitude strength: Antecedents and consequences* (pp. 247–282). Hillsdale, NJ: Lawrence Erlbaum Associates.

Fazio, R. H., Chen, J. M., McDonel, E. C., & Sherman, S. J. (1982). Attitude accessibility, attitude–behavior consistency, and the strength of the object–evaluation association. *Journal of Experimental Social Psychology, 18,* 339–357.

Fazio, R. H., & Olson, M. A. (2003a). Implicit measures in social cognition research: Their meaning and use. *Annual Review of Psychology, 54,* 297–327.

Fazio, R. H., & Olson, M. A. (2003b). Reducing the influence of extrapersonal associations on the Implicit Association Test: Personalizing the IAT. *Journal of Personality and Social Psychology, 86*(5), 653–667.

Fishbein, M., & Ajzen, I. (1975). *Beliefs, attitude, intention and behavior: An introduction to theory and research.* Reading, MA: Addison-Wesley.

Forehand, M. R., & Perkins, A. (2004). Implicit assimilation and explicit contrast: A Set/Reset model of response to celebrity voiceovers. *Journal of Consumer Research.*

Fournier, S. (1998). Consumers and their brands: Developing relationship theory in consumer research. *Journal of Consumer Research, 24,* 343–373.

Gorn, G. J. (1982). The effects of music in advertising on choice behavior: A classical conditioning approach. *Journal of Marketing, 46,* 94–101.

Greenwald, A. G., Banaji, M. R., Rudman, L. A., Farnham, S. D., Nosek, B. A., & Mellott, D. S. (2002). A unified theory of implicit attitudes, stereotypes, self-esteem, and self-concept. *Psychological Review, 109*(1), 3–25.

Greenwald, A. G., McGhee, D. E., & Schwartz, J. L. K. (1998). Measuring individual differences in implicit cognition: The Implicit Association Test. *Journal of Personality and Social Psychology, 74,* 1464–1480.

Greenwald, A. G., Nosek, B. A., & Banaji, M. R. (2003). Understanding and using the Implicit Association Test: I. An improved scoring algorithm. *Journal of Personality and Social Psychology, 85*(2), 197–216.

Heider, F. (1958). *The psychology of interpersonal relations.* New York: Wiley.

Hong, S.-T., & Wyer, R. S., Jr. (1989). Effects of country-of-origin and product-attribute information on product evaluation: An information processing perspective. *Journal of Consumer Research, 16,* 175–187.

Hoyer, W. D., & MacInnis, D. J. (1997). *Consumer behavior.* Boston: Houghton Mifflin.

Janiszewski, C., & Van Osselaer, S. M. J. (2000). A connectionist model of brand–quality associations. *Journal of Marketing Research, 37,* 331–350.

Kardes, F. (1994). Consumer judgment and decision processes. In R. S. Wyer, Jr., & T. K. Srull (Eds.), *Handbook of social cognition: Vol. 2. Applications* (pp. 399–466). Hillsdale, NJ: Lawrence Erlbaum Associates.

Keller, K. L. (1993). Conceptualizing, measuring, and managing customer-based brand equity. *Journal of Marketing, 57*, 1–22.

Keller, K. L. (1998). *Strategic brand management.* Upper Saddle River, NJ: Prentice-Hall.

Kleine, S. S., Kleine, R. E., III, & Allen, C. T. (1995). How is a possession 'me' or 'not me'? Characterizing types and an antecedent of material possession attachment. *Journal of Consumer Research, 22*, 327–343.

LeClerc, F., Schmitt, B. H., & Dube, L. (1994). Foreign branding and its effect on product perceptions and attitudes. *Journal of Marketing Research, 31*, 263–270.

Loken, B., & Ward, J. (1990). Alternative approaches to understanding the determinants of typicality. *Journal of Consumer Research, 16*, 39–54.

MacKenzie, S. B., & Lutz, R. J. (1996). An empirical examination of the structural antecedents of attitude toward the ad in advertising pretesting context. *Journal of Marketing, 53*(2), 48–65.

MacKenzie, S. B., Lutz, R. J., & Belch, G. E. (1986). The role of attitude toward the ad as a mediator of advertising effectiveness: A test of competing explanations. *Journal of Marketing Research, 23*(2), 130–143.

Maheswaran, D. (1994). Country of origin as a stereotype: Effects of consumer expertise and attribute strength on product evaluations. *Journal of Consumer Research, 21*, 354–365.

Maison, D., Greenwald, A. G., & Bruin, R. H. (2004). Predictive validity of the Implicit Association Test in studies of brands, consumer attitudes, and behavior. *Journal of Consumer Psychology, 14*(4), 405–415.

McAlexander, J. H., Schouten, J. W., & Koenig, H. F. (2002). Building brand community. *Journal of Marketing, 66*(1), 38–54.

McSweeney, F. K., & Bierley, C. (1984). Recent developments in classical conditioning. *Journal of Consumer Research, 11*, 619–631.

Mitchell, A. A. (1986). The effect of verbal and visual components of advertisements on brand attitudes and attitude toward the advertisement. *Journal of Consumer Research, 13*(1), 12–24.

Mitchell, A. A., & Olson, J. C. (1981). Are product attribute beliefs the only mediator of advertising effects on brand attitude? *Journal of Marketing Research, 18*(3), 318–332.

Moon, Y. (2002). Personalization and personality: Some effects of customizing message style based on consumer personality. *Journal of Consumer Psychology, 12*(4), 313–325.

Muniz, A. M., Jr., & O'Guinn, T. C. (2001). Brand community. *Journal of Consumer Research, 27*(4), 412–432.

Nord, W. R., & Peter, J. P. (1980). A behavior modification perspective on marketing. *Journal of Marketing, 44*, 36–47.

Park, C. W., Jun, S. Y., & Shocker, A. D. (1996). Composite branding alliances: An investigation of extension and feedback effects. *Journal of Marketing Research, 33*(4), 453–466.

Peterson, R. A., & Jolibert, A. J. P. (1995). A meta-analysis of country-of-origin effects. *Journal of International Business Studies, 26*(4), 883–900.

Samu, S., Krishnan, H. S., & Smith, R. E. (1999). Using advertising alliances for new product introduction: Interactions between product complementarity and promotional strategies. *Journal of Marketing, 63*(1), 57–74.

Sen, S., & Johnson, E. J. (1997). Mere-possession effects without possession in consumer choice. *Journal of Consumer Research, 24*(1), 105–117.

Simonin, B. L., & Ruth, J. A. (1998). Is a company known by the company it keeps? Accessing the spillover effects of brand alliances on consumer brand attitudes. *Journal of Marketing Research, 35*, 30–42.

Sujan, M., Bettman, J. R., & Baumgartner, H. (1993). Influencing consumer judgments using autobiographical memories: A self-referencing perspective. *Journal of Marketing Research, 30*, 422–436.

Van Osselaer, S. M. J., & Janiszewski, C. (2001). Two ways of learning brand associations. *Journal of Consumer Research, 28*(2), 202–223.

Wyer, R. S., Jr., & Srull, T. K. (1989). Person memory and judgment. *Psychological Review, 96*(1), 58–83.

CHAPTER SEVEN

Advancing Theory on Consumer Plans, Actions, and How Marketing Information Affects Both

Roger March
University of New South Wales

Arch G. Woodside
Boston College

We explore consumer plans and actions from three perspectives. First, the influence of product information on both planned and realized consumption behavior is considered by grouping respondents into users and nonusers of product information and investigating possible differences in consumption patterns.

Second, changes that occur between planned and realized behavior are examined in the context of customer characteristics, such as product experience, income, and geographical origin. These two areas of inquiry represent the major managerial applications of this chapter.

Third, the chapter probes theory by applying Mintzberg's 1978 model of planned and unplanned organizational strategy to consumer strategies for the purchases of products and services (see Fig. 7.1). Heretofore, Mintzberg's (1978) model is untested in the consumer behavior academic literature. The model has two advantages for consumer behavior researchers: It offers a new technique for matching intentions to actual behavior, and, by extension, enables the identification of products whose actual consumption levels have failed to match the intended consumption levels. Most importantly, it offers a rich interpretation of how people behave.

The illustrated area of application (tourism behavior) is not the dominant fast moving consumer goods (FMCGs) focus found in the literature on planned and actual buyer behavior. Previous research into the intentions and consumption has overwhelmingly focused on planned behavior, or intentions, and specifically with two aims: to improve the use of intention measurement to improve the predictive power of future behavior and to influence purchase behavior. Although a multi-

FIG. 7.1.   Types of strategies. Source: Mintzberg (1978, p. 945).

tude of factors and situations interfere or constrain an individual's ability to act on his or her intentions (e.g., Belk, 1974, 1975; Filiatrault & Ritchie, 1988), intention is still an important construct found to be related to actual behavior.

Although an increasing number of scholars have developed an interest in impulse buying since the 1980s (Agee & Martin, 2001; Beatty & Ferrell, 1998; Dittmar, Beattie, & Friese, 1996; Gardner & Rook, 1988; Rook & Fisher, 1995; Weun, Jones, & Beatty, 1998), the characteristics and antecedents of unplanned behavior in the broader sense remain unexplored and unknown. Indeed, some scholars neglect to mention the subject altogether. East, for example, in his 1997 book on consumer behavior, makes no mention of the concept, although he briefly outlines compulsive shopping, a variation of the term. Table 7.1 summarizes the empirical research undertaken into unplanned and impulse-purchase behavior.

The complexity of the *unplanned* concept may be one of the reasons for this lack of interest. Behavior can be unplanned yet done, either in the form of impulse buying (e.g., purchase of a chocolate bar at the supermarket checkout counter) or (for the want of a better term) unplanned purchases (when knowledge of and interaction with the task environment and time pressure combine to force a decision that otherwise would have been foregone; see Bettman, 1979). To complicate matters more, not all impulse buying may be totally unplanned. Rook and Hoch (1985) found that some people "*plan* on being impulsive" as a shopping strategy (p. 25; emphasis added). Cobb and Hoyer (1986) drew an interesting distinction between impulse planners and partial planners. Although both cohorts appear to be impulse purchasers because they delay brand decisions until entering the consumption environment, impulse planners act almost entirely in a spontaneous manner, whereas partial planners exhibited careful in-site purchase behavior and were price sensitive.

Unplanned behavior may also be unplanned and not done, as conceptualized in the Mintzberg matrix. Three scenarios are possible: The product may have been considered and rejected, it may have not been considered and rejected, or it may have not entered the consumer's awareness set. Reflecting on Weick's approach

TABLE 7.1

Summary of Empirical Research on Unplanned and Impulse Purchasing

Investigator(s)	Percent of Unplanned Purchases	Research Setting	Tested for Influence of		Identified Precursor Variables of Unplanned or Impulse Behavior
			Product Information	Demographics	
Clover, 1950	60–15	19 store types	No	No	Unplanned purchases differed across product category
West, 1951	44/27/42	Grocery, drug, variety	No	No	Shelf space
Cox, 1964	n.a.	Supermarket	No	No	Display location
Kelly, 1965	n.a.	Supermarket	No	No	Unplanned purchases increased with money spent and size of shopping list
Kollat & Willett, 1967	50.5	Supermarket	No	Income/education/ occupation	Low level of brand awareness indicates propensity for unplanned purchases
Williams & Dardis, 1972	33/37/31	Specialty/department/variety	No	Income/gender	The greater the transaction size, the more likely are unplanned purchases
Prasad, 1975	35.3/62.4	Department/discount stores	No	Income/education	
Bellenger, Robertson, & Hirschman, 1978	38.7	Supermarket	No	Age/race/gender	Age and race were significant for certain product lines
McGoldrick, 1982	7	Pharmacies	No	No	In-store displays
Cobb & Hoyer, 1986	12	Supermarket	No	Age/sex/house-hold size	Gender (males more likely to make unplanned purchases)
Rook & Fisher, 1995	n.a	CD retail store purchases	No	No	Normative evaluations influence subsequent impulse buying behavior
Dittmar et al., 1996	n.a.	Survey of shopping habits	No	Yes	Attitudes to shops and gender were key variables
Beatty & Ferrell, 1998	n.a.	Recall of recent shopping trip	No	No	Time in store; enjoyment of shopping; impulse buying tendency
Bayley & Nancarrow, 1998	n.a.	Survey of product items	No	No	Sociopsychological models developed to explain impulse purchase behavior
Weun et al., 1998	n.a.	Develop and test an instrument to predict impulse purchases	No	No	Antecedents of impulse behavior were not investigated
Agee & Martin, 2001	n.a.	Purchasing from infomercials	Yes	Yes	Exposure to advertising increases likelihood of purchase; only demographic to influence purchase was age of children

to intention–behavior dichotomy, Bettman, Luce, and Payne (1998) highlighted a growing belief among consumer-decision researchers that preferences for options of any complexity or novelty are often constructed and not simply revealed in making a decision. They cite the analogy used by Gregory, Lichenstein, and Slovic (1993) whereby consumer preference formation is "more like architecture, building some defensible set of values, rather than archaeology, uncovering values that are already there" (p. 181). Little wonder therefore that Rook and Gardner (1993) concluded that impulse buying is still in a relatively immature state, especially compared to other areas of consumer research, such as attitude research (Beatty & Ferrell, 1998).

As Table 7.1 indicates, previous research into the nature of planned, unplanned and actual consumption has happened mainly in the supermarket setting. Key findings are summarized now:

- Despite the large number of items that customers usually intend buying in supermarkets, Peterson (1987) found that just 30% of shoppers made shopping lists (cited by Shapiro & Krishnan, 1999).
- The incidence of unplanned purchases rises with the size of the shopping bill and the numbers of items purchased (Kollett & Willett, 1967; Prasad, 1975).
- Because supermarkets often require a high degree of searching and scanning for desired items, the likelihood of the customer being distracted and engaging in unplanned purchase behavior is increased. Most of this scanning is done completely subconsciously by the peripheral vision, which sifts out those items that are worthy of closer scrutiny (Bruce & Green, 1991).

BUILDING FROM THE WORK OF MINTZBERG

Mintzberg (1978) proposed a model to illustrate the relationship between planned behavior and behavioral outcomes (see Fig. 7.1). Mintzberg explored planning and outcomes as they related to organizations in pursuit of strategic goals. Although he never subsequently attempted to empirically verify his parsimonious model, Mintzberg's conceptual contribution is useful if untested. He was the first to illustrate the variety of outcomes—planned and unplanned—that arise from intended and unintended actions.

Mintzberg identifies three main types of strategies: *deliberate* strategies that are planned and enacted and *emergent* strategies that occur even though they were not intended (both of these he termed *realized* strategies), and *unrealized* strategies that are planned but not enacted. Of these, Mintzberg suggests deliberate strategies are the most commonly examined in the management-planning literature (Mintzberg, 1994). His third case, emergent strategy, where a realized "pattern" was not intended, has been of less interest to researchers and practitioners. Deliberate strategies will hereinafter be called realized. We believe that the term better embodies the twin notions of both planning and completion. According to *The Australian Oxford Dictionary* (Moore, 2004, p. 349), *deliberate* is defined as *intentional*, a term that focuses more on the cognitive decision to act and less on the process that culminates in the act being carried out. *Realized* more appropriately emphasizes an end result rather than *deliberate*, which, notwithstanding Mintzberg's own views, focuses more on the initial act rather than the culmination of behavioral actions.

We now add a fourth behavioral category. Termed *unplanned/not done* behavior, it refers to, as the name suggests, outcomes that are neither planned nor done; these four possible outcomes are illustrated in Fig. 7.2. The importance of this fourth outcome lies in the implications it has for organizations when their marketing communications elicit such nonresponse from consumers. The need for management to identify and understand behavior that is both unplanned and not realized is, arguably, as important as that for purchases that are planned and carried out. Put another way, the customer that organizations do not have may be its most important. But even this hitherto ignored outcome of *unplanned/not done* has a further dimension: Consumers may have considered the product but rejected it, or they may have not considered it and therefore rejected it. Clearly, a firm's understanding of its existing and potential customers would be enhanced by insights into the factors underlying rejection of its product at the planning and the actual consumption stage.

Consider Mintzberg's three strategies in the consumer context. Deliberate strategies are self-explanatory and need little comment. Everyday we decide on and then enact a range of consumption behavior, from buying morning coffee to filling the tank with gas on the way home from work. Similarly, unrealized strategies are not uncommon. We plan to go shopping at lunchtime only to have an urgent job at work intervene and cause postponement of the shopping. Or a decision to buy a new Sony™ stereo system is changed after finding information about a less expensive and seemingly equally good system from Panasonic™. (For the

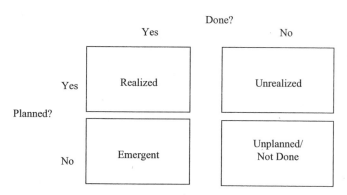

FIG. 7.2. The planned and done strategy grid: realized, emergent, unrealized, and unplanned/not done strategies.

present purposes, it is does not matter whether the unrealized action relates to a product category or brand.) Emergent strategies, which occur when unplanned behavior is enacted, most commonly take the form of impulse purchasing in consumer-shopping situations. As was discussed earlier, no empirical research has been undertaken beyond this research setting.

To summarize therefore, Mintzberg's work offers both conceptual and managerial insights for the marketing discipline. In terms of theoretical development, his typology can be applied to individual consumer behavior as well as to its original context, organizational behavior. Just as he extended the conceptualization of strategy in the management domain, marketers can generate deeper insights into consumer planning and implementation of consumption intentions by "teasing out" the influences that explain the shifts that occur between the expression of intention and the performance of consumption behavior (cf. Engel, Blackwell, & Miniard, 1993; Howard & Sheth, 1969; Peter & Olson, 1999). Logic suggests that it is conceivable for individuals not to succeed in pursuing the strategies they intended. Equally, it is probable that individuals end up pursuing strategies they never envisaged. What it adds is the notion that an intention is a preliminary stage of a process that may or may not culminate in a consumption behavior.

Managerially, the model provides marketing strategists a strategic tool that facilitates a richer understanding of reasons for a product's lack of appeal in the marketplace. The Mintzberg grid can be used to classify products of an organization's product mix by comparing the amount of intended consumption of each product with the amount that was actually consumed; then generating an arithmetic measure for each product to represent that difference; and finally using that measure to allocate each product to one of the four consumption-behavioral outcomes. The differences between intentions and actual consumption behavior require greater attention for several reasons. First, there is a need to more accurately identify and quantify the intervening and unforeseen factors that divert intentions away from eventual behavioral outcomes. Lilien, Kotler, and Moorthy (1992), in a review of marketing models, argued that there is a lack of exploration into the mechanisms that underlie the link between intentions and behavior. More recently, Shapiro and Krishnan (1999) argued that memory represents an intervening variable between intention formation and behavior, and not only one antecedent of intentions.

Second, given differences in intention–behavior link between durables and low-involvement products (Kalwani & Silk, 1982), the typical consumer-behavior model may not capture the dynamics of consumption behavior in, for example, a services context (cf. Hawkins & Hoch, 1992). Morwitz (1997b), for example, has shown that the intention–behavior relationship will differ across product types.

Third, Morwitz (1997a) urged further research into factors that moderate the relationship between intention and behavior in consumption environments that entail a sequence of transactions or a bundle of products. Fourth, limiting research to prepurchase settings (as often occurs) can understate the amount and influence of information that customers have at their disposal at the time of actual purchase (Bloch, Sherrell, & Ridgway, 1986). Fifth, an increasingly prominent theme in recent behavioral-decision research is that preferences are—rather than retrieved from memory and real experience—often constructed when consumers need to choose one alternative from a set of alternative products, services, or courses of action (Bettman et al., 1998; Kardes, 1994). Sixth, there is a need to improve our understanding of the influence of information on consumer behavior (Bettman & Park, 1980). Prior information is obviously very useful in narrowing the scope of the choice task early in the decision process by allowing the consumer to focus on certain brands and attributes. Lastly, unforeseen situational opportunities and constraints arise, which are extremely difficult to predict (Belk, 1975).

PLANNED, UNPLANNED AND REALIZED BEHAVIOR
IN LEISURE & TOURISM

Because the focus of this chapter is consumption (and nonconsumption) undertaken by tourists in a tourism destination, we turn to the tourism and leisure literature for further theoretical or empirical insights. Unfortunately, work carried out in these academic domains reveals a similar scarcity in identifying the influences on either unplanned or planned behavior. In an exhaustive review of research in leisure and tourism, Ritchie (1994) lamented the lack of attention paid to the context of decision making in consumer behavior, whereas Otto and Ritchie (1996) highlighted the challenge of examining consumer behavior in the tourism setting.

Young and Kent (1985) examined planned and actual behavior related to leisure campers, and found that intentions were slightly more influenced by the respondents' motivations than by the composition of the social group with which they were traveling. Crotts and Reid (1993) found that most visitors to Alachuca County in Florida had decided on recreational activities prior to arrival. Those travelers who made activity decisions after arrival were typically long-haul, international visitors. In Tsang's (1993) survey of information-search and travel-planning behavior of international visitors to New Zealand, over 40% of respondents indicated they preplanned no vacation activities (cited by Hyde, 2000). Only a minority of visitors had preplanned their length of stay in each subdestination within New Zealand.

Jeng (1997) asked respondents to imagine a 2- to 4-day domestic-vacation trip, and consider what elements they might plan before departure. He identified a set of core subdecisions made before departure, including date of trip, primary destination, location of overnight stay, and travel route. He went on to identify a set of secondary subdecisions, made before departure but considered to be flexible, including choice of attractions and activities. This subset made way for a third set of *en route* decisions, including where to dine, where to shop, and where to stop and rest. The one important caveat in this study was that dependents were asked to consider a short domestic trip, not an overseas one. Stewart and Vogt (1999) adopted a case-based decision theory to understand how consumers plan for, and actuate, vacation travel. This approach assumes that consumers deal with uncertainty by basing their judgments of the current situation (or alternatives) on similar cases they have encountered previously—in other words, on past experience. The tourist plans for a series of activities and experiences for a future trip, but while he/she is on-site, a cycle of actuation-failure-revision-actuation occurs. Intuitively, this scenario approximates the complex process by which many of us decide on plans, and then alter, abandon, or implement them.

Perdue (1986) touched on the subject in a modest investigation that sought to empirically verify the proposition that unplanned yet realized behavior yielded higher spending than unplanned and unrealized behavior. He found that consumers who purchase a product that they had not planned for are likely to express satisfaction with the product as a means of justifying the purchase to themselves and other members of their traveling party.

Ajzen and Driver (1992) used leisure activities as the research setting for testing the theory of planned behavior. They found that the theory was useful in predicting influences on intentions and actual behavior from intentions. The research had the limitation of being confined to college students and only five leisure activities were studied. Existing models of decision behavior such as theory of planned behavior (TPB) have been developed for tangible products, rather than intangible services such as tourism products. The tourism product is an experiential product with emotional undertones whose decision process differs vastly from the rational, problem-solving scenario applied to many tangible products. Mayo and Jarvis (1990) argued "travel is a special form of consumption behavior involving an intangible, heterogeneous purchase of an experiential product" (cited in Gilbert, 1991, p. 98). As a consequence, existing models omit important realities of tourist behavior. To cite Um and Crompton (1990): "It should be noted that perceptions of alternative destinations' physical attributes in the awareness set . . . are susceptible to change during the period of active solicitation of information stimulated by an intention to select a travel destination" (p. 437).

Finally, several writers argue that the benefits realized from a consumption experience may be more useful to understand than the benefits that consumers say they intend to seek (Dann, 1981; Pearce & Caltabiano, 1983; Shoemaker, 1994; Woodside & Jacobs, 1985). Research that investigates the process by which intentions are actualized into actual behavior and elucidates the influences that result in unplanned as well as planned behavior has a valuable contribution to make to the marketing discipline. Vacation space (or any leisure environment), by its very nature, encourages the consumer to engage in spontaneous consumption behavior. The decision task environment in the tourist consumption system is complex and the decision process that tourists initiate can be highly arbitrary (Zajonc & Markus, 1982). Society's norms embodying rational behavior are weakened, to be replaced by stimulus-seeking behavior; and the imperatives on fiscal rectitude fewer. So irrational is much of tourist behavior that some scholars portray it as "play" (Berlyne, 1960, cited by Godbey & Graefe, 1991; Graburn, 1977) whereas others have conceptualized it as "novelty seeking" (Cohen, 1972; Crompton, 1979; Dann, 1981; Plog, 1974) and sought empirical testing of the concept (see, e.g., Basala & Klenosky, 2001; Mo, Howard, & Havitz, 1993; Snepenger, 1987; Yiannakis & Gibson, 1992). Parr (1989) summed it up: ". . . some [travelers] had little idea of what they wanted to see and do . . . Some people enjoyed the element of the unknown . . . they felt they were on an adventure, full of surprises and spontaneity" (p. 194). In short, impulsiveness is okay when you're having fun. This premeditated "irrational" dimension of the tourist/leisure experience contrasts starkly with the supermarket or shopping-mall environment investigated by Rook and Fisher (1995) where consumers are more likely to experience, monitor, and evaluate buying impulses. Although the prevalence of unplanned behavior, regardless of dimension, may be greater in these environments, the usefulness and strategic importance of better understanding the nature of unplanned consumption activities in tourist and leisure environments is without question.

This chapter focuses on: (a) the differences between planned and realized discretionary tourism behavior, (b) the influence of product information on planned and realized tourism behavior, and (c) the influence of customer characteristics on planned and realized tourism behavior.

RELATIONSHIP BETWEEN PLANNED AND REALIZED CONSUMPTION BEHAVIOR

Investigating the discrepancies between planned and realized consumption activities is the core research focus here. Six consumption behaviors common to the tourism & leisure experience are used as dependent variables: spending (planned budget vs. actual money spent), length of stay in the destination (planned number of days vs. actual days stayed), attractions (planned to visit and actually visited), destinations (planned to visit and actually visited), accommodations (planned to use and actually used), and activities (planned and actually carried out). A starting point for our investigation is whether consumers will, overall, consume or spend more or less than they plan. An obvious enough question perhaps, but few studies have sought an answer. In a pioneering study, Kollat and Willett (1967) concluded, "There is a strong tendency for actual expenditure to approximate spending intentions" (p. 29) and that shoppers are "more likely to spend less than they anticipated than they are to spend more than planned" (p. 30). They surmise, "that measured purchase intentions should correspond more closely to actual purchase intentions when the customers' time and effort are minimized" (p. 29). Taken at face value, this early finding is puzzling. How could consumers engage in unplanned purchases and adhere to their intended budget—unless they abandon

some planned purchases? In the absence of evidence that people abandon significant amounts of purchases to compensate for their unplanned-purchase behavior,
it would seem likely that spending intentions are exceeded, to varying degrees, by
actual expenditures. Indeed, the work of Abratt and Goodey (1990) confirmed
this logic. In their study of supermarket-shopping behavior, 41% of respondents
reported that they had spent more than their expressed spending intention, which
suggests, "the proposition that consumers tend to spend more than they planned
may hold" (p. 119).

Pertinent to this research setting is the vacation planning study of Hyde (2000).
Hyde's work was the only longitudinal study examining the differences between
travelers' plans and their eventual behavior. He reported several interesting findings related to the present investigation: (a) respondents had fewer than seven specific planned elements in their planning and that almost half were subdestinations
(and this despite the fact that travelers' vacations had a mean of 33 elements); (b)
few attractions or activities had been planned; and (c) a minority of travel parties
had a preplanned travel route. He found that of the vacation elements that travelers had specifically planned, a large proportion—a mean of 73%—were actioned.
(It should be noted that a limitation of his work was the small qualitative sample
of 20 travel parties; all respondents were first-time visitors, none of whom were
visiting friends or relatives.) Based on the preceding discussion, the following
proposition is now formally stated:

P_1:   Realized consumption behavior is greater than planned for most specific services related to a purchased service system.

Numerous studies in the marketing field examined the relationship between
planned purchases and actual purchase behavior (Manski, 1990; Warshaw, 1980;
Young, DeSarbo, & Morwitz, 1998). Although the observed relationships are
generally positive, the strength of the relationship has differed from study to
study, depending on the contingencies inherent in the research setting. Three contingencies critical in tourist behavior and consumption plans are product experience, motivation and, in the tourist consumption system, composition of the travel
party.

Past experience affects consumers' plans (Fazio & Zanna, 1981; Morwitz &
Schmittlein, 1992). Product experience is critical when studying the dynamic
choice processes of consumers new to a market (Heilman, Bowman, & Wright,
2000). Experience teaches people how to plan and that the actual behavior of consumers with product experience will more closely approximate their plans than
consumers with no or little product knowledge (Stewart & Vogt, 1999). Routine
and habitual buyer behavior allows for purposeful and intelligent behavior without deliberation (Katona, 1975). Visitors who vacation at the same place regularly
are likely to engage in little prearrival planning, relying instead on their accumulated knowledge and experience from previous visits (Fodness & Murray, 1999).

Underlying motivations have a significant influence on the traveler's behavior (Morrison, 1996). Travelers visiting friends or relatives are more likely to rely on the advice of their hosts, less likely to use product information, and therefore more likely to deviate between planned and eventual behavior (Gitelson & Crompton, 1983). Leisure travelers, on the other hand, are more likely to engage in prearrival planning by obtaining information, particularly if they are first-time visitors. Novelty seekers, operationalized in this study as seekers of new culture, tend to seek more information, to undertake more activities, but also to engage in more unplanned activities (Gitelson & Crompton, 1983), in contrast to visitors seeking familiarity in the destination, whose behavior are more likely to approximate their eventual behavior.

In the general marketing environment, the social setting (presence or absence of others) that characterizes the consumption of a product or service influences both planned and actual behavior, as it does other consumer behavior (Stayman & Deshplande, 1989). Fisher (2001) found that greater collaboration led to higher decision quality and smaller deviations between consumers' planned and actual expenditures. In leisure settings, the behavior of travelers is heavily influenced by the composition of the traveling party (McIntosh & Goeldner, 1990). Leisure travel is a product that is jointly consumed, and leisure travel activities reflect the influence of—directly and indirectly—all those traveling together (Chadwick, 1987). This phenomenon is particularly noticeable when children are present (or absent). It is safe to assume that traveling with children in a tourist destination requires greater planning and forethought than is required by couples or tourists traveling alone. Therefore, groups with children are likely to plan their trip itinerary prior to, rather than after, arrival in the destination (Fodness & Murray, 1999). Also, large travel parties comprising friends require greater coordination in order to meet differential needs than will couples or individuals traveling alone.

In the context of contingencies, the following proposition is now formally stated based on the foregoing discussion:

P_2: The level of matching between planned and realized actions varies as a function of contingency factors: composition of travel party, product experience, and motivations. (a) For composition of travel party, the fewer the number of members, the more likely will planned behavior match actual behavior; (b) For product experience, the greater the experience, the more likely will planned behavior match actual behavior; (c) For motivation, the planned behavior of novelty-seeking individuals will be less likely to match their actual behavior, whereas the planned behavior of familiarity-seeking individuals will be more likely to match their actual behavior.

The third proposition related to this section examines the relationship between shifts in planned and realized behavior according to increases in the time spent in the consumption system. Although research into time pressure effects has a long and deep history in both economics and psychology (Bishop & Witt, 1970; Hendrick, Mills, & Kiesler, 1968; Wright, 1974), consumer researchers arrived late to the topic (Feldman & Hornik, 1981; Gross, 1994; Hornik, 1982; Iyer, 1989; Leclerc, Schmitt, & Dube, 1995; Nickols & Fox, 1983). Howard and Sheth (1969) included time pressure as an exogenous variable in their classic, *The Theory of Buyer Behavior*, and they commented that little was known about it. Writing in the marketing literature, Jacoby, Szybillo, and Berning (1976) provided an excellent synthesis of work in the field, but felt compelled to subtitle their paper, "An Interdisciplinary Overview," due to the "scant attention" (p. 320) the topic had received in the marketing field. Payne, Bettman, and Johnson (1987, cited in Iyer, 1989) alluded to, but did not examine, the time variable in a conference paper. Time has been shown to constrain unplanned purchases (Iyer, 1989) whereas time availability was linked to search activity in a retail setting (Beatty & Smith, 1987). Iyer (1989) found that time pressure, and the lack thereof, reduced unplanned purchases. In the tourism literature, determinants of planning time have been investigated (Zalatan, 1996), but the interaction between time in the consumption system and consumption behavior has not. In this study, time is operationalized as *length of stay* and categorized as a *contingency influence*.

All other things being equal, we may assume that the longer the length of stay, the greater is the likelihood that individuals will engage in unplanned behavior. In one study, Beatty and Ferrell (1998) treated time available as an external exogenous variable (along with budget available). In this study however, because our main focus is to identify the characteristics of individuals engaged in planned, unplanned, and actual consumption, time is defined as *length of stay in the destination* and treated as a dependent variable.

Kollat and Willett's (1967) research suggested that unplanned purchases were more likely to occur on a large shopping (grocery) trip than on a small one to buy just a few items. (This finding was confirmed years later by Inman & Winer, 1998.) Prasad (1975) found that the level of unplanned purchases increased with the size of the shopper's total transaction. Beatty and Ferrell (1998) found that *time available*, an exogenous variable, was particularly influential in the length of time devoted to browsing and purchasing. Based on the preceding discussion, the following proposition is formally stated:

P₃: Increases in length of stay in a destination region for planned and realized behavior relate to increases in the number of destination-area consumption activities, although the increase in the number of activities by length of stay is greater for realized rather than for planned behavior.

The ability of individuals to anticipate outcomes is related to the availability of information, as well as to the individual's cognitive abilities. If information is available in the consumption environment, *ceteris paribus*, the more accurately individuals should be able to anticipate their future outcomes; conversely, the absence of information heightens uncertainty and makes decision making more difficult and the outcomes less predictable. Although marketing communications are widely assumed to have a positive impact on consumption behavior, the extent of the influence has long been debated. The supply of tourist information, typically in the form of a visitor information guide (VIG), is a critical element of the communication strategy of tourism marketing organizations. The VIG is important for three reasons: first, because a leisure trip is a high-risk purchase, involving the use of discretionary dollars, a VIG serves to reassure the consumer that his/her decision is the correct one; second, because the intangibility of the tourism product means that the consumer is heavily reliant on information, whether it be printed, word-of-mouth, or electronic; and third, because the majority of holiday makers visiting a particular place are likely to be first-time visitors, information about the destination is essential (Wicks & Schuett, 1991).

Despite this importance, little research has been undertaken in the tourism field to substantiate the widespread belief that visitors who use printed information will, all other things being equal, consume more than those visitors who do not. Ritchie (1994) lamented, "[W]e are still far from a clear understanding of the effectiveness of the various forms of advertising and promotion which are used so extensively by tourism marketers" (p. 10). For example, although the investigation of trip-planning behavior was a main research objective of the authors' research into travel preferences of the U.S. outbound travel market, Rao, Thomas, and Javalgi (1992) did not ask respondents the degree to which different information sources influenced their trip decisions. Fesenmaier, Vogt, and Stewart (1993) examined the influence of information on future travel plans (defined as trip purpose, travel route, and information search strategies), and although the impact of information on the actual behavior was neglected, general support was found for their propositions. In a related study, Fodness and Murray (1999) identified a strong correlation between the number of information sources accessed and the length of stay, and the number of information sources accessed and overall spending. Little wonder, therefore, that in his study of VIGs produced by regional tourism bodies (RTBs) in the United Kingdom, Alford (1998) concluded that although the guides "represent a major slice of the RTB marketing budget, [the RTBs] have little means of gauging the effectiveness of this publication, other than receiving general feedback from suppliers, distributors, and information gathered through surveys" (p. 67). Co-authors of one of the most recent studies of tourist information search and usage drew the conclusion that "additional research on tourist information search is needed in many areas" (Fodness & Murray, 1999, p. 229).

Destination marketing organizations need to better understand the extent to which printed information influences consumer choices and consumption outcomes. As studies have shown, the more activities and opportunities an individual is aware of at the intended destination, the greater is the individual's likely level of consumption (Chadwick, 1987; McIntosh & Goeldner, 1990; Moutinho, 1987). In addition, Etzel and Wahlers (1985) reported a positive relationship between increasing levels of information search and increasing travel expenditures. One of the core propositions is that product information significantly increases the level of consumption behavior undertaken by consumers, relative to those individuals who do not receive product information. When this assumption is applied to the proposition generated earlier, that realized behavior exceeds planned behavior, we can postulate that the consumers who have received versus have not received the VIG and who have completed their visit to the destination report higher consumption behavior.

Based on the foregoing discussion, the following propositions are offered:

P₄: Consumers with product information are more likely to both plan and engage in more tourist consumption behavior than those without product information (see Fig. 7.3, Panel A).

P₅: Consumers use product information more while in the consumption site than prior to entering the consumption site (see Fig. 7.3, Panel B).

P₆: Consumers who use product information plan and report higher consumption behavior (such as spending and length of stay) than consumers who do not use product information (see Fig. 7.3, Panel C).

Studies have shown that experience of the destination plays a significant role in various aspects of travel planning and activities, including information use (Etzel & Wahlers, 1985), time spent planning (Zalatan, 1996), and destination attractiveness (Hu & Ritchie, 1993).

Although conventional wisdom suggests that consumers with little or no product experience are likely to require and seek more information than experienced consumers, Bettman and Park (1980) argued that consumers with little prior knowledge will engage in less information search if the nature of the search task appears overwhelming. Individuals in the exit survey who received the VIG are likely to record the highest number of (realized) activities, while their counterparts in the entry survey who did not receive the VIG will register the smallest number of (planned) activities.

The foregoing discussion results in the following proposition:

P₇: Within a given time period (period the consumer is in the tourism destination), first-time consumers planning and actually doing the trip use product information more than experienced consumers (see Fig. 7.3, Panel D).

Famous destinations and major tourist attractions benefit, by definition, from high brand awareness. Iconic attractions are "pull factors," or motivators that influence tourists to visit. Information plays a minor role in prompting purchase or visit. For example, for visitors to Prince Edward Island, the home of *Anne of Green Gables*, Charlottetown, is the island province's major (and probably only) icon. Conversely, unknown destinations require information to generate visita-

Tourist Activities   Percent Using Product Information

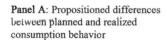

Panel A: Propositioned differences between planned and realized consumption behavior

Panel B: Propositioned differences between planned and realized use of information

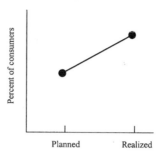

Spending   Use of VIG by Experience

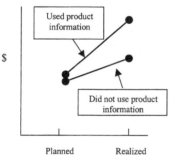

Panel C: Propositioned differences between planned and realized spending according to use of information

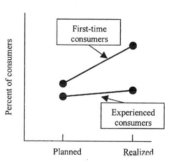

Panel D: Propositioned differences between planned and realized use of information according to product experience

FIG. 7.3.   Impact of product information on planned and realized consumption behaviors (Panels A–E).

tion. For that reason, consumers exposed to product information are more likely to visit unknown places than consumers not exposed to such information.

P8:   The more unknown an attraction is, the greater the influence of product information about that attraction on planning and actual consumption of the experience.

This examination informs our understanding of how customer characteristics shape both planned and unplanned consumption behavior. One of the main shortcomings in research on unplanned consumption has been the inadequate consideration of consumer characteristics. As Table 7.1 reveals, only five empirical studies on the subject of planned and unplanned behavior incorporate demographics or other consumer characteristics. Cobb and Hoyer (1986) felt sufficiently concerned about the neglect of research into customer characteristics associated with unplanned and impulse purchasing that they labeled it a "shortcoming" (p. 389). From a strategic marketing viewpoint, understanding the characteristics of target segments is fundamental in creating an effective communication mix.

The relationship between distance traveled and behavior is especially pertinent in the tourism context. There are a number of perspectives. First, the distance traveled to a consumption site has been used as a surrogate for risk in previous marketing studies, namely, Newman and Staelin's (1974) study of information-seeking behavior related to new cars and household durables, and the tourism-related study by Fesenmaier and Johnson (1989) into involvement in the vacation-planning process. These investigations suggest that individuals traveling long distances will plan more due to higher perceived risk associated with the distance involved. Schul and Crompton (1983) confirmed this: "information search [is] likely to be greater for major (that is long-distance travel) rather than minor (short-distance) investments" (p. 25). Greater planning may suggest that eventual behavior will more likely match intended behavior. On the other hand, the very fact that long distances are required are likely to compel consumers to purchase low-risk package tours, rather than attempt to make their own travel arrangements.

P9:   The greater the distance that consumers travel to engage in destination-specific consumption activities, the greater the difference in expenditures between planned and realized activities.

The influence of experience on planned and actual behavior is a fascinating area of our study. Research shows that intention formation is affected by past experience (Fazio & Zanna, 1981; Morwitz & Schmittlein, 1992). Product experience is critical when studying the dynamic choice processes of consumers new to a market (Heilman et al., 2000). Because experience teaches people how to plan, the consumption actions of experienced consumers will more closely approximate their plans than consumers with little or no product knowledge (Stewart & Vogt, 1999). Routine and habitual buyer behavior allows for purposeful and intelligent behavior without deliberation (Katona, 1975). Experienced consumers should be better able to assess the risks associated with engaging in particular behavior and to understand the factors that will influence the decision than less-experienced consumers. For example, how long it takes to drive to particular destinations on an island, which route offers the best scenery, which attractions are worth spending time and money on, and what accommodation is of value for the money are all questions more readily answered by the experienced rather than the inexperienced visitor. Consequently, proposition P10 states that experienced consumers differ from inexperienced consumers in two ways: They plan fewer consumption activities and the difference between planned and realized consumption activities will be less for experienced consumers than for inexperienced consumers.

P_{10}:   Experienced consumers plan fewer consumption activities and are less likely to engage in unplanned activities compared to inexperienced consumers.

Product experience in this study relates to the number of times a respondent has visited Prince Edward Island. Consumers with previous experience should have more accurate predictions of whether or not they will engage in particular future behavior than consumers with little or no experience. Again, experienced consumers should be better able to assess the risks associated with engaging in particular behavior and to understand the factors that will influence the decision than less experienced consumers. For example, how long it takes to drive to particular destinations on the island, which route offers the best scenery, which attractions are worth spending time and money on, and what accommodation is of value for the money are all questions more readily answered by the experienced rather than the inexperienced tourist.

Experienced shoppers in a supermarket environment, for instance, were found to repeat the same choice as the previous consumption experience and to have well-articulated preferences when they are familiar with the preference object (Bettman et al., 1998). Morwitz and Schmittlein (1992) found that past usage of a durable good moderated the accuracy of future purchase intentions. Among individuals who stated an intention to purchase a personal computer (PC) in the following 6 months, 48% of those with experience of a PC fulfilled their intentions, whereas only 29% with no experience fulfilled their intentions. Similarly, Verplanken, Aarts, and van Knippenberg (1997) reported that respondents who frequently performed a certain behavior (a particular mode of transport) searched for less information about which travel mode to use and were more likely to focus on information about the habitual choice than alternative choices, compared to those who less frequently performed the behavior. Past behavior therefore acts as an internal source of information. And as consumers' experience with a product increases, consideration sets are likely to be increasingly stable over time (Klenosky & Rethans, 1988; Mitra, 1995). This would suggest that first-time customers would display less consistency that will, in return, be reflected in greater discrepancies between planned and actual behavior. Aarts, Verplanken, and van Knippenberg (1998) argued that habitual behavior become capable of being automatically activated by features of the situation and context in which the behavior occurs.

Much of the consumer research in this area has dealt with product brands rather than product categories. Brand loyalty and awareness become, therefore, critical issues for the researcher to understand. But what of product categories that lack powerful brands—or in situations when the powerful brands are simply not available? If we consider the variety of typical leisure consumption activities in a destination such as Prince Edward Island, few involve products with which travelers register any brand recognition whatsoever. There are no international hotel chains such as Hilton and Sheraton, and no famous natural or man-made attractions such as Canadian Rockies or Disneyland, and no famous restaurants. The only study adopting this perspective found that preference reversals are less prevalent for familiar product categories (Coupey, Irwin, & Payne, 1996). Given the large amount of consumption occurring in product categories in which brands are not important, this finding needs to be verified.

As discussed earlier, the influences on unplanned purchasing that have been identified include characteristics of the shopping party (Kollat & Willett, 1967), personality traits (Raju, 1980), and proclivity to visit stores (Granbois, 1968). Neither Kollat and Willett (1967) nor Prasad (1975) found that socioeconomic characteristics were a significant explanatory factor in shoppers performing unplanned buying behavior. Supporting the argument that inexperience and information-seeking behavior are positively related is the finding by Bloch, Sherrell, and Ridgway (1986) who, in investigating consumer search procedures for clothing and PCs, found that heavy searchers were heavy spenders within the product class. Higher spending was associated with higher product awareness and frequent contact with information providers and retailers. (They also identified two types of searchers: ongoing/hedonistic searchers and prepurchase searchers. Hedonistic searchers enjoyed the activity of seeking out information, perhaps even more than any actual consumption experience.)

Within the tourism literature, customer experience is commonly defined as whether the visitor is a first-time or repeat traveler. Similar to other consumption systems, it is assumed that first-time visitors to a destination have little product knowledge and will likely therefore spend more than their experienced counterparts. Woodside, Trappey, and MacDonald (1997), for instance, supported findings in other fields that experienced consumers undertake fewer consumption activities than inexperienced ones. Etzel and Wahlers (1985) sought to identify the characteristics of people who request travel information and those who do not. Several interesting findings emerged: First, information seekers tend to spend more than consumers who do not seek out information; second, the greater the frequency in product consumption, the less likely consumers would seek information; and third, experienced travelers were more likely to request information. However, a major weakness in the study was the assumption that request for information equated with information used and, ultimately, actual behavior.

The influence of experience on consumption behavior in the travel context is well documented. Studies show product experience of the destination plays a significant role in various aspects of travel planning and activities, including information use (Etzel & Wahlers, 1985); time spent planning (Zalatan, 1996); risk perception (Roehl & Fesenmaier, 1992); site choice (McFarlane et al., 1998); destination attractiveness (Hu & Ritchie, 1993); and satisfaction with a destination (Mazursky, 1989).

P_{11}:   Experienced consumers are less likely to engage in unplanned activities compared to inexperienced consumers.

Attitudes toward planning differ between individuals. For some individuals, the planning of holidays, including the collection of vast amounts of information, is an integral part of the whole experience; for others, a holiday is a spontaneous experience, in which predetermined activities and time allocations are an anathema; and there are many individuals who fit somewhere in between. Greater planning of a holiday would, arguably, reflect greater involvement and commitment in the destination, which would then be reflected in higher expenditures. Vacation behavior has been shown to differ according to specific sociodemographic variables (Gitelson & Kerstetter, 1990). Morwitz and Schmittlein (1992) suggested that economic factors such as wealth will increase the likelihood of intentions matching actual behavior. On the other hand, individuals with greater discretionary income would presumably be capable of engaging in a greater degree of unplanned, impulsive consumption.

P_{12}:   The higher the income level and therefore the greater ability to undertake consumption behavior, the greater the likelihood of unplanned consumption activity.

Early research in the tourism and leisure field flagged the association between social context and the individual's decision process. Burch (1969) was one of the earliest to discuss the importance of the social group in relation to recreation and tourist behavior. His personal community proposition suggested that such behavior is seldom an isolated individual decision. Christensen and Yoesting (1973) confirmed his thesis, and argued that the choice and use of recreational facilities are related to the social context in which the individual is located.

Leisure travel is a product that often is jointly consumed, and tourist activities reflect the influence (both direct and indirect) of all those traveling together (Chadwick, 1987). The behavior of tourists is heavily influenced by the composition of the traveling party (McIntosh & Goeldner, 1990). Travel-party size can influence behavior in several ways. First, a group of travel companions, whether extended family, friends, or colleagues, require more time for planning and a stronger need for information than do couples or singles (Fesenmaier & Lieber, 1988, cited in Stewart & Vogt, 1999). Conversely, independent travelers are more likely to engage in unplanned behavior. According to Hyde (2000), "the [independent] tourist avoids vacation planning because flexibility of action and experiencing the unknown are key amongst the hedonic experiences they are seeking" (p. 188). Second, groups including children require greater planning efforts to coordinate schedules and differential needs than groups without children (Fodness

& Murray, 1999). Third, Fisher (2001) found that collaboration led to higher decision quality and smaller deviations between consumers' planned and actual expenditures. Fourth, a respondent traveling alone has more flexibility in changing plans than a respondent traveling with children or with a group of friends. Morwitz (1997b) posited that the intent–behavior relationship for durable products might actually be weaker when the approval of more than one person is required than products involving a single decision maker. Fifth, preferences for travel experiences can differ according to travel-party composition (Basala & Klenosky, 2001). Here the role of the family members is highly influential (Dimanche & Havitz, 1994; Moutinho, 1987).

P$_{13}$:   The smaller the travel party size, the less the difference between planned and realized behavior.

SUMMARY

This chapter examines the influences on consumers' planned and unplanned strategies in the purchases of products and services in a tourist consumption system. The rationale underlying proposed theory relates to the need to better understand some of the determinants of consumption behavior, particularly when they differ

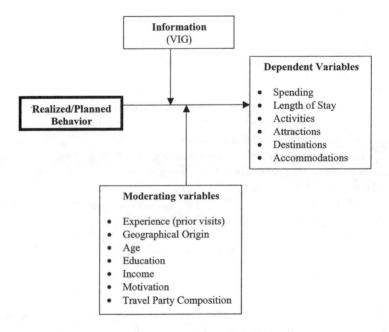

FIG. 7.4.   Modeling the hypothesized relationships.

significantly from planned behavior. Two critical determinants are product information and demographics such as income, age, and geographical location.

The application of the Mintzberg strategy matrix offers a useful conceptual tool for future examinations of divergences between planned, unplanned, and actual behavior. Managerially, this chapter highlights the importance of product information as a means of positively influencing consumer demand for products and services.

Theory related to planned and unplanned behavior was examined. Beginning with empirical and conceptual research in the field of social psychology, the discussion then summarized the contributions made in the marketing and tourism fields in the area of intentions and behavior. Figure 7.4 summarizes the marketing-related empirical research carried out in the topic area.

REFERENCES

Aarts, H., Verplanken, B., & van Knippenberg, A. (1998). Predicting behavior from actions in the past: Repeated decision making or a matter of habit. *Journal of Applied Social Psychology, 28,* 1355–1374.

Abratt, R., & Goodey, S. D. (1990). Unplanned buying and in-store stimuli in supermarkets. *Managerial and Decision Economics, 11,* 111–121.

Agee, T., & Martin, B. A. S. (2001). Planned or impulse purchases? How to create effective infomercials. *Journal of Advertising Research, 41,* 35–42.

Ajzen, I., & Driver, B. L. (1992). Application of the theory of planned behavior to leisure choice. *Journal of Leisure Research, 24*(3), 207–224.

Alford, P. (1998). Positioning the destination product—Can regional tourist boards learn from private sector practice? *Journal of Travel & Tourism Marketing, 7,* 53–68.

Basala, C. L., & Klenosky, D. B. (2001). Travel-style preferences for visiting a novel destination: A conjoint investigation across the novelty–familiarity continuum. *Journal of Travel Research, 40,* 172–182.

Bayley, G., & Nancarrow, C. (1998). Impulse purchasing: A qualitative exploration of the phenomenon. *Qualitative Market Research: An International Journal, 1,* 99–114.

Beatty, S. E., & Ferrell, M. E. (1998). Impulse buying: Modeling its precursors. *Journal of Retailing, 74,* 169–191.

Beatty, S. E., & Smith, S. M. (1987). External search effort: An investigation across several product categories. *Journal of Consumer Research, 14,* 83–95.

Belk, R. W. (1974). An exploratory assessment of situational effects in buyer behavior. *Journal of Marketing Research, 11,* 156–163.

Belk, R. W. (1975). Situational variables and consumer behavior. *Journal of Consumer Research, 2,* 157–163.

Bellenger, D. N., Robertson, D. H., & Hirschman, E. C. (1978). Impulse buying varies by product. *Journal of Advertising Research, 18,* 15–18.

Bettman, J. R. (1979). Memory factors in consumer choice: A review. *Journal of Marketing, 43,* 37–53.

Bettman, J. R., & Park, C. W. (1980). Effects of prior knowledge and experience and phase of the choice process on consumer decision processes: A protocol analysis. *Journal of Consumer Research, 7,* 234–248.

Bettman, J. R., Luce, M. F., & Payne, J. W. (1998). Constructive consumer choice processes. *Journal of Consumer Marketing, 25,* 187–217.

Bishop, D. W., & Witt, P. A. (1970). Sources of behavioral variance during leisure time. *Journal of Personality and Social Psychology, 16*, 352–360.

Bloch, P. H., Sherrell, D. L., & Ridgway, N. M. (1986). Consumer search: An extended framework. *Journal of Consumer Research, 13*, 119–126.

Bruce, V., & Green, P. R. (1991). *Visual perception*. Hillsdale, NJ: Lawrence Erlbaum Associates.

Burch, W. R. (1969). The social circles of leisure: Competing explanations. *Journal of Leisure Research, 1*, 125–147.

Chadwick, R. A. (1987). Concepts, definitions, and measures used in travel and tourism research. In J. R. B. Ritchie & C. R. Goeldner (Eds.), *Travel, tourism and hospitality research* (pp. 110–116). New York: Wiley.

Christensen, J. E., & Yoesting, D. R. (1973). Social and attitudinal variants in high and low use of outdoor recreational facilities. *Journal of Leisure Research, 5*, 6–15.

Clover, V. T. (1950). Relative importance of impulse buying in retail stores. *Journal of Marketing, 25*, 66–70.

Cobb, C. J., & Hoyer, W. D. (1986). Planned versus impulse purchase behavior. *Journal of Retailing, 62*, 384–409.

Cohen, E. (1972). Towards a sociology of international research. *Social Research, 39*, 164–182.

Coupey, E., Irwin, J. R., & Payne, J. W. (1996). *Product category familiarity and preference evaluation*. Working paper, Stern School of Business, New York University.

Cox, K. (1964). The responsiveness of food sales to shelf space changes in supermarkets. *Journal of Marketing Research, 1*, 63–67.

Crompton, J. (1979). Motivations for pleasure vacation. *Journal of Leisure Research, 6*, 408–424.

Crotts, J. C., & Reid, L. J. (1993). Segmenting the visitor market by the timing of their activity decisions. *Visions in Leisure and Business, 12*, 4–7.

Dann, G. M. S. (1981). Tourist motivation: An appraisal. *Annals of Tourism Research, 8*, 187–219.

Dimanche, F., & Havitz, M. E. (1994). Consumer behavior and tourism: Review and extension of four study areas. *Economic Psychology of Travel and Tourism, 3*, 37–57.

Dittmar, H., Beattie, J., & Friese, S. (1996). Gender identity and material symbols: Objects and decision considerations in impulse purchases. *Journal of Economic Psychology, 15*, 391–511.

East, R. (1997). *Consumer behavior: Advances and applications in marketing*. London: Prentice-Hall.

Engel, J. F., Blackwell, R. D., & Miniard, R. W. (1993). *Consumer behavior* (7th ed.). New York: Dryden Press.

Etzel, M. J., & Wahlers, R. G. (1985). The use of requested promotional material by pleasure travelers. *Journal of Travel Research, 12*, 2–61.

Fazio, R. H., & Zanna, M. P. (1981). Direct experience and attitude behavior consistency. *Advances in Experimental Social Psychology, 14*, 161–202.

Feldman, L. P., & Hornik, J. (1981). The use of time: An integrated conceptual model. *Journal of Consumer Research, 7*, 407–419.

Fesenmaier, D. R., & Johnson, B. (1989). Involvement-based segmentation. *Journal of Tourism Research, 28*, 293–300.

Fesenmaier, D. R., Vogt, C. A., & Stewart, W. P. (1993). Investigating the influence of welcome center information on travel behavior. *Journal of Travel Research, 34*, 47–52.

Filiatrault, P., & Ritchie, J. R. B. (1988). The impact of situational factors on the evaluation of hospitality services. *Journal of Travel Research, 26*, 29–37.

Fisher, R. J. (2001). The role of collaboration in consumers' in-store decisions. *Advances in Consumer Research, 28*, 251.

Fodness, D., & Murray, B. (1999). A model of tourist information search behavior. *Journal of Travel Research, 37*, 220–230.

Gardner, M. P., & Rook, D. W. (1988). Effects of impulse purchases on consumers affective states. *Advances in Consumer Research, 15*, 127–130.

Gilbert, D. C. (1991). An examination of the consumer behavior process related to tourism. In *Progress in tourism, recreation and hospitality management, 3*, 78–105.

Gitelson, R. J., & Crompton, J. L. (1983). The planning horizons and sources of information used by pleasure vacationers. *Journal of Travel Research, 23*, 2–7.

Gitelson, R. J., & Kerstetter, D. L. (1990). The relationship between sociodemographic variables, benefits sought and subsequent vacation behavior: A case study. *Journal of Travel Research, 29*, 24–29.

Godbey, G., & Graefe, A. (1991). Repeat tourism, play and monetary spending. *Annals of Tourism Research, 18*, 213–225.

Graburn, N. H. H. (1977). Tourism: The sacred journey. In V. Smith (Ed.), *Hosts and guests: The anthropology of tourism* (pp. 21–36). Philadelphia: University of Pennsylvania.

Granbois, D. H. (1968). Improving the study of customer in-store behavior. *Journal of Marketing, 32*, 28–33.

Gregory, R., Lichenstein, S., & Slovic, P. (1993). Valuing environmental resources: A constructive approach. *Journal of Risk and Uncertainty, 7*, 177–197.

Gross, B. L. (1994). Consumer responses to time pressure: A qualitative study with homeowners in foreclosure. *Advances in Consumer Research, 21*, 121–125.

Hawkins, S. A., & Hoch, S. J. (1992). Low-involvement learning: Memory without evaluation. *Journal of Consumer Research, 19*, 212–225.

Heilman, C. M., Bowman, D., & Wright, G. P. (2000). The evolution of brand preferences and choice behavior of consumers new to a market. *Journal of Marketing Research, 37*, 139–155.

Hendrick, C., Mills, J., & Kiesler, C. A. (1968). Decision time as a function of the number and complexity of equally attractive alternatives. *Journal of Personality and Social Psychology, 8*, 313–318.

Hornik, J. (1982). Situational effects on the consumption of time. *Journal of Marketing, 40*, 44–55.

Howard, J. A., & Sheth, J. N. (1969). *The theory of buyer behavior*. New York: Wiley.

Hu, Y., & Ritchie, J. R. B. (1993). Measuring destination attractiveness: A contextual approach. *Journal of Travel Research, 32*, 25–34.

Hyde, K. F. (2000). A hedonic perspective on independent vacation planning, decision-making and behavior. In A. G. Woodside, G. I. Crouch, J. A. Mazanec, M. Oppermann, & M. Y. Sakai (Eds.), *Consumer psychology of tourism, hospitality and leisure* (pp.). New York: CABI Publishing.

Inman, J. J., & Winer, R. S. (1998). *Where the rubber hits the road: A model of in-store consumer decision making*. Cambridge, MA: Marketing Science Institute.

Iyer, E. S. (1989). Unplanned purchasing: Knowledge of shopping environment and time pressure. *Journal of Retailing, 65*, 40–57.

Jacoby, J., Szybillo, A. J., & Berning, C. K. (1976). Time and consumer behavior: An interdisciplinary overview. *Journal of Consumer Research, 2*, 320–329.

Jeng, J. (1997, June). *Facets of the complex trip decision making process*. Paper presented at the Travel and Tourism Research Association's 28th Annual Conference, Norfolk, VA.

Kalwani, M. U., & Silk, A. J. (1982). On the relationship and predictive ability of purchase intention measures. *Marketing Science, 1*, 243–286.

Kardes, F. R. (1994). Consumer judgment and decision processes. In R. S. Wyer & T. K. Srull (Eds.), *Handbook of social recognition* (2nd ed.). Hillsdale, NJ: Lawrence Erlbaum Associates.

Katona, G. (1975). *Psychological economics*. New York: Elsevier.

Kelly, R. (1965). *An evaluation of selected variables of end display effectiveness*. Unpublished doctoral dissertation, Harvard University.

Klenosky, D. B., & Rethans, A. J. (1988). The formation of consumer choice sets: A longitudinal investigation at the product class level. *Advances in Consumer Research, 15*, 13–18.

Kollat, D. T., & Willett, R. P. (1967). Customer impulse purchasing behavior. *Journal of Marketing, 6*, 21–31.

Leclerc, F., Schmitt, B., & Dube, L. (1995). Waiting time and decision making: Is time like money? *Journal of Consumer Research, 22*, 110–119.

Lilien, G. L., Kotter, P., & Moorthy, K. S. (1992). *Marketing models*. Englewood Cliffs, NJ: Prentice-Hall.

Manski, C. (1990). The use of intentions data to predict behavior: A best-case analysis. *Journal of American Statistical Association, 85*, 934–940.

Mazursky, D. (1989). Past experience and future tourism decisions. *Annals of Tourism Research, 16*, 333–344.

McFarlane, B., Boxall, P., & Watson, D. (1998). Past experience and behavioral choice among wilderness users. *Journal of Leisure Research, 30*, 195–213.

McGoldrick, P. J. (1982). How unplanned are impulse purchases? *Retail & Distribution Management, 56*, 27–30.

McIntosh, R. W., & Goeldner, C. R. (1990). *Tourism: Principles, practices, philosophies.* New York: Wiley.

Mintzberg, H. (1978). Patterns in strategy formation. *Management Science, 24*, 934–948.

Mintzberg, H. (1994). *The rise and fall of strategic planning: Reconceiving roles for planning, plans, planners.* New York: The Free Press.

Mitra, A. (1995). Advertising and the stability of consideration sets over multiple purchase considerations. *International Journal of Research in Marketing, 12*, 81–94.

Mo, C., Howard, D. R., & Havitz, M. E. (1993). Testing an international tourist role typology. *Annals of Tourism Research, 20*, 319–335.

Moore, B. (Ed.). (2004). *Australian Oxford Dictionary.* Sydney: Oxford University Press.

Morrison, A. (1996). *Hospitality and travel marketing.* Albany, NY: Delmar.

Morwitz, V. G. (1997a). It seems like only yesterday: The nature and consequences of telescoping errors in marketing research. *Journal of Consumer Psychology, 6*(1), 1–29.

Morwitz, V. G. (1997b). Why consumers don't always accurately predict their own future behavior. *Marketing Letters, 8*, 57–70.

Morwitz, V. G., & Schmittlein, D. C. (1992). Using segmentation to improve sales forecasts based on purchase intent: Which 'intenders' actually buy? *Journal of Marketing Research, 29*, 391–405.

Moutinho, L. (1987). Consumer behavior in tourism. *European Journal of Marketing, 21*, 5–44.

Newman, J. W., & Staelin, R. (1974). Prepurchase information seeking for new cars and major household appliances. *Journal of Marketing Research, 9*, 249–257.

Nickols, S. Y., & Fox, K. D. (1983). Buying time and saving time: Strategies for managing household production. *Journal of Consumer Research, 10*, 197–208.

Otto, J. E., & Ritchie, J. R. B. (1996). The service experience in tourism. *Tourism Management, 17*, 165–174.

Parr, D. (1989). *Free independent travelers.* Master's thesis, Lincoln College, Canterbury, New Zealand.

Pearce, P. L., & Caltabiano, M. (1983). Inferring travel motivations from travelers' experiences. *Journal of Travel Research, 22*, 25–30.

Perdue, R. R. (1986). The influence of unplanned attraction visits on expenditures by travel-through visitors. *Journal of Travel Research, 25*, 14–19.

Peter, J. P., & Olson, J. C. (1999). *Consumer behavior and marketing strategy* (5th ed.). Boston: McGraw-Hill.

Peterson, L. (1987, October 12). Study confirms impulse buying on the rise. *Promote, 6*–10.

Plog, S. (1974). Why destination areas rise and fall in popularity. *Cornell Hotel Restaurant and Administration Quarterly, 14*, 55–58.

Prasad, V. K. (1975). Unplanned buying in two retail settings. *Journal of Retailing, 51*, 3–12.

Raju, P. S. (1980). Optimum stimulation level: Its relationship to personality, demographics, and exploratory behavior. *Journal of Consumer Research, 7*, 272–282.

Rao, S. R., Thomas, E. G., & Javalgi, R. G. (1992). Activity preferences and trip planning behavior of the U.S. outbound pleasure travel market. *Journal of Travel Research, 30*, 3–13.

Ritchie, J. R. B. (1994). Research on leisure behavior and tourism—state of the art. In R. V. Gasser & K. Weiermair (Eds.), *Spoilt for choice: Decision making processes and preference changes of tourists—Intertemporal and intercountry perspectives* (pp. 3–27). Frankfurt, Germany: Kultur.

Roehl, W., & Fesenmaier, D. (1992). Risk perception and pleasure travel: An exploratory analysis. *Journal of Travel Research, 30*, 17–26.

Rook, D. W., & Fisher, R. J. (1995). Normative influences on impulsive buying behavior. *Journal of Consumer Research, 22*, 305–313.

Rook, D. W., & Gardner, M. P. (1993). In the mood: Impulse buyings' affective antecedents. In J. Arnold-Costa & R. W. Belk (Eds.), *Research in consumer behavior* (Vol. 6, pp. 1–28). Greenwich, CT: JAI Press.

Rook, D. W., & Hoch, S. J. (1985). Consuming impulses. *Advances in Consumer Research, 12*, 23–27.

Schul, P., & Crompton, J. L. (1983). Search behavior of international vacationers: Travel-specific lifestyle and socio-demographic variables. *Journal of Travel Research, 21*, 25–30.

Shapiro, S., & Krishnan, H. S. (1999). Consumer memory for intentions: A prospective memory perspective. *Journal of Experimental Psychology, 5*, 169–189.

Shoemaker, S. (1994). Segmenting the U.S. travel market according to benefits realized. *Journal of Travel Research, 32*, 8–21.

Snepenger, D. (1987). Segmenting the vacation market by novelty seeking role. *Journal of Travel Research, 26*, 8–14.

Stayman, D. M., & Deshpplande, R. (1989). Situational ethnicity and consumer behavior. *Journal of Consumer Research, 16*, 361–371.

Stewart, S. I., & Vogt, C. A. (1999). A case-based approach to understanding vacation planning. *Leisure Sciences, 21*, 79–95.

Tsang, G. K. Y. (1993). *Visitor information network study: Visitors' information seeking behavior for on-site travel-related sub-decision making and evaluation of service performance.* Unpublished master's thesis, University of Otago, Dunedin, NZ.

Um, S., & Crompton, J. L. (1990). Attitude determinants in tourism destination choice. *Annals of Tourism Research, 17*, 432–448.

Verplanken, B., Aarts, H., & van Knippenberg, A. (1997). Habit, information acquisition, and the process of making travel mode choices. *European Journal of Social Psychology, 27*, 539–560.

Warshaw, P. R. (1980). Predicting purchase and other behavior from general and contextually specific intentions. *Journal of Marketing Research, 17*, 26–33.

West, C. J. (1951). Results of two years of study into impulse buying. *Journal of Marketing, 15*, 362–363.

Weun, S., Jones, M. A., & Beatty, S. E. (1998). The development and validation of the impulse buying tendency scale. *Psychological Reports, 82*, 1123–1133.

Wicks, B., & Schuett, M. (1991). Examining the role of tourism promotion through the use of brochures. *Tourism Management, 12*, 301–313.

Williams, J., & Dardis, R. (1972). Shopping behavior for soft goods and marketing strategies. *Journal of Retailing, 48*, 32–41.

Woodside, A. G., & Jacobs, L. W. (1985). Step two in benefit segmentation: Learning the benefits realized by major travel markets. *Journal of Travel Research, 24*, 7–14.

Woodside, A. G., Trappey, R. J., & MacDonald, R. (1997). Measuring linkage-advertising effects on customer behavior and net revenue: Using quasi-experiments of advertising treatments with novice and experienced product-service users. *Canadian Journal of Administrative Sciences, 14*, 214–228.

Wright, P. L. (1974). The harassed decision maker: Time pressure, distraction, and the use of evidence. *Journal of Applied Psychology, 59*, 555–561.

Yiannakis, A., & Gibson, H. (1992). Roles tourists play. *Annals of Tourism Research, 19*, 287–303.

Young, M. R., DeSarbo, W. S., & Morwitz, V. G. (1998). The stochastic modeling of purchase intentions and behavior. *Management Science, 44*(2), 188–202.

Young, R. A., & Kent, A. T. (1985). Using the theory of reasoned action to improve the understanding of recreation behavior. *Journal of Leisure Research, 17*, 90–106.

Zajonc, R. B., & Markus, H. (1982). Affective and cognitive factors in preferences. *Journal of Consumer Research, 9*, 123–131.

Zalatan, A. (1996). The determinants of planning time in vacation travel. *Tourism Management, 17*, 123–131.

III. NEW PERSPECTIVES ON MOTIVATION AND CONSUMER INFORMATION PROCESSING

CHAPTER EIGHT

Goals, Policies, Preferences, and Actions

Arthur B. Markman
University of Texas, Austin

C. Miguel Brendl
INSEAD

Research on judgment and decision making has often focused on the rules people use to make choices and the information used in decision making at the expense of the prediction of what people like and dislike. For example, much of the heuristics and biases literature examined strategies people used when making choices such as satisficing and elimination-by-aspects (Payne, Bettman, & Johnson, 1993; Simon, 1957; Tversky, 1972). As another example, studies have examined people's tendency to focus their choices on information that matches across a set of options rather than on properties that are unique to one of the options (Hsee, 1996; Markman & Medin, 1995; Slovic & MacPhillamy, 1974; Zhang & Markman, 1998, 2001).

Research on consumer behavior can ill-afford to focus only on choice strategies and information processing. In order to understand consumption behavior and factors that influence purchase decisions, it is important to understand the constituents of preference and action. Central to this enterprise is a focus on the motivational processes that drive attitudes and purchases. For this reason, consumer behavior has benefited from an upsurge in research on the influence of motivation on cognitive processes (Brendl & Higgins, 1996; Carver & Scheier, 1998; Gollwitzer, 1999; Higgins, 1997; Markman & Brendl, 2000).

There have been many proposals for the structure of the goal and motivational systems (Carver & Scheier, 1998; Kruglanski et al., 2002; Lewin, 1926, 1935). Unfortunately, it has proven difficult to provide evidence for specific proposals about the relationship between goals and motivation because key aspects of the motivational system are not consciously accessible. Happily, there is quite a bit of data that bears on the structure of the motivational system, and from this work, it is possible to extract a good working framework that can be used to drive further research.

In this chapter, we outline such a framework that draws on past research. We begin by sketching nine empirical phenomena that constrain a theory of goal systems. Then, we present a framework for thinking about goals and motivation. We use this framework to suggest new lines of research, and sketch some of our recent work that addresses these questions.

PHENOMENA THAT CONSTRAIN AN ACCOUNT OF GOALS

Goals and *motivations* are key terms that are used quite broadly within the psychology literature. Motivation is typically used to refer to the impetus to perform an action, while goal is typically used to refer to an outcome that an agent has a tendency to work toward bringing about (i.e., to approach) or to keep from occurring (i.e., to avoid). Agents (people, animals, perhaps autonomous systems like robots) also have objects and strategies that can be used to fulfill their goals. These objects and strategies are called the *means* for goal satisfaction.

The motivational system has been difficult to characterize because there are many conflicting findings in the literature that have influenced the development of theories of the structure of the system that drives people's actions. In this section, we briefly describe nine phenomena that bear on the structure of the motivational system. Some of these phenomena may appear to be contradictory, although we try to resolve these contradictions later in this chapter. A list of these phenomena is now presented:

Nine Phenomena That a Theory of Goals and Motivation Must Explain

1. People can talk about their actions.
2. Talking about actions can interfere with choices.
3. People have difficulty predicting future preferences and future affective states.
4. People express attitudes, but their attitudes do not always coincide with their future actions.
5. Affective states are taken to reflect underlying motivational states, although they correlate with such states only loosely.
6. States of the world can prime goals.
7. Goals prime means.
8. Means can remind people of goals.
9. Explicit intentions to perform actions can influence behavior.

Loosely, these phenomena bear on three aspects of the motivational system. First, there are findings that suggest that people have some conscious access to their goals. Second, there are findings that suggest that aspects of the motivational system are inaccessible to consciousness. Third, the are findings on the relationships between the world, cognitive states, and the activation of goals and motivations.

ACCESSIBILITY OF GOALS

When people are asked why they performed a particular action, they give a response. For example, if a person is asked why they are eating breakfast, they might say that they are hungry or that they always eat breakfast. People's explanations of their behavior are typically sensible and seem to reflect some aspect of their environment or their internal state. Given the importance of introspective reports as data in psychology and applied psychological work (e g., the laddering technique, thought listings, and verbal protocols in studies and focus groups), it is hard to believe that people's explanations of their own behavior have no relationship to the factors that affect their behavior (Ericsson & Simon, 1993).

Indeed, there are many cases in which people are able to provide information about their goals. In their classic book on the use of protocols as data, Ericsson and Simon (1993) described a number of contexts in which people's verbal reports can be taken as a good narration of the thought processes underlying behaviors. People can often give accurate reports about the way that they intend to process information in problem solving and choice contexts.

Furthermore, there are a number of cases in which choices are made because an explicitly available reason or rationale is available to justify the choice (Shafir, Simonson, & Tversky, 1993; Simonson, 1989). For example, Simonson (1989) explored the role of reasons in the attraction effect (Huber, Payne, & Puto, 1982). In the attraction effect, the likelihood that people will choose an alternative increases when a new option is added to a choice set that is dominated only by that alternative. Simonson (1989) found that the attraction effect increases in magnitude when people are asked to justify their choices, suggesting that the availability of a justification for selecting a particular option is an important factor in this effect.

Indeed, there are cases in which explicitly forming the intention to achieve some end state increases the likelihood that the actor will succeed in reaching it. Gollwitzer's (1999) work demonstrates that when people make a conscious commitment to an action, they are much more likely to take actions congruent with their commitment. Furthermore, people who have made this commitment can report it as a rationale for their actions. Thus, their intentions predict future behavior.

People are also able to provide information about values that are important to them (Baron & Spranca, 1997; Irwin & Spria, 1997; Tetlock, Kristel, Elson,

Green, & Lerner, 2000). For example, Baron and Spranca (1997) discussed the concept of a *protected value*, which is a strong belief held by people for which they are not willing to accept tradeoffs. For example, someone might not be willing to accept taking a human life at any cost. People who express that they have a protected value in a particular arena modify their behavior accordingly. That is not to say that they do not actually accept tradeoffs under any circumstances (e.g., Irwin & Baron, 2001), but rather that the expression of a protected value for a dimension coincides with a behavioral consequences for that dimension.

This discussion suggests that some aspects of the goal system are clearly accessible to consciousness. The phenomena explored in the next section focus on cases in which aspects of goals and motivations are not accessible to consciousness.

INACCESSIBILITY OF MOTIVATIONS

The fact that people can successfully talk about some aspects of their pursuit of goals does not mean that the entire motivational system is accessible to consciousness (Wilson & Dunn, 1986; Wilson & Schooler, 1991). The nonverbalizable parts consist both of aspects that are not accessible to consciousness at all as well as of perceptual representations that are not compatible with verbal descriptions of the same elements (Barsalou, 1999; Schooler & Engstler-Schooler, 1990).

Wilson and his colleagues demonstrated that many choices rest on factors that cannot be verbalized (Wilson et al., 1993; Wilson & Schooler, 1991). For example, in one study, people chose from a set of humorous and art-reprint posters and either were or were not asked to justify this choice (Wilson et al., 1993). People were much more likely to choose an art-reprint poster (and much more likely to be satisfied with their choice) when they did not give a verbal justification of their choice than when they did. Assuming that most people do not have a good vocabulary for talking about why they like artwork, this result suggests that giving a justification biases people away from options whose good qualities cannot be verbalized easily. These kinds of phenomena are relatively easy to explain, because there is no need to assume that people are good at talking about all aspects of their cognitive representations (Markman, 1999). There is no need to assume that these phenomena reflect a lack of accessibility of aspects of the goal system. Somewhat more difficult to explain are findings reviewed by Berridge (1999). In these studies, drug addicts will work much harder in a button-pressing task to intravenously self-administer solutions containing a very low dosage of drugs than drug-free ones. However, they were unable to identify the solutions containing drugs. In other words, their motivational system drove them to want a solution, but they were not aware that they liked that solution better than others. These findings are consistent with the idea that motivation is not accessible to consciousness, though it is always hard to interpret null effects.

Much research has begun to examine a pervasive phenomenon that people have difficulty predicting future affective states and future preferences. As we will see, this phenomenon also suggest that aspects of the motivational system are also inaccessible to consciousness. For example, Kahneman and Snell (1992) found that people could not predict the amount of ice cream that they would want to consumer at some future time. Similarly, Read, Loewenstein, and Kalyanaram (1999) found that students choosing between a comedy movie and a serious movie were more likely to choose the comedy when selecting a movie to watch that day, but more likely to choose a serious movie when selecting a movie to watch on another night. Thus, their prediction for a future preference was not the same as their actual preference for that moment.

A third example of the inability to predict future preferences comes from a study we conducted with smokers (Brendl, Markman, & Messner, 2003). German students who were smokers were approached after a long lecture class during which they could not smoke. Half remained in the classroom, and half went outside. The half that remained in the classroom drank a cup of coffee to enhance their need to smoke. The half that went outside smoked a cigarette and drank a cup of coffee (to provide time for the nicotine to diffuse through their systems). Then, participants bought raffle tickets. For half of the participants, the prize in the raffle was three cartons of cigarettes. For the other half, the prize was an amount of cash about equal to the cost of three cartons of cigarettes. Participants given the cigarette raffle bought slightly (and nonsignificantly) more tickets if they were in the classroom (and hence had a high need to smoke) than if they were outside the classroom (and thus had a low need to smoke). Of interest, participants given the cash raffle bought significantly fewer tickets if they had a high need to smoke than if they had a low need to smoke. Thus, they showed a decreased preference for cash in the presence of the strongly active competing goal of smoking. We refer to this finding as a *devaluation effect*, because cash was devalued when there was a strong need to smoke.

Of importance for this discussion, people inside the classroom would probably be having a cigarette soon after leaving the classroom. Thus, their assessment of the attractiveness of the cash prize (as measured by the willingness to buy tickets) would be changing just moments after participating in the experiment. These participants were all habitual smokers who should have had a lot of experience with the effects of smoking, yet they seemed unaware that the need to smoke was having an influence on their preferences. Indeed, in an unpublished, follow-up study, we found that when we described this setting to smokers, they were unable to predict that having a high need to smoke would decrease their willingness to purchase raffle tickets to win cash relative to having a low need to smoke.

This finding is similar to a more general observation that people's behavior is often inconsistent with their attitudes (Fazio & Roskos-Ewoldsen, 1994). Ajzen and Fishbein (1977) suggested that many cases in which attitudes are inconsistent with behaviors reflect cases in which the elicited attitude is expressed about a different behavior or object of behavior than is actually measured. In the examples discussed here, however, the elicited preferences are well aligned to the objects and actions that are measured. Instead, there are situational factors that influence the strength of people's goals that fall outside of people's awareness, and so people are unable to recognize how these situational factors might have a different influence on their behavior at some later time.

Despite the fact that people do not have conscious access to the motivational states that drive behavior, they will give sensible explanations of their behaviors in situations where other factors are governing their performance. We raise this point, because, as discussed, the presence of such seemingly sensible justifications of behavior may be taken as *prima facie* evidence that people do have access to their motivational states. If sensible explanations occur in situations where they must be false, then it suggests that any explanations people give for their actions are potentially suspect.

As an example of people's ability to generate sensible explanations, Kruglanski et al. (2002) replicated a study by Nisbett and Wilson (1977) in which people selected from among an array of identical pairs of socks (that they were told were different qualities). People with a high need for cognitive closure (that is a high need to complete their decision) were more likely to select the rightmost pair in the array than were people with a low need for closure. Presumably this preference comes about because people are scanning the array from left to right and then selecting the last pair they examined, since that provides an easy solution to the problem of selecting the best pair. Despite this preference for the right-most pair, people in this study justified their choice with comments about the quality of the socks, suggesting that they were unaware of the factors that were actually affecting their choice.

Finally, the factors people use to assess the strength of their own goals are typically only loosely related to the actual strength of their goals as measured by behavior. Tiffany and his colleagues (Tiffany, 1990; Tiffany & Conklin, 2000) demonstrated that cravings for drugs are not strongly related to the underlying physiological factors related to the need to use drugs (see Kassel & Shiffman, 1992, for a related discussion about eating and hunger). Instead, people experience cravings or hunger when they have a need and are blocked from their habitual means of satisfying the need. People will attempt to satisfy an active need using automatic behaviors first, and will be consciously aware of the activity of this need only in cases where they are unable to satisfy the need through these automatic behaviors.

In one study, we attempted to dissociate physiological needs from conscious feelings triggered by interrupted goals (Brendl et al., 2003). For all participants, we triggered a goal to eat popcorn by announcing that they would participate in a popcorn taste test and by exposing them to the smell of popcorn. (The smell should have also raised the need to eat for all respondents.) The "low hunger–high need" group tasted a handful of popcorn right away. This supported the goal of eating an accordingly this group reported relatively low feelings of hunger. But it presumably raised the need to eat even further because a small amount of carbohydrates increases rather than decreases the physiological need to eat (Rodin, 1985). In contrast, the "high hunger–low need" group was told that they would have to do another task before tasting the popcorn. Hence, their goal of eating was interrupted and accordingly they reported relatively high feelings of hunger. However, compared to the other group, their need to eat was lower because it was not activated by additional carbohydrates. Preferences for various objects were driven by unconscious physiological needs, showing that conscious feelings of hunger were not diagnostic of the physiological need to eat. Thus, affective states provide an imperfect conscious window into the activity of the motivational system.

To summarize, goals are often active without people being consciously aware of their activation. Because many factors that drive behavior are not consciously accessible, people are often unable to predict their future preferences and actions. Furthermore, because the link between situational factors and goal activation is not available to conscious experience, people have difficulties correcting their future predictions for the effects of the current situation. Finally, the affective states that people use as markers of their current needs are imperfectly related to the underlying state of the motivational system, which decreases the accuracy of self-reports of the activation of goals.

PRIMING OF GOALS AND MOTIVATIONAL STATES

The goal system has a clear cognitive structure that relates people's goals to the means of achieving them. This structure is visible in the ways that goals can cause the means of achieving them to be activated and also in how means can activate goals. In particular, desired end states and means appear to be connected in a network that permits activation of any one of them to activate others.

A classic example of this priming is the Zeigarnik effect (Zeigarnik, 1927). This effect refers to cases where a person has an unfulfilled goal. People are more likely to remember unfinished actions than finished actions, that is, an active goal (e.g., to complete a clay figure) primes means to reach that outcome (e.g., form a clay figure). Patalano and Seifert (1997) obtained a similar result. Lewin (1926) also hypothesized that objects in the environment that can facilitate satisfaction of a goal are more easily noticed as long as the goal has not been reached (see Gollwitzer, 1993, for evidence).

Kruglanski and colleagues have explored the relationships among elements of the goal system (Kruglanski et al., 2002; Shah, Friedman, & Kruglanski, 2002; Shah, Kruglanski, & Friedman, 2003). They use a variety of cognitive measures of priming to examine this issue. For example, Kruglanski et al. (2002) described a study in which people made speeded responses about whether a particular word described an activity or an attribute that a person could have. The activities and attributes used in their study were pretested to find pairs for which participants believed that the activity would lead to attainment of the attribute. Thus, the activities could be viewed as means to obtain the goal of possessing an attribute. In those cases where people had an active goal to possess an attribute, presentation of that attribute led to significantly faster decisions about the activities in the speeded task. This pattern of results suggests that goals prime means. Kruglanski et al. (2002) described studies demonstrating that means prime goals as well.

One consequence of the conceptual relationships between goals and means is that the structure of human memory will influence the likelihood of goal satisfaction. That is, in order for people to consciously pursue some end state, specific goals that facilitate bringing about that end state must be activated in appropriate circumstances. One way to ensure that goal satisfaction occurs is to form specific intentions that relate to the implementation of the goal (Gollwitzer, 1999). Intentions to implement a goal are effective, because they increase the accessibility of the goal in those instances in which the goal can be satisfied (Gollwitzer, 1993).

For example, a particular woman might want to quit smoking. This end state is abstract, but the woman will live in specific circumstances that probably have strong connections to specific goals of smoking. For example, she might go to a bar where she used to meet friends and smoke. This environment would prime the goal to have a cigarette, and this behavior might be carried out automatically (or at least lead to a strong craving for a cigarette if the goal to smoke is blocked). Bringing about the end state to quit smoking will be more effective if the woman envisions this circumstance in advance and develops a plan for how to deal with the urge to smoke in that setting. In this way, the actual circumstance of sitting in a bar will also activate the specific intention to stop smoking and will facilitate satisfaction of this desire. Indeed, Wertenbroch (1998) showed that smokers prefer buying small amounts of cigarettes allowing them to control future temptations to smoke that a larger stock of cigarettes would create.

The central point of this section is that the informational content of goals is interconnected. Thus, motivation has its influence in part by affecting information that is active in the cognitive system. This point is important, because it makes clear that motivation does not lead to actions that are preprogrammed by some evolutionary process. Instead, the connections among goals and the means for satisfying them are learned.

THE STRUCTURE OF THE GOAL SYSTEM

We have summarized the nine phenomena relating to goals and motivation. Any theory of goal systems must account for all of the phenomena listed. In this section, we develop a view of goals that is related to the one posited by Kruglanski et al. (2002). Their theory is a cognitive view of goals that consists of interconnections among goals, subgoals, and means for achieving them. In their view, *goals* are abstract desired and undesired end states. *Subgoals* are more specific end states that connect to objects and activities in the world that satisfy them. *Means* are the particular objects and activities that are used to satisfy subgoals.

In this system, goals, subgoals, and means are connected in a semantic network. Goals are connected via excitatory connections to their subgoals so that activating a goal will lead to priming of the connected subgoals (and vice versa). Similarly subgoals have excitatory connections to their means. Competing goals are connected via inhibitory links, so that activation of one goal decreases activation of competing goals. Similarly, competing subgoals have inhibitory connections as do competing means.

Not surprisingly, this structure is compatible with the goal priming phenomena already given. Indeed, Kruglanski et al.'s (2002) proposal was developed with these goal priming phenomena in mind and was used to motivate additional studies of the degree to which goals, subgoals, and means prime each other.

There are limitations to this proposal, however. First, it is silent on the degree to which elements of the goal system are consciously accessible. As discussed, the manifest difficulty people have in predicting their future preferences suggests that some goals—and some relationships between the environment and goal activation—are not accessible to consciousness. Thus, it is important to make a clear distinction between those aspects of the goal system that will be consciously accessible and those that will not.

Second, the relationship between affective states and motivational states is not incorporated into this theory. As discussed, there is a complex relationship between the activation of some motivational state and the consciously accessible affective states that relate to it. For example, activation of a need to use a drug or to eat need not give rise to a craving or to hunger. Because consciously accessible states such as cravings and hunger can influence the activation and pursuit of goals, it is important to clarify this relationship.

In the remainder of this chapter, we develop an extended version of Kruglanski et al.'s (2002) proposal that addresses these limitations. After we describe this proposal, we present a line of research motivated by issues relating to this architecture.

An Extended Goal-Systems Architecture

The goal-systems architecture we propose is sketched in Fig. 8.1. Embedded within this figure is a system that contains the elements of Kruglanski et al.'s proposal. The circles at the top of the figure labeled *policies* are related to what they called goals. The *focal goals* in the figure are related to their subgoals. The *means* in the figure play the same role as the means in Kruglanski et al.'s proposal. In this figure, links with solid lines are excitatory connections. Links that terminate in circles are inhibitory connections. Thus, policies connect to their relevant focal goals via excitatory connections and focal goals connect to means via excitatory

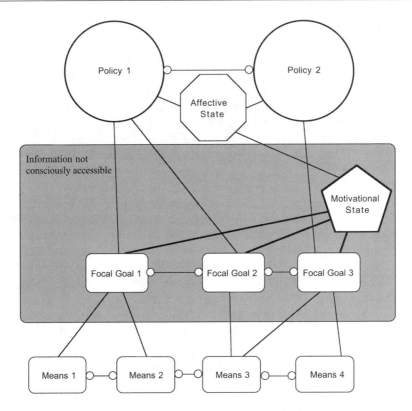

FIG. 8.1.   An overview of the proposed view of goals and motivation.

connections. As for Kruglanski et al., competing elements have inhibitory links (some of which are shown in Fig. 8.1 for the purposes of clarity).

In the framework we present, policies are distinguished from goals in their accessibility to consciousness. Policies are accessible to consciousness, but focal goals are not. This distinction is designed to account for the observed dissociations between action and attitude (that involve cases in which the attitude and behavior are being measured at the same level of abstraction; Ajzen & Fishbein, 1977). Focal goals rather than policies are the more proximate drivers of actions, because they are more closely connected to means and because policies are connected to means only through the focal goals. Focal goals are activated by policies through their direct excitatory connections. In addition, the current motivational state (to come) and the environment can affect the activity of focal goals.

There are three key assumptions here. First, there are two different cognitive components in the goal system, but only one of them is accessible to consciousness. Second, it is the focal goals (which are relatively specific and are connected to means) that are inaccessible to consciousness, whereas the more abstract policies are accessible to consciousness. Third, consciously accessible policies are connected to means only indirectly through focal goals. On this view, when people guide their actions consciously (e.g., through willpower), they are doing so by maintaining activation of a policy, which activates a focal goal and in turn activates a particular means.

Figure 8.1 contains a box labeled *motivational state* in the section of the figure that is inaccessible to consciousness. This box is a placeholder for many aspects of the motivational system that go beyond the scope of this chapter. For example, one key component of motivational state is the activity among the set of focal goals. The total amount of such activation may fluctuate with factors such as arousal. The mechanisms underlying regulatory focus are also important components of motivational state. Higgins (1997) distinguished between promotion and prevention focus (i.e., sensitivity to potential positive vs. negative outcomes). A more complete discussion of this model of the goal system would have to unpack further the notion of motivational state.

An important aspect of our framework is that motivational state is separated from affective state. As discussed, consciously accessible markers of goal activation—such as drug cravings and hunger—are at best loosely related to the actual activation of underlying goals. People appear to infer which goals are activated in part by monitoring their affective state. Thus, it is important to make an explicit distinction between consciously accessible affect and underlying motivational states.

Means in this framework function like means in Kruglanski et al.'s (2002) work. They can be activated either by focal goals or by the environment. If the environment activates a means, then goals relating to those means may also become activated.

Obviously, this framework is just a sketch of the relationships among core factors within the motivational system. The value of such frameworks, however, is that they may lead us to ask questions that have not otherwise been addressed. In the next section, we give one example of how this framework can lead to new research.

TESTING THE GOAL-SYSTEMS ARCHITECTURE: WHAT IS A FOCAL GOAL?

Our goal framework raises an important question. If focal goals are not accessible to consciousness, then how can we know their content? We believe that one reason why it has been so difficult to make progress on understanding the structure of the motivational system is that key aspects of it are not accessible to consciousness. It is crucial to find a way to provide data that bears on the structure of focal goals.

The valuation and devaluation of means in the presence of an active goal may provide a method for exploring the nature of focal goals (Markman, Brendl, & Kim, 2004). In the example described earlier, smokers were somewhat more likely to purchase raffle tickets to win cigarettes when they needed a cigarette than when they did not. Thus, they showed a small valuation effect for a means related to the goal of smoking. Smokers were significantly less likely to buy a raffle ticket to win cash when they needed a cigarette than when they did not. This devaluation effect occurred for an item that was not a direct means for satisfying the need to smoke (i.e., cash cannot be smoked).

This result suggests that objects which are means that are directly connected to an active focal goal may show valuation effects. In contrast, objects that are means that are connected to focal goals that are not active may show devaluation effects. Thus, if we understood the function that relates goal activation to the pattern of valuation and devaluation, then we could infer the scope of active focal goals from the observed pattern of valuations and devaluations of various means.

To accomplish this task, we first assessed the relationship between the strength of the need to smoke and patterns of valuation and devaluation (see Markman et al., 2004, for a detailed description of the methods and data). Need to smoke was manipulated either by having habitual smokers read stories involving the pleasure of smoking and depriving them of the chance to smoke or having them read stories that did not involve smoking and having them smoke a cigarette. Then, participants rated their preference for a series of items that varied in their relatedness to smoking. From most to least related to smoking, the items were: brands of cigarettes, items instrumentally related to smoking (e.g., lighters and ashtrays), foods typically consumed while smoking, products with cigarette brands imprinted on them, smoking-unrelated items (e.g., a DVD player).

In this study, both the cigarette brands and the instrumentally related items showed significant valuation. That is, their rated preference was higher for people with a high need to smoke than for people with a low need to smoke. The smoking-unrelated items showed significant devaluation. That is, their rated preference was lower for people with a high need to smoke than for people with a low need to smoke. Finally, the foods consumed while smoking and the cigarette branded products showed neither valuation nor devaluation. That is, their rated preference was about the same for people with a high need to smoke and for people with a low need to smoke.

A followup study suggests that this pattern of data is consistent with the idea that active goals lead to the activation of concepts describing the means that can be used to satisfy a goal. In this study, after a manipulation of the need to smoke, people were given a Stroop task in which they had to identify the color of the font used to print out words. The words described the five types of items from the study of preferences that we just described. In this task, the more accessible a concept, the longer it should take to identify the color of the font of the word. Overall, there was a reliable correlation between the difference in Stroop color identification times for items in the high-need and low-need conditions and the size of the valuation/devaluation effects for those items. Thus, goal activation influenced both preference and accessibility of the items.

These data suggest that items that are directly related to an active focal goal show reliable valuation. Items that are unrelated to an active focal goal show devaluation. Items that are of intermediate relatedness to an active focal goal show a pattern intermediate between valuation and devaluation.

Given this pattern, it is possible to explore the specificity of people's focal goals by varying the relatedness of the items to the goal and looking at the patterns of valuation and devaluation that arise. We used this method in a study examining preferences for foods (see Markman et al., 2004, for details of the method and data). In this experiment, college men were given a manipulation of "need to eat." A low need to eat was created by giving participants a large slice of bread with unsalted butter to eat. A high need to eat was created by giving participants a small amount of bread with salted butter. The combination of the small amount of bread and the salt increases people's need to eat (Fedoroff, Polivy, & Herman, 1997; Herman, 1996).

In addition, subjects were run either at 9:00 a.m. or at 4:00 p.m., in order to provide a contextual manipulation of the appropriateness of types of foods. The morning context would facilitate access to mental representations of foods appropriate to breakfast. The evening context would facilitate access to mental representations of foods appropriate to dinner.

Subjects rated the attractiveness of a set of breakfast foods, dinner foods, and nonfoods. If focal goals are specific, then we would expect to see valuation for foods appropriate to the time of day when the study was run, and devaluation for nonfoods. In contrast, if focal goals are general, then we would expect to see valuation for all foods and devaluation for nonfoods. At the outset, it is worth recognizing that the fact that researchers do not have a strong intuition about the outcome of this experiment suggests that people do not have insight into the generality of their focal goals.

The results were consistent with the view that focal goals are specific. Subjects who run in the morning showed valuation for breakfast foods (i.e., higher preference ratings if they had a high need to eat than if they had a low need to eat), devaluation for nonfoods, and approximately equal preference ratings in the high and low need conditions for the dinner foods. In contrast, subjects run in the evening showed reliable valuation for dinner foods, devaluation for nonfoods, and the intermediate pattern for breakfast foods.

These data demonstrate how the goal framework discussed here can be used to motivate research. By acknowledging that focal goals are not directly accessible to consciousness, we make clear that indirect measures must be used to gather information about the semantic content of the goals. In the studies described in this section, we used patterns of valuation and devaluation as such an indirect measure. First, we presented studies demonstrating that the degree of valuation goes up with similarity to the active focal goal, and that devaluation occurs for objects that are distant from the active focal goal. Furthermore, as we would expect if these goals exist in a semantic network (see also Kruglanski et al., 2002), the degree of valuation and devaluation observed in the preference ratings was systematically related to the accessibility of the items as measured by a Stroop task. Finally, valuation and devaluation were used in the domain of eating to demonstrate that focal goals were specific to the time of day in which the study was run. This finding suggests that focal goals are activated by a combination of physiological factors (e.g., the need to eat) as well as cognitive factors (knowledge of the types of food appropriate to a time of day). We believe that this method can be used in future research to explore the content of focal goals in a variety of settings.

CONCLUSIONS

We have tried to demonstrate in this chapter that psychology has learned enough about the goal system to make concrete proposals about the structure of goals as well as the degree to which information about active goals is accessible to consciousness. The model sketched in Fig. 8.1 is consistent with the extant data, and it makes predictions that can be used to guide future research.

This model also has important implications for the study of consumer behavior. First, it suggests that marketers should be careful when using protocol methods (both individual protocols and focus groups) to test the effectiveness of marketing campaigns and product launches. Verbal protocols require that the information of interest be consciously accessible. If purchase behavior is driven by focal goals, then people will not have conscious access to important elements that guide choice behavior. In these cases, observations of purchase behavior and indirect methods of assessing goals will be more effective than will introspective measures.

Second, the model suggests that introspective methods will also have systematic biases to focus on the relationship between affective states and consciously accessible policies. There are two potential problems with this focus. First, affective states result from motivational states, but are not a veridical readout of the underlying motivational state. Second, policies are more abstract than the focal goals that drive behavior (through their connection to means). Thus, people's justifications of their behavior will tend to focus on end states that are more abstract than the ones that drive behavior. Again, methods that observe behavior in context will be more effective than introspective reports in this case.

Future research must clarify key aspects of this framework. For example, the diagram in Fig. 8.1 contains a single box labeled *motivational state*. Obviously, motivation is itself a complex system consisting of both approach and avoidance motivations as well as states of readiness for approach and avoidance states (Carver & Scheier, 1998; Higgins, 1997). Motivational states are also influenced by physiological needs. Furthermore, the details of the relationship between affective states and underlying motivational states remain to be worked out. Finally, the methods that allow individuals to learn the relationships between policies, focal goals, and means must be elucidated. We believe, however, that this framework provides a firm basis for addressing important gaps in our understanding of the relationships among goals, motivation, and preferences.

ACKNOWLEDGMENTS

This research was supported by NIDA Grant R21 DA015211-01A1 given to the first author. The authors would like to thank Kyungil Kim and Claude Messner for their help with empirical studies that have been central to this enterprise. The authors also thank Frank Kardes, Levi Larkey, Claude Messner, Lisa Narvaez, Leora Orent, and C. Hunt Stilwell for helpful discussions during the evolution of this project.

REFERENCES

Ajzen, I., & Fishbein, M. (1977). Attitude–behavior relations: A theoretical analysis and review of empirical research. *Psychological Bulletin, 84*(5), 888–918.

Baron, J., & Spranca, M. (1997). Protected values. *Organizational Behavior and Human Decision Processes, 70*(1), 1–16.

Barsalou, L. W. (1999). Perceptual symbol systems. *Behavioral and Brain Sciences, 22*(4), 577–660.

Berridge, K. C. (1999). Pleasure, pain, desire, and dread: Hidden core processes of emotion. In D. Kahneman, E. Diener, & N. Schwartz (Eds.), *Well-being: The foundations of hedonic psychology* (pp. 525–557). New York: Russell Sage Foundation.

Brendl, C. M., & Higgins, E. T. (1996). Principles of judging valence: What makes events positive or negative. *Advances in Experimental Social Psychology, 28*, 95–160.

Brendl, C. M., Markman, A. B., & Messner, C. (2003). Devaluation of goal-unrelated choice options. *Journal of Consumer Research, 29*, 463–473.

Carver, C. S., & Scheier, M. F. (1998). *On the self-regulation of behavior.* New York: Cambridge University Press.

Ericsson, K. A., & Simon, H. A. (1993). *Protocol analysis: Verbal reports as data* (Rev. ed.). Cambridge, MA: MIT Press.

Fazio, R. H., & Roskos-Ewoldsen, D. R. (1994). Acting as we feel: When and how attitudes guide behavior. In S. Shavitt & T. C. Brock (Eds.), *Persuasion: Psychological insights and perspectives* (pp. 71–93). Needham Heights, MA: Allyn & Bacon.

Fedoroff, I. C., Polivy, J., & Herman, C. P. (1997). The effect of pre-exposure to food cues on the eating behavior of restrained and unrestrained eaters. *Appetite, 28*, 33–47.

Gollwitzer, P. M. (1993). Goal achievement: The role of intentions. *European Review of Social Psychology, 4*, 141–185.

Gollwitzer, P. M. (1999). Implementation intentions: Strong effects of simple plans. *American Psychologist, 54*, 493–503.

Herman, C. P. (1996). Human eating: Diagnosis and prognosis. *Neuroscience and Biobehavioral Reviews, 20*(1), 107–111.

Higgins, E. T. (1997). Beyond pleasure and pain. *American Psychologist, 52*(12), 1280–1300.

Hsee, C. K. (1996). The evaluability hypothesis: An explanation for preference reversals between joint and separate evaluations of alternatives. *Organizational Behavior and Human Decision Processes, 67*(3), 247–257.

Huber, J., Payne, J. W., & Puto, C. (1982). Adding asymmetrically dominated alternatives: Violations of regularity and the similarity hypothesis. *Journal of Consumer Research, 9*, 90–98.

Irwin, J. R., & Baron, J. (2001). Response mode effects and moral values. *Organizational Behavior and Human Decision Processes, 84*(2), 177–197.

Irwin, J. R., & Spria, J. S. (1997). Anomalies in the values for consumer goods with environmental attributes. *Journal of Consumer Psychology, 6*(4), 339–363.

Kahneman, D., & Snell, J. S. (1992). Predicting a changing taste: Do people know what they will like? *Journal of Behavioral Decision Making, 5*(3), 187–200.

Kassel, J. D., & Shiffman, S. (1992). What can hunger teach us about drug craving? A comparative analysis of the two constructs. *Advances in Behavioural Research and Therapy, 14*, 141–167.

Kruglanski, A. W., Shah, J. Y., Fishbach, A., Friedman, R., Chun, W. Y., & Sleeth-Keppler, D. (2002). A theory of goal systems. *Advances in Experimental Social Psychology, 34*, 331–378.

Lewin, K. (1926). Vorsatz, Wille und Bedürfnis [Intention, will, and need]. *Psychologische Forschung, 7*, 330–385.

Lewin, K. (1935). *A dynamic theory of personality*. New York: McGraw-Hill.

Markman, A. B. (1999). *Knowledge representation*. Mahwah, NJ: Lawrence Erlbaum Associates.

Markman, A. B., & Brendl, C. M. (2000). The influence of goals on value and choice. In D. L. Medin (Ed.), *The psychology of learning and motivation* (Vol. 39, pp. 97–129). San Diego, CA: Academic Press.

Markman, A. B., Brendl, C. M., & Kim, K. (2004). *The structure of people's goals: Evidence from valuation and devaluation*. Manuscript in preparation.

Markman, A. B., & Medin, D. L. (1995). Similarity and alignment in choice. *Organizational Behavior and Human Decision Processes, 63*(2), 117–130.

Nisbett, R. E., & Wilson, T. D. (1977). Telling more than we can know: Verbal reports on mental processes. *Psychological Review, 87*, 231–259.

Patalano, A. L., & Seifert, C. M. (1997). Opportunistic planning: Being reminded of pending goals. *Cognitive Psychology, 34*, 1–36.

Payne, J. W., Bettman, J. R., & Johnson, E. J. (1993). *The adaptive decision maker*. New York: Cambridge University Press.

Read, D., Loewenstein, G., & Kalyanaram, S. (1999). Mixing virtue and vice: Combining the immediacy effect and diversification heuristic. *Journal of Behavioral Decision Making, 12*(4), 257–273.

Rodin, J. (1985). Insulin levels, hunger, and food intake: An example of feedback loops in body weight regulation. *Health Psychology, 4*(1), 1–24.

Schooler, J. W., & Engstler-Schooler, T. Y. (1990). Verbal overshadowing of visual memories: Some things are better left unsaid. *Cognitive Psychology, 22*, 36–71.

Shafir, E., Simonson, I., & Tversky, A. (1993). Reason-based choice. *Cognition, 49*, 11–36.

Shah, J. Y., Friedman, R., & Kruglanski, A. W. (2002). Forgetting all else: On the antecedents and consequents of goal shielding. *Journal of Personality and Social Psychology, 83*(6), 1261–1280.

Shah, J. Y., Kruglanski, A. W., & Friedman, R. (2003). Goal systems theory: Integrating the cognitive and motivational aspects of self-regulation. In S. J. Spencer, S. Fein, M. P. Zanna, & J. M. Olson (Eds.), *Motivated social perception: The Ontario Symposium, Volume 9* (pp. 247–275). Mahwah, NJ: Lawrence Erlbaum Associates.

Simon, H. A. (1957). *Models of man: Social and rational*. New York: Wiley.

Simonson, I. (1989). Choice based on reasons: The case of attraction and compromise effects. *Journal of Consumer Research, 16*, 158–174.

Slovic, P., & MacPhillamy, D. (1974). Dimensional commensurability and cue utilization in comparative judgment. *Organizational Behavior and Human Performance, 11*, 172–194.

Tetlock, P. E., Kristel, O. V., Elson, S. B., Green, M. C., & Lerner, J. S. (2000). The psychology of the unthinkable: Taboo trade-offs, forbidden base rates, and heretical counterfactuals. *Journal of Personality and Social Psychology, 78*(5), 853–870.

Tiffany, S. T. (1990). A cognitive model of drug urges and drug-use behavior: Role of automatic and nonautomatic processes. *Psychological Review, 97*, 147–168.

Tiffany, S. T., & Conklin, C. A. (2000). A cognitive processing model of alcohol craving and compulsive alcohol use. *Addiction, 95*, S145–S154.

Tversky, A. (1972). Elimination by aspects: A theory of choice. *Psychological Review, 79*(4), 281–299.

Wertenbroch, K. (1998). Consumption self-control by rationing purchase quantities of virtue and vice. *Marketing Service, 17*(4), 317–337.

Wilson, T. D., & Dunn, D. S. (1986). Effects of introspection on attitude–behavior consistency: Analyzing reasons versus focusing on feelings. *Journal of Experimental Social Psychology, 22*, 249–263.

Wilson, T. D., Lisle, D. J., Schooler, J. W., Hodges, S. D., Klaaren, K. J., & LaFleur, S. J. (1993). Introspecting about reasons can reduce post-choice satisfaction. *Personality and Social Psychology Bulletin, 19*(3), 331–339.

Wilson, T. D., & Schooler, J. W. (1991). Thinking too much: Introspection can reduce the quality of preferences and decisions. *Journal of Personality and Social Psychology, 60*(2), 181–192.

Zeigarnik, B. (1927). Das Behalten erledigter unt unerledigter Handlungen [The retention of completed and uncompleted actions]. *Psychologische Forschung, 9*, 1–85.

Zhang, S., & Markman, A. B. (1998). Overcoming the early entrant advantage: The role of alignable and nonalignable differences. *Journal of Marketing Research, 35*, 413–426.

Zhang, S., & Markman, A. B. (2001). Processing product-unique features: Alignment and involvement in preference construction. *Journal of Consumer Psychology, 11*, 13–27.

CHAPTER NINE

Consumption as a Multiple-Goal Pursuit Without Awareness

Woo Young Chun
Hallym University

Arie W. Kruglanski
University of Maryland

This chapter examines how multiple-goal pursuit without awareness affects individuals' judgment, decision making, and behavior, especially within the domain of product consumption. The evaluation and selection of products in everyday life are often directed by consumers' multiple goals. In some cases, consumers are consciously aware of what goals they are pursuing. One may buy a hybrid car because he or she is explicitly aware that it is not only the most fuel-efficient vehicle, but that it also promises the cleanest emissions for the environment. An interesting question, however, is if in fact consumers have such volitionally pursued goals, are their decisions still susceptible to the influence of goals of which they are unaware? For example, would an individual make a different decision regarding the car based on his or her unconscious goal of identification with his or her own country, even if the goal of finding a fuel-efficient car with clean emissions is still clearly in mind? Another question of interest is whether such unconscious multiple-goal pursuits are more chronically accessible to some individuals than to others. That is, are there individual differences in the desire for multiple-goal pursuit in product consumption?

To address these questions, we first propose that an individual's conscious and unconscious goals may be cognitively connected to a single means of attainment. Consumers' unconscious goal pursuit, while striving to attain conscious goals, is enabled through the choice of a product linked to both types of goals. We specifically propose that consumers' choices are likely to be influenced by unconscious goals as long as their choices also satisfy goals that they are consciously pursuing. We posit additionally that a consumer's desire for multiple-goal pursuit may depend on the extent of his or her permanency strivings induced by a heightened need for cognitive closure (Kruglanski & Webster, 1996). We argue that consumers motivated to attain cross-situational consistency and in that sense, epistemic "permanence" in the use of products are likely to prefer and choose a product that allows consumers to achieve multiple goals without changing products. In other words, we are proposing that individuals high (vs. low) in the need for cognitive closure will prefer and choose products with multifunctions likely to lend them a sense of epistemic permanence, rather than products with only a single function, because the latter will leave them with a growing sense of uncertainty with respect to the fulfillment of other needed functions.

In the following four sections, we first describe the mental structure of goals and means that predicts the structural possibility of the effects of unconscious goals on preferences and choices of products. We then discuss two issues regarding the application of social cognitive research paradigms in investigating unconscious consumer behavior. Next, we review research testing the effects of unconscious goals on choices and the effects of need for closure on multiple-goal pursuit. Finally, we discuss the implications of this research program for consumer research.

GOAL SYSTEMS AS INTERCONNECTED COGNITIVE NETWORKS

According to *goal systems theory* (Kruglanski et al., 2002), goals are mentally represented within intricate cognitive networks (see also Bargh & Gollwitzer, 1994; Wyer & Srull, 1986) wherein a high-level goal is cognitively connected to lower-level subgoals that, in turn, are linked to their own means of attainment and to alternative goals as well. An interesting aspect of the structure of the interconnected goal systems is that the number of means attached to a given goal may vary and so may the number of goals linked to a given means. These enable respectively the configurations of equifinality and multifinality.

Equifinality Set

The number of means linked to a given goal defines the *equifinality* set (e.g., Heider, 1958) encapsulated in the notion that "all roads lead to Rome." A given goal can be achieved by any one of the single means that are linked to it. For example, the goal of buying a car can be fulfilled by purchasing either a hybrid car or a SUV. The size of the equifinality set determines the amount of available choice between the means and the range of substitutability of one means for another (Kruglanski, 1996). The more means are connected to a given goal, the greater the perceived substitutability of each means and hence the greater the perceived freedom of choice afforded in this situation.

One of the most commonly adopted ways to make a decision in the presence of multiple means to achieve goals is to choose the means that promises the greater perceived value of the outcome. According to the goal systems theory, this is determined by another configurational property of goal systems referred to as multifinality (Kruglanski et al., 2002).

Multifinality Set

The *multifinality* configuration is known as the set of goals linked to a given means of attainment. The old proverb of "killing two birds with one stone" exemplifies the idea of multifinality. That is, multiple goals can be satisfied by a single means of attainment. For example, by purchasing a hybrid car one can satisfy the goal of finding a fuel-efficient vehicle as well as finding a car with the cleanest emissions at the same time. The size of the multifinality set may partially affect the perceived value that a given means may afford. For example, the more goals a given product can facilitate, the greater should be its perceived value. Therefore, a multifinal product that affords the attainment of several goals may be chosen over a unifinal product because it may promise greater value, or "more bang for one's buck."

Focal Versus Background Goals

In goal systems theory, we distinguish between focal goals that a person is consciously and deliberately pursuing, and background goals of which he or she may not be consciously aware. Often, a means may be multifinal because it serves not only the focal goal, but also a background goal or goals. By choosing such a multifinal means people can fulfill their focal and background goals at the same time. In other words, the multifinal choice may often be driven by a background goal of which the person is not explicitly aware. Suppose an undergraduate student, who has a background goal of identifying with his or her university, is looking for a durable sweatshirt and finds two equally durable ones. Which one will he or she pick? According to the goal systems theory, it may depend on which shirt has the university color. Although he or she is not consciously aware of their background goal, as long as the background goal of identification with their university is activated, the person would choose the university colored shirt in order to satisfy not only his or her focal goal of finding a durable sweatshirt, but also background goal of attaining one's school identification.

The distinction between focal goals and background goals provides a significant advantage in research on the unconscious aspects of consumer behavior and decision making. Before we review our own studies on these issues, it is worthwhile to discuss some issues regarding the research paradigm utilized in investigating unconscious consumer behavior and related to the benefit of distinguishing between focal and background goals.

APPLYING SOCIAL COGNITIVE RESEARCH PARADIGM
TO UNCONSCIOUS CONSUMER BEHAVIOR

As Bargh (2002) aptly pointed out in his article, the dominant approach to consumer behavior assumes that consumers make their judgments and decisions consciously and deliberately, even though the unconscious nature of human judgment, decision making, and behavior has been widely accepted in the domain of social cognition since the 1980s (Bargh & Chartrand, 1999; Fazio, Sanbonmatsu, Powell, & Kardes, 1986; Nisbett & Willson, 1977). A possible reason why research on unconscious consumer behavior is lacking is that consumers' purchase decisions generally involve spending money, which makes the nature of their decisions volitional. That does not necessarily mean, however, that consumers are completely aware of the forces that may prompt their choices. Instead, it identifies a need for a research paradigm that can address the question as to how unconscious goals or motivations may affect consumer behavior even when that behavior is under influence of a deliberately pursued goal.

Because the main purpose of most social cognitive research on the role of unconscious goals in judgment and decision making has been to show the existence of unconscious goals and their impact on social behavior, controlling possible influences of conscious goals on dependent measures might have been the key to success in testing the impact of unconscious goals on social behavior (e.g., Chartrand & Bargh, 1996). Ironically, however, incorporating conscious goals in the experimental paradigm may be the key to success in investigating the unconscious impact of goals on consumer behavior.

Another methodological question concerns the most appropriate way of priming unconscious goals in the investigation of unconscious consumer behavior. Should it be a subliminal priming or supraliminal one? Although many social cognitive studies have been using subliminal priming to activate unconscious goals, consumers' unconscious goals in real life are mostly activated supraliminally. That is, "most stimuli in real life as well as in advertising are in one's plain view" (Bargh, 2002, p. 283). Therefore, another reason that the wave of work on unconsciousness in social cognition failed to attract attention from the field of consumer research could be found in the lack of studies applicable to consumer research, that is, research using supraliminal priming, or real-life situations as a source of background goals. As long as individuals are unaware of how supraliminal priming or how their experiences in real-life settings affect their consumption behavior, it will have a greater "ecological validity" (McKechnie, 1997).

In summary, we argue that in order to understand and investigate unconscious consumer behavior in and of itself, a participant's focal goals should be explicitly activated with the background goals still in operation. In addition, using supraliminal priming or real experiences in everyday life as a source of background goals will provide a closer and more ecologically valid look at consumers' behavior.

We now discuss the implications of the multifinality configuration regarding unconscious consumer judgment, decision making, and behavior. We first examine how the multifinality pursuit can influence choice without awareness. Next, we explore how individual differences in need for cognitive closure affect multifinality pursuits. In the concluding section, we discuss the implications of goal systems theory and the need for cognitive closure in understanding consumer behavior.

THE MULTIFINALITY PRINCIPLE IN CHOICE
WITHOUT AWARENESS

A fascinating implication regarding the multifinality set is that a consumer may choose a multifinal product even if he or she is not consciously aware of the multifinal nature of their choice. In order to test this possibility, Chun, Kruglanski, Keppler, and Friedman (2004) used identification or disidentification goals with one's university or country to manipulate participants' background goals. This research is now described.

The Influence of Background Goals on Choice

In spring 2001, two significant events happened on the College Park campus of the University of Maryland (UM); one was positive and the other was negative. The positive event was that the Maryland basketball team reached the "final four" in the NCAA (National Collegiate Athletic Association) tournament. The negative event was an outbreak of vandalism in College Park after the loss to Duke in the semifinal game. Chun et al. (2004, Study 2) took advantage of these two events to manipulate the participants' background goals to either identify or disidentify with their university.

In this experiment, participants, undergraduates at the University of Maryland, were presented a series of questions in order to recall the events of "reaching the final four" or "vandalism" and then reported their feelings about it. Not surprisingly, participants reported "feeling proud" in the final four condition (i.e., goal of identification with UM), and "feeling ashamed" in the vandalism condition (i.e., goal of disidentifying with UM).

Subsequently, participants were invited for an ostensibly separate joint experiment of the department of psychology and marketing on campus. Participants were presented with two patches of fabric. Participants were *explicitly* instructed that their task was to feel the two fabric patches and choose the one that felt more durable. This constituted participants' explicitly introduced "focal goal." Although they were told that the two different fabrics produced by two different companies used different raw materials, in fact, both patches were of exactly the same material. One was colored red, representing the University of Maryland color, whereas the other was purple, representing a control color.

Due to the fact that in this study, participants' focal goal of finding the more durable fabric could be equally satisfied by either the red patch or the purple patch, we expected that the participants' choices would be determined by their background goals. In the final four condition, by selecting the University of Maryland color, which was a red patch, they could fulfill both the focal goal, which was to find a durable patch, while simultaneously accomplishing the background goal, which was to satisfy their identification goal. By contrast, in the vandalism condition, the multifinal choice induced selecting the control color, which was a purple patch. This choice afforded fulfillment of the focal goal, as well as background goal, which was to disidentify with their university.

As predicted, the results indicated that in the final four condition, most participants selected the red patch as the more durable patch. However, in the vandalism condition, this tendency was reversed. These results support the notion that the pursuit of multiple goals by choosing a single product can be directed by consumers' background goals, even when the individuals are explicitly pursuing their focal goals.

Following their choice, participants were asked to list their reasons for choosing the patch that they did. The content analysis on the reasons participants gave for their choices revealed that participants exhibited no awareness that their choices might have anything to do with the background goal of identifying or disidentifying with their university, or with the color of the patches. Their reported reasons for their choices were phrased invariably in terms of their focal goal, namely, the durability of fabrics. Typical such reasons include statements such as "The red is stiffer" or "The red is more tightly woven." These reasons indicate that participants were totally unaware of the multifinal nature of their choices, and of the background goals that affected it.

Overriding Effects of the Focal Goal

Does the Maryland Color Study implicitly depict consumers as passive and helpless victims of their unconscious goals? We think not. It is possible that unconscious goals in the Maryland Color Study could influence participants' choices of fabrics because both fabric patches being chosen from were equally capable of satisfying their focal goal. In other words, unconscious goals could have played an important role in participants' decision making because participants chose among items that identically satisfied the focal goal. It is indeed plausible that if the focal goal were not satisfied by the choice objects, the power of the background goals would be overridden, and they would no longer influence the consumers' decision.

To test this possibility, Chun et al. (2004, Study 3) used two events related to the September 11th terrorist attack on the Twin Towers—one positive, the other negative. The positive event was that so many Americans volunteered their time at Ground Zero (e.g., see BBC News, September 25, 2001). The negative event was the possibility that an American could be responsible for the anthrax cases (e.g., see BBC News, November 10, 2001). In this experiment, participants were asked to describe their feelings about either volunteering or the anthrax cases. The results of the content analysis on the participants' description about their feelings show that participants in the "volunteering" condition felt greater pride of as well as greater identification with the United States than did those in the "anthrax" condition.

Subsequently, participants were asked to participate in joint research with the marketing department to choose the tastiest cola between: (a) a caffeine-free diet Pepsi™, (b) a caffeine-free diet Coke™, and (c) a generic cola, actually a Shoppers brand diet cola. In a pilot study, it was found that most of the participants, all American citizens, perceived Coke as the representative or typical American brand of soda. Therefore, it was expected that the proportion of participants choosing Coke over Pepsi or Shoppers cola would be greater when participants desired to identify with the United States (in the "volunteering" condition) than to disidentify with the United States (in the "anthrax" condition). However, this should be the case only when participants could satisfy their focal goal by selecting Coke! Although the bottles of cola were presented in their original packaging of caffeine-free diet Pepsi, caffeine-free diet Coke, and Shoppers diet cola, the content of all three beverages were composed of regular Shoppers cola and water. In the "Shoppers superior" condition, the Shoppers cola was composed of pure cola without water but in the "Shoppers inferior" condition, Shoppers cola was composed of 2000 ml water and 500 ml cola. Furthermore, in both conditions, Coke and Pepsi were composed of half Shoppers cola and half water. Therefore, in the "Shoppers superior" condition, Shoppers cola was tastier than Coke and Pepsi. But in the "Shoppers inferior" condition, Coke and Pepsi were tastier than Shoppers cola.

In the "Shoppers superior" condition, the focal goal could be fulfilled only by choosing the Shoppers cola. Therefore, in this condition, participants should select Shoppers cola regardless of their background goal. However, in the "Shoppers inferior" condition, the focal goal could be equally well satisfied by choosing either Coke or Pepsi. But only one of these beverages would satisfy participants' background goal, depending on whether they identified or disidentified with their country.

In the volunteering condition, by choosing Coke, which is the most "American" of the colas, they could realize their focal goal of choosing the tastiest cola, while at the same time achieving their background goal of identifying with their country. However, in the anthrax condition, it was opting for the alleged Pepsi cola instead of the Coke that allowed participants to achieve their focal goal, and at the same time satisfy their background goal of disidentifying with the United States.

The results indicate that in the "Shoppers superior" condition, regardless of whether they desired to identify or disidentify with the United States, participants indeed selected Shoppers cola as the tastiest soda. This result indicates that participants were actually attending to their focal goal. However, in the "Shoppers inferior" conditions, participants' choices depended on their background goals. In the "volunteering" condition, most participants selected Coke, but in the "anthrax" condition, most participants chose Pepsi. These results support our prediction that the multifinality pursuit in product choice can be directed by a consumer's background goals even if he or she is explicitly pursuing other, focal, goals. However, this effect of consumers' background goals on choices is in operation only when their choices guarantee the attainment of focal goals as well.

As in the Maryland Color Study, participants' reasons for their choices indicated that their choices were directed by the focal goal. The reasons participants gave for their choices include, "The Coke seemed just slightly more bubbly and slightly sweeter than the Pepsi," "It was sweeter and more carbonated," and "You can taste more sugar, more bubbles, more flavor." These statements indicate that participants were unaware of the multifinal nature of their choices.

Summary

The studies reviewed demonstrate that (a) the pursuit of multiple goals via a single product can be directed by consumers' background goals even when they are explicitly pursuing their focal goals, and (b) consumers' background goals seem to affect their decisions only when their choices for multiple-goal pursuit promise the attainment of focal goals. Taken together, these findings provide evidence for our basic assumption that the pursuit of multiple goals can take place without people's conscious awareness of the multifinal nature of their choices even when they are pursuing their focal goals in full consciousness. That is, all else being equal, individuals may indeed desire to "kill two birds with one stone" and implement this desire in their choices.

THE INFLUENCE OF THE NEED FOR COGNITIVE CLOSURE ON MULTIFINALITY PURSUIT IN CONSUMER BEHAVIOR

Though generally people desire to attain multiple goals, not all persons may experience such a desire equally. Different people may have different needs, motivations, or goals. Some of these may affect individuals' predilection toward multifinality. The need for cognitive closure (Kruglanski, 1989; Kruglanski & Webster, 1996) is of particular importance in this regard.

The Need for Cognitive Closure

The need for closure (NFC) has been defined as a desire for a definite answer to a question as opposed to uncertainty, confusion, or ambiguity (Kruglanski, 1989). This need has been treated both as a dispositional variable (Webster & Kruglanski, 1994) and as a situationally evocable state (Chiu, Morris, Hong, & Menon, 2000; Kruglanski, Webster, & Klem, 1993; Mayseless & Kruglanski, 1987). The NFC has been shown to moderate a wide range of consumer judgmental phenomena, including the alignability effect (Zhang, Kardes, & Cronley, 2002), consideration set overvaluation (Kardes, Sanbonmatsu, Cronley, & Houghton, 2002), the noncomplementarity effect (Houghton & Kardes, 1998), and price–quality inference (Kardes, Cronley, Kellaris, & Posavac, in press). A number of studies have found that individuals under high NFC, after having attained closure immediately, desire to retain it permanently (see Kruglanski & Webster, 1996; Webster & Kruglanski, 1998, for a review). It has been shown that individuals high (vs. low) in NFC, presumably due to their permanency strivings, prefer knowledge that affords cross-situational consistency and lessens the need to reconsider one's knowledge from one social situation to the next (Boudreau, Baron, & Oliver, 1992; Rubini & Kruglanski, 1997; Webster, Kruglanski, & Pattison, 1997). For instance, Webster et al. (1997) found that individuals high (vs low) in NFC exhibited greater linguistic abstraction in describing behaviors of in- and out-group members, and Rubini and Kruglanski (1997) also found that participants under high (vs. low) NFC selected more abstract interview questions, because the abstract (vs. concrete) expressions satisfied their permanency strivings. Whereas the concrete term (e.g., A *hits* B) portrays a specific event, which may potentially hinder the application of the term to different situations, the abstracted language (e.g., A is *aggressive*) can be generalized beyond specific situations to other various future circumstances (Semin & Fiedler, 1988). In other words, because the abstract expressions are more applicable to other events or situations and hence promise greater permanency than the concrete ones, they can fulfill the permanency goals of high NFC individuals to a greater extent than the concrete ones. Therefore, in terms of goal systems theory (Kruglanski et al., 2002), abstract expressions are more multifinal than concrete expressions whose uses are confined to relatively limited situations compared to abstract ones.

The Multifinality Pursuit for a Permanency Goal

If high (vs. low) NFC individuals' desire for permanency is a chronically accessible goal, we can also expect that their permanency strivings would impact not only the use of language, but also the use of products and consumer behavior more generally. Therefore, a product that can be used to achieve various goals should be more appealing to high (vs. low) NFC individuals. For example, a Swiss Army Knife™, which can be used as a pair of scissors, a bottle opener, a knife, and so forth, is more multifinal than a regular knife, whose functions are confined to relatively limited goals at least when compared to the Swiss Army Knife. Accordingly, the Swiss Army Knife may be more appealing to high (vs. low) NFC individuals. We now examine the implication of the foregoing notions.

Conflicts Between Multifinality Pursuit and Product Quality

An interesting question to consider is whether the preference for the choice of multifinal products by high (vs. low) need for closure individuals may occasionally override consideration of product quality. To test this possibility, Chun and Kruglanski (2004, Study 2) asked participants to report their willingness to buy two different cameras. One camera had only one function and was portrayed as of a very good quality, which was an unifunctional camera from our definition. The other camera had several functions and was portrayed as of only a good quality, which was regarded as a multifunctional camera. Thus, participants' preferences between the two cameras could be determined by a joint function of the number of goals that they could achieve by each camera and the quality of goals that each camera could provide.

The results showed that for individuals high in NFC, the willingness to buy the multifunctional camera of good quality was greater than that to buy the unifunctional one of very good quality. As we expected, when the number of goals that can be attained by a means is in conflict with the quality of the goals, the judgment of individuals high in NFC is more likely to be influenced by the number of goals than by the goals' quality.

These findings also indicate that individuals high (vs. low) in NFC are likely to adopt the multifinality pursuit as their strategy for their judgment, even when its efficacy is limited. Even though the multifinality pursuit in this experiment involved a certain sacrifice (namely in terms of quality), individuals high (vs. low) in NFC showed a stronger preference for the multifunctional over the unifunctional camera.

Conflicts Between Multifinality Pursuit and the Price of Products

Another possible limitation of the multifinality pursuit in product consumption has to do with a price to be paid for a multifunctional product. For instance, it is not difficult to find cellular phones that include features of games, e-mails, and pictures, as well as high reception. Yet such cellular phones are usually more expensive than phones with more limited functions. The question then is whether people high in NFC would pursue multifinality even if this would mean paying a higher price for the selected products.

To test this possibility, Chun and Kruglanski (2004, Study 3) investigated the influence of NFC on choice for multifinality in a situation wherein the price of a multifunctional product was higher than that of a unifunctional product in the same category. Specifically, participants were given information regarding two cellular phones: One had several functions, including high reception, camera capabilities, e-mail accessibility, and a very high price. The other cellular phone had only one function, namely, high reception, and a very low price. Note that in this study, unlike the previous one, the number of goals that the cellular phones provided was not in conflict with the quality of the goals because the multifunctional cellular phone offered the same level of reception rate as did the unifunctional cellular phone. Therefore, the participants' choices in this study confronted a conflict between the number of goals a product was offering and its price. A choice of the unifunctional cellular phone would entail giving up additional functions, yet a choice of the multifunctional phone entails paying a higher price.

The results showed that the proportion of participants who chose the multifunctional cellular phone was greater in the high (vs. the low) NFC group even if they were supposed to pay more money to purchase it. That is, high (vs. low) NFC individuals seem to be less sensitive to price of a product possibly because of their concern with multifinality.

The Multifinality Pursuit in Product Use

It seems now evident that high (vs. low) NFC individuals' preferences (The Camera Study) and product choices (The Cellular Phone Study) are more likely to be influenced by the number of goals that the products promise rather than the quality or cost of products. But note that these findings pertain to a predecision period, before the individuals actually acquired a product. The next question is how does the multifinality pursuit influence high (vs. low) NFC individuals' behavior after making a decision. One possibility is that after selecting a product, individuals high (vs. low) in NFC might try to find more possible ways of using it. Put differently, because individuals high (vs. low) in NFC have a stronger motivation not to change their means across situations, once they find a single means, they might use it for multiple purposes.

To test this possibility, Chun and Kruglanski (2004, Study 4) asked participants to list the goals that they wanted to attain from using computers. In addition, they were asked to report the average number of hours they used computers daily, and to rate how often they used the computers. The results show that individuals high in NFC wanted to attain more goals by using computers than did those low in NFC. However, there was no significant difference between high versus low NFC individuals in hours and frequency of reported computer use. In other words, the fact that individuals high (vs. low) in NFC desire to attain more goals by using computers is not because they spend more time with computers or use them more frequently, but because they want to keep using the same means across goals. Individuals high (vs. low) in NFC prefer not to change a single product depending on goals because they strive for permanency in the use of means.

Multifinality Pursuit and the Use of Fewer Products

An alternative interpretation for the foregoing studies is that individuals high in NFC might have more goals compared to those low in NFC and, as a consequence, they have a higher need for multifinal products. The question, then, is whether high (vs. low) NFC individuals would prefer a multifinal product over a number of unifinal products that, *collectively*, afford the attainment of the same number of goals.

To address this question, Chun and Kruglanski (2004, Study 5) asked participants simply to report products they were using to wash their face and body. Because everyone has the same number of goals in this case, we expected that the desire for multifinal products would result in choosing and hence using fewer products for the same number of goals. That is, we predicted that individuals high in NFC would choose as well as use fewer products (e.g., soap) for the same number of goals (i.e., for washing face and body) compared to those low in NFC (who might use, e.g., facial cleanser for washing the face and soap for washing the body). Given that soap is the most common product for washing the face and the body and that individuals high (vs. low) in NFC have a desire not to change their means across different goals, they should be likely to use one soap for washing both their face and their body, instead of using two different products for the same purposes.

We additionally expected, however, that this tendency would be moderated by gender (e.g., Iacobucci & Ostrom, 1993). Because a pilot study has shown that females are more motivated to take care of their skin as compared to males, they may have a greater *fear of invalidity* (Kruglanski & Freund, 1983) for selecting the right products for their skin and hence might experience a low need for closure in this particular choice context.

Consistent with our predictions, the results of our study showed that most female participants reported that they were using two different products for washing their face and their body, and this was independent of the individual differences in NFC. In contrast, the choices of males were strongly dependent on individual differences in NFC. Males low in NFC were likely to use two different products for washing their face and their body, whereas males high in NFC were likely to use only one soap for the same purposes.

These results support our assumption that individuals high (vs. low) in NFC would tend to use fewer means to achieve the same number of goals. These findings also indicate that individuals high in the NFC are more likely to pursue multiple goals, not because they have more goals compared to individuals low in NFC, but because they prefer to use a single multifinal product for the attainment of the same number of goals that could be collectively afforded by a number of unifinal products.

Summary

In summary, research reviewed in this section demonstrates that because individuals high (vs. low) in need for closure have a stronger desire for permanency, they favor products with multiple functions over products with a single function even if (a) this involves a sacrifice in quality or (b) it comes at a particularly high price. Moreover, high need for closure individuals (c) are more likely to use the same product across various situations without changing it depending on goals, and (d) they tend to use fewer products to achieve the same number of goals. Taken together, these findings provide evidence for our basic assumption that the degree of implementation of a desire for achieving multiple goals by using a single means in the domain of product consumption may depend on individual differences in need for closure. Across a broad range of goals and means, the multifinality pursuit of individuals high in need for closure results in the use, preference, and choice of multifunctional over unifunctional products.

IMPLICATIONS AND APPLICATIONS

The foregoing goal-systemic analysis of consumer behavior has a variety of important implications. In this, our final, section we discuss them in turn.

Consumer Life Satisfaction

Consumption, at least in capitalistic countries, is now regarded as a culturally accepted means of seeking happiness (Burroughs & Rindfleisch, 2002). Research in the domain of subjective well-being suggests that possessing a product that satisfies the consumers' goals may enhance their subjective well-being. For example, Cantor and Sanderson (1999) found that possessing resources or means allowing individuals to pursue and attain their intrinsic and distinct goals is an important factor in subjective well-being. Diener and Fujita (1995) also found that having means (e.g., money, family support, social skills, physical attractiveness, and intelligence) relevant to an individual's personal goals is related to subjective well-being. Therefore, it seems that having products, especially allowing consumers' to achieve their focal goals for a relatively long period of time (e.g., durables), may increase their subjective life satisfaction. The question then is whether the possession of products enabling consumers to attain their background goals may similarly affect subjective well-being. According to Chun et al. (2004), consumers' subjective well-being may be enhanced by such products as long as these products allow them to achieve their focal goals as well.

A more interesting question is whether the effects on subjective well-being of acquiring a product allowing consumers to attain both focal and background goals may be moderated by consumers' individual difference in need for closure. Based on the findings of Chun and Kruglanski (2004), we predict that high (vs. low) NFC individuals' subjective life satisfaction may be more strongly influenced by whether they have a multifinal product that allows them to attain both focal and background goals. It should be noted, however, that in this case, high NFC people's choice can be based on their "immediacy" as well as their "permanency" strivings (Kruglanski & Webster, 1996). For example, a person may purchase an American brand hybrid car because it can satisfy his or her permanency goal. That is, it can satisfy the focal goal of having an economical car at one moment but it may also fulfill the background goal of identification with one's own country at the other moment when the identification goal is activated. Note that the same purchasing behavior can satisfy the same focal and background goals immediately at the moment he or she purchases it.

Although studies reviewed in this chapter entirely focus on permanency concerns, it is noteworthy that people's immediacy concerns can also be addressed via a multifunctional product. For instance, products such as orange juice with calcium are designed to satisfy consumers' immediacy goal rather than their permanency goal. People could satisfy their multiple goals (e.g., taking vitamin C and calcium) immediately by drinking orange juice with calcium. Therefore, we could expect that multifunctional products designed to satisfy multiple goals immediately may also be more appealing to individuals high (vs. low) in NFC even if it requires sacrificing other goals such as a higher quality, which unifunctional products may provide. In addition, having a product with multifunctions that satisfies immediacy needs may be more closely related to the subjective well-being of individuals high (vs. low) in NFC.

Variety Seeking

Consumers seek variety in their choices even though it may provide less pleasure than does the repeated exercise of the very same option (Ratner, Kahn, & Kahneman, 1999). For example, one may visit a new coffee shop occasionally even though he or she is completely satisfied with coffee from Starbucks, one's usual source of this drink. The question is whether the variety seeking is related to the structure of goals and means or whether it could be influenced by the need for closure.

First of all, a conceptual distinction should be drawn between multifinality pursuit and variety seeking (Bawa, 1990; Givon, 1984; McAlister, 1982; Ratner et al., 1999). Although two concepts may sound somewhat similar to one another, *variety seeking* is about the pursuit of various means to fulfill a single goal, rather than the pursuit of multiple goals with a single means. Therefore, variety seeking is more closely related to the equifinality configuration, known as the set of means linked to a given goal (Kruglanski et al., 2002). Because the size of the equifinality set determines the amount of available choice among the means and the range of substitutability (Kruglanski, 1996), a presence of a greater equifinality set, that is, of many available means or options for a goal may be a necessary condition for variety seeking. Unlike with multifinality, variety seeking may not be a strategy preferred by individuals with a high (vs. low) NFC. Such persons are likely to prefer a small (vs. a large) equifinality set requiring less deliberation and affording greater immediacy. Thus, we predict that high (vs. low) NFC individuals will exhibit a lesser tendency of variety seeking. This possibility should be explored in subsequent research.

Consumer Loyalty

Why are some individuals more likely than others to be frustrated on finding out that a local Starbucks coffee shop was unexpectedly closed? Maybe it is, in part, because they are more committed to drinking the Starbucks coffee every morning. The question then is whether consumer loyalty is related to the need for closure and also the goals and means structure.

The findings of studies reviewed in this chapter imply that individuals high (vs. low) in NFC may be more likely to be reluctant to change their current means. Put differently, individuals high (vs. low) in NFC may be less willing to change the products and services that they are currently enjoying. Because they have a stronger desire for permanency, they may be motivated to stay with the same means, and thus be loyal to the same products, brands, and services.

In addition to the motivational reason above, cognitive structures of goals and means also imply that individuals high (vs. low) in need for closure may be more likely to be committed to products, brands, and services that they are currently consuming. According to Chun and Kruglanski (2004, Study 5), individuals high (vs. low) in NFC may associate fewer products with a given goal. Their tendency toward multifinality may result in fewer means per goal ratio. This, in turn, may imbue each means with greater importance, increasing commitment to the means. Therefore, both motivational and cognitive factors suggest that high (vs. low) NFC people may be more likely to rely on the same products, brands, and services over time, and hence be more loyal customers overall.

CONCLUSION

In this chapter, we proposed that individuals' judgment and decision making regarding product consumption are often directed by a multiple-goal pursuit without awareness. The pursuit of multiple goals by choosing a single product can be influenced by consumers' background goals while they are explicitly pursuing focal goals as long as their choices promise the attainment of the focal goals. Such unconscious multiple-goal pursuit through a single product may be more characteristic of individuals high (vs. low) in NFC. Across a broad range of goals and means, the multifinality pursuit of individuals high in NFC may result in the use, preference, and choice of products with multifunctions over those affording a single functionality. On the basis of this research, it seems plausible that consumers' goal-systemic structure and its relationship to need for closure may underlie a wide range of behavioral phenomena of considerable interest to consumer psychologists.

REFERENCES

Bargh, J. A. (2002). Losing consciousness: Automatic influences on consumer judgment, behavior, and motivation. *Journal of Consumer Research, 29,* 280–285.

Bargh, J. A., & Chartrand, T. L. (1999). The unbearable automaticity of being. *American Psychologist, 54*, 462–479.

Bargh, J. A., & Gollwitzer, P. M. (1994). Environmental control of goal-directed action: Automatic and strategic contingencies between situations and behavior. In W. D. Spaulding (Ed.), *Nebraska Symposium on Motivation* (pp. 71–124). Lincoln: University of Nebraska Press.

Bawa, K. (1990). Modeling inertia and variety seeking tendencies in brand choice behavior. *Marketing Science, 9*, 263–278.

Boudreau, L. A., Baron, R., & Oliver, P. V. (1992). Effects of expected communication target expertise and timing of set on trait use in person description. *Personality and Social Psychology Bulletin, 18*, 447–452.

BBC News. (2001, November 10). Anthrax culprit 'probably domestic.' Available at http://news.bbc.co.uk/go/em/fr/-/1/hi/world/americas/1648159.stm

BBC News. (2001, September 25). Generation Y's chance to shine? Available at http://news.bbc.co/uk/go/em/fr/-1/hi/world/americas/1562112.stm

Burroughs, J. E., & Rindfleisch, A. (2002). Materialism and well-being: A conflicting values perspective. *Journal of Consumer Research, 29*, 348–370.

Cantor, N., & Sanderson, C. A. (1999). Life task participation and well-being: The importance of taking part in daily life. In D. Kahneman, E. Diener, & N. Schwarz (Eds.), *Well-being: The foundations of hedonic psychology* (pp. 230–243). New York: Russell Sage Foundation.

Chartrand, T. L., & Bargh, J. A. (1996). Automatic activation of impression formation and memorization goals: Nonconscious goal priming reproduces effects of explicit task instructions. *Journal of Personality and Social Psychology, 71*, 464–478.

Chiu, C., Morris, M. W., Hong, Y., & Menon, T. (2000). Motivated cultural cognition: The impact of implicit cultural theories on dispositional attribution varies as a function of need for closure. *Journal of Personality and Social Psychology, 78*, 247–259.

Chun, W. Y., & Kruglanski, A. W. (2004). *Killing two birds with one soap: The multifinality pursuit and the need for closure.* Unpublished manuscript.

Chun, W. Y., Kruglanski, A. W., Keppler, D. S., & Friedman, R. (2004). *The multifinality principle in choice without awareness.* Unpublished manuscript.

Diener, E., & Fujita, F. (1995). Resources, personal strivings, and subjective well-being: A nomothetic and idiographic approach. *Journal of Personality and Social Psychology, 68*, 926–935.

Fazio, R. H., Sanbonmatsu, D. M., Powell, M. C., & Kardes, F. R. (1986). On the automatic activation of attitudes. *Journal of Personality and Social Psychology, 50*, 229–238.

Givon, M. (1984). Variety-seeking through brand switching. *Marketing Science, 3*, 1–22.

Heider, F. (1958). *The psychology of interpersonal relations.* New York: Wiley.

Houghton, D. C., & Kardes, F. R. (1998). Market share overestimation and the noncomplementarity effect. *Marketing Letters, 9*, 313–320.

Iacobucci, D., & Ostrom, A. (1993). Gender differences in the impact of core and relational aspects of services on the evaluation of services encounters. *Journal of Consumer Psychology, 2*, 257–286.

Kardes, F. R., Cronley, M. L., Kellaris, J. J., & Posavac, S. S. (in press). The role of selective information processing in price–quality inference. *Journal of Consumer Research.*

Kardes, F. R., Sanbonmatsu, D. M., Cronley, M. L., & Houghton, D. (2002). Consideration set overevaluation: When impossibly favorable ratings of a set of brands are observed. *Journal of Consumer Psychology, 12*, 353–361.

Kruglanski, A. W. (1989). *Lay epistemics and human knowledge: Cognitive and motivational bases.* New York: Plenum.

Kruglanski, A. W. (1996). Motivated social cognition: Principles of the interface. In E. T. Higgins & A. W. Kruglanski (Eds.), *Social psychology: Handbook of basic principles* (pp. 493–520). New York: Guilford.

Kruglanski, A. W., & Freund, T. (1983). The freezing and un-freezing of lay-inferences: Effects on impressional primacy, ethnic stereotyping and numerical anchoring. *Journal of Experimental Social Psychology, 19*, 448–468.

Kruglanski, A. W., Shah, J. Y., Fishbach, A., Friedman, R., Chun, W. Y., & Keppler, D. S. (2002). A theory of goal system. In M. P. Zanna (Ed.), *Advances in experimental social psychology* (Vol. 34, pp. 331–376). New York: Academic Press.

Kruglanski, A. W., & Webster, D. M. (1996). Motivated closing of the mind: "Seizing" and "freezing." *Psychological Review, 103*(2), 263–283.

Kruglanski, A. W., Webster, D. M., & Klem, A. (1993). Motivated resistance and openness to persuasion in the presence or absence of prior information. *Journal of Personality and Social Psychology, 65*, 861–876.

Mayseless, O., & Kruglanski, A. W. (1987). What makes you so sure? Effects of epistemic motivations on judgmental confidence. *Organizational Behavior and Human Decision Processes, 39*, 162–183.

McAlister, L. (1982). A dynamic attribute satiation model of variety-seeking behavior. *Journal of Consumer Research, 9*, 141–150.

McKechnie, G. E. (1997). Simulation techniques in environmental psychology. In D. Stokols (Ed.), *Perspectives on environment and behavior: Theory, research and applications* (pp. 169–189). New York: Plenum.

Nisbett, R. E., & Willson, T. D. (1977). Telling more than we can know: Verbal reports on mental processes. *Psychological Review, 87*, 231–259.

Ratner, R. K., Kahn, B. E., & Kahneman, D. (1999). Choosing less-preferred experiences for the sake of variety. *Journal of Consumer Research, 26*, 1–15.

Rubini, M., & Kruglanski, A. W. (1997). Brief encounters ending in estrangement: Motivated language-use and interpersonal rapport. *Journal of Personality and Social Psychology, 12*, 1047–1060.

Semin, G. R., & Fiedler, K. (1988). The cognitive functions of linguistic categories in describing persons: Social cognition and language. *Journal of Personality and Social Psychology, 54*, 558–567.

Webster, D. M., & Kruglanski, A. W. (1994). Individual differences in need for cognitive closure. *Journal of Personality and Social Psychology, 67*, 1049–1062.

Webster, D. M., & Kruglanski, A. W. (1998). Cognitive and social consequences of the motivation for closure. *The European Review of Social Psychology, 8*, 133–173.

Webster, D. M., Kruglanski, A. W., & Pattison, D. A. (1997). Motivated language use in intergroup contexts: Need for closure effects on the linguistic intergroup bias. *Journal of Personality and Social Psychology, 72*, 1122–1131.

Wyer, R. S., & Srull, T. K. (1986). Human cognition in its social context. *Psychological Review, 93*, 322–359.

Zhang, S., Kardes, F. R., & Cronley, M. L. (2002). Comparative advertising: Effects of structural alignability on target brand evaluations. *Journal of Consumer Psychology, 12*, 303–311.

ACKNOWLEDGMENTS

This work was supported by the Research Grant from Hallym University, Korea and NSF grant 0314291/0313483.

CHAPTER TEN

Using Implementation Intentions to Increase New Product Consumption: A Field Experiment

Frank R. Kardes
University of Cincinnati

Maria L. Cronley
Miami University

Steven S. Posavac
University of Rochester

The best-laid plans of mice and men often go astray.

—Robert Burns

People often form good intentions that never reach fruition. New Year's resolutions, promises, and assurances are often quickly forgotten before they have a chance to influence behavior. Intentions are particularly ineffective when forgetting, procrastination, or distraction from other goals or activities increase the difficulty of self-regulation. One way to overcome these obstacles is to form *implementation intentions*, or intentions that are supplemented with detailed plans and contextual cues that serve as reminders to perform intention-relevant activities (Gollwitzer, 1999). In addition to specifying a desired end state, implementation intentions link goals to situations by taking the form, "I intend to do *y* whenever situation *z* is encountered." If sufficiently strong action-situation associations are formed in memory, the action is performed automatically whenever the relevant situation is encountered. When this occurs, behavioral control shifts from the individual to the situation.

Intentions increase commitment to a goal or a desired end state, and implementation intentions specify precisely how a goal will be executed. This entails *predecision making*, or making a decision before a situation requiring action is encountered. Expending cognitive effort at an early stage in the decision process reduces the amount of effort needed at later stages. Implementation intentions also involve reflecting on the appropriate times and circumstances for goal-relevant activities. This enables consumers to seize opportunities more quickly, and to pursue goals more efficiently and persistently. Implementation intentions also facilitate goal-relevant behavior by encouraging consumers to form action-situation associations in memory and to rehearse these associations until an action sequence can be triggered automatically by an appropriate situational cue. Automatically activated intentions are mentally represented in a single efficient cognitive unit that emphasizes general plans and goals rather than specific action details, and are capable of controlling relatively complex sequences of behavior (Bargh, Gollwitzer, Lee-Chai, Barndollar, & Trotschel, 2001).

Implementation intentions have been shown to be effective in increasing the intention–behavior relation in a wide variety of contexts—including completing class assignments (Gollwitzer & Brandstatter, 1997), solving puzzles (Webb & Sheeran, 2003), remembering to take daily vitamin supplements (Sheeran & Orbell, 1999), screening for cervical cancer (Sheeran & Orbell, 2000), performing breast self-examinations (Orbell, Hodgkins, & Sheeran, 1997), and eating healthy foods (Verplanken & Faes, 1999). Implementation intentions can also facilitate self-regulation by enhancing the prospective memory performance of older adults (Chasteen, Park, & Schwarz, 2001).

In a classic experiment, undergraduates from the University of Munich were asked to write a report over the Christmas holidays about what they did on Christmas Eve (Gollwitzer & Brandstatter, 1997, Experiment 2). Half of the participants were randomly assigned to the implementation intentions condition and half were assigned to the control condition. In the implementation intentions condition, participants were asked to indicate precisely when and where they intended to begin writing their reports. They were also asked to visualize this situation and to silently say, "I intend to write the report in situation z."

The cover story stated that the purpose of the study was to investigate how people spend their leisure time, and that it was important to write the report during the holidays before their memories began to fade. Anonymity was ensured by asking participants to create their own code number using the first letter of their mother's first name, the first letter of her maiden name, and the first letter of their own place of birth, and the first digit of their date of birth. This procedure was used to control for experimenter bias and demand effects.

Although all participants agreed to write a report over the Christmas holidays, 71% of the participants in the implementation intentions condition completed this assignment by the deadline, whereas only 32% of the participants in the control condition did so. Moreover, the assignment was completed more quickly in the implementation intentions condition than in the control condition, and most of the participants in the implementation intentions condition indicated that they worked on the assignment at the times and places that they previously indicated that they intended to work on the assignment. Hence, the results indicate that implementation intentions dramatically increase completion rates for a relatively onerous task.

The present study applied Gollwitzer and Brandstetter's (1997, Experiment 2) paradigm to a consumer context in which participants were given a free sample of a new product for use at home. Nonstudent participants were randomly assigned to implementation intention or control conditions. In the implementation intention condition, participants received a calendar and were asked to indicate the exact dates, times, places, and usage situations in which they intended to use the new product and were asked to visualize using the new product during these dates, times, places, and usage situations. In the control condition, participants were asked if they intended to use the new product, but no questions about plans or contextual details were presented. Attitudes, intentions, and intention latencies were measured in a controlled laboratory setting in Session 1. At the end of Session 1, all participants received a free sample of the new product to take home.

Session 2 was conducted in the field. Two weeks after Session 1, participants received an unexpected questionnaire containing attitudinal, intention-related, and behavioral measures by mail and were asked to complete these measures at home. During the critical 2-week, in-home-use period, it was predicted that participants would use the new product more frequently, use up a greater amount of the new product, and use the new product for a greater number of different purposes in implementation intention than in control conditions. It was also predicted that more favorable attitudes and intentions toward the new product would be formed in implementation intention than in control conditions. Finally, it was predicted that greater effort would be expended at early stages in the decision process, and that, consequently, response latencies to intention measures would be slower, in implementation intention than in control conditions.

METHOD

Because this was a proprietary study, details about the new product or the sponsor cannot be revealed. The new product is a liquid product used for cleaning a wide variety of everyday household objects. The new product had not yet been launched during this experiment. The cover story stated that the purpose of the study was to examine the effects of several different personality variables on responses to new products. To bolster the cover story, participants were asked to complete a battery of personality scales at the end of Session 1.

Participants

Two hundred and six consumers participated in a laboratory setting in Session 1, and in a field setting in Session 2. Participants were adults recruited from a local church group and a local school. Age ranged from 19 to 79 years, 85% were female, and 86% were primarily responsible for grocery shopping for the household. Household size ranged from 2 to 10 persons. Anonymity was ensured by asking participants to create their own code number, using the first letter of their mother's first name, the first letter of her maiden name, and the first letter of their own place of birth, and the first digit of their date of birth. This procedure was used to control for experimenter bias and demand effects. Participants received $25 for participating.

Procedure

On arrival, each participant received a demonstration of how to use the new product, and an explanation of the benefits of the new product. Participants were randomly assigned to implementation intention or control conditions. In implementation intention conditions, participants received a calendar and were asked to indicate the exact dates, times, places, and purposes for which they intended to use a free sample of the new product over the next 2 weeks. They were also asked to visualize themselves using the new product in each of these situations. In control conditions, participants were merely asked to indicate whether or not they intend to try the free sample over the next weeks. At the end of Session 1, all participants received a free sample of the new product to take home.

Attitude and Intention Measures. All participants were asked to indicate their attitudes and intentions concerning the new product on 11-point semantic differential scales. Participants indicated "Do you intend to try [the new product]" on a scale ranging from *0* (Definitely will not try [the new product]) to *10* (Definitely will try [the new product]); "Do you intend to try [the new product] more than once?" on a scale ranging from *0* (Definitely will not) to *10* (Definitely will); "How much do you like this product idea?" on a scale from *0* (Dislike very much) to *10* (Like very much); "The idea of this product is:" *0* (Ridiculous) to *10* (Great idea); "If it were available where you shop, how likely would you be to buy [the new product]?" on a scale from *0* (Not at all likely) to *10* (Very likely).

Response Latency Measure. Paper-and-pencil and computer-administered intention ("Do you intend to try [the new product]") measures were used, and order of measurement was counterbalanced. This procedure was used to test the hypothesis that forming implementation intentions requires greater cognitive effort than forming simple goal intentions, and to test the hypothesis that implementation intentions are formed spontaneously.

Spontaneous intention formation was assessed using the Fazio, Lenn, and Effrein (1984) *spontaneous attitude formation paradigm*. This paradigm involves manipulating the presence or absence of cues suggesting that it would be functional to form an evaluation of an attitude object for future use. Fazio et al. (1984) investigated the influence of two functional cues, the expectation of future questioning concerning an attitude object (via standard paper-and-pencil attitude scales; Experiment 1) and the expectation of future interaction with an attitude object (Experiment 2). Both types of expectations were effective in eliciting spontaneous attitude formation as evidenced by patterns of response latencies to questions about the attitude object. Response latencies did not differ as a function of order of measurement (either the response latency task was administered first or the standard attitude scales were administered first) when expectations encouraged participants to form attitudes spontaneously. By contrast, response latencies were faster when standard attitude scales were administered first than when the response latency task was administered first when spontaneous attitude formation was unlikely. This pattern was observed because completing standard paper-and-pencil attitude scales forces participants to consolidate their evaluations of an attitude object and this facilitates response speeds on a subsequent response latency task.

Personality Measures. At the end of Session 1, several personality scales were administered to bolster the cover story and to permit the investigation of moderating variables. The Need to Evaluate Scale (Jarvis & Petty, 1996) was the most relevant scale. Several less relevant scales were also administered including the Need for Cognitive Closure Scale (Webster & Kruglanski, 1994), the Rational-Experiential Inventory (Epstein, Pacini, Denes-Raj, & Heier, 1996), the Behavior Identification Form (Vallacher & Wegner, 1989), and the Five-Factor Personality Inventory (Saucier, 1994).

Session 2: Attitude, Intention, and Behavior Measures. In Session 2, 2 weeks later, participants received an unexpected follow-up questionnaire by mail. The follow-up questionnaire contained the same attitude and purchase intention measures used in Session 1. It also included several behavioral measures concerning whether, when, and how often consumers used the free sample of the new product. Participants were also asked to indicate exactly how much of the sample they used by drawing a line on a cardboard shadow picture to indicate the amount of the product that remained in the container.

RESULTS

Session I: Laboratory Experiment

Attitudes toward the new product and intentions to use the new product as a function of implementation intention versus control conditions are presented in Fig. 10.1. As Fig. 10.1 indicates, intentions to use the new product were greater in implementation intention than in control conditions [Ms = 9.09 vs. 8.46, $F(1, 205)$ = 3.86, $p < .05$]. Intentions to use the new product more than once [Ms = 8.48 vs. 7.85, $F(1, 205)$ = 3.11, $p < .08$] and purchase intentions [Ms = 7.36 vs. 6.62, $F(1, 205)$ = 3.29, $p < .07$] also tended to be greater in implementation intention than in control conditions. These results indicate that implementation intention-formation procedures are effective at increasing intentions to use a favorably evaluated

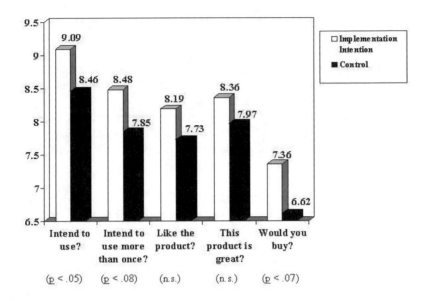

FIG. 10.1.   Attitudes and intentions as a function of implementation intention versus control conditions before in-home trial.

new product. Attitudes toward the new product were equally favorable across
conditions in Session 1.

Session 2: Two-Week Follow-Up Field Experiment

Attitudes toward the new product and intentions to buy the new product as a function of implementation intention versus control conditions are presented in Fig.
10.2. Although attitudes did not differ across conditions in Session 1, more favorable attitudes were found in implementation intention than in control conditions
in Session 2. As Fig. 10.2 indicates, this pattern was found for both attitude measures: How much do you like this product idea? [$Ms = 7.96$ vs. 6.73, $F(1, 156) =
8.28$, $p < .01$], and the idea of this product is ridiculous/great [$Ms = 8.08$ vs. 7.08,
$F(1, 156) = 5.01$, $p < .03$]. Participants also indicated that they would be more
likely to buy the new product, if it were available, in implementation intention
than in control conditions [$Ms = 7.39$ vs. 5.42, $F(1, 156) = 13.51$, $p < .001$].
    The effects of implementation intentions on behavior are presented in Fig.
10.3. As Fig. 10.3 indicates, the number of times the new product was used was
greater in implementation intention than in control conditions [$Ms = 13.26$ vs.
6.06, $F(1, 156) = 42.69$, $p < .001$]. Moreover, the amount of the new product that
was used (in ounces using the shadow picture measure) was greater in implementation intention than in control conditions [$Ms = 9.60$ vs. 2.63, $F(1, 156) = 34.03$,

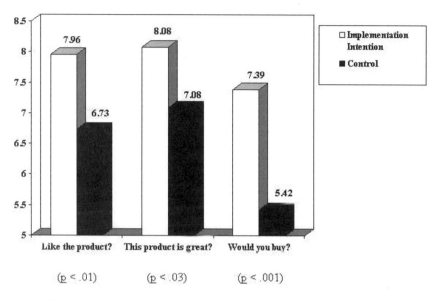

FIG. 10.2. Attitudes and intentions as a function of implementation intention versus control conditions after in-home trial.

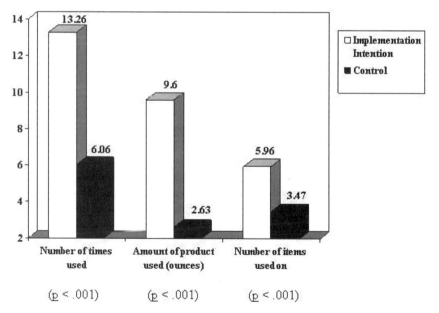

FIG. 10.3. Behavioral responses as a function of implementation intention versus control conditions after in-home trial.

$p < .001$]. The new product was also used for a greater number of purposes in implementation intention than in control conditions [$Ms = 5.96$ vs. 3.47, $F(1, 156) = 37.02$, $p < .001$]. Together, these results indicate that implementation intentions dramatically increase usage of a new product.

Ancillary Analyses

Response Latency Analyses. During the laboratory study (Session 1), response latencies to the purchase intention measure were assessed via computer and the Fazio et al. (1984) paradigm was used to determine the conditions under which spontaneous intention formation was likely to occur. Because implementation intentions require greater effort during the early stages of the decision process, relative to simple goal intentions, it was predicted that purchase intentions should be formed spontaneously in implementation intention conditions, but not in goal intention (control) conditions. Purchase intention latencies as a function of implementation intention (vs. control) conditions and order of measurement (computer measurement task first or paper-and-pencil measurement task first) are presented in Fig. 10.4. As Fig. 10.4 indicates, a significant implementation intention by order of measurement interaction was observed, $F(1, 203) = 4.77, p < .03$.

Follow-up tests showed that, in control conditions, purchase intention latencies were faster when they were measured via paper-and-pencil first, as opposed to via computer first, [$Ms = 4.3608$ vs. 6.0251, $t(203) = 3.32$, $p < .001$]. This result was observed because the paper-and-pencil measurement task encouraged participants to form purchase intentions prior to the computer measurement task and this facil-

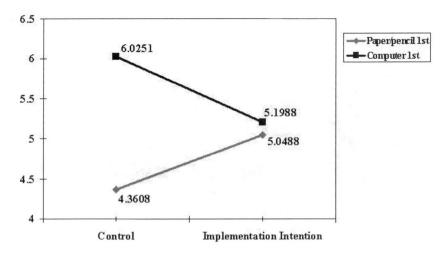

FIG. 10.4.   Purchase intention latencies as a function of implementation intention versus control conditions and order of measurement before in-home trial.

itated performance on the computer measurement task. By contrast, no order of measurement effect was found in implementation intention conditions, [Ms = 5.0488 vs. 5.1988, $t(203) < 1$]. This result was observed because forming implementation intentions encouraged participants to form purchase intentions prior to the paper-and-pencil measurement task, as well as prior to the computer measurement task. When purchase intentions are formed spontaneously, or without prompting due to exposure to potentially reactive measures, similar results are observed regardless of measurement order. Hence, the response latency results suggest that purchase intentions were formed spontaneously in implementation intention conditions, but not in control conditions.

Interestingly, in paper-and-pencil measurement task first conditions, purchase intention latencies tended to be faster in control conditions than in implementation intention conditions, [Ms − 4.3608 vs. 5.0488, $t(203) = 1.64$, $p < .10$]. This pattern of results suggests that forming implementation intentions encourages consumers to expend greater levels of cognitive effort during the early stages of the decision process. Presumably, expending high levels of cognitive effort during the early stages of the decision process frees up cognitive resources and allows consumers to expend much lower levels of cognitive effort during the later stages of the decision process.

Correlational Analyses.   Correlations among intention measures administered in Session 1 (before in-home trial) and behavior and intention measures administered in Session 2 (after in-home trial) are presented in Table 10.1. As Table 10.1 indicates, intentions to use the new product measured in Session 1 were correlated significantly with all of the behaviors and intentions measured in Session 2 in implementation conditions. Moreover, the correlation coefficients tended to be greater in implementation intention than in control conditions. This difference was significant for the amount of the product that was used. Intentions to use the new product were not correlated with the amount of the product that was used in control conditions. A similar pattern was observed for intentions to use the new product more than once measured in Session 1 and behaviors and intentions measured in Session 2.

Need to Evaluate Analyses.   The amount of the new product used in the field study (Session 2) was influenced by the need to evaluate as well as by implementation intentions. The Need to Evaluate Scale assesses the degree to which individuals form opinions toward a wide variety of objects and evaluate these objects quickly (Jarvis & Petty, 1996). Those who score high on this scale are highly opinionated and are quick to judge objects and issues. Those who score low on this scale are less opinionated and judgmental. New product usage as a function of implementation intention (vs. control) conditions and the need to evaluate are pre-

TABLE 10.1

Correlations Among Intention to Use the Product Before In-Home Trial and Behavior and Purchase Intention Measures After In-Home Trial as a Function of Implementation Intention Versus Control Conditions

	Intend to use? (before trial)	Intend to use more than once? (before trial)	Would you buy? (before trial)	Number of times used (after trial)	Amount of product used (after trial)	Number of items used on (after trial)	Would you buy? (after trial)
	Implementation Intention Versus Control Conditions						
Intend to use? (before trial)	1.00/1.00						
Intend to use more than once? (before trial)	.85/ .79	1.00/1.00					
Would you buy? (before trial)	.52/ .47	.63 / .49	1.00/1.00				
Number of times used (after trial)	.25/ .25	.29 / .28	.28/ .38	1.00/1.00			
Amount of product used (ounces) (after trial)	.25/–.04[a]	.29/–.02[b]	.33/ .12	.58/ .60	1.00/1.00		
Number of items used on (after trial)	.36/ .28	.42/ .20[c]	.38/ .16	.58/ .46	.61 / .28[d]	1.00/1.00	
Would you buy? (after trial)	.40/ .40	.49/ .36	.69/ .72	.39/ .42	.34 / .23	.52/ .36	1.00 / 1.00

Note. Correlation coefficients greater than $r = .15$ are significant at $p < .05$. Tests of significance of the difference between the correlation coefficients for implementation intention (left side coefficients) versus control conditions revealed the following significant differences:

[a]$r_{rs} = .25$ versus -0.04, $z = 1.84$, $p < .07$.

[b]$r_{rs} = .29$ versus -0.02, $z = 1.98$, $p < .05$.

[c]$r_{rs} = .42$ versus $.20$, $z = 1.78$, $p < .08$.

[d]$r_{rs} = .61$ versus $.28$, $z = 2.56$, $p < .01$.

All correlation coefficients were converted to z scores prior to testing for differences. No other significant differences were found.

sented in Fig. 10.5. As Fig. 10.5 shows, a significant implementation intention by need to evaluate interaction was observed, $F(1, 146) = 4.88$, $p < .03$.

Follow-up tests showed that although usage volume was greater in implementation intention than in control conditions for participants high in the need to evaluate [$Ms = 11.98$ vs. 2.97, $t(146) = 5.39$, $p < .001$] and low in the need to evaluate [$Ms = 6.29$ vs. 2.61, $t(146) = 2.13$, $p < .04$], this effect was more pronounced when the need to evaluate was high [$Ms = 11.98$ vs. 6.29, $t(146) = 3.37$, $p < .001$]. Although implementation intentions were effective at increasing usage volume for both types of individuals, the results suggest that implementation intentions are particularly influential and useful for individuals who are high in the need to evaluate. Presumably, such individuals are particularly likely to expend high levels of cognitive effort during the early stages of the decision process in order to reduce the levels of cognitive effort required during the later stages.

This pattern of results also suggests that the manner in which cognitive effort is allocated during intention formation is more important than the amount of cognitive effort allocated during intention formation in influencing the use of a new product. If the amount of cognitive effort allocated was influential, greater consumption rates would have been observed in high need to evaluate than in low need to evaluate conditions when simple goal intentions were elicited because consumers high in the need to evaluate are likely to invest more time and effort in judgment formation. Instead, the results showed that consumption rates did not differ as a function of the need to evaluate in the control condition. Hence, the manner in which cognitive effort is allocated (i.e., forming action-situation associations in memory) appears to be a more important determinant of usage rates, relative to the nonspecific expenditure of cognitive effort.

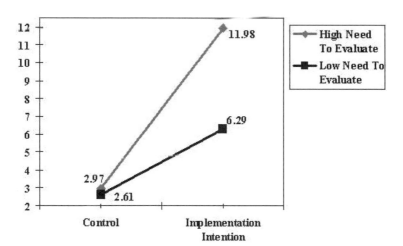

FIG. 10.5. New product usage as a function of implementation intention versus control conditions and the need to evaluate after in-home trial.

DISCUSSION

The results of the present experiment indicate that procedures that encourage consumers to form implementation intentions (as opposed to simple goal intentions) increase intentions to use a new product, increase usage volume, and increase purchase intentions. Following product trial, more favorable evaluations of a new product are also formed when implementation intentions are formed than when simple goal intentions are formed. Implementation intentions are also less susceptible to order of measurement effects, presumably due to the expenditure of greater amounts of cognitive effort during the early stages of the decision process.

In a recent review of 64 studies of the relationships among habits, intentions, past behaviors, and future behaviors, Ouellette and Wood (1998) found that past behavior influences future behavior through two different processes. When behaviors are performed regularly (daily or weekly) in stable contexts (at the same time and place), the processes that regulate behavior become automatic and habitual. Automatic, habitual behaviors are likely to be repeated because they can be performed quickly, relatively effortlessly, in parallel with other behaviors, and with minimal attention. This pattern was observed for many different types of habitual behaviors, including grocery coupon clipping, coffee consumption, class attendance, church attendance, seat belt use, and exercise routines.

By contrast, when behaviors are performed occasionally (annually or biannually), the processes that regulate behavior are deliberative and time and energy consuming. Nonautomatic, nonhabitual behaviors are unlikely to be repeated frequently because they require time, effort, and careful attention. Opportunity costs are also greater for nonautomatic than for automatic behaviors. This pattern was observed for many different types of nonhabitual behaviors, including blood donation, flu shots, nuclear protest behavior, and new mothers exercising after childbirth. Intentions guide behavior in these contexts. However, over time and under the right conditions, intentions (a) can become automatic; (b) can be specified in an efficient, stable, and general form that stresses plans and goals rather than action details; and (c) can be combined into a single efficient cognitive unit that initiates and controls a string or sequence of behaviors.

Ouellette and Wood's (1998) analysis suggested that to become habitual, new behaviors must be repeated frequently in a stable context. When contexts are unstable, intentions guide behavior and strategies should be devised to encourage consumers to develop automatic intentions. One way to achieve this is by encouraging consumers to form implementation intentions (Gollwitzer & Brandstatter, 1997), as opposed to the more commonly formed goal intentions ("I intend to achieve x"). Implementation intentions take the form "I intend to do y when situation z is encountered." Implementation intentions link specific behaviors to specific contexts. Behavior-context associations in memory trigger the behavior whenever the appropriate context is encountered. Gollwitzer and Brandstatter (1997) found that people were nearly three times more likely to perform a task when implementation intentions (rather than goal intentions) were formed, and conceptually similar results were found in the present study even though the studies were conducted in completely different contexts.

In the present research, consumers who stated implementation intentions consumed more than three times of the target product than did those who did not. Accordingly, our results suggest that there may be tremendous upside for managers who can induce consumers to form implementation intentions regarding their products. Participants in our research were induced to form implementation intentions via the *calendar method*, in which they were given a calendar and were asked to indicate the precise dates, times, and usage situations in which they intended to use a free sample of a new product. Although such a procedure would likely affect consumption of a variety of product types, it is likely that there are multiple additional possibilities by which managers can induce implementation intention formation, and thereby increase product consumption.

The consequences of implementation intention formation may be leveraged by an advertisement that leads consumers to think about time- and place-specific details concerning when they could use a particular new product. Advertising that shows consumers precisely when and how to use a new product, and that ideally leads consumers to generate their own implementation intentions, may be particularly effective. Rhetorical questions could also stimulate thinking about the specific contexts in which a new product could be particularly useful.

Although creative advertising may be used to stimulate implementation intention formation, other elements of the marketing communication mix may be even more efficacious. Although consumers are typically passive recipients of advertising, the key to the behavioral effects we report is active cognitive work by consumers. Thus, marketing interventions should be aimed at facilitating consumers generating their own implementation intentions, versus having times and contexts suggested to them. For example, a salesperson in a personal selling context could ask the consumer to describe how and when he or she would use a target product. Although this would not appear to be a heavy-handed sales pitch to the consumer (after all, the consumer, and not the salesperson, would be doing the talking) our results suggest that such a strategy may account for more behavioral variance than any pitch that the salesperson could offer.

Consumer sales promotion may also be fertile ground for inducing consumers to generate implementation intentions. For example, a firm may sponsor a contest where prizes are given to consumers who write essays that explicitly must include details about when and how a product should be used. A ratcheting effect may be obtained by sending coupons to every consumer who enters the contest. Alternatively, a firm could sponsor a sweepstakes in which the entry form requires that the consumer write a few sentences describing their product implementation intentions.

Although to this point we have focused on consequences of implementation intention formation on consumer behavior, the effects we report could also be leveraged in trade sales promotion. For example, incentives such as contests and sweepstakes are often offered to retailers to encourage stocking of a given brand. In the same way that these sales promotion tools can be creatively used to induce consumers' implementation intention formation, the behavior of the purchasing agent for a retailer may be similarly influenced if he or she were led to generate specific plans for purchase of a given brand.

However implementational thinking is induced, the effortful process of thinking about specific plans and contextual details during the early stages of decision making frees up cognitive resources and reduces the amount of effort required during the later stages. Moreover, strong action-situation associations in memory facilitate the translation of intentions into behavior by automatically priming goal-relevant behavior when the appropriate situational cues are encountered, and by increasing goal pursuit and goal persistence.

REFERENCES

Bargh, J. A., Gollwitzer, P. M., Lee-Chai, A., Barndollar, K., & Trotschel, R. (2001). The automated will: Nonconscious activation and pursuit of behavioral goals. *Journal of Personality and Social Psychology, 81*, 1014–1027.

Chasteen, A. L., Park, D. C., & Schwarz, N. (2001). Implementation intentions and facilitation of prospective memory. *Psychological Science, 12*, 457–461.

Epstein, S., Pacini, R., Denes-Raj, V., & Heier, H. (1996). Individual differences in intuitive-experiential and analytical-rational thinking styles. *Journal of Personality and Social Psychology, 71*, 390–405.

Fazio, R. H., Lenn, T. M., & Effrein, E. A. (1984). Spontaneous attitude formation. *Social Cognition, 2*, 217–234.

Gollwitzer, P. M. (1999). Implementation intentions: Strong effects of simple plans. *American Psychologist, 54*, 493–503.

Gollwitzer, P. M., & Brandstatter, V. (1997). Implementation intentions and effective goal pursuit. *Journal of Personality and Social Psychology, 73*, 186–199.

Jarvis, W. B. G., & Petty, R. E. (1996). The need to evaluate. *Journal of Personality and Social Psychology, 70*, 172–194.

Orbell, S., Hodgkins, S., & Sheeran, P. (1997). Implementation intentions and the theory of planned behavior. *Personality and Social Psychology Bulletin, 23*, 945–954.

Ouellette, J. A., & Wood, W. (1998). Habit and intention in everyday life: The multiple processes by which past behavior predicts future behavior. *Psychological Bulletin, 124*, 54–74.

Saucier, G. (1994). Mini-markers: A brief version of Goldberg's unipolar big-five markers. *Journal of Personality Assessment, 63*, 506–516.

Sheeran, P., & Orbell, S. (1999). Implementation intentions and repeated behavior: Augmenting the predictive validity of the theory of planned behavior. *European Journal of Social Psychology, 29*, 349–369.

Sheeran, P., & Orbell, S. (2000). Using implementation intentions to increase attendance for cervical cancer screening. *Health Psychology, 19*, 283–289.

Vallacher, R. R., & Wegner, D. M. (1989). Levels of personal agency: Individual variation in action identification. *Journal of Personality and Social Psychology, 57*, 660–671.

Verplanken, B., & Faes, S. (1999). Good intentions, bad habits, and effects of forming implementation intentions on healthy eating. *European Journal of Social Psychology, 29,* 591–604.

Webb, T. L., & Sheeran, P. (2003). Can implementation intentions help to overcome ego-depletion? *Journal of Experimental Social Psychology, 39,* 279–286.

Webster, D. M., & Kruglanski, A. W. (1994). Individual differences in need for cognitive closure. *Journal of Personality and Social Psychology, 67,* 1049–1062.

CHAPTER ELEVEN

Regulatory Focus and Consumer Information Processing

Arnd Florack
Universität Basel, Switzerland

Martin Scarabis
Stefanie Gosejohann
Universität Münster, Germany

When making a purchase decision, consumers differ with respect to two basic motivational orientations: Some consumers attempt to maximize their benefits and to realize their ideals, others are more concerned with avoiding a negative outcome. For example, imagine that you intend to purchase a mobile phone. In thinking about your decision, you may consider whether the mobile phone is equipped with the newest technology and has an appealing design, or you may wonder whether the product falls short of your expectations and the purchase could be a serious mistake. Recent research in social cognition has shown that these different orientations have far-reaching consequences on judgments and information processing.

Higgins (1997, 1998) offered a broad framework for integrating research in this area with his regulatory focus theory. He postulates two motivational subsystems: the *promotion system* and the *prevention system*. The promotion system is concerned with needs of development and self-actualization. The goal of this system is to approach a desired state. In contrast, the prevention system is more concerned with approaching a secure rather than ideal state and avoiding negative outcomes. A similar framework is offered by Carver, Lawrence, and Scheier (1999), who differentiated between motivational systems with a positive or negative point of reference. However, even if the reference points and the goals are different in a promotion and prevention focus, in both cases the goal is a desired end state that increases in relevance as one moves closer to attaining the goal (Förster, Higgins, & Idson, 1998).

The purpose of this chapter is to illustrate the impact of regulatory focus on consumer behavior and consumer information processing. We begin with a brief summary of possible variations in regulatory focus and basic findings in research on regulatory focus. We then provide a detailed overview of influences that self-regulation toward promotion or prevention goals might have on persuasion and product choice. We divided this part of the chapter into different sections. First, we put forward that individuals prefer products that have an outcome value that is related to an activated regulatory goal. Then we discuss the importance of a regulatory focus that is emphasized in an advertising message. In particular, we refer to research that demonstrates the effectiveness of a message focus that matches other elements within an ad and that fits with the regulatory focus of the recipient. Furthermore, we consider effects of the regulatory focus on systematic information processing and the reliance on cues (e.g., a celebrity endorser) in persuasion. Finally, we conclude the chapter with an outlook on implications for advertising and marketing practices.

SOURCES OF REGULATORY FOCUS

Regulatory focus, which is predominant when a consumer makes a decision, can be affected by three different sources: the chronic regulatory focus of the decision maker, contextual priming during or before the decision task, and the decision task itself. Higgins (1997, 1998) supposed that one of the two foci increasingly dominates across a person's lifespan as a result of socialization. An important determinant of this chronic regulatory focus is said to be rooted in caretaker–child interactions (Higgins & Silberman, 1998). If the caretaker regulates the behavior of a child predominantly through the presence or absence of positive reinforcement, the child should develop sensitivity toward promotion goals. In contrast, a child should be more likely to develop a chronic prevention focus if he or she is trained to be alert to potential dangers.

Because the accessibility of ideal self-guides is believed to be associated with a chronic promotion focus, whereas the accessibility of ought self-guides should accompany a prevention focus, the time participants need to access ideals or oughts from memory should depend on their chronic regulatory focus. Therefore, chronic regulatory focus can be assessed indirectly with reaction time tasks (e.g., Amodio, Shah, Sigelman, Brazy, & Harmon-Jones, 2004; Förster et al., 1998; Higgins, Shah, & Friedman, 1997; Liberman, Idson, Camacho, & Higgins, 1999). A common feature of these methods is that participants are asked to list and then rate attributes that describe either an ideal or ought self. Participants with a chronic promotion focus should be faster at listing ideals than oughts, whereas the reverse should be true for participants in a prevention focus. A more direct way to measure the regulatory focus is the self-assessment of participants. Lockwood, Jordan, and Kunda (2002), for instance, developed a questionnaire to measure chronic regulatory goals. In this questionnaire, participants have to indicate the degree to which items relevant to promotion or prevention goals apply to them. Higgins et al. (2001) assessed a different aspect of the regulatory focus. They asked participants to indicate past success in pursuing promotion or prevention goals.

Like other motivational orientations, regulatory focus may vary between individuals not only dispositionally, but also momentarily. Recent or momentary experiences may activate a specific regulatory focus that may be independent of chronic regulatory goals. For a variety of reasons, in one context ideals may be more salient, whereas in another context individuals may be especially aware of their responsibilities and duties. In experiments, this variability of the regulatory focus is used to induce a promotion or prevention focus—e.g., by priming of ideals or oughts (Higgins, Roney, Crowe, & Hymes, 1994)—and to examine the consequences of this induced regulatory focus on information processing and behavior.

Finally, a decision task or a product can also be associated with a certain regulatory focus (Zhou & Pham, in press). For example, the purchase of casualty insurance may evoke a prevention focus and may be less likely to be associated with a promotion focus. In contrast, thoughts of making a speculative investment may evoke a promotion focus more than a prevention focus. Consequently, the purchase of a brand from a product category that is strongly associated with either of the two regulatory foci may evoke the associated self-regulation in the individual. Zhou and Pham impressively demonstrated this effect. They asked participants to make several decisions that involved either individual stocks offered in a trading account (a more speculative investment product), or mutual funds offered in retirement accounts (a more secure investment product). Afterward, participants had to choose between two brands of grape juice and toothpaste. Importantly, the two choices in grape juice and toothpaste differed in characteristics that were related to promotion (e.g., tooth whitening) or prevention benefits (e.g., cavity prevention). In line with the prediction, making an investment had an effect on the subsequent choice of juice and toothpaste. Participants who made decisions that involved prevention-related investment products were subsequently more likely to prefer brands with prevention characteristics than were participants who made decisions that involved more risky investment products.

BASIC FINDINGS OF RESEARCH ON REGULATORY FOCUS

Numerous studies have documented that the importance of regulatory focus for information processing, judgment, and decision making is multifaceted (e.g., Higgins et al., 1997; Higgins & Tykocinski, 1992; Förster, Grant, Idson, & Higgins, 2001; Liberman, Molden, Idson, & Higgins, 2001; Shah & Higgins, 1997, 2001). Higgins et al. (1994), for instance, reported that individuals are more likely to recall information that fits their regulatory focus. In this study, participants were primed with a promotion or a prevention focus and then read about several life episodes. Later, participants were asked to recall the episodes. Participants in a promotion focus were better at recalling life episodes that were related to approach strategies. Participants in a prevention focus were better at recalling life episodes that were concerned with avoidance strategies. Shah, Higgins, and Friedman (1998) found that the performance of individuals in a promotion focus increased when the incentives were framed as gains, whereas the performance of individuals in a prevention focus increased when the incentives were framed as nonlosses.

Similarly, Zhou and Pham (in press) proposed that individuals are differentially sensitive to gains and losses depending on whether a decision task evokes a promotion or a prevention focus. In their studies, participants were more sensitive toward possible gains when they thought about a risky investment (promotion focus), and more sensitive toward possible losses when they thought about a more secure investment (prevention focus). Furthermore, individuals in a promotion focus are inclined to use more risky and less conservative strategies to pursue a goal compared to participants in a prevention focus. In a simple drawing task, Förster, Higgins, and Taylor Bianco (2003), for instance, observed faster performances, but also more errors, for participants in a promotion focus compared to participants in a prevention focus, who were more careful and made fewer mistakes, but also worked more slowly on the task. Altogether, the results of the research on regulatory focus demonstrate that individuals in a promotion focus are sensitive to different types of information and also apply different strategies to reach their regulatory goals.

There is even evidence for psychophysiological correlates of the different regulatory foci. Amodio et al. (2004) measured the chronic regulatory focus with a latency-based method (cf. Higgins et al., 1997). In a separate session, the resting electroencephalogram (EEG) was recorded. The analyses revealed that a chronic promotion focus was associated with greater left frontal activity, whereas a prevention focus was associated with greater right frontal activity. These findings are congruent with previous research that demonstrated an asymmetrical activity of the frontal cortex for approach and avoidance processes, with approach motivations or emotions associated with greater left frontal activity, and avoidance motivations or emotions associated with greater right frontal activity (Coan & Allen, 2003).

REGULATORY GOALS AND PRODUCT CHOICE

One of the basic predictions of regulatory focus theory is that a promotion orientation is associated with a sensitivity toward positive outcomes, and a prevention focus is associated with a sensitivity toward negative outcomes. For example, picture yourself lying on the beach of your favorite holiday destination on a warm summer day. In this situation, you might enjoy the sun, hoping to get a good tan. However, you might also be afraid of getting sunburned and damaging your skin. In a Web experiment (Florack, Scarabis, & Gosejohann, 2004a), we examined whether—in such a situation—regulatory focus would have an influence on the purchase and evaluation of sun lotions (cf. Lee & Aaker, 2004). We asked participants to evaluate two different brands of sun lotion and to indicate which one they would purchase on their summer holidays at the sea. The two sun lotions were presented by two pictures with an advertising claim for each. For one brand, we used a claim that was concerned with the avoidance of sunburn ("Give sunburn no chance. Avène™ provides safe protection. Avène™—The double protection"), whereas for the other brand we used a claim that emphasized the enjoyment of the sun and a tan ("Enjoy the warm rays of the sun. Clarins™ for healthy tan. Clarins™—Enjoy the sun."). In addition, we induced a promotion or prevention focus with a few questions just before participants evaluated the sun lotions. In the promotion focus condition, we provided participants with a list of positive things that could happen during their holidays (e.g., meeting nice people, fun with sports) and asked them to indicate which of these things they would actively pursue. In the prevention focus condition, we provided participants with a list of negative things that could occur during holidays and asked them to indicate those they would actively try to avoid (e.g., through planning). As predicted, participants in a prevention focus were more likely to choose the sun lotion that stressed protection against sunburn, whereas participants in a promotion focus preferred the sun lotion that focused on a tan and fun. The results suggest that a product may be instrumental for reaching a goal that is linked to the regulatory focus. In our simple experiment, the product (sun lotion) was a means of approaching a positive outcome (getting tanned) or avoiding a negative one (sunburn).

Investment products belong to another product category that could also be supposed to have instrumental value for pursuing a specific regulatory goal. If a person has money to invest, he or she can focus on possible gains or on possible losses from investing the money. Indeed, modern banks and investment firms offer a huge spectrum of investment products that are customized to these different foci. Florack and Hartmann (2003) demonstrated that a manipulation of the regulatory focus does in fact influence the choice of such investment products. In this study, participants first worked on a cognitive task that was used to manipulate the regulatory focus. In the prevention focus condition, the experimenter, at the beginning of the task, allotted a certain number of small chocolate bars to each participant and then told participants that they would have to give back chocolate bars for wrong solutions. In the promotion focus condition, the experimenter did not allot any chocolate before participants worked on the tasks. But he told participants that they would receive small chocolate bars for correct answers. It is important that after working on the task, all participants received the same feedback and in the end were given the same number of chocolate bars. For participants in the prevention focus condition, this was a moderate prevention success. For participants in the promotion focus condition, this was a moderate success of a promotion strategy.

Afterward, participants worked on what was supposedly a second experiment. In fact, this "second experiment" included the dependent measure of the study. In this part of the experiment, participants received some information about different investment funds and then had to decide how much money they would invest in the different funds. The experiment was varied as to whether or not there was time pressure to make the decision. Our main interest was the amount of money participants invested in the most secure fund, which was described as having low chances of achieving high rates of return, but a great quota of secure annuity funds. Florack and Hartmann (2003) hypothesized that this investment product would be more attractive for participants in a prevention focus than for those in a promotion focus. Because it is reasonable that individuals rely on information that is perceived as most diagnostic, especially under time pressure, they also predicted that this effect of the regulatory focus on the investment decision will be strengthened if the decision time is limited.

The results provided support for these predictions. When the decision time was limited, participants in a prevention focus invested more money in the secure investment product than did participants in a promotion focus. When the decision time was not limited, no difference between participants in a promotion and a prevention focus was found. However, even if time pressure may strengthen a regulatory focus effect, it is not a necessary precondition for the emergence of such effects. Indeed, Zhou and Pham (in press) obtained results similar to those of Florack and Hartmann (2003) without the induction of time pressure. They found that participants in a promotion focus preferred more speculative financial assets than did those in a prevention focus. But as we have mentioned before, Zhou and Pham point to the fact that making an investment decision can also induce different regulatory foci, depending on the investment product that is being considered.

This finding is particularly interesting if we look at what people do with money that is a return from either a promotion- or prevention-related investment. If an investment product can evoke a specific regulatory focus, this should also apply to the returns from these products. Indeed, this is what Zhou and Pham (in press) found in a further study. Participants in this study preferred higher risks when the money to be invested was a return on a high-risk investment than when it was a return on a low-risk investment.

Investment products and sun lotion can be regarded as means to approaching a positive outcome or avoiding a negative one. In other situations, the product itself is the outcome and choosing or not is the means to achieving a specific regulatory goal. When it comes to the judgment or choice of products with specific regulatory outcome value, regulatory focus theory postulates that consumers prefer products which are superior on dimensions that are relevant to the activated regulatory goal (Higgins, 2002). Indeed, there is some evidence that advertising appeals congruent with the recipients' activated self-concept are more effective than those that are incongruent (Bettman & Sujan, 1987; Higgins, 2002; Hong & Zinkhan, 1995; Snyder & DeBono, 1985). Snyder and DeBono (1985, Study 3), for instance, found that participants are more likely to test a product that is superior on a dimension that corresponds to the viewers' level of self-monitoring. Specifically, they carried out a telephone survey asking people which of two shampoo products they would prefer. One product was described as superior in how it makes the hair look, and the other as superior in how it cleans. In line with the assumption that image aspects are more relevant for high self-monitoring individuals, whereas product utility is more relevant for low self-monitoring individuals, participants high in self-monitoring were more likely to prefer the product that was described as superior in how it makes the hair look, whereas participants low in self-monitoring were likely to prefer the shampoo with the superior cleaning ability.

Bettman and Sujan (1987) examined the effects of a situationally activated decision criterion that is also more closed to differences in promotion and prevention self-regulation. Having first primed a reliability or creativity orientation, they asked participants to evaluate two products and to choose one. As expected, participants were more likely to prefer an alternative that was superior on the activated decision criterion. Even if reliability is related to a prevention focus and creativity to a promotion focus, the object of the study by Bettman and Sujan (1987) was not to examine regulatory focus effects. A study that did examine regulatory focus effects more directly is described by Higgins (2002), who was referring to an unpublished doctoral dissertation by Safer (1998).

In one of the studies carried out by Safer (1998), the task of participants was to choose between products (cars and apartments) that differed with respect to their reliability or luxury. Because luxury is more related to accomplishment and promotion concerns, and reliability reflects more prevention concerns, the author predicted that individuals in a promotion focus would regard the differences between the products in luxury as more important, whereas the reverse should be true for individuals in a prevention focus. The results supported this assumption. Participants with a predominant promotion focus were more likely to choose alternatives that were more luxurious. Participants with a predominant prevention focus preferred alternatives that were higher in reliability. Thus, participants chose a product that was superior on the dimension that was most relevant to their regulatory focus.

Furthermore, a product might not only be superior on a dimension that is relevant to a specific regulatory focus, for example, reliability or luxury, but the choice of a product might also come with the risk of making the wrong decision or the chance for a benefit. Because a main goal for individuals in a promotion focus is to attain benefits, and for those in a prevention focus to avoid junk, the regulatory focus should also have an impact on the choice of products that are differentially associated with risk or stability. For example, imagine that you have been using a certain brand for quite some time and might consider buying a new brand in the future. The switch to the new brand could imply a positive outcome for you if it surpasses the old brand, but it could also imply a negative outcome if the new brand is a dud.

Because a promotion focus is concerned with ensuring hits and avoiding errors of omission, regulatory focus theory would predict that in a promotion focus, the brand change would be more likely than in a prevention focus, which is more concerned with ensuring correct rejections and avoiding errors of false alarm. Indeed, there are some results that point in this direction. For example, Liberman et al. (1999) found that participants with a promotion focus were more willing than participants in a prevention focus to exchange objects they owned for alternative objects. They argue that individuals in a prevention focus feel more obliged to rely on the original alternatives as long as they are satisfactory. In contrast, individuals with a promotion focus are willing to change if they think that the new alternative is an improvement over the original object. However, it is important to stress that promotion-focused individuals do not change without considering the alternatives. If they do not see a good chance for a benefit from the new alternative, they should be content with a satisfactory item.

However, it is not simply the case that individuals rely more often than not on strategies that are appropriate means for reaching their regulatory goals, they also feel more comfortable when they rely on strategies that fit their regulatory goals. As Higgins (2000, 2002) proposed, several studies have shown that independent of valued outcomes, people experience a regulatory fit when they pursue a goal in a manner that sustains their regulatory focus. This fit increases people's feeling that the strategy used was the right strategy (Cesario, Grant, & Higgins, 2004). Higgins, Idson, Freitas, Spiegel, and Molden (2003) and Avnet and Higgins (2003) demonstrated that this "feeling right" can be transferred to monetary evaluations of an object. For example, in one study by Higgins et al. (2003), participants were asked to choose between a coffee mug and an inexpensive pen as reward for participating in an experiment. To produce fit or nonfit with the regulatory focus, participants were asked to think either about what they would gain by choosing the pen or the mug, or, in another condition, what they would lose. Fit was produced when participants in a promotion focus applied the gain strategy, or when participants in a prevention focus applied the lose strategy. In the other focus/strategy combinations there was nonfit. As Higgins and colleagues expected, participants assigned a higher price to the same coffee mug when they had chosen it with a strategy that fit their regulatory focus than with a strategy that did not.

PERSUASION AND REGULATORY FIT WITHIN A MESSAGE

In advertising, it is less likely, if not impossible, that the marketer could influence which strategy a consumer would use to select a product. However, more interesting for the advertiser is the question whether regulatory focus theory has implications for the design of ads and marketing campaigns. One point that may be of special interest regarding the design of ads is the compatibility of goals that are highlighted in a persuasive message and the regulatory focus that is made salient in the message. Although any specific goal may be pursued with either a promotion or a prevention focus, some goals are more compatible than others with a particular self-regulatory strategy (Higgins, 2002). For example, as we have stressed before, goals that are concerned with approaching a desired end state are more compatible with a promotion focus than with a prevention focus, whereas goals that involve the avoidance of an undesirable end state are more compatible with a prevention focus than with a promotion focus. A few studies have shown that persuasive messages are more persuasive when mentioned goals or means are compatible with the regulatory focus of the message (Lee & Aaker, 2004).

Lee and Aaker (2004, Study 1) presented participants with an ad for grape juice. The content of the ad was either related to promotion concerns (energy boost) or prevention concerns (disease prevention). Additionally, the authors varied whether a gain or a loss frame was used in the ad. For example, in the promotion condition, a gain frame was "Get energized!," whereas a loss frame was "Don't miss out on getting energized!" In the prevention condition, an example of a gain frame was "Prevent clogged arteries!," and a loss frame was "Don't miss out on preventing clogged arteries!" Lee and Aaker found that promotion and prevention appeals were differently effective depending on how they were framed. Promotion appeals were more persuasive when presented in a gain rather than in a loss frame, whereas prevention appeals were more persuasive when presented in a loss rather than in a gain frame. The authors propose that a message becomes easier to process when the frame of the message is consistent with the way in which "individuals naturally think about issues that involve positive or negative outcomes" (Lee & Aaker, 2004, p. 207). Moreover, they argue that individuals transfer the experienced ease to more favorable attitudes toward the ad (cf. Wänke, Bohner, & Jurkowitsch, 1997). Indeed, participants in one of the studies of Lee and Aaker found the messages with regulatory fit easier to understand than the messages lacking fit, and mediational analyses showed that this processing ease does in fact mediate the impact of regulatory fit on attitudes. Altogether, the studies of Lee and Aaker demonstrate that fit between a gain or loss frame and the regulatory goals that are stressed in a message leads to a processing ease that elicits a positive feeling, which in turn affects the perceived persuasiveness of a message.

Another factor that may be of importance as regards the regulatory focus of a message is whether an ad speaks to one's individual or interdependent self. Aaker and Lee (2001) modified the Web site of Welch's Grape Juice™ in order to activate either an independent or an interdependent self-view. They used a picture of a family or a single person on the Web site and supported the picture with suitable text. Aaker and Lee hypothesized that the activation of an interdependent self would fit better with a prevention message emphasizing the health benefits of the juice than it would with a promotion message containing arguments for higher personal effectiveness and energy. The results supported the hypotheses. Participants evaluated the Web site more positively when the family picture was combined with a prevention message and when the picture of the individual was combined with a promotion message than in the other two combinations. Thus, the study of Aaker and Lee suggests that an advertisement is more effective when the regulatory focus of a message fits the self-view of the recipient, which can also be influenced, for example by pictures in an advertisement.

Taking into account that such an activated self-view has an impact on the processing of an advertisement, it is reasonable to assume that it is not only the activation of the self-view by an ad that is important, but also differences in self-view that are caused by other sources. Indeed, Aaker and Lee (2001; see also Briley & Wyer, 2002) found differences in the perception of promotion and prevention-related messages between an individualistic (United States) and a collectivist culture (Hong Kong). Thus, the fit of the regulatory focus of a message with aspects of the recipient not induced by an advertisement are important. For that reason, we shall take a more detailed look in the next section at the effects that different regulatory foci of consumers have on the way in which a persuasive message is perceived.

REGULATORY FIT BETWEEN MESSAGE AND RECIPIENT

Cesario et al. (2004) measured the chronic regulatory focus of participants and also induced experimentally a promotion or prevention focus. They found that participants were more likely to be persuaded by a message that stressed eager means to reach a goal when participants were in a promotion focus. A message that emphasized the use of vigilant means was, in contrast, more persuasive when participants were in a prevention focus. Because eager means fit with a promotion focus and vigilant means are typical for a prevention focus, it seems that fit between the content of a message and the regulatory focus of the recipient enhances the persuasive impact of the message. There are several possible explanations for such fit effects.

One explanation is that the fit of a message with a person's regulatory focus leads to enhanced persuasion because individuals evaluate messages more positively when they are in line with their attitudes, motivations, and needs (e.g., Snyder & DeBono, 1985). The perception of fit may be used in this sense as a heuristic that the message is all right. Similarly, it can be argued that fit or nonfit leads to processing of message arguments in a biased manner. Fit may lead to the generation of more favorable thoughts and nonfit to more unfavorable thoughts (cf., Cacioppo, Petty, & Sidera, 1982; Lavine & Snyder, 1996). Evans and Petty (2003) provided data that points to a further explanation. They suggest that the perception of fit enhances the motivation to process the message, presumably because fit indicates that a message is relevant for the individual. The two authors tested this hypothesis by first measuring the chronic strength of accessible ideal or ought self-guides. Subsequently, they presented participants with a persuasive message that was framed in terms of either ideals or responsibilities and contained either strong or weak arguments. Since ideal self-guides are typical for a promotion focus and ought self-guides are typical for a prevention focus, the self-guide measure can be regarded as a measure of regulatory focus. The authors found that participants with a promotion focus were more likely to consider the arguments of the message when they were framed in terms of ideals and hopes. In contrast, participants with a prevention focus were more likely to consider the arguments of the message when they were framed in terms of responsibilities and duties. In other words, fit led to more positive thoughts when the message arguments were strong, but it led to more negative thoughts when the message arguments were weak. In the nonfit condition, there were no significant differences in thoughts depending on the message arguments. Thus, fit between the concerns of a message and the regulatory focus of a recipient appears to increase message processing.

Besides the effect that regulatory fit has on the effort to process a message, it might also affect persuasion through a transfer of feeling onto the perceived persuasiveness of a message. Indeed, one proposition of regulatory focus theory holds that decisions are evaluated more positively when they are made with strategies that fit with the regulatory focus of the decision maker (Higgins, 2000, 2002). The reasoning is that the regulatory fit elicits a feeling of correctness or importance ("feeling right"), which, in turn, is attributed to the decision or the chosen alternative and interpreted as a positive evaluation. As previously mentioned, there is evidence that tasks and decisions are evaluated more positively when individuals experience fit between their regulatory focus and applied strategic means, which elicits feeling right (Avnet & Higgins, 2003; Freitas & Higgins, 2002; Freitas, Liberman, & Higgins, 2002; Higgins, et al., 2003). If, in a similar vein, the transfer of a feeling has an impact on the efficiency of persuasive messages, two conditions should be fulfilled: First, individuals who experience regulatory fit should evaluate a message as more persuasive than individuals who do not. Second, if the basis for this effect is a misattribution of the unspecific feeling right, the persuasive effect of regulatory fit should disappear when individuals' attention is directed to the source of the feeling (Schwarz & Clore, 1983, 1996). Cesario et al. (2004) tested these predictions and found strong support for the assumed processes. They demonstrated that participants experiencing regulatory fit perceived messages as more persuasive, and that this effect disappeared—or was at least reduced—when participants attended to the correct source of feeling right from regulatory fit prior to the message.

However, even if individuals do not correct the feeling right, this feeling from regulatory fit does not inevitably lead to a more positive attitude toward the attitude object. Rather, the feeling right enhances their own response toward the message. It means something like feeling right about the own response for the individual. Consequently, Cesario et al. (2004) found in one study that regulatory fit and the associated feeling right can also lead to reduced persuasion when the thoughts about the message topic were negative. In this case, presumably, individuals feel right in their response that the message is weak. Thus, regulatory fit increases the effect of generated thoughts by the perception that the thoughts are correct and right.

REGULATORY FOCUS AND SYSTEMATIC INFORMATION PROCESSING

So far, we have illuminated three different kinds of impact regulatory focus might have. First, we have shown that individuals may choose products that are instrumental for their regulatory goals, or products that have specific outcome values compatible with their regulatory focus. Second, we reported evidence that a regulatory fit between different components of a message makes it easier to process a message. Third, we mentioned different effects of the fit between the regulatory focus of a message and a recipient. One point we did not mention so far is that the regulatory focus can also have a direct impact on the processing of information. For example, Friedman and Förster (2001) found that participants in a creativity task relied more on explorative and risky information-processing strategies when a promotion focus was primed than when a prevention focus was primed. Thus, there is evidence that the risk-aversive strategy of individuals in a prevention focus compared to those in a promotion focus can also be found in information processing itself.

Pham and Avnet (2004) applied these ideas to the area of consumer judgment. Like Friedman and Förster (2001), they postulated that a prevention focus should be accompanied by a less risky information-processing strategy. Further, they argue that regulatory focus affects which information is used to form a judgment. Consequently, consumers should rely on information that leads to a reasonable and less risky decision when a prevention focus versus a promotion focus is predominant. In the view of Pham and Avnet (2004), affective information is a less reliable source for the decision than information that is more related to the central merits of a product. Therefore, individuals in a prevention focus should rely less on their affective reaction to a product appeal or other peripheral cues than on the central merits that the product is claimed to have. In a series of experiments, Pham and Avnet tested this prediction. After first manipulating the regulatory focus with a priming procedure, they exposed participants to the ad for a dictionary. The attractiveness of the ad was varied along with the persuasive strength of the claims. In line with their expectations, the authors found that the judgment of the dictionary was influenced to a stronger degree by the ad's attractiveness when a promotion focus was primed than when a prevention focus was primed. The claim was more important for participants with a prevention focus than for those with a promotion focus. Altogether, Pham and Avnet have provided evidence that the regulatory focus has an impact on the processing of information in the area of consumer judgment.

Florack et al. (2004b) attempted to furnish additional support for the assumption that a promotion focus and a prevention focus are linked to different processing strategies, and to illuminate the conditions under which the differential effects of regulatory focus on consumer behavior occur. In a first experiment, they examined the hypothesis that individuals in promotion focus are more likely than individuals in a prevention focus to rely on their automatic product preferences when forming an impression of a product. The experimenter told participants that they could choose between fruit and chocolate as a reward for their participation, and that they should indicate their preferences on a few items. To induce a promotion focus in one condition and a prevention focus in the other, the researchers applied a priming procedure before participants indicated their preferences. This priming procedure was adapted from Pham and Avnet (2004). In the promotion focus condition, participants were asked to think about their current and past hopes, aspirations, and dreams, and to list at least two of each. In the prevention focus condition, participants were asked to think about their current and past duties, obligations, and responsibilities, and to list at least two of each. In addition, Florack et al. (2004b) measured automatic product preferences with the Implicit Association Test (IAT; Greenwald, McGhee, & Schwartz, 1998). In line with their expectations, they found a significant correlation between the automatic preferences and the self-reported preferences only for participants in the promotion-priming condition, but not for those in the prevention-priming condition. Thus, it seems that individuals in a prevention focus rely on other information than just their automatic preferences when making a choice. Presumably, they do not consider their automatic preference or their affective response as valid information that ensures a good decision, hence they look out for other sources of information. In contrast, the results of Florack et al. (2004b) and those of Pham and Avnet (2004) suggested that individuals in a promotion focus trust their immediate responses. Because for these people the attainment of their individual goals has priority, we suppose that the reliance on their own responses and knowledge structures is very functional.

REGULATORY FOCUS AND CUE RELEVANCE IN PERSUASION

If we regard systematic processing as a way of obtaining security, it seems reasonable to assume that individuals in a prevention focus are motivated to process all relevant information more systematically than individuals in a promotion focus. Taking into account that studies in persuasion with high reliability found that peripheral cues have increased effects on persuasion when the processing motivation is low, it seems reasonable to assume that individuals in a prevention focus are also less likely to be influenced by peripheral cues than individuals in a promotion focus. Indeed, a core assumption of the classic two-process models in persuasion research (Chaiken, Liberman, & Eagly, 1989; Petty & Cacioppo, 1986b) is that peripheral or heuristic cues have relatively little impact on attitudes under high-elaboration conditions.

If we examine these theories in greater detail, it appears that the perceived relevance of cues is the crucial point. For example, Petty and Cacioppo (1986b) proposed that peripheral cues have a reduced impact under high-elaboration conditions because highly motivated people do not consider peripheral cues as particularly relevant for making their judgments. Indeed, in a recent analysis of persuasion research, Pierro, Mannetti, Kruglanski, and Sleeth-Keppler (2004) found that in almost all of the studies that tested the two-process models in persuasion, peripheral cues were perceived as less relevant than high-quality message arguments.

However, cues like the source of a message might also be more relevant for a judgment or a decision than message arguments, and may affect attitudes under systematic processing as well as under heuristic or peripheral processing (Kruglanski & Thompson, 1999; Petty & Wegener, 1999). This may be the case especially if the issue is important to a person, but the person is unable to understand the arguments being presented. Consider a consumer who would like to buy a detergent. She or he may have difficulties finding strong arguments for a particular choice when standing in front of a shelf in the supermarket. Even if the ingredients of the detergents are listed on the packages, the consumer is probably unable to understand them. Furthermore, detailed information about a product is virtually absent in other contexts, such as some print or TV ads. In these cases, consumers who are motivated to engage in effortful information processing do not have the possibility to elaborate on central arguments that are given. Rather, they might think extensively about the relevance of peripheral cues or might attempt to generate arguments (Petty, Wheeler, & Bizer, 1999).

If we consider the argument of Petty and Cacioppo (1986a) that "the kind of information that is relevant to evaluating the central merits of a product may vary from situation to situation and from person to person" (p. 17), this may apply especially to individual differences in regulatory focus. As we have suggested, some cues—such as the affective reaction toward a product—may be more relevant for participants in a promotion focus than for those in a prevention focus. Other cues may be more diagnostic for a safe and responsible decision, and may therefore be especially relevant for participants in a prevention focus.

There is some evidence from mood research that is congruent with this proposition. Indeed, there are similarities in the information-processing strategies used by individuals in a bad mood and by individuals in a prevention focus. Bless and Schwarz (1999) postulated that mood provides the individual with important information about his or her status. They argued that good mood indicates that everything is all right, whereas bad mood signals that something is wrong and that the individual has to carefully think about his or her behavior and decisions. Several studies provided broad support for this assumption and documented that individuals in bad mood process information more systematically than individuals in good mood, and that they are less likely to rely on heuristics, stereotypes, or peripheral cues in persuasion (e.g., Bless, Bohner, Schwarz, & Strack, 1990; Bless, Mackie, & Schwarz, 1992; Bodenhausen, Kramer, & Süsser, 1994; Mackie & Worth, 1989). However, Bohner, Crow, Erb, and Schwarz (1992, Experiment 2) also showed that individuals in a bad mood do not disregard peripheral cues in every case. In one of their experiments, they advised an assistant to collect money for disabled persons. The assistant supported the request either by a strong argument ("Money for the construction of ramps for wheel chairs") or a weak one ("Money for a separate library for the disabled"). Furthermore, participants were shown a list of contributors that contained as few as two or as many as 19 names. The results demonstrated that individuals in a negative mood considered not only the message strength, but also the consensus cue. They were more likely to donate money for the disabled when 19 names were on the list of contributors rather than only two names. This effect was not found for participants in a positive mood. Because consensus information is a cue that may be related to a secure and valid decision, it seems that individuals who are motivated to avoid erroneous decisions— as are those in a bad mood—may rely on cues that signal safeness. Therefore, we assume that individuals in a prevention focus may also rely more heavily on cues than individuals in a promotion focus when these cues are more relevant to them than to individuals in a promotion focus.

In fact, Florack et al. (2004b) found first support for this assumption in an experiment in which they tested whether individuals in a prevention focus are more likely to rely on the preferences of others. In this experiment, the authors again primed a promotion or a prevention focus with the adapted procedure of Pham and Avnet (2004). Participants then saw a comparative ad for a burger that promoted either the Whopper (Burger King™) or the Big Mac (McDonalds™). In the Whopper-promotion condition, the ad reported that in a market study, 62% of consumers would prefer the Whopper over the Big Mac if they had to make a choice between the two products. In the Big Mac-promotion condition, the opposite percentages were depicted on the ad, with a majority of 62% of respondents preferring a Big Mac. After participants saw the ad, they indicated their purchase intention for either a Whopper or a Big Mac on a few items. Furthermore, the automatic product preferences were assessed with an IAT and the chronic regulatory focus with a questionnaire of Lockwood et al. (2002).

A first step examined whether the differences in correlations of the automatic preferences with the choice intention were similar to the results obtained in the previous experiment for automatic preferences and self-reported attitudes. The authors obtained consistent results for the induced regulatory focus as well as for the chronic regulatory focus. For participants who thought about their ideals, they found a significantly higher correlation between the automatic preference and choice intention than for participants who thought about their obligations. Similarly, when they divided the sample by median split on the chronic regulatory-focus measure into a group with a prevention focus and a group with a promotion focus, they obtained a higher correlation of the automatic product preference with choice intentions for participants with a chronic promotion focus compared to those with a chronic prevention focus.

Furthermore, the authors analyzed the effects of the experimental conditions and of chronic regulatory focus on choice intentions. They found a main effect for the presented ads. Participants were more likely to report intentions to buy a Big Mac when the ad claimed that most people preferred a Big Mac. However, when the opposite was claimed, this tendency was reduced. Importantly, this main effect was qualified by an interaction between the presented ad and the chronic regulatory focus. Indeed, participants in a prevention focus were more likely to be influenced by the ad than participants in a promotion focus (see Fig. 11.1). For participants with a chronic promotion focus, no significant differences between the two ad presentations were found. Altogether, this experiment demonstrated that individuals in a promotion focus are more likely than individuals in a prevention focus to follow their intuition or automatic preferences. Individuals in a chronic prevention focus seem to rely more on the majority preferences, presumably because the preference of the majority is diagnostic for a safe decision.

Another consequence of a prevention focus is a preference for the status quo over change. We have already referred to the research of Liberman et al. (1999), who demonstrated that individuals in a prevention focus were less willing than individuals in a promotion focus to exchange objects they already possessed for other objects. An explanation for this finding is that change entails the danger of worsening a status that one has already achieved. In a certain sense, the choice between a well-established brand and a newcomer in the market can be seen also as a choice between stability and change. One important argument for choosing a well-established brand is that the buyer knows what he or she is getting. Indeed, that might be one reason why consumers often accept that well-established brands are much more expensive than comparison brands of comparable quality. In contrast, the choice of a newcomer in the market or a product with an unknown brand

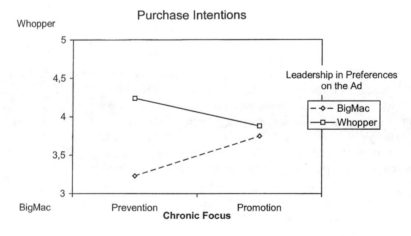

FIG. 11.1.   Purchase intentions as a function of the chronic regulatory focus and consensus information on the ad. High values indicate a preference for a Whopper, low values a preference for the Big Mac. Data from Florack, Scarabis, and Gosejohann (2004b).

label offers the chance for an extra benefit, for example, new product features or the same quality for a lower price. However, the choice of an unknown brand is also associated with the risk of a mispurchase.

If we take into account that individuals in a prevention focus are less willing than individuals in a promotion focus to accept a risk to improve an acceptable status, individuals in a prevention focus should prefer well-established brands more so than individuals in a promotion focus. Indeed, a third study of Florack et al. (2004b) provided results that are to some extent congruent with this assumption. In this study, participants saw a print ad for a new mobile phone. However, even if the layout of the ad was the same for all participants, the brand of the mobile phone and the claim of the ad were varied. Half of the participants received an ad for a well-established brand (Sony Ericsson™), while the other half received an ad for a fictitious brand (Kiotel). In one condition, the claim of the ad was related to a prevention goal ("With this mobile phone you always have a reliable partner") or a promotion goal ("With this mobile phone you are always a step ahead").

Furthermore, the authors measured the chronic regulatory focus with a scale of Lockwood et al. (2002), and divided the sample into a group with a predominant promotion focus and another with a predominant prevention focus by median split. When the claim addressed a prevention goal, the statistical analyses revealed the expected interaction between the predominant goal and the brand label. Participants with a predominant prevention focus, but not those with a predominant promotion focus, evaluated the mobile phone more positively when the ad carried a well-known brand label as compared to when it carried an unknown brand label. However, it is important to note that when the claim of the ad addressed a promotion goal, the brand label had no effect on the product evaluation, either for participants with a predominant promotion focus or for those with a predominant prevention focus. Thus, the key finding of this study is that individuals in a prevention focus rely on the brand label, but they do so only when the claim of the ad addresses a goal that corresponds to their regulatory focus.

An explanation for the results of Florack et al. (2004b) is rooted in the research on regulatory fit (Cesario et al., 2004; Higgins, 2000, 2002). As mentioned before, Cesario et al. (2004) argued that a fit between a persuasive message and the regulatory focus of the recipient elicits a "feeling right" that can be transferred to the evaluation of a message. Going one step further, a consumer might also rely on such a feeling right when evaluating the validity of heuristic cues like the brand. Following this reasoning, the perceived relevance of a brand should be higher when the claim fits with the predominant focus of the participants. This might explain why participants with a predominant prevention focus relied on the well-known brand when the claim addressed a goal that matched their focus, and why they did not when there was a mismatch. However, this still leaves open the question why fit does not lead to an enhanced brand effect for participants in a promotion focus. If regulatory fit leads to a feeling right about the cues, this should also be true for promotion-focused people. It is possible that because of their superficial processing style, participants with a predominant promotion focus did not care about the brand information in any condition (cf. Pham & Avnet, 2004). In making their judgment, the may have relied on their immediate response that was driven by the product appeal, but not by the brand name.

A main implication of the study by Florack et al. (2004b) is that the relevance of a cue might depend on the context of a judgment or choice. The study we have mentioned showed that a cue that was relevant for participants with a predominant prevention focus in one condition was not relevant for them in another condition. Indeed, this might be even more true for cues other than a brand name. Consider the example of a celebrity endorser. The personality of a celebrity endorser, like that of every individual, consists of many different traits, and he or she might be associated with a lot of attributes and social categories. A celebrity might fit the expectations of a consumer on one attribute but not on another, and which information about the celebrity is salient will vary a lot between different contexts. All in all, whether or not a consumer perceives a celebrity endorser as trustworthy and relevant might depend on many different things and may vary contextually (Silvera & Laufer, chap. 3, this volume). Because the perception of the celebrity endorser is variable, affective reactions as well as the feeling right from regulatory fit may also have an impact on the trustworthiness of a celebrity endorser.

Indeed, Florack et al. (2004b) argued that one of the context variables that might determine whether individuals perceive a cue as valid is the regulatory fit between characteristics of an advertisement and the regulatory focus of the consumer. In particular, they propose that a fit between regulatory goals that are addressed in the claim of an ad and the predominant regulatory focus of the consumer might induce a feeling right. Because previous research has shown that such a feeling right is to some extent an unspecific feeling that, as we know from research on mood, may be attributed to different causes, consumers may also interpret this feeling as an indicator of the validity and the relevance of the celebrity in the ad. If the regulatory fit elicits a feeling right, consumers might think that the celebrity is in the right place on the ad and they might rely on this cue in making their judgment. This implies that a cue like a celebrity endorser can be more relevant for individuals in a prevention focus than for those in a promotion focus when an ad addresses prevention goals, but that the same cue can also be more relevant for participants in a promotion focus than for those in a prevention focus when the claim of the ad addresses promotion goals. In a fourth study, Florack et al. (2004b) tested this assumption.

In this study, the authors again applied Pham and Avnet's (2004) priming procedure for inducing a promotion or a prevention focus. Afterward, they presented an ad for a mobile phone on the computer screen. Participants then evaluated the product on several items. The presented ads were similar to those in the previous experiment, with the exception that the brand label was the same in all conditions. Instead, in one condition a celebrity endorser appeared in the ad, while in another condition participants only saw an unknown person. The variation of the claims, which either addressed a promotion or a prevention goal, was the same as in the previous experiment. As the authors hypothesized, an analysis of variance (ANOVA) with the primed regulatory focus (promotion vs. prevention), the claims (promotion vs. prevention), and the endorsers (celebrity vs. unknown person) as independent variables and the evaluation of the mobile phone as dependent measure yielded a significant three-way interaction (Fig. 11.2).

a) Promotion Priming Condition

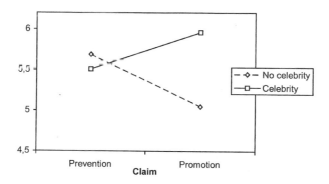

b) Prevention Priming Condition

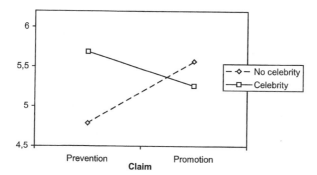

FIG. 11.2.   Evaluation of the mobile phone as a function of the induced regulatory focus, the focus of the claim, and the endorser. Data from Florack, Scarabis, and Gosejohann (2004b).

Let us first consider the results for the induced promotion focus. When a promotion focus was primed, the celebrity endorser did indeed have a positive effect on the evaluation of the mobile phone, but only when the claim of the ad addressed a promotion goal. Interestingly, the shape of the interaction was different when a prevention focus was primed. For these participants, there were no significant differences in the evaluation of the mobile phone between the conditions with a celebrity or an unknown endorser when the claim addressed a promotion goal. But when the claim addressed a prevention goal, these participants also evaluated the mobile phone more positively when they were exposed to an ad with a celebrity endorser than when they were exposed to an ad with an unknown endorser. Altogether, the results demonstrated that the celebrity endorser had a higher persuasive impact on the evaluation of the mobile phone when the claim addressed a goal that was compatible with the induced regulatory focus. Thus, the results suggest that a peripheral cue like a celebrity endorser in this experiment might be differentially relevant for participants in a promotion focus and for those in a prevention focus. However, they also suggest that the relevance of the cues may flip when the claim of the message changes.

Even if the results are completely congruent with the regulatory-fit explanation, further research is necessary to clarify the underlying process. Because the primary goal of the studies of Florack et al. (2004b) was to identify the phenomena that regulatory focus and regulatory fit have an impact on the relevance of heuristic cues, they did not test whether the obtained cue effects are indeed a consequence of the misattribution of a feeling right that has its source in perceived regulatory fit. We have already examined the work of Cesario et al. (2004) and Lee and Aaker (2004), who showed that regulatory fit leads to a feeling right and that this feeling right can be misattributed as a positive affective reaction to the issue of the advertisement. However, they did not test cue effects like those that appeared in the studies of Florack et al. (2004b). Thus, the field would benefit if future research were to address the underlying processes of the described phenomena. In fact, the studies just discussed cannot rule out some alternative explanations. Two possible explanations that are important to mention are (a) that the claim might prime a different view of the cues, and (b) that the claim affects the motivation of the participants.

We discussed earlier that a cue might be perceived in many different ways. A well-known brand may stand for quality, reliability, or even for overpriced products. Similarly, a celebrity may be associated with a lot of different benefits or disadvantages. The message may operate as a prime, which activates a certain concept that is applied to the cues. For example, if a message activates the concept reliability, the cue may be perceived in relationship to reliability. If we apply this to the brand study of Florack et al. (2004b), it is possible that in one condition, but not in the other, participants perceived the well-known brand as warranting reliability. Taking into account that reliability is an important issue for individuals in a prevention focus, it would be reasonable to assume that, in this case, they rely on the well-known brand. Because priming research has shown that a primed concept must be applicable (Higgins, 1996), it may be that the concept of *reliability* was not applicable to the unknown brand. Thus, the message may prime how the cue is perceived.

Furthermore, it remains an open question whether the effects of regulatory fit are consequences of enhanced motivation. Evans and Petty (2003) already demonstrated that fit between a message and the regulatory goals of a recipient leads to a greater elaboration of the message. At first glance, this seems to contradict the findings that cues may be especially important under conditions of regulatory fit. However, if we consider that the ads presented in the studies of Florack et al. (2004b) contained no information other than a simple claim, a picture, and a cue, participants had no chance to further elaborate given information. Perhaps they thought more about the information that was present, including cues like the brand name or the endorser. In particular, it may be possible that, in the brand study, the brand was only noticed by those participants who were motivated to study the advertisement very carefully. As for the study with the celebrity endorser, it may be that highly motivated participants generated thoughts about the celebrity like "He would not make advertisements for an inferior product that would ruin his name." Thus, the findings could also be explained as a consequence of a higher motivation to elaborate on the ads that goes hand in hand with regulatory fit.

SUMMARY: REGULATORY FOCUS, INFORMATION PROCESSING, AND PRODUCT CHOICE

The main objective of this chapter has been to illustrate the impact of regulatory focus on consumer information processing and consumer choice. First, we discussed results that were related to the proposition of regulatory focus theory that "decision makers in a promotion orientation will treat promotion-relevant outcomes as more important in their decision than prevention-relevant outcomes, whereas the reverse will be true for decision makers in a prevention orientation" (Higgins, 2002, p.186). Several studies provided support for two implications of this proposal. Primarily, there is evidence that individuals prefer products that are instrumental for pursuing a regulatory goal.

Our sun-lotion study (Florack et al., 2004a) was based on the idea that individuals have different goals in mind when buying a sun lotion: the goal to protect the skin and to avoid sunburn, which is associated with a prevention focus; and the goal to get tanned, which is associated with a promotion focus. In agreement with the postulate of the regulatory focus theory, we found that participants in a prevention focus, more so than participants in a promotion focus, preferred a sun lotion with a claim that stressed the importance of skin protection instead of the goal of getting well tanned. However, in this particular example, the outcome related to a promotion or prevention focus is not the product. Rather, the product is the means to attaining a superordinate goal (getting tanned, avoiding sunburn). In other cases, a product or certain attributes of a product have direct outcome values that are differently related to a promotion or prevention focus. For instance, Safer (1998) found that when participants make a choice, they pay more attention to attribute dimensions of a product that are relevant to their regulatory focus than to other dimensions. Thus, there is evidence that consumers prefer products that provide a means to reach a regulatory goal or have an outcome value relevant to a regulatory goal.

However, there is research showing not only the impact of a consumers' regulatory focus on a choice, but also that different products can differently elicit a promotion or prevention self-regulation. Consider the study by Zhou and Pham (in press), who asked participants, first, to make investment decisions, and, then, to choose between unrelated products with either a promotion or a prevention benefit. The authors found that the act of making decisions had an impact on the regulatory focus in subsequent choices unrelated to investment (e.g., choice of a juice). Participants who had just made decisions about risky investment products preferred consumer products with promotion benefits, whereas those who had just made decisions about more secure investment products preferred products with prevention benefits.

Another aspect we have stressed in this chapter is the importance of the regulatory focus as regards the design of advertisements. The studies of Lee and Aaker (2004) illustrated that an advertising claim is more effective when there is a fit between different elements of the message. In particular, they showed that it is easier for participants to understand a claim when a promotion benefit is highlighted in a gain frame, and when a prevention benefit is highlighted in a loss frame. These frame and focus combinations, unlike the reversed ones, also lead to a feeling right that, in turn, increases the perceived persuasiveness of an advertising claim. In addition, Aaker and Lee (2001) demonstrated that elements of a message can also induce different self-views, and that an advertisement is evaluated more positively when the activated self-view fits with other regulatory issues of the advertisement. For example, in one study, the Web site for a juice was rated more positively when pictures and text activated an independent self and when, simultaneously, the ad asserted promotion benefits (e.g., power, energy) rather than prevention benefits (e.g., disease prevention). When an interdependent self-view was activated, a prevention claim had a more positive effect on the evaluation of the Web site.

The effects of different kinds of fit were also discussed regarding the fit between the regulatory focus of an advertising message and the regulatory focus of the recipient. Evans and Petty (2003) found that fit motivates participants to elaborate on the arguments of a message more extensively. Moreover, Cesario et al. (2004) proposed that fit between the regulatory focus of a message elicits a feeling right that can be interpreted by individuals as an indicator of the persuasive strength of an advertisement, a claim, or a message. Indeed, they found strong support for their assumption. In their studies, the feeling right from regulatory fit influenced the persuasive impact of a message as long as the participants were not directed to the correct source of this feeling. If they were, participants corrected for the influence of the feeling right. Cesario et al. (2004) suggested as the main mechanism that individuals interpret the feeling right as the perceived correctness of their own responses. In support of this assumption, they found that the feeling right amplified the effect of message-related thoughts. When the thoughts were primarily positive, the feeling right led to more positive evaluations of the attitude object, whereas more negative evaluations resulted when the thoughts were primarily negative. Taking into account the research of both Evans and Petty (2003) and of Cesario et al. (2004), there is evidence that regulatory fit between a message and a recipient (a) signals that the message is relevant and should be elaborated more extensively, and (b) evokes a feeling right that serves as an indicator of the correctness of one's own responses toward a message.

In addition, we have also discussed the fact that a consumer's regulatory focus might have a direct impact on information-processing strategies. Pham and Avnet (2004) as well as Florack et al. (2004b) assumed that the conservatism and risk aversion that characterized individuals in a prevention focus in contrast to those in a promotion focus is also reflected in information-processing strategies. As support for this assumption, we referred to a study by Pham and Avnet. In this study, participants were more likely to be influenced by substantive information than by the appeal of a product when a prevention focus versus a promotion focus was primed. Similarly, Florack et al. (2004b) found that individuals in a prevention focus were less likely than individuals in a promotion focus to rely on their automatic preferences. However, the impact of regulatory focus is not limited to the amount of processing; regulatory focus also affects which information is relevant and diagnostic for the consumer. The research of Florack et al. (2004b) showed that the automatic preference is a relevant cue for people in a promotion focus, but not for those in a prevention focus. In contrast, consensus information was proved to have greater impact on the judgments of participants in a prevention focus than on those of participants in a promotion focus. Thus, it seems that people in a prevention focus, more so than those in a promotion focus, apply information-processing strategies that allow for a secure and less risky decision. For instance, individuals in a prevention focus may elaborate on the given information or look out for information that indicates safeness, for example, consensus information.

Extending this view, we stressed another argument in this chapter: the variability of cue relevance. Some cues may have a meaning that does not vary much over different contexts, but a lot of cues can be associated with several different meanings. There was evidence in the studies of Florack et al. (2004b) that a celebrity endorser is an informative cue for participants in a promotion focus in one context, and is relevant for participants in a prevention focus in other contexts. Indeed, the same celebrity endorser may be associated with characteristics that are relevant for people in a prevention focus (e.g., reliability) or for people in a promotion focus (e.g., ideals). Depending on the context, different characteristics of the celebrity endorser may be salient. The studies of Florack et al. (2004b) have shown that another variable also has an influence on the relevance of a cue: That variable is, once again, the regulatory fit between the focus of the recipient and the focus of an advertising claim. It was found that a celebrity endorser had a greater impact on the evaluation of a product when the claim matched the regulatory goals of the recipient. We have argued that in this condition, the feeling right associated with the regulatory fit also serves as an indicator that the celebrity is trustable or in the right place. However, we also pointed out that, in the fit conditions, participants possibly relied more on the celebrity because he was associated with a claim that was relevant to them. Further research is necessary to evaluate our cue variability proposition more extensively. In particular, it is important to examine directly the supposed mediating role of the feeling right as well as the effects of the salience of differential cue characteristics.

IMPLICATIONS FOR MARKETING

The impact of a promotion or prevention focus on consumer information processing also has implications for advertising and marketing. One implication that is easy to implement is that advertisers should avoid a mismatch of different elements of an advertisement as regards regulatory focus. Since Lee and Aaker (2004) showed that loss frames fit better with a prevention claim, and gain frames fit better with a promotion claim, advertisers should use only framing/focus combinations that fit. Furthermore, advertisers should be aware that a specific self-view or self-regulation can be evoked by elements of an ad (Aaker & Lee, 2001). Regulatory focus theory predicts that ads should be more persuasive when the regulatory focus of the highlighted benefits is congruent with the self-view or self-regulation of the recipient that is evoked by picture or text elements.

More difficult to realize is the design of an advertisement with reference to the regulatory focus of a target group. Even if there are cultural differences relevant to regulatory focus (e.g., Aaker & Lee, 2001), which may be of special interest for global marketing campaigns, often the target group consists of promotion as well as prevention-focused individuals. However, there might be products that are advertised in specific market segments that are strongly related to a specific regulatory focus, such as investment products that are addressed to people who seek a secure retirement arrangement, or family-related products (e.g., a child-safety seat). Indeed, products can be strongly associated with a promotion or prevention focus and can induce the associated self-regulation in the individual (Zhou & Pham, in press). In these cases as well, advertisers may avail themselves of the processes of regulatory fit.

To get an idea which products are related to which focus, practitioners could rely on product typologies like the *product color matrix* (PCM; e.g., Spotts, Weinberger, & Parsons, 1997). This matrix categorizes products into one of four categories on the basis of two dimensions: (a) risk of purchase (high vs. low); (b) the consumer's objective (functional tools vs. expressive toys). One can speculate, for example, that "big toys" (expressive products with a high purchase risk, e.g., sports cars) are more promotion connected, while "little tools" (functional products with a low risk, e.g., detergents and household cleaners) are more prevention connected, because they mainly serve to preserve or reestablish the status quo.

To induce regulatory fit, advertisers may also display specific emotions in an advertising campaign. For example, Higgins (1998) argued that a promotion focus is more connected to cheerfulness-related and dejection-related emotions (e.g., happiness or disappointment) compared to a prevention focus, which is connected rather to quiescence-related or agitation-related emotions (e.g., calmness or tension). These emotional aspects can be used to construct stories that appeal to different groups of consumers. A very simple idea is to target the prevention-oriented consumer by showing a situation that stresses the uneasiness of a person in face of a potential loss. Besides the recommendation to use fitting content, this aspect could help to find the right emotional undertone. Incidentally, with the exception of the feeling-right effect, the emotional dimension of regulatory focus theory is so far untested in the context of consumer psychology.

Finally, even if products may be associated with a certain regulatory focus, it was shown that the regulatory focus of participants varies depending on the context of a judgment or choice. This variability is not only a problem for marketing managers and advertisers, who might be able to utilize this effect to their advantage. For example, a product may be placed in different locations within a store. Consider the sun-lotion experiment that we described at the beginning of this chapter. Depending on which focus we made salient, participants preferred a sun lotion with a claim that stressed the protective characteristics of the product, or a sun lotion with a claim that was concerned with getting tanned. Similarly, the context within a supermarket varies. Sun lotion can be placed close to holiday-related products such as color film or sunglasses. However, it can also be placed in a section that is related to health products. The product claims could be designed to fit with the respective placement to enhance the purchase probability.

CONCLUSION

In this chapter, we have reviewed research on the impact of regulatory focus in the area of consumer psychology. In our view, the regulatory focus approach is helpful for understanding consumer behavior and also allows us to make predictions that could be beneficial for advertisers and marketers. Although regulatory focus is, needless to say, only one of many variables that drive consumer behavior, we have attempted to demonstrate that it is, in many contexts, an important one. This can be seen from the variety of effects that have been described in this chapter. Nevertheless, the relationship to other constructs needs further study. In many respects, regulatory focus theory makes predictions that are similar to mood research. For example, it is assumed that individuals in a bad mood—like individuals in a prevention focus—search for strong arguments and reliable cues to make sure of their decisions or judgment (Bless & Schwarz, 1999). In fact, the regulatory focus manipulations reported in this chapter were shown not to affect mood (e.g., Florack & Hartmann, 2003; Pham & Avnet, 2004). However, there might be a more basic process that underlies both effects. Furthermore, the relationship between a regulatory focus and personality differences in risk aversion or other related constructs (Lopes, 1987) should be further illuminated in future research. The aim should be to gain a deeper understanding of the processes that underlie the effects of regulatory focus on different domains (e.g., persuasion, memory, and decision making). Finally, we would like to propose that regulatory focus theory could make a huge contribution also in the applied context of marketing and advertising. In our view, practitioners can benefit a lot from considering the mechanisms we have discussed in this chapter.

REFERENCES

Aaker, J. L., & Lee, A. Y. (2001). "I" seek pleasure and "we" avoid pains: The role of self-regulatory goals in information processing and persuasion. *Journal of Consumer Research, 28*, 33–49.

Amodio, D. M., Shah, J. Y., Sigelman, J., Brazy, P. C., & Harmon-Jones, E. (2004). Implicit regulatory focus associated with asymmetrical frontal cortical activity. *Journal of Experimental Social Psychology, 40*, 225–232.

Avnet, T., & Higgins, E. T. (2003). Locomotion, assessment, and regulatory fit: Value transfer from "how" to "what". *Journal of Experimental Social Psychology, 39*, 525–530.

Bettman, J. R., & Sujan, M. (1987). Effects of framing on evaluation of comparable and non-comparable alternatives by expert and novice consumers. *Journal of Consumer Research, 14*, 141–154.

Bless, H., Bohner, G., Schwarz, N., & Strack, F. (1990). Mood and persuasion: A cognitive response analysis. *Personality and Social Psychology Bulletin, 21*, 766–778.

Bless, H., Mackie, D. M., & Schwarz, N. (1992). Mood effects on encoding and judgmental processes in persuasion. *Journal of Personality and Social Psychology, 63*, 585–595.

Bless, H., & Schwarz, N. (1999). Sufficient and necessary conditions in dual-process models: The case of mood and information processing. In S. Chaiken & Y. Trope (Eds.), *Dual process theories in social psychology* (pp. 423–440). New York: Guilford.

Bodenhausen, G. V., Kramer, G. V., & Süsser, K. (1994). Happiness and stereotypic thinking in social judgment. *Journal of Personality and Social Psychology, 66*, 621–632.

Bohner, G., Crow, K., & Erb, H.-P. (1992). Affect and persuasion: Mood effects on the processing of message content and context cues and on subsequent behavior. *European Journal of Social Psychology, 22*, 511–530.

Briley, D. A., & Wyer, R. S. (2002). The effect of group membership salience on the avoidance of negative outcomes: Implications for social and consumer decisions. *Journal of Consumer Research, 29*, 400–415.

Cacioppo, J. T., Petty, R. E., & Sidera, J. A. (1982). The effects of a salient self-schema on the evaluation of proattitudinal editorials: Top–down vs. bottom–up processing. *Journal of Experimental Social Psychology, 18*, 324–338.

Carver, S., Lawrence, J. W., & Scheier, M. F. (1999). Self-discrepancies and affect: Incorporating the role of feared selves. *Personality and Social Psychology Bulletin, 25*, 783–792.

Cesario, J., Grant, H., & Higgins, E. T. (2004). Regulatory fit and persuasion: Transfer from "feeling right". *Journal of Personality and Social Psychology, 86*, 388–404.

Chaiken, S., Liberman, A., & Eagly, A. H. (1989). Heuristic and systematic processing within the persuasion context and beyond. In J. S. Uleman & J. A. Bargh (Eds.), *Unintended thought* (pp. 212–252). New York: Guilford.

Coan, J. A., & Allen, J. J. B. (2003). The state and trait nature of frontal EEG asymmetry in emotion. In K. Hugdahl & R. J. Davidson (Eds.), *The asymmetrical brain* (pp. 565–615). Cambridge, MA: MIT Press.

Evans, L. M., & Petty, R. E. (2003). Self-guide framing and persuasion: Responsibly increasing message processing to ideal levels. *Personality and Social Psychology Bulletin, 29*, 313–324.

Florack, A., & Hartmann, J. (2003). *Die Bedeutung des regulatorischen Fokus bei Investitionsentscheidungen in Kleingruppen* [The importance of regulatory focus as regards investment decisions in small groups]. Paper presented on the 9th conference of the social psychology division of the Deutsche Gesellschaft für Psychologie (DGPs), Heidelberg.

Florack, A., Scarabis, M., & Gosejohann, S. (2004a). *Regulatory focus and the choice of sun cream.* Unpublished raw data, University of Basel.

Florack, A., Scarabis, M., & Gosejohann, S. (2004b). *Regulatory focus and cue relevance in product choice and persuasion.* Manuscript in preparation, University of Basel.

Förster, J., Grant, H., Idson, L. C., & Higgins, E. T. (2001). Success/failure feedback, expectancies, and approach/avoidance motivation: How regulatory focus moderates classic relations. *Journal of Experimental Social Psychology, 37*, 253–260.

Förster, J., Higgins, E. T., & Taylor Bianco, A. (2003). Speed/accuracy decisions in task performance: Built-in trade-off or separate strategic concerns? *Organizational Behavior and Human Decision Processes, 90*, 148–164.

Förster, J., Higgins, E. T., & Idson, L. C. (1998). Approach and avoidance strength during goal attainment: Regulatory focus and the "goal looms larger" effect. *Journal of Personality and Social Psychology, 75*, 1115–1131.

Freitas, A. L., & Higgins, E. T. (2002). Enjoying goal-directed action: The role of regulatory fit. *Psychological Science, 13*, 1–6.

Freitas, A. L., Liberman, N., & Higgins, E. T. (2002). Regulatory fit and resisting temptation during goal pursuit. *Journal of Experimental Social Psychology, 38*, 291–298.

Friedman, R. S., & Förster, J. (2001). The effects of promotion and prevention cues on creativity. *Journal of Personality and Social Psychology, 81*, 1001–1013.

Greenwald, A. G., McGhee, D. F., & Schwartz, J. L. K. (1998). Measuring individual differences in implicit cognition: The implicit association test. *Journal of Personality and Social Psychology, 74*, 1464–1480.

Higgins, E. T. (1996). Knowledge activation: Accessibility, applicability, and salience. In E. T. Higgins, & A. W. Kruglanski (Eds.), *Social psychology: Handbook of basic principles* (pp. 133–168). New York: Guilford.

Higgins, E. T. (1997). Beyond pleasure and pain. *American Psychologist, 52*, 1280–1300.

Higgins, E. T. (1998). Promotion and prevention: Regulatory focus as a motivational principle. In M. P. Zanna (Ed.), *Advances in experimental social psychology* (Vol. 30, pp. 1–46). San Diego, CA: Academic Press.

Higgins, E. T. (2000). Making a good decision: Value from fit. *American Psychologist, 55,* 1217–1229.

Higgins, E. T. (2002). How self-regulation creates distinct values: The case of promotion and prevention decision making. *Journal of Consumer Psychology, 12,* 177–191.

Higgins, E. T., Friedman, R. S., Harlow, R. E., Idson, L. C., Ayduk, O. N., & Taylor, A. (2001). Achievement orientations from subjective histories of success: Promotion pride versus prevention pride. *European Journal of Social Psychology, 31,* 3–23.

Higgins, E. T., Idson, L. C., Freitas, A. L., Spiegel, S., & Molden, D. C. (2003). Transfer of value from fit. *Journal of Personality and Social Psychology, 84,* 1140–1153.

Higgins, E. T., Roney, C. J. R., Crowe, E., & Hymes, C. (1994). Ideal versus ought predilections for approach and avoidance: Distinct self-regulatory systems. *Journal of Personality and Social Psychology, 66,* 276–286.

Higgins, E. T., Shah, J., & Friedman, R. (1997). Emotional responses to goal attainment: Strength of regulatory focus as moderator. *Journal of Personality and Social Psychology, 72,* 515–525.

Higgins, E. T., & Silberman, I. (1998). Development of regulatory focus: Promotion and Prevention as ways of living. In J. Heckhausen & C. S. Dweck (Eds.), *Motivation and self-regulation across the life span* (pp. 78–113). New York: Cambridge University Press.

Higgins, E. T., & Tykocinski, O. (1992). Self-discrepancies and biographical memory: Personality and cognition at the level of psychological situation. *Personality and Social Psychology Bulletin, 18,* 527–535.

Hong, J. W., & Zinkhan, G. M. (1995). Self-concept and advertising effectiveness: The influence of congruency, conspicuousness, and response mode. *Psychology & Marketing, 12,* 53–77.

Kruglanski, A. W., & Thompson, E. P. (1999). Persuasion by a single route: A view from the unimodel. *Psychological Inquiry, 10,* 83–109.

Lavine, H., & Snyder, M. (1996). Cognitive processing and the functional matching effect in persuasion: The mediating role of subjective perceptions of message quality. *Journal of Experimental Social Psychology, 32,* 580–604.

Lee, A. Y., & Aaker, J. L. (2004). Bringing the frame into focus: The influence of regulatory fit on processing fluency and persuasion. *Journal of Personality and Social Psychology, 86,* 205–218.

Liberman, N., Idson, L. C., Camacho, C. J., & Higgins, E. T. (1999). Promotion and prevention choices between stability and change. *Journal of Personality and Social Psychology, 77,* 1135–1145.

Liberman, N., Molden, D. C., Idson, L. C., & Higgins, E. T. (2001). Promotion and prevention focus on alternative hypotheses: Implications for attributional functions. *Journal of Personality and Social Psychology, 80,* 5–18.

Lockwood, P., Jordan, C. H., & Kunda, Z. (2002). Motivation by positive or negative role models: Regulatory focus determines who will best inspire us. *Journal of Personality and Social Psychology, 83,* 854–864.

Lopes, L. L. (1987). Between hope and fear: The psychology of risk. In L. Berkowitz (Ed.), *Advances in experimental social psychology* (Vol. 20, pp. 255–295). New York: Academic Press.

Mackie, D. M., & Worth, L. T. (1989). Cognitive deficits and the mediation of positive affect in persuasion. *Journal of Personality and Social Psychology, 57,* 27–40.

Petty, R. E., & Cacioppo, J. T. (1986a). *Communication and persuasion: Central and peripheral routes to attitude change.* New York: Springer.

Petty, R. E., & Cacioppo, J. T. (1986b). The elaboration likelihood model of persuasion. In L. Berkowitz (Ed.), *Advances in experimental social psychology* (Vol. 19, pp. 123–205). New York: Academic Press.

Petty, R. E., & Wegener, D. T. (1999). The elaboration likelihood model: current status and controversies. In S. Chaiken & Y. Trope (Eds.), *Dual-process theories in social psychology* (pp. 41–72). New York: Guilford.

Petty, R. E., Wheeler, S. C., & Bizer, G. Y. (1999). Is there one persuasion process or more? Lumping versus splitting in attitude change theories. *Psychological Inquiry, 10,* 156–163.

Pham, M. T., & Avnet, T. (2004). Ideals and oughts and the reliance on affect versus substance. *Journal of Consumer Research, 30*, 503–518.

Pierro, A., Mannetti, L., Kruglanski, A. W., & Sleeth-Keppler, D. (2004). Relevance override: On the reduced impact of "cues" under high-motivation conditions of persuasion studies. *Journal of Personality and Social Psychology, 86*, 251–264.

Safer, D. A. (1998). *Preferences for luxurious or reliable products: Promotion and prevention focus as moderators.* Unpublished doctoral dissertation, Department of Psychology, Columbia University.

Schwarz, N., & Clore, G. L. (1983). Mood, misattribution, and judgments on well-being: Informative and directive functions of affective states. *Journal of Personality and Social Psychology, 45*, 513–523.

Schwarz, N., & Clore, G. L. (1996). Feelings and phenomenal experiences. In E. T. Higgins, & A. Kruglanski (Eds.), *Social psychology: Handbook of basic principles* (pp. 433–465). New York: Guilford Press.

Shah, J., & Higgins, E. T. (1997). Expectancy × value effects: regulatory focus as a determinant of magnitude and direction. *Journal of Personality and Social Psychology, 73*, 447–458.

Shah, J., & Higgins, E. T. (2001). Regulatory concerns and appraisal efficiency: The general impact of promotion and prevention. *Journal of Personality and Social Psychology, 80*, 693–705.

Shah, J., Higgins, E. T., & Friedman, R. S. (1998). Performance incentives and means: How regulatory focus influences goal attainment. *Journal of Personality and Social Psychology, 74*, 285–293.

Snyder, M., & DeBono, K. G. (1985). Appeals to image and claims about quality: Understanding the psychology of advertising. *Journal of Personality and Social Psychology, 49*, 568–597.

Spotts, H. E., Weinberger, M. G., & Parsons, A. L. (1997). Assessing the use and impact of humor on advertising effectiveness: A contingency approach. *Journal of Advertising, 26*, 17–32.

Wänke, M., Bohner, G., & Jurkowitsch, A. (1997). There are many reasons to drive a BMW: Does imagined ease of argument generation influence attitudes? *Journal of Consumer Research, 24*, 170–177.

Zhou, R., & Pham, M. T. (in press). Promotion and prevention across mental accounts: When financial products dictate consumers' investment goals. *Journal of Consumer Research.*

IV. NEW PERSPECTIVES ON CONSUMER INFORMATION PROCESSING AND PERSUASION

CHAPTER TWELVE

Subliminal Priming and Persuasion:
How Motivation Affects the Activation
of Goals and the Persuasiveness of Messages

Erin J. Strahan
Wilfrid Laurier University

Steven J. Spencer
Mark P. Zanna
University of Waterloo

In the late 1950s, James Vicary, an advertising executive, made news headlines when he declared that he had increased Coca Cola® sales by 18% and popcorn sales by more than 50% by subliminally flashing the words "Drink Coke" and "Eat Popcorn" onto a movie screen at a New Jersey theater. People were angry and stunned by the claim: The idea that someone could influence their behavior to such a great extent without their knowledge was scary. By most accounts, Vicary hadn't really flashed anything onto a movie screen at all. The claim was just a hoax to try and save his struggling advertising company. Nevertheless, the general public still harbors a lingering fear that subliminal persuasion can and does work.

People's reaction to subliminal priming is not merely fear, however, they also harbor hopes that subliminal processes can work. Every day hundreds of people buy subliminal self-help tapes to help them lose weight, improve their self-esteem, and increase their memory (Natale, 1988). Such tapes hold out the promise of a low effort way to improve one's life: Simply press play on the tape and let your subconscious do the work.

Although the general public both hopes and fears that subliminal persuasion can work, social and cognitive psychologists who have empirically studied subliminal persuasion have concluded that direct subliminal persuasion is ineffective. For example, Greenwald, Spangenberg, Pratkanis, and Eskenazi (1991) tested the effectiveness of commercially available subliminal self-help tapes. Participants were given either tapes that they believed would improve their self-esteem or their memory. The actual content of the subliminal tapes, however, was varied so that half of participants who believed that they were using memory tapes were actually using self-esteem tapes and half of the participants who believed they were using self-esteem tapes were actually using memory tapes. Greenwald and his colleagues found that after a month of use, there was no evidence that either the self-esteem tapes or the memory tapes produced their claimed effects. More generally, Pratkanis and Aronson (1992) examined more than 350 mass media and scientific papers and concluded there was no evidence that subliminal messages influence attitudes or behavior.

Greenwald and his colleagues (1991) speculated that one reason subliminal messages cannot influence behavior is because people cannot process an entire sentence when it is presented subliminally. They argued that people are incapable of processing the meaning of a whole sentence, such as "Drink Coke," when it is presented below their threshold of awareness (Greenwald, 1992; Greenwald & Liu, 1985). For example, Greenwald and Liu (1985) tested whether participants could process simple sentences presented subliminally. They subliminally flashed two-word sentences on a computer screen that were designed so the individual word meanings differed from the meaning of the sentences as a whole. For example, in the sentence "enemy loses," both "enemy" and "loses" are negative words. When placed together in a sentence however, the meaning is positive. Greenwald and Liu found that the effects of such stimuli were determined by the meaning of the individual words, rather than by the meaning of the sentence. This finding suggested that the participants were incapable of processing the meaning of even a two-word sentence when it was presented subliminally. Such findings seem to suggest that subliminal persuasion would be difficult if not impossible to enact.

In contrast to the lack of evidence for subliminal persuasion, a large literature suggests that subliminal priming techniques can be quite influential. Previous research has demonstrated that subliminal priming techniques can have a range of powerful effects (Bargh & Barndollar, 1996; Chartrand & Bargh, 1999; Chartrand & Bargh, 1996; Gollwitzer & Bargh, 1996). For example, Bargh, Chen, and Burrows (1996) had participants complete a frustrating computer task and then subliminally presented either an African-American or a Caucasian face to participants on a computer screen. They found that participants who were exposed to the African-American face displayed more hostility to a bothersome request made by the experimenter than did participants exposed to the Caucasian face. In another series of experiments, Chartrand and Bargh (1996) illustrated that they could prime both an impression formation goal and a memorization goal using only subliminal priming techniques.

Murphy and Zajonc (1993) also demonstrated that subliminal priming techniques can influence people's affective reactions to an unfamiliar object. In a series of experiments, Murphy and Zajonc found that participants liked Chinese ideographs that were preceded by a subliminally presented smiling face better than the same ideographs preceded by a subliminally presented scowling face. Using a similar paradigm, Krosnick, Betz, Jussim, and Lynn (1992) have shown that the subliminal presentation of positive and negative images can classically condition people's impressions of others. Thus, a number of studies have shown that subliminal priming procedures can activate a number of concepts, affect a range of behaviors, and influence affective reactions to various stimuli.

If subliminal priming techniques can have such powerful influences on people's behaviors and evaluations, why can't subliminal priming procedures be used to enhance persuasion? We think they can. Although we do not challenge the contention of Greenwald and his colleagues (1991) that direct subliminal persuasion is unlikely to ever be effective, we do believe that subliminal priming techniques can activate concepts that may make people more likely to be influenced by a standard persuasive appeal. More concretely, we propose that subliminal priming can be used to prime goal-relevant cognitions, and that when this priming is combined with a motive to pursue the goal, persuasive appeals that target the goal are particularly effective.

In the first half of this chapter, we describe three lines of research that highlight the important ways that motivation interacts with subliminal priming to affect behavior. In the first line of research, we demonstrate how chronic hunger, due to a motivation to restrain one's eating, affects women's decisions to drink more of a high calorie beverage when subliminally primed with words related to overeating. In a second set of studies, we describe how subliminally priming thirsty people with words related to thirst can lead them to drink more, and to prefer an advertisement for a sports drink that is especially thirst-quenching. And, in a final set of studies, we show that when people are motivated to repair their mood, subliminally priming them with sad faces leads them to prefer an advertisement for a rock band that plays mood-enhancing music. In the remainder of the chapter, we discuss why motivation is such a crucial component of our subliminal priming effects. More specifically, we discuss why our subliminal priming procedure affects people who are motivated, but has no impact on people who are not motivated.

Subliminal Priming and Restrained Eating

In one line of research (Strahan, Spencer, & Zanna, 2004) we have examined how subliminal priming can influence women who chronically restrain their eating and therefore, presumably, are chronically hungry. More specifically, we tested whether women who were restrained eaters would respond differently to subliminal primes related to overeating than were women who were unrestrained eaters. Restrained eating has been defined as the "intentional efforts to achieve or maintain a desired weight through reduced caloric intake" (Stice, Ozer, & Kees, 1997, p. 145). Women who are classified as restrained eaters are extremely focused on their weight and body shape and try to restrict their food intake to lose weight (Herman & Mack, 1975; Herman & Polivy, 1980). Although they are chronically motivated to lose weight, their efforts to limit how much food they consume often fail. In fact, the restraint mechanisms of restrained eaters are quite fragile

(Herman & Polivy, 1980). Researchers found that a number of factors, such as forced preloading (Herman & Mack, 1975; Hibscher & Herman, 1977; Polivy, 1976; Spencer & Fremouw, 1979), alcohol (Polivy & Herman, 1976a, 1976b), and emotional arousal (Baucom & Aiken, 1981; Herman & Polivy, 1975) can all lead restrained eaters to lose their restraint and overeat.

We were interested in studying whether subliminally priming restrained eaters with the concept of overeating would lead them to abandon their restraint and drink more of a high-calorie beverage. Female participants came to the lab for what they believed was a market research study. Several weeks before the experimental session they had all filled out a Restraint Scale (Herman & Polivy, 1980), and on the basis of their responses, we divided them into two groups: Restrained and unrestrained eaters.

When participants arrived at the lab, they were told that they would be evaluating a number of different products in the study, and that to allow time for their senses to clear between evaluations, they would also participate in an unrelated computer-based study. To bolster our cover story, participants began the study by evaluating the appearance and scent of two different candles. After this evaluation, we had participants complete the computer task. The computer task presented participants with various strings of letters, some of which were words and some of which were not. Their task was to decide whether each letter string was a word or a non-word. This task, often called a *lexical decision-making task* (LDT), allowed us to administer our subliminal priming manipulation. Half of the participants were subliminally primed with words related to overeating (i.e., eat and binge) that were flashed before half of the letter strings in the LDT, whereas the other half were subliminally primed with neutral words (i.e., won and pirate).

After completing the LDT, participants were asked to conduct a taste test of two different beverages. The beverages were cherry Kool-Aid® made with either real sugar or with a low calorie sweetener. We made certain that participants were aware that they were drinking both a low calorie and a high calorie drink in the taste test, so they could take this information into account when deciding how much of each beverage to drink.

We expected that restrained eating status would interact with subliminal priming condition and that is what we found (see Fig. 12.1). The subliminal priming procedure had no impact on how much of the high calorie beverage unrestrained eaters drank, but it had a dramatic impact on how much restrained eaters drank. When primed with neutral words, restrained eaters drank significantly less of the high calorie beverage than unrestrained eaters. But when they were primed with words related to overeating, their restraint was lost and they consumed more of the high calorie beverage—in fact, just as much as unrestrained eaters. No differences were found between the groups for consumption of the low calorie beverage. This study demonstrated how subliminal priming can lead restrained eaters to abandon their restraint. As restrained eaters limit the amount of calories they consume they are likely to be chronically hungry. Their typical pattern of restraint of-

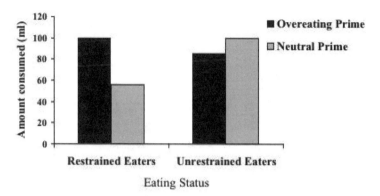

FIG. 12.1. Amount of high calorie beverage consumed as a function of restrained eating status and subliminal prime.

ten keeps this motivation in check, but in this study when they were primed with words related to overeating their restraint was lost and they consumed just as much of the high calorie beverage as did unrestrained eaters.

Subliminal Priming and Thirst

In a second line of research, we examined the role that motivation can play in the relation between subliminal priming and persuasion (Strahan, Spencer, & Zanna, 2002). In this research we asked people to come to the lab for what they believed was a market research study. They were told that they would be tasting and eating a variety of products, and that because people are better at evaluating products on an empty stomach, they should refrain from eating or drinking anything for three hours before the session. When participants arrived at the lab, we had them taste a dry cookie and then we gave them either some water to drink, to 'cleanse their palate,' or nothing. Therefore, half of the participants were thirsty and half were not. After this cookie taste test, we told participants that they would take a break from the evaluation of products and complete a computer task. The computer task used in this study was a standard LDT. The LDT afforded us the opportunity to administer our subliminal priming manipulation. Half of the participants were subliminally primed with thirst-related words (i.e., thirst and dry) and the other half were subliminally primed with neutral words (i.e., pirate and won).

After completing the LDT, we had participants conduct a second taste test on two different beverages. The beverages were actually two different types of Kool-Aid, made with extra sugar so that they would be quite sweet, and therefore, not overly thirst quenching. We expected the subliminal priming procedure would affect how much participants drank when they were thirsty, but not when they were satiated and that is exactly what we found (see Fig. 12.2). When participants were thirsty, they drank more liquid when they were subliminally primed with thirst-

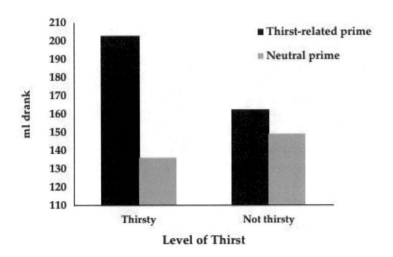

FIG. 12.2.   Amount of liquid consumed as a function of level of thirst and subliminal prime.

related words than when they were primed with neutral words. However, when
they were not thirsty, the subliminal prime had no impact on drinking behavior.

In this study, we demonstrated that thirst-related subliminal primes can influence people's drinking behavior when they are thirsty. In the second study, we
wanted to determine whether subliminal priming could be used to enhance the
persuasiveness of an advertisement. In the first study, we manipulated motivation
by making half of the participants feel thirsty before the subliminal priming procedure and making the other half feel satiated. Given the fact that the subliminal
priming procedure only affected thirsty participants, we included only thirsty participants in the second study.

In this second study, participants were again brought to the lab for a market research study and were again asked not to eat or drink anything for 3 hours before
the experimental session. However, in this study all of the participants remained
thirsty for the entire session, and instead of engaging in the drinking taste test, the
participants were next asked to rate two supposedly new sports drinks: Super-
Quencher and PowerPro. The Super-Quencher ad claimed that studies have found
that it "quenches your thirst 25% better than any other sports drink on the market." It also included the tag line, "When you are super thirsty, drink Super-
Quencher." The PowerPro ad claimed that studies found that it "replaces your
electrolytes 45% better than any other sports drink," and included the tag line "Do
your body a favor: Drink PowerPro!" Participants were asked to evaluate both of
the beverages, and when they were finished evaluating them, were told that the
company that developed the beverages wanted to thank participants by giving
them up to nine coupons, each worth 50 cents off the purchase price of the bever-

ages. Participants were told to indicate how many coupons they wanted for Super-Quencher and how many coupons they wanted for PowerPro.

We predicted that our thirsty participants who received the thirst-related primes would be more persuaded by the Super-Quencher ad than were participants who received the neutral primes. We found that the subliminal prime did affect participant's preference for the ads and their choice of coupons. When participants were primed with the thirst-related words they preferred Super-Quencher over PowerPro, but when they were primed with the neutral words they showed no preference.[1] Taken together the results of these two studies demonstrate that subliminal priming influences people's behavior, primarily when they are motivated. When people were thirsty, subliminal priming led to increased drinking in the first study and enhanced persuasion in the second study.

Subliminal Priming and Mood

In a third line of research (Study 3, Strahan et al., 2002), we conceptually replicated the studies just mentioned by investigating whether subliminally priming people with a sad face would enhance the persuasiveness of an ad for a mood-restoring product primarily in situations in which people are motivated to restore their mood. In this study, we had participants come to the lab believing that they were going to complete a number of tasks. In the last task, they expected to either be alone or to interact with another person. Erber and his colleagues (Erber, Wegner, & Therriault, 1996) showed that such a manipulation affects people's motivation to repair their mood. When people expect to interact with another person they engage in mood repairing activities, but when they expect to be alone they do not. After explaining the nature of the tasks in which participants would be participating, we then had them complete an LDT in which we either subliminally primed them with a sad face or a neutral stimuli.

After the LDT, we had participants rate CDs from two new bands and decide the number of songs that they wanted to listen to from each CD. One band called the Tweed Monkeys was described as playing upbeat music, and the tag line for the ad said "If you are looking for a CD that will put you in a good mood, this is the CD for you." The other band called Crystal Hammer was described as musically talented, and the tag line for the ad said "If you like music with a strong sound, you will love this CD."

We found that when participants were primed with the sad face and were motivated to repair their mood they preferred the upbeat Tweed Monkeys CD, and wanted to listen to more songs from this band. However, when participants were not motivated to repair their mood or were not primed with the sad face they showed no preference for either ad, and chose about the same number of songs from each band. These results suggest that when people are subliminally primed

---

[1]We replicated this effect in two other experiments. See Strahan et al. (2002) for details.

with the concept of sadness, and are in a situation in which they are motivated to restore their mood, they will be persuaded more by an ad that targets this motive.

Why Is Motivation Necessary?

We have clearly demonstrated that motivation interacts with subliminal priming to affect people's behavior. When people are motivated, in our studies, the subliminal prime affects their choices and their behavior, but when they are not motivated the subliminal prime has no affect on them. The question is: Why is motivation such a crucial component of our subliminal priming effects? We believe the answer lies in the specific thoughts that are activated when people who are either motivated (or not) are exposed to a subliminal prime. When people are not motivated, subliminal priming activates concepts related to the subliminal prime, however when people are motivated, it activates a goal.

The idea that motivation can affect the nature of concepts that are activated when people are exposed to a stimulus is not entirely new. Bruner and his colleagues (Bruner, 1957; Bruner, Postman, & McGinnies, 1947) in the "New Look" perspective in perception, certainly believed that motivation could determine what people perceived when exposed to a given stimulus. More recently, Bargh (1990) in his auto-motive model of cognition also proposed that motives, when combined with cues in the environment, can lead to the automatic activation of particular thoughts.

In our research on subliminal priming and persuasion (Strahan, Spencer, & Zanna, 2002), we noticed the important role that motivation can play in the activation of unconscious thoughts. Recall that in the first thirst study, described earlier, we had people who were thirsty or not thirsty and who were subliminally primed with either thirst-related words or neutral words complete an LDT. Among the words in the LDT, we included some words related to the concept of quenching one's thirst (i.e., liquid, moist, and rain). The logic behind the LDT is that when a concept is activated it facilitates the identification of words related to that concept, and therefore, participants make the appropriate lexical decision faster for these words (but not for other items) than if the concept is not activated.

What we noticed when we examined the data from the LDT in this study is that motivation and the subliminal prime interacted to affect people's responses to words related to quenching one's thirst on the LDT. As can be seen in Fig. 12.3, when people were thirsty and were subliminally primed with the thirst-related words they activated words related to quenching thirst (i.e., liquid, moist, and rain). When people weren't thirsty or they weren't primed with thirst-related words, they did not activate these concepts. In addition, motivation and the subliminal prime had no effect on the activation of neutral words. Finally, we found that activation of the thirst-quenching words was related to participants' drinking behavior. That is, we found that activation of the thirst-quenching words predicted how much people drank when they were thirsty and primed with thirst-

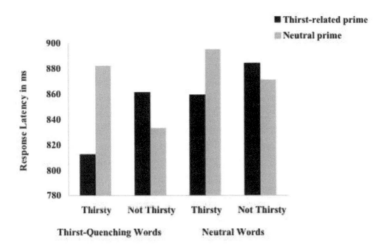

FIG. 12.3.   Activation of thirst-quenching and neutral words as a function of subliminal prime.

related words, such that the more these words were activated, the more liquid our participants drank in our taste test. In other conditions, there was no relation between activation of the thirst-quenching words and the amount that people drank.

In our second thirst study, we again found that thirsty participants who were subliminally primed with thirst-related words activated words related to quenching thirst. In addition, we found that when subliminally primed with thirst-related words the more the thirst-quenching words were activated the more participants preferred Super-Quencher ($r = -.59, p < .05$). In the neutral prime condition, however, the activation of the thirst-quenching words was not reliably related to preferences for either sports drink.

In our mood study, we had participants complete an LDT in which we subliminally primed either a sad face or a neutral stimuli. Some of the words that participants responded to in the LDT were related to the concept happiness. In examining the results we again found that motivation and the subliminal prime interacted to affect participants' responses to some of the words on the LDT. More specifically, we found that when participants expected to interact with another person (i.e., when they were motivated to repair their mood) and they were primed with the sad face they activated words related to happiness (i.e., happy, cheerful, joyous). In contrast, when participants expected to be alone—and thus were presumably less motivated to repair their mood—and when they were primed with the neutral stimulus they showed no activation of these words. In addition, we found that when participants were primed with the sad face and were motivated to repair their mood the more they activated happy words the greater their preference for the upbeat band. In the other conditions, however, the activation of happy words was not reliably related to preferences for either band.

Thus, in both these studies, when participants were motivated and subliminally primed with stimuli that were motivationally relevant, they activated concepts that were related to satisfying their motives although these concepts were semantic opposites of the concepts that were primed. In contrast, when participants were not motivated they showed no such activation. These intriguing results led us to conduct two carefully designed studies to test these ideas more fully (Spencer, Fein, Strahan, & Zanna, 2005).

The first study was identical to the thirst study described above (participants were either thirsty or not and were primed with thirst-related words or not) except that participants only completed an LDT that included a longer list of critical words. In particular, we had participants identify 6 words related to "thirst" and 6 words related to "quenching thirst" when completing the LDT. What we found was that when primed with the thirst-related words, both thirsty and satiated participants activated words related to thirst (e.g., desert, hot), but only participants who were thirsty activated words related to quenching thirst (e.g., beverage, quench). Participants primed with the neutral words did not activate either concept.

The second study was identical to the mood study just described (participants were either motivated to repair their mood and were primed with a sad face or a neutral stimulus), except that again participants completed an LDT that included a longer list of critical words. In particular, we had participants identify 10 words related to sadness and 10 words related to happiness. We found that when primed with the sad face, participants both motivated and not motivated to repair their mood activated words related to sadness (e.g., sad, gloomy), but only participants who were motivated to repair their mood activated words related to happiness (e.g., happy, joyous). Participants primed with the neutral stimulus did not activate either concept.

Taken together, these studies demonstrate that when people are not motivated subliminal primes activate semantically similar concepts. However, when people are motivated, the subliminal primes activate a goal. Thus, these studies provide strong evidence that our motives can lead to the activation of concepts that will satisfy our motives. When people were thirsty and subliminally primed with thirst-related words, they activated the goal of quenching one's thirst. And when people were motivated to repair their mood and were subliminally primed with a sad face, they activated the goal of repairing their mood.

GENERAL DISCUSSION

We reviewed evidence from our research on subliminal priming that suggests that when subliminal priming is combined with a motive to pursue the goal, it can affect people's behavior. In our research on subliminal priming and restrained eating, we find that subliminally priming restrained eaters with words related to overeating leads them to abandon their restraint and drink more of a high calorie beverage. The subliminal prime has no impact on unrestrained eaters. In our research on subliminal priming and thirst, we find that when people are motivated to quench their thirst and are presented with thirst-related subliminal primes, they drink more and prefer an advertisement for a sports drink that is especially thirst-quenching. The subliminal prime does not affect participants who are not thirsty or who are not primed with thirst-related words. Finally, in our research on subliminal priming and mood, we find that when people are motivated to repair their mood and are subliminally primed with a sad face, they prefer an advertisement for a rock band that plays mood-enhancing music, however, the subliminal prime does not affect participants who are not motivated to repair their mood or who are not primed with a sad face. Thus, we have demonstrated that when people are motivated in our studies, the subliminal prime affects their choices and their behavior, but when they are not motivated, the subliminal prime has no affect on them.

The reason that motivation is such a crucial component of our subliminal priming effects is because of the specific thoughts that are activated when people who are motivated are exposed to a subliminal prime. We find that when people are motivated to quench their thirst, they activate concepts related to quenching thirst (e.g., liquid) even when they are presented with stimuli that are related to the semantic opposite (e.g., dryness). Likewise, when people are motivated to repair their mood, they activate concepts related to mood repair (e.g., cheerfulness) even when they are presented with stimuli that are related to the semantic opposite (e.g., sadness). This sort of activation does not occur in the absence of motivation.

In addition, we find that such activation influences people's behavior. When thirsty participants are subliminally primed with thirst-related words, they activate concepts related to quenching thirst, and this activation leads them to drink more and to prefer an advertisement for a thirst-quenching beverage. Similarly, when people who are motivated to repair their mood are exposed to a sad face they activate concepts related to happiness, and this activation leads them to prefer a band that plays mood-enhancing music. Together, these results provide evidence that people's motivations can affect the way activated concepts shape behavior even when the activation of the concepts occurs outside of conscious awareness. When thirst and sadness were activated by subliminal primes, people's motivations channeled this activation into goals: When primed with thirst, thirsty people preferred a thirst-quenching beverage and drank more; when primed with a sad face, people motivated to repair their mood preferred an upbeat band and wanted to listen to upbeat music. These results provide compelling evidence that our motives can channel our activated thoughts into actions that are functional: When people are not motivated, subliminal priming activates concepts related to the subliminal prime, however, when people are motivated, it activates a goal.

These findings have important implications for subliminal priming and persuasion. Our results suggest that subliminal priming can be used to enhance persuasion, but only when the subliminal primes activate a goal to complete an action.

Let's return to the James Vicary story from the beginning of the chapter. Based on our findings, is there any way that Vicary could have used subliminal priming to sell more Coke? We think there is. Let's say that everyone in the audience arrived at the theater without drinking anything for a few hours beforehand, or at least, as they walked into the theater they were given a free sample of dry popcorn to eat. This would ensure that everyone was feeling thirsty. Then, during the time that they waited for the movie to start, everyone was asked to direct their attention to the movie screen where some movie promotions were being described. During the movie promotions, the words "thirst" and "dry" could be subliminally flashed on the screen. And, directly following the subliminal priming manipulation, an advertisement for Coke could appear discussing the thirst-quenching attributes of the drink. If a salesperson then walked into the theater and announced that they were selling bottles of Coke, people might be particularly likely to buy them. Such an effect might occur because the people in the audience would be in the correct motivational state for the subliminal priming to be most effective (i.e., they feel thirsty), the subliminal prime would have activated concepts related to satisfying a goal (i.e., to quench their thirst), and by offering to sell them Coke, they have a straightforward way to attain their goal (i.e., drink Coke and you will no longer feel thirsty).

In future research, it will be interesting to test whether directly priming a goal subliminally can create the same types of effects seen in our research. Could directly priming people to eat or drink cause everyone to eat popcorn or drink Coke? Although we have not tested this hypothesis directly, our restrained eating studies suggest that such a possibility is unlikely. In that study, all participants were primed with the injunction to eat and binge, but not all participants did. Only those who were chronically motivated to eat followed the injunction. In our view, such findings provide an important limitation on the power of subliminal priming to affect persuasion: Only those motivated to pursue a goal are likely to succumb to subliminal prods to pursue it.

AUTHOR'S NOTE

This research was supported by grants from the Social Sciences and Humanities Research Council of Canada to the second and third authors.

Correspondence concerning this chapter should be addressed to Erin J. Strahan, Wilfrid Laurier University, Brantford Campus, 73 George Street, Brantford, Ontario, N3T 2Y3. Email may be sent to estrahan@wlu.ca.

REFERENCES

Bargh, J. A. (1990). Auto-motives: Preconscious determinants of thought and behavior. In E. T. Higgins & R. M. Sorrentino (Eds.), *Handbook of motivation and cognition* (Vol. 2, pp. 93–130). New York: Guilford Press.

Bargh, J. A., & Barndollar, K. (1996). Automaticity in action: The unconscious as repository of chronic goals and motives. In P. M. Gollwitzer & J. A. Bargh (Eds.), *The psychology of action: Linking cognition and motivation to behavior* (pp. 457–481). New York: Guilford Press.

Bargh, J. A., Chen, M., & Burrows, L. (1996). Automaticity of social behavior: Direct effects of trait construct and stereotype activation. *Journal of Personality and Social Psychology, 71*, 230–244.

Baucom, D. H., & Aiken, P. A. (1981). Effect of depressed mood on eating among obese and nonobese dieting and nondieting persons. *Journal of Personality and Social Psychology, 41*, 577–585.

Bruner, J. S. (1957). On perceptual readiness. *Psychological Review, 64*, 340–358.

Bruner, J. S., Postman, L., & McGinnies, E. (1947). Personal values as determinants of perceptual selection. *American Psychologist, 2*, 285–286.

Chartrand, T. L., & Bargh, J. A. (1999). The chameleon effect: The perception-behavior link and social interaction. *Journal of Personality and Social Psychology, 76*, 893–910.

Chartrand, T. L., & Bargh, J. A. (1996). Automatic activation of impression formation and memorization goals: Nonconscious goal priming reproduces effects of explicit task instructions. *Journal of Personality and Social Psychology, 71*, 464–478.

Erber, R., Wegner, D. M., & Therriault, N. (1996). On being cool and collected: Mood regulation in anticipation of social interaction. *Journal of Personality and Social Psychology, 70*, 757–766.

Gollwitzer, P. M., & Bargh, J. A. (Eds.). (1996). *The psychology of action: Linking cognition and motivation to behavior.* New York: Guilford Press.

Greenwald, A. G., & Liu, T. J. (1985, November). Limited unconscious processing of meaning. Presented at meeting of the Psychonomic Society, Boston, MA.

Greenwald, A. G. (1992). New Look 3: Unconscious cognition claimed. *American Psychologist, 47*, 766–779.

Greenwald, A. G., Spangenberg, E. R., Pratkanis, A. R., & Eskenazi, J. (1991). Double-blind tests of subliminal self-help audiotapes. *Psychological Science, 2*, 119–122.

Herman, C. P., & Mack, D. (1975). Restrained and unrestrained eating. *Journal of Personality, 43*, 647–660.

Herman, C. P., & Polivy, J. (1975). Anxiety, restraint and eating behavior. *Journal of Abnormal Psychology, 84*, 666–672.

Herman, C. P., & Polivy, J. (1980). Restrained eating. In A. J. Stunkard (Ed.), *Obesity*. Philadelphia: Saunders.

Hibscher, J. A., & Herman, C. P. (1977). Obesity, dieting, and the expression of "obese" characteristics. *Journal of Comparative and Physiological Psychology, 91*, 374–380.

Krosnick, J. A., Betz, A. L., Jussim, L. J., & Lynn, A. R. (1992). Subliminal conditioning of attitudes. *Personality and Social Psychology Bulletin, 18*, 152–162.

Murphy, S. T., & Zajonc, R. B. (1993). Affect, cognition, and awareness: Affective priming with optimal and suboptimal stimulus exposures. *Journal of Personality and Social Psychology, 64*, 723–739.

Natale, J. A. (1988). Are you open to suggestion? *Psychology Today*, 28–30.

Polivy, J. (1976). Perception of calories and regulation of intake in restrained and unrestrained eaters. *Addictive Behaviors, 1*, 237–243.

Polivy, J., & Herman, C. P. (1976a). Effects of alcohol on eating behavior: Disinhibition or sedation? *Addictive Behaviors, 1*, 121–125.

Polivy, J., & Herman, C. P. (1976b). Effects of alcohol on eating behavior: Influences of mood and perceived intoxication. *Journal of Abnormal Psychology, 85*, 601–606.

Pratkanis, A. R., & Aronson, E. (1992). *Age of propaganda: The everyday use and abuse of persuasion.* New York: W. H. Freeman and Company.

Spencer, J. A., & Fremouw, W. J. (1979). Binge eating as a function of restraint and weight classification. *Journal of Abnormal Psychology, 88*, 262–267.

Spencer, S. J., Fein, S., Strahan, E. J., & Zanna, M. P. (2005). The role of motivation in the unconscious: How our motives control the activation of our thoughts and shape our actions. In J. P.

Forgas, K. Williams, & S. M. Laham (Eds.), *Social motivation: Conscious and unconscious processes. The Sydney Symposium* (Vol. 6, pp. 113–132). New York: Psychology Press.

Stice, E., Ozer, S., & Kees, M. (1997). Relation of dietary restraint to bulimic symptomatology: The effects of the criterion confounding of the restraint scale. *Behavior Research and Therapy, 35,* 145–152.

Strahan, E. J., Spencer, S. J., & Zanna, M. P. (2004). Unpublished data. University of Waterloo.

Strahan, E. J., Spencer, S. J., & Zanna, M. P. (2002). Subliminal priming and persuasion: Striking while the iron is hot. *Journal of Experimental Social Psychology, 38,* 556–568.

CHAPTER THIRTEEN

Consumer Responses to False Information: Is Believability Necessary for Persuasion?

Claudiu V. Dimofte
Georgetown University

Richard F. Yalch
University of Washington

Advertising is legalized lying.

—Herbert G. Wells

THE IMPACT OF FALSE MARKETPLACE INFORMATION ON SOCIAL WELFARE

Exposed to numerous persuasion attempts each day, consumers are expected to critically evaluate the believability of the product information they encounter. As most of this information is truthful or slightly enhanced with some element of exaggeration or puffery, consumers are generally dealing with credible, legitimate information cues. However, infomercials are a prime example of promotional messages wherein extraordinary claims abound. For example, an infomercial for "The 6-Second Abs" claims that a four-minute daily use of the equipment will result in a perfectly sculpted stomach. Although most consumers express skepticism about these claims, reported sales indicate that many individuals are nevertheless influenced enough by such information to place orders for the advertised product. At the opposite side of this phenomenon, consumers are exposed to product-disparaging rumors. Notable recent examples include Procter & Gamble (long plagued by rumors of an affiliation with devil-worshipers) and the American Red Cross (reportedly endangering blood donors in the past through exposure to AIDS). Organizational efforts to combat rumors are often frustrated by the finding that rumors that stretch credibility even to the point of being obviously false

281

still adversely affect them. Businesses and nonprofits are challenged to dispel this information and regain their reputation and finances.

These phenomena have both consumer and organizational welfare implications. In the case of misleading product information, consumer welfare is harmed when untruthful information in the form of product oversell motivates consumers to make purchases that fail to meet their expectations, leading to regret and psychological discomfort. In addition, businesses wrongly profit from their deceptive behavior. In the case of rumors and other forms of untrue and unfavorable product information, businesses suffer lost sales, profits, and a tarnished image. Consumers lose by avoiding products that would otherwise satisfy them. Here the organization's competitors (who frequently originate rumors), wrongly gain from their actions.

Both phenomena are a challenge to the economic system because they appear resistant to standard methods of consumer education: people often act on information even though they acknowledge that the claims are "too good" (infomercial) or "too bad" (rumor) to be true. This chapter reviews research that looks at the effects of explicitly disbelieved information on consumer attitudes and reports on studies of both falsely positive (infomercial) and falsely negative (rumor) information.

After setting up the discussion framework, we first consider literature that refers to the (unwarranted) inferences consumers make from the promotional messages they are exposed to, in the context of the curious nonbelief phenomenon (Maloney, 1963) and the Spinozan/Cartesian approaches to discourse comprehension. We then consider literature that refers to the origination and diffusion of rumor information, in the context of information processing theory. In both instances we present a novel theoretical account that explains why consumer beliefs (or more accurately, nonbeliefs) are often not directly related to subsequent behavior. The view that emerges from the research reviewed here argues that cognitive processing of the automatic kind is responsible for some of the paradoxical effects observed in the literature.

SOURCES OF PRODUCT INFORMATION

Consumer behavior is largely driven by the information consumers are exposed to either in the process of actively seeking to aid decision making (e.g., reading product reviews in *Consumer Reports*) or incidentally in their everyday lives (e.g., watching commercials presented during a television program). This information may be favorable or unfavorable to the product and it may be true or false. Advertising is considered favorable information because it is illogical to think that advertisers would knowingly pay for information that is unfavorable to the product they are offering. Furthermore, most product advertising presents truthful claims about products, partially in recognition that it is illegal to present false and deceptive information to consumers in order to sell products. Truthful sources of unfavorable product information would be product reviews presented in the media and word of mouth from dissatisfied customers. False or untruthful product information often serves as the basis for disparaging rumors. The Internet offers an inexpensive and effective channel for disseminating these rumors. A recent example is an internet rumor that Canola Oil contains ingredients from a genetically modified plant and is the source of many illnesses, some related to Mad Cow disease. Most, but not all rumors appear to be false and unfavorable based on a review of the many posted at urbanlegends.com. Table 13.1 categorizes the different sources of product information based on their favorability toward the product and truthfulness.

True product information is quite useful to consumers as it aids in making informed product choices and is essential to maintaining an efficient market-based economy. Research on consumer decision making looks at how consumers make their choices by presenting them with product information and observing how they use it to evaluate one or more products. In these studies, consumers are expected to assume that this information is accurate. However, in everyday decision making, consumers may have been exposed to and possess product information that is not true. This should complicate decision making as consumers must judge the truthfulness of various claims as well as their relevance to the decision at hand.

Some consumer research deals with the issue of judging product information's truthfulness in the process of evaluating products. It documents the difficulties consumers often have in recognizing false or misleading statements (Richards, 1990). For example, Harris (1977) illustrates how pragmatic implications (e.g., *"Winter is cold season. Use Listerine every winter day"*) can lead to false impressions about product benefits (e.g., *"Listerine prevents winter colds"*). In past research, consumers are processing information when they are unaware that it is false. More recent research looks at situations in which consumers are aware that the product information is false. This approach enhances our understanding of this process by advancing the counterintuitive notion that consumer judgments are affected by product information even when consumers are aware that the information may not be true.

TABLE 13.1
Sources of Product Information Categorized by Favorableness and Truthfulness

	Favorable	*Unfavorable*
True	• Most Advertising/Selling • Publicity • Third Party Reviews (+) • Word of Mouth (+)	• Third Party Reviews (−) • Word of Mouth (−)
False	• Deceptive Advertising/Selling (Infomercials)	• Product/Corporate Rumors

THE CASE OF FALSE POSITIVE INFORMATION

The Problem

Since the mid-1990s, the infomercials consumers deny watching on television have sold more than one billion dollars' worth of merchandise annually (Hutheesing, 1995; Donthu & Gilliland, 1996). Knives, washing machines, fitness equipment and exercise videotapes, cookware, sunglasses, tool kits, and many other things consumers did not know they needed are paraded on screen in half-hour blocks (typically) in the pursuit of the consumer's disposable income. Infomercial producers appear to have an intimate knowledge of their target audience and have developed an intuitive approach to selling that is universally alluring (Donthu & Gilliland, 1996) and that ultimately makes use of a layman's social psychology. Appealing to basic human needs related to consumers' hopes and desires is an effective way to influence people (MacInnis & de Mello, 2005). Consequently, a faster lawn mower is not better because it gets your grass cut in less time; it is better because of the extra free time you have to spend with your family (servicing your need to socialize). According to Cialdini (1998), the 30 minutes of the infomercial are also sprinkled with stunts and gimmicks that build up expectations and lead to confirmation bias. Furthermore, the use of testimonials and similar techniques exploit another of consumers' needs—that for social validation (Cialdini, 1998) and shrewdly precipitate purchase decisions. Despite FTC rules against deception in advertising (e.g., requiring disclaimers in situations where a misleading impression might be created), infomercials abound with claims that are nothing short of outrageous in the eyes of any discriminate observer. The overselling of product attributes or benefits essentially amounts to conveying false positive product information. Surprisingly, even when consumers are suspicious or even explicitly aware of the likelihood that the claims are not valid, persuasion occurs and they still buy. How does this happen?

Theoretical Accounts

That some advertising is misleading has been both common knowledge and a matter of concern for consumer advocates for years. In an early survey of consumer perceptions of advertising, about 40% of the sample perceived "most" or "all" television advertising to be misleading (Schutz & Casey, 1981). The most common research interest in the area has focused on the more subtle varieties of deception, such as the inferences consumers make from implied (i.e., not explicitly stated) advertising claims and about information missing from the presentation.

To make human communication more efficient, people typically process discourse using numerous heuristics. Along theses lines, consumers are often inclined to personally conclude what have been termed incomplete comparisons in advertisements (Johar, 1995) and to misattribute these pragmatic implications (Harris, 1977) or inferences to the ad. No clear theoretical explanation for this effect has been provided, although it would appear that schema-driven encoding and recall of information should prove fruitful avenues of inquiry. Boundary conditions have been established by looking at moderating variables such as age (Gaeth & Heath, 1987; Brett, Bhimy, & Agee, 2002), accessibility (Dick, Chakravarti, & Biehal, 1990), expertise (Compeau, Grewal, & Chandrashekaran, 2002), and involvement (Johar, 1995; Kardes, 1988). Furthermore, several researchers have challenged the processing explanation behind the inference effect by showing little or no inference making by consumers (e.g., Simmons & Lynch, 1991). Accordingly, it has been proposed that extant explicit measures are deficient in terms of capturing these processes with an apparent implicit flavor (Kardes, 1988; Johar, 1995).

Relying on consumers' self-originated inferences as a form of persuasion through conclusion omission (see Kardes, 1988) may constitute deception, but surely not outright fraud. Furthermore, other consumer research has shown that perhaps no such delivery subtlety is actually needed for persuasion. Suter and Burton (1996) demonstrated how reference price advertisements that make explicit use of clearly implausible price levels are nonetheless capable to influence consumers' willingness to pay a higher price for the promoted brand. Even more surprisingly, the believability of the price offer has a stronger impact on non-price related evaluative dependent variables than on pertinent price-related estimates (Suter & Burton, 1996). Similar results were recently obtained by Compeau et al. (2002), who argued that even when reference prices in an advertisement are obviously inflated and consumers are not inclined to believe them, consumer perceptions of the value of the deal are nevertheless influenced in the promoted brand's favor.

In extending their finding that consumers have largely negative explicit evaluations of the infomercials they are exposed to, Agee and Brett (2001) suggested that the infomercial is not necessarily a device that only prompts impulse purchases. Many purchases take place after repeated exposures to the same message, when presumably the rehearsal of negative attitudes would work against the promoted product. This paradox can be resolved by proposing that persuasion occurs despite explicit nonacceptance of the product claims because the claims are not completely rejected. In other words, there is neither belief nor disbelief about the claims.

In a consumer research classic, Maloney (1962) proposed that the disbelief most people experience when encountering exaggerated product claims is often overwhelmed by an innate curiosity. When advertising information conflicts with extant beliefs, the resulting dissonance must be somehow appeased. This is often done by yielding to the message and trying out the product in an attempt to readjust personal attitudes toward the brand (Maloney, 1963). In his study, a sample of housewives was exposed to advertisements for food products and was subsequently divided into two groups: those participants that found the ad claims to be believable and the others that thought they were hard to believe. The latter group was further divided into two groups, those who confidently disbelieved the claims and those who had what Maloney (1963) described as a *curious nonbelief.* The latter was tied into beliefs that actual product experience was necessary to fully judge the claims. Few consumers who clearly disbelieved the message were interested in trying the product (18%). However, relevant to our interest in explaining the success of infomercials, Maloney's results showed that more consumers who were in the curious nonbelief group were ready to try the product (44%) than in the group that expressed no concerns about (i.e., believed) the advertising claims (34%). The results suggest that advertising that causes consumers to not believe the message claims but makes them curious may be the most effective form of new product advertising. Convincing consumers that the claims about a new product are true is not necessary to create interest in product trial.[1]

Social psychology research provides a parsimonious explanation for the persuasion-despite-nonbelief effect by juxtaposing two long-standing conceptual accounts. Gilbert and his colleagues (Gilbert, Krull, & Malone, 1990; Gilbert, Tafarodi, & Malone, 1993) and more recently Koslow and Beltramini (2002) looked at views of information believability espoused by philosophers René Descartes and Benedict Spinoza. The Cartesian account proposes that messages are at once comprehended and accepted if assessed to be believable or rejected if judged unbelievable. The Spinozan view, in contrast, argues that all information is first accepted as believable during comprehension and only subsequently rejected after a believability assessment (Gilbert et al., 1990). A series of studies compared the Cartesian and Spinozan views. The results showed that under conditions of cognitive load or time pressure individuals failed to reject false information and instead used it to make consequential judgment decisions (Gilbert et al., 1993). In effect, when the subjects merely comprehended information and were unable to judge its believability, the information tended to be judged true. This argues in favor of Spinoza's two-stage comprehension process mentioned above consisting of initial acceptance of an assertion followed by a subsequent evaluation of its truthfulness. However, in the absence of a conscientious effort to evaluate incoming information's truthfulness, the default bias appears to be to accept new information as true.

Explicit Accounts for Infomercial Successes

Little research has looked at ways in which the social welfare cost associated with consumers' acceptance of product benefit oversells can be mitigated. This is perhaps not surprising, as providing solutions to a problem requires its clear a priori understanding. As the previous paragraphs suggest, the mechanisms underlining consumers' indiscriminate response to false positive information are not yet ap-

---

[1]It is probably important that the claims be about a new product or a product for which the consumer lacks direct experience. Otherwise, the exaggerated claims would easily be refuted by recalling the prior experience.

parent. Singh, Balasubramanian, and Chakraborty (2000) suggested that the infomercial works better than a regular ad (also see Tom, 1995) because of its closer resemblance to a direct experience with the product (although, they argue, the optimal length of an infomercial should be 15 minutes). The presence of both search and experience attributes was an element suggested as important (Singh et al., 2000), and further research by Hetsroni and Asya (2002) supported this assertion. The latter authors looked at the value system components and found that functionalism is emphasized as much as three times more and hedonism is mentioned 25% more frequently in infomercials compared to regular commercials, whereas affective cues are less present (Hetsroni & Asya, 2002). It appears that performance, component, and availability-related information cues are the most common aspects of infomercials (Elliott & Lockard, 1996). If so, encouraging consumers to consciously compare product attributes across similar offerings in the marketplace should be one way to build in some discrimination.

Although attitude change emerges somewhat differently across consumer groups along variables such as depth and breadth of viewing experience (see Elliott & Speck, 1995; for a somewhat different view see Donthu & Gilliland, 1996), extant research on the topic suggests that deceptive messages (e.g., infomercials) change attitudes and increase purchase intentions. In a rare piece of work addressing ways in which consumers can be inoculated against deception, Lord and Kim (1995) found that consumers are better able to detect false claims when their frame of reference (cognitive or affective) is incongruent with the infomercial's executional style. However, with most of the typical infomercial's claims consisting of affect-free cues that appeal to relatively basic human needs on Maslow's (1943) hierarchy, the chance of self-referent mismatch—and thus resistance to undue persuasion—is low.

The Implicit Account

The fact that consumers appear to have difficulty exhibiting more discriminating evaluations of the promotional claims of an infomercial (i.e., relative to regular advertising or other marketing mix elements) hints at the likelihood that the information processing they engage in does not follow the central route (Petty & Cacioppo, 1981). Given that the products being evaluated are usually one time only purchases (durable goods such as mixers, exercise equipment, or self-help courses), consumers may have difficulty assessing the believability of the specific claims (i.e., they lack a repertoire of direct counterarguments). Alternately, consumers' explicit assessments of the veracity of infomercial claims based on the source suggest they are not gullible and naïve individuals (Chapman & Beltramini, 2000). Furthermore, infomercials have a well-deserved notorious reputation with numerous exposés on television and in consumer-education magazines. Despite discounting of the source, and arguably because of the curious nonbelief phenomenon, favorable attitudes are formed and products associated with dubious claims are ordered. As popular persuasion models (e.g., Elaboration Likelihood Model, Petty & Caccioppo, 1981) do not easily explain this phenomenon, it is proposed that the processing of these messages uses resources or knowledge outside conscious control. A direct evaluation of this implicit processing account appears warranted and may provide new insights into the mechanisms underlining the heretofore puzzling effects.

Dimofte and Yalch (2004) proposed that what underlies these contradictory effects is the automatic association between incoming information cues (the false claim) and the brand name that emerges during ad exposure. In addressing the curious nonbelief phenomenon, an experiment was run that involved exposing subjects to a videotaped excerpt from an infomercial or the same information content in a verbal presentation format. The infomercial was presented alone or preceded or followed by a disclaimer (discounting cue). Explicit measures were collected (brand rating, believability, curiosity, etc.) after the presentation. Finally, participants performed two Implicit Association Tests (Greenwald, McGhee, & Schwartz, 1998) looking at novel automatic associations created for the brand featured in the infomercial and a well-known competing brand. The items used in the IATs assessed the relative association between the brands and the attributes of truthfulness (believable/unbelievable in IAT_1) and curiosity (boring/interesting in IAT_2).

Results showed that presenting the infomercial alone was the most persuasive at both explicit and implicit levels, suggesting that the specific format of this marketing communication is indeed conducive to attitude change. Conversely, the same information presented in a text format was deemed most believable but performed the worst in terms of eliciting curiosity and attaining persuasion. Finally, exposure to the discounting cues either before or after the infomercial was successful in eliciting suspicion and hurt both explicit believability and curiosity. However, despite the explicit effects of the discounting cues, the infomercial was nevertheless perceived as believable and elicited curiosity at implicit levels. In summary, it appears that infomercials are successful because they stimulate a curious nonbelief and that operates differently at the explicit and implicit levels. Explicitly, consumers are curious but reject the product claims as unbelievable. However, at an implicit level, consumers are both curious and slightly accepting of the product claims (i.e., they now have a stronger implicit association between the claims and the advertised brand compared to a nonadvertised brand). The implicit effects are most critical because they seem resistant to efforts to undermine the credibility of the infomercial by providing disclaimers.

THE CASE OF FALSE NEGATIVE INFORMATION

The Problem

Periodically, a negative rumor about a brand or company emerges from an unknown source, circulates among consumers, and eventually fades into disregard. Rumors of worm meat in hamburgers, beer tainted by urine, carcinogenic shampoo, and many other claims have plagued powerful brand names around the world. For example, Procter & Gamble has been fighting rumors of links to Satanism since the late 1970s and even sued a competitor (Amway) for aiding the persistence of such information (Del Castillo, 2001). Although this case predictably ended in court, its ultimate dismissal and continued evidence of the rumor on the Internet and other places is testimony to the difficulty of coping with such problems.

There appears to be no clear way to effectively preempt the initial launch of such rumors. The fact that these claims are nothing short of outrageous in the eyes of any thoughtful observer may even aid in their diffusion. After all, it is a human predisposition to convey negative experiences much more so than positive ones. This keeps such gossip alive, potentially causing significant brand or company damage. The malicious origination and the subsequent dissemination of rumors about specific product attributes or benefits essentially amounts to conveying false negative information and, surprisingly, consumers are often explicitly aware of its falsity. Nevertheless, persuasion occurs and individuals alter their behavior. How does this happen?

Theoretical Accounts

Allport and Postman (1947) first defined the rumor as a specific proposition or belief passed along from person to person without any secure standards of evidence. Their model of rumor dynamics argued that the reach, intensity, duration, and reliance on a rumor are roughly equivalent to the importance that one attaches to the rumor if true, multiplied by the ambiguity surrounding the rumor. Subsequent approaches have used more cognitive views. Rosnow (1980) postulated that a rumor results from combinations of uncertainty and anxiety that are related to its strength differently as state and trait factors. Rossignol (1973) introduced an implicit component by proposing that at the origin of rumor lies an unconscious desire that is transferred by certain facts into the conscious, a hypothesis suggesting perhaps that measures of implicit cognition (available today) could offer novel insights into the issue.

What is it that makes negative information more likely to be conveyed than positive information? According to Mizerski (1982), the expectation among consumers is that positive cues should generally be associated with product-related messages. The subsequent encounter of negative cues is therefore likely to elicit surprise and be more salient during product evaluations (Mizerski, 1982). This would explain the basic marketing maxim that a satisfied consumer raves about the pleasant product or service experience on average to three others, but a dissatisfied one rants about an unpleasant experience to seven others.

Wegner et al. (1981) looked at innuendos and the extent to which their presence in the media is sufficient for acceptance by readers. Several of their experiments demonstrated that innuendos are persuasive even when lacking source credibility and when the audience is aware of the sensationalistic nature of the innuendo. If rumors are so insidious and difficult to prevent, how can one adequately fight false negative claims?

Marketing Research on Combating Rumors

Appropriate ways to deal with rumors have been proposed by several researchers. For example, Kamins, Folkes, and Perner (1997) found that rumors—although explicitly lacking credibility—are easily spread, but even more so when they are personally relevant and favorable. Iyer and Debevec (1991) looked at the type of stakeholder refuting the rumor and confirmed that rumors are less credible when propagated by someone with something to gain out of its acceptance and further dissemination.

Explaining a rumor's origin to consumers via positive advertising (see Koller, 1992) and its honest denial (see Bordia, DiFonzo, & Schulz, 2000) have been suggested as appropriate ways to quell it, but others dispute this. Tybout, Calder, and Sternthal (1981) employed information processing theory (availability-valence) and demonstrated that directly refuting rumors may be the least effective way of dealing with them. More useful were two memory altering devices. One, labeled a storage strategy, involves exposing consumers to a secondary stimulus at the time the rumor information is presented, making the rumor more likely to be associated with the secondary stimulus instead of the affected brand. The alternative method, labeled a retrieval strategy, consists of providing consumers with the secondary stimulus at the time of retrieval, thereby lessening the chance of the joint retrieval of brand and rumor information. In Tybout et al.'s (1981) single experiment, the two memory based strategies proved superior to a refutation procedure similar to the one being employed by the affected organization.

Although concern with managing rumors and other forms of organizational crises has attracted much interest since Tybout et al. (1981) was published (there is even a journal focused on the topic—the *Journal of Contingencies and Crisis Management*), the issue appears to have generated little empirical or theoretical interest in the ensuing decades among consumer psychologists. This is particularly surprising because, as the authors pointedly acknowledged, the precise mechanisms underlining the success of their storage and retrieval procedures were not demonstrated and their results could have "multiple theoretical grounds" (Tybout et al., 1981, p. 78). In terms of the storage strategy for example, it could be that the secondary stimulus disrupts the association of the brand with the negative rumor because the item in the rumor becomes more strongly associated with the secondary stimulus than the brand. Or, the secondary stimulus could reduce the rumor's negative valence by priming its association with the positive stimulus.

Interestingly, Tybout et al. (1981) cited Maloney (1962) in noting that their rumor research could be an example of a broader phenomenon wherein consumers are persuaded by information although they explicitly do not accept its veracity.

This *curious nonbelief* effect[2] mentioned earlier and originally suggested by Maloney (1963) has to our knowledge never been directly addressed since the original study described earlier in this chapter. The *Journal of Advertising Research* appears in agreement with our view of its potential importance as it recently republished the original article (Maloney, 1962/2000), maintaining its history of surfacing and resurfacing every twenty years.

The Implicit Account

The observation that consumers exhibit difficulty ignoring the slandering claims of a rumor (i.e., relative to positive accounts of brands or service experiences) when making discriminating product evaluations is consistent with the suggestion that the influence of this information is not occurring through the central route of persuasion (Petty & Cacioppo, 1981). If it did, individuals with the resources and motivation to adequately tease apart (likely) fact from (likely) fiction would easily note the illogical elements present in most rumors (e.g., Procter & Gamble is one of the world's largest publicly owned corporations with hundreds of thousands of employees and stockholders and therefore not plausibly controlled by a Satan worshipping cult). That shifts in attitudes still occur after exposure to such rumors suggests that it may be the processing of these messages with resources or knowledge outside conscious control that causes the shifts. An implicit processing account appears once again warranted.

Having established the fact that the emergence of automatic associations is the underlying driver of persuasion despite nonbelief, Dimofte and Yalch (2004) also looked (in two studies) at the storage and retrieval strategies proposed by Tybout et al. (1981). In the first experiment, subjects read several news stories, one of which mentioned a McDonald's worm rumor similar to that employed by Tybout et al. (1981). In the storage condition, one of the stories also reported about a new trend in high-class cuisine: worm dishes. Participants in a control condition read an irrelevant story. A 10-minute filler task followed, then IATs looking at novel automatic associations between target brands and attributes (McDonald's, Burger King, and food-related or worm-related in IAT$_1$; Foods or worms and pleasant or unpleasant in IAT$_2$). Finally, explicit measures were collected on brand rating. Results showed that the storage strategy was successful at an explicit level in altering evaluations of McDonald's. The implicit association explanation that the storage strategy works by neutralizing the consumers' negative thoughts associated with the negative aspects of the rumor was supported by the IAT data. Consumers exposed to the storage strategy maintained the association between McDonalds and worms but associated worms with more positive thoughts than did consumers in the control condition.

---

[2]Tybout et al. (1981) used the term *disbelief*, but a careful reading of Maloney (1962) reveals that he was differentiating between disbelief and nonbelief. Therefore, the phenomenon is properly described as *curious nonbelief*.

The second rumor study of Dimofte and Yalch (2004) looked at what exactly drives the success of the retrieval strategy and whether refutation is as ineffective, as Tybout et al. (1981) concluded. The same general procedure was employed with the additional manipulation of delay between exposure and measures collection (5 vs. 30 minutes). A single implicit association task was performed (IAT_1 from the storage study). In terms of the explicit measures, both the retrieval strategy and direct refutation worked when there was a short delay (supporting Bordia et al., 2000) but not when the delay was long (supporting Tybout et al., 1981). IAT data are once again useful in explaining these results. They suggest that the automatic association between McDonald's and worms emerges but does not have time to solidify if alternative or contradictory information is shortly available. However, if this information only comes much later, the original association represents a priming instance that leads to the evaluation of subsequent refutation cues as mere rumor repetition.

CONCLUSIONS

Both consumers and organizations are victimized by the spreading of false product information in the marketplace. Consumers suffer by buying products that do not live up to their exaggerated claims or by avoiding products based on alleged faults. Organizations lose when consumers waste their money on competitors' oversold products or avoid their legitimate offerings for illegitimate reasons. Understanding the psychological bases for consumers' susceptibility to false product information is a necessary first step in developing effective programs to counter these threats to societal welfare.

The research reviewed in this chapter indicates that infomercials are a particularly powerful implementation of the "too good to be true" phenomenon that consumers find difficult to resist. The FTC estimated in 2003 that 40% of the 300 fitness and weight loss infomercials they had studied made at least one false representation, and 55% of them had at least one unsubstantiated claim. It found altered before and after pictures, paid client testimonials, actors impersonating health experts, and misrepresented results of pertinent scientific studies. Although all this is surely not surprising to any consumer, the fact that purchases still occur speaks toward the power of implicit processing as a viable alternative (from the marketers' perspective) to central route engagement of cognitive resources.

Our explanation is that resistance is difficult for several reasons. First, as we demonstrated, much of the effectiveness occurs below the level of conscious awareness as the infomercials build implicit associations between brands and the claims made in the commercial. Given a human tendency to first accept claims as true (cf. Gilbert et al., 1990, 1993), the consumer burden is to convince themselves why the claims should be rejected. This may be difficult for many infomercials because they usually present visual "proof" of the claim or strong "testimonials" from satisfied users. Often, these testimonials are supported by on-camera product trials (taking advantage of the "seeing is believing" phenomenon). The fact that most of these visuals involve a variety of camera tricks and other deceptive methods is not easily determined by a naïve viewer. Finally, we maintain that infomercials are also successful because they address fundamental and frustrating consumer problems such as weight loss, financial wealth, and easy meal preparation. Here, the advertiser is exploiting the consumer hope that the product will perform as claimed (see MacInnis & de Mello, 2005). Thus, even skeptical consumers may be willing to take a chance that this product might be the one that actually works. Furthermore, failure might not materially increase rejection of future claims because consumers might attribute the past failure to task difficulty (losing weight is hard) rather than to the product's inability to live up to its exaggerated claims. To be sure, consumers are no more gullible when exposed to infomercials than in other situations (for a similar point, see Chapman & Beltramini, 2000), but the unusually lengthy extent of the message, its repetitive nature, and its appeal to ultimately the most basic human needs combine to produce and rehearse automatic associations that subsequently operate through unconscious routes.

As the number of channels of cable television available to the typical household explodes, it appears that the number of infomercials is expanding to fill the airtime. Infomercials represent a win–win proposition for the sponsor and station because the station is typically compensated as a percent of the sales. Thus, the sponsor has an easily calculated cost of doing business. There are several possible ways to prevent or reduce the number of consumers duped by infomercials. One suggestion is for the FTC to require periodic, or even continuous, disclaimers during the infomercial to remind those in the viewing public that the program is paid use of public airways to promote a sponsor's products. The research reviewed here suggests that a single such notice at the beginning of the program can be missed or forgotten, and any post-exposure notices will not prevent a sleeper effect, as described by Dimofte and Yalch (2004). However, the research shows that latent skepticism toward infomercials is ineffective in preventing the implicit associations created by the infomercial. If the skepticism is not strong enough to counter the powerful visuals, it will not matter if consumers are primed about it. However, if consumers are not consciously aware of their skepticism, then it may be effective.

Three alternative approaches should be considered. One is to stiffen the penalty for deceptive advertising. Too often, advertisers merely include the small fines as a cost of business, and as such, the current regulations provide little deterrence. A second approach is to provide consumers with access to other customers' unfiltered product experiences, much as is done by Amazon, eBay, and other Internet shopping sites. The advertisers might be required to inform viewers of the existence and location of this information. A third is to require the stations broadcasting an infomercial to offer time to those who want to offer a different perspective about the advertised product, much as was done just before cigarette advertising was banned from broadcast on television or radio. Testimonials from those suffering health effects caused by smoking were claimed to result in greater decline in smoking than were removal of both cigarette and anti-smoking messages (Hamilton, 1972). Ready access to truth verification information would make it easier for consumers to overcome the initial acceptance of new information.

Also, despite the acknowledgment that rumors are both damaging and pervasive, we propose that information processing theory offers ways to combat it that are generally superior to direct refutation. Furthermore, the dissociation between explicit attitudes and subsequent behavior can be accommodated by the implicit account just discussed. Admittedly, previous literature has hinted at the possibility that something such as implicit processing may be at work. In an early book on rumors in the marketplace, Koenig (1985) argued that—in the context of the McDonald's rumor for example—"the negative image suggested by the rumor could exist at various levels of consciousness and could lead one to get a pizza or a taco without being aware of why one did so" (Koenig, 1985, p. 140). The present implicit account proposes that false information persuades via an automatic route by easily building automatic associations between brands and the information cues. While explicitly rejecting the veracity of rumors, consumers lack control over the associations occurring at exposure and practiced during subsequent instances of decision making.

In terms of specific procedures for developing effective counter messages for rumor control, direct refutation is largely ineffective because of its temporal detachment from the moment of negative automatic association encoding. When refutation is prompt enough to not allow this association to emerge, honesty is indeed the best policy (Bordia et al., 2000). Unfortunately, this is very rarely the case, especially because automatic associations emerge relatively fast. As Koenig (1985) put it, "time is the worst enemy" (p. 167). Consequently, different strategies must be used. Storage works by improving implicitly the evaluation of the negative cue, but this is also rather impractical. The best corporate strategy would therefore involve prompt promotional campaigns that focus on attributes relevant to the rumor, but in less than obvious ways. This has been previously described as the "do something—but discreetly" strategy (Koenig, 1985) and seems to fit the intuition of corporate PR personnel well. Another approach that could be employed refers to slowing the rumor diffusion in the media—where the appeal to journalistic integrity or the threat of legal action can prove fruitful avenues in the attempt to limit the geographical expansion of negative information.

As positive and negative effects of information are often better observed at implicit levels, the research reviewed herein further demonstrates how recent advances in our ability to capture and quantify automatic cognition processes (such as the Implicit Association Test) provide the proper conceptual and methodological tools necessary to explain previously inaccessible phenomena of interest.

In the end, is advertising truly legalized lying? Whereas the FTC would argue that things are not quite that bleak, the ease with which advertising, rumors, or any similar marketing-related information can automatically impact consumer behavior suggest that another quote by an industry insider (Chester L. Posey, Senior V.P. and Creative Director with McCann Erickson) may be getting closer to the truth: "[Advertising is a] ten billion dollar a year misunderstanding with the public."

REFERENCES

Agee, T., & Brett, M. A. (2001). Planned or impulse purchases? How to create effective infomercials. *Journal of Advertising Research, 41*(6), 35–42.

Allport, G. W., & Postman, L. J. (1947). *The psychology of rumor.* New York: Holt.

Bordia, P., DiFonzo, N., & Schulz, C. A. (2000). Source characteristics in denying rumors of organizational closure: Honesty is the best policy. *Journal of Applied Social Psychology, 30*(11), 2309–2321.

Brett, M. A., Bhimy, A. C., & Agee, T. (2002). Infomercials and advertising effectiveness: An empirical study. *The Journal of Consumer Marketing, 19*(6), 468–480.

Cialdini, R. C. (1998). *Influence (rev.): The psychology of persuasion.* New York: William Morrow and Co.

Chapman, P. S., & Beltramini, R. F. (2000). Infomercials revisited: Perspectives of advertisers and advertising agencies. *Journal of Advertising Research, 40*(5), 24–31.

Compeau, L. D., Grewal, D., & Chandrashekaran, R. (2002). Comparative price advertising: Believe it or not. *The Journal of Consumer Affairs, 36*(2), 284–294.

Del Castillo, D. (2001). Rumors & lies: The parameters of liability for commercial speech. *Academy of Marketing Science Journal, 29*(3), 328–330.

Dick, A., Chakravarti, D., & Biehal, G. (1990). Memory-based inferences during consumer choice. *Journal of Consumer Research, 17*(1), 82–93.

Dimofte, C. V., & Yalch, R. F. (2004). Is advertising believability really important? The response is automatic. (working paper).

Donthu, N., & Gilliland, D. (1996). The infomercial shopper (observations). *Journal of Advertising Research, 36*(2), 69–76.

Elliott, M. T., & Speck, P. S. (1995). Antecedents and consequences of infomercial viewership. *Journal of Direct Marketing, 9*(2), 39–41.

Elliott, M. T., & Lockard, P. (1996). An analysis of information content in infomercial programs. *Journal of Direct Marketing, 10*(2), 44–55.

Gaeth, G. J., & Heath, T. B. (1987). The cognitive processing of misleading advertising in young and old adults: Assessment and training. *Journal of Consumer Research, 14*(1), 43–54.

Gilbert, D. T., Krull, D. S., & Malone, P. S. (1990). Unbelieving the unbelievable: Some problems in the rejection of false information. *Journal of Personality and Social Psychology, 59*(4), 601–613.

Gilbert, D. T., Tafarodi, R. W., & Malone, P. S. (1993). You can't not believe everything you read. *Journal of Personality and Social Psychology, 65*(2), 221–233.

Greenwald, A. G., McGhee, D. E., & Schwartz, J. L. K. (1998). Measuring individual differences in implicit cognition: The implicit association test. *Journal of Personality and Social Psychology, 74*, 1464–1480.

Hamilton, J. L. (1972). The demand for cigarettes: Advertising, the health scare and the cigarette advertising ban. *Review of Economics and Statistics, 54*, 401–411.

Harris, J. R. (1977). Comprehension of pragmatic implications in advertising. *Journal of Applied Psychology, 62*(October), 603–608.

Hetsroni, A., & Asya, I. (2002). A comparison of values in infomercials and commercials. *Corporate Communications, 7*(1), 34–45.

Hutheesing, N. (1995). The wild west of advertising. *Forbes, 155*(2), 50–52.

Iyer, E. S., & Debevec, K. (1991). Origin of rumor and tone of message in rumor quelling strategies. *Psychology & Marketing, 8*(3), 161–175.

Johar, G. V. (1995). Consumer involvement and deception from implied advertising claims. *Journal of Marketing Research, 32*(3), 267–279.

Kamins, M. A., Folkes, V. S., & Perner, L. (1997). Consumer responses to rumors: Good news, bad news. *Journal of Consumer Psychology, 6*(2), 165–187.

Kardes, F. R. (1988). A nonreactive measure of inferential beliefs. *Psychology & Marketing, 5*(3), 273–286.

Koenig, F. (1985). *Rumor in the marketplace: The social psychology of commercial hearsay.* Dover, MA: Auburn House.

Koller, M. (1992). Rumor rebuttal in the marketplace. *Journal of Economic Psychology, 13*(1), 167–186.

Koslow, S., & Beltramini, R. F. (2002). Consumer skepticism and the 'Waiting room of the mind:' Are consumers more likely to believe advertising claims if they are merely comprehended? *Advances in Consumer Research, 29,* 473–479.

Lord, K. R., & Kim, C. K. (1995). Inoculating consumers against deception: The influence of framing and executional style. *Journal of Consumer Policy, 18*(1), 1–22.

MacInnis, D., & de Mello, G. (2005). The concept of hope and its relevance to product evaluation and choice. *Journal of Marketing, 69*(1), 1–14.

Maloney, J. C. (1962). Curiosity versus disbelief in advertising. *Journal of Advertising Research, 2*(2), 2–8.

Maloney, J. C. (1963). Is advertising believability really important? *Journal of Marketing, 27*(4), 1–8.

Maloney, J. C. (2000). Curiosity versus disbelief in advertising. *Journal of Advertising Research* (November–December), 7–13. (Original work published 1962)

Maslow, A. H. (1943). A theory of human motivation. *Psychological Review, 50,* 370–396.

Mizerski, R. W. (1982). An attribution explanation of the disproportionate influence of unfavorable information. *Journal of Consumer Research, 9*(3), 301–311.

Petty, R. E., & Caccioppo, J. T. (1981). *Attitudes and persuasion: Classic and contemporary approaches.* Boulder, CO: Westview Press.

Richards, J. (1990). *Deceptive advertising: Behavioral study of a legal concept.* Hillsdale, NJ: Lawrence Erlbaum Associates.

Rosnow, R. L. (1980). Psychology of rumor reconsidered. *Psychological Bulletin, 87*(3), 578–591.

Rossignol, C. (1973). Phenomena of rumor process of association and study of social representations. *Psychologie Française, 18*(1), 23–40.

Schutz, H. G., & Casey, M. (1981). Consumer perceptions of advertising as misleading. *The Journal of Consumer Affairs, 15*(2), 340–357.

Simmons, C. J., & Lynch, Jr., J. G. (1991). Inference effects without inference making? Effects of missing information on discounting and use of presented information. *Journal of Consumer Research, 17*(4), 477–491.

Singh, M., Balasubramanian, S. K., & Chakraborty, G. (2000). A comparative analysis of three communication formats: Advertising, infomercial, and direct experience. *Journal of Advertising, 29*(4), 59–75.

Suter, T. A., & Burton, S. (1996). Believability and consumer perceptions of implausible reference prices in retail advertisements. *Psychology & Marketing, 13*(1), 37–54.

Tom, G. (1995). The information content of infomercials. *Review of Business, 17*(2), 42–45.

Tybout, A. M., Calder, B. J., & Sternthal, B. (1981). Using information processing theory to design marketing strategies. *Journal of Marketing Research, 18*(1), 73–79.

Wegner, D. M., Wenzlaff, R., Kerker, M. R., & Beattie, A. E. (1981). Incrimination through innuendo: Can media questions become public answers? *Journal of Personality & Social Psychology, 40*(5), 822–832.

CHAPTER FOURTEEN

Implications for Advertising Effectiveness of Divergence Among Measured Advertising Effects

Philip J. Mazzocco
Derek D. Rucker
Timothy C. Brock
The Ohio State University

At some level, a goal of any advertisement is to increase the ability of a company to sell their product or service. Of course, ads also cost money. Hence, *advertising effectiveness* can be thought of as a reasonable return on investment (ROI). This very general definition of advertising effectiveness begs the questions of how to create ads that increase ROI, and how to diagnose the problem when satisfactory ROI is not achieved. For both questions, latent factors and constructs thought to enhance or detract from advertising success will play a central role. When an ad can be shown to influence one of these latent constructs, the ad can be said to have an advertising effect (see also Wright-Isak, Faber, & Horner, 1997, for the distinction between advertising effectiveness and advertising effects). Because practitioners can rarely pretest ads by following recipients over long periods of times to check on actual purchase behavior, they will often rely on the measurement of advertising effects to make predictions about general advertising effectiveness (ROI). Researchers, more interested in the interrelationships between constructs and theory, may be primarily interested in advertising effects, though they may often venture to generalize into the realm of advertising effectiveness. For both researchers and practitioners, the generalizability of a given measure of an advertising effect to other measures of advertising effects, or advertising effectiveness in general, is of paramount importance.

Consider one example where researchers generalized from ad effects to ad effectiveness. Bushman and Bonacci (2002) reported poorer recall and recognition for ads shown during violent and sexual programming as compared to neutral programming. They concluded, ". . . advertisers should think twice about sponsoring violent and sexually explicit TV programs." (p. 563). Hence, ad effects were used to make an inference about likely ad effectiveness (seemingly in terms of ROI). Bushman (1998) and Bushman and Phillips (2001) concluded with similar advice to would-be advertisers. Though the social significance of these studies can be applauded, it is reasonable to question whether the specific advertising effects relating to recall and recognition can and should be generalized to advertising effectiveness in general. For example, effects on recall may not generalize to either attitudes or behavior, other important indicators of advertising effectiveness.

There are some obvious (and less obvious) reasons why recall, on one hand, and other measures of advertising effectiveness, on the other hand, would not be associated with one another. These reasons are reviewed in this chapter. However, we intend to make a more general point: Correct measurement of advertising effectiveness depends on the particular definition of advertising effectiveness used for any given ad. For example, most advertising campaigns have multiple stages, and each stage may be designed to achieve a different goal. Although a variety of specific advertising effects might be argued to be linked to advertising effectiveness, three psychological constructs, in particular, have received considerable attention as indicators of ad effectiveness: reception (e.g., day after recall, recognition, comprehension, etc.), evaluation (e.g., attitudes, thoughts, feelings, etc.), and behavior (e.g., hypothetical choice, initial or repeat sales, word-of-mouth).

Each of these general constructs can be operationalized in numerous ways. If all of these specific measures were highly correlated, there would be no need for matching a particular type of measurement with a given measurement goal. Recall, for example, could be used to estimate evaluation and behavior. In fact, early measurements of advertising effectiveness by practitioners such as Daniel Starch and George Gallup took just this tack (Biel, 1996). Subsequent research and theorization, however, has uncovered numerous ways that measures of advertising effectiveness can diverge; both within and between the three broad construct categories already mentioned.

CHAPTER OVERVIEW AND GOALS

In this chapter we focus on three key constructs associated with advertising effectiveness: reception, evaluation, and behavior. For each of these constructs, we discuss why similar measures within the construct may not often correlate (e.g., evaluative constructs such as thoughts and attitudes). Furthermore, we examine why natural, theory-guided, links between constructs may not always exist. In particular, we organize our chapter based on the natural order in which these variables often take part in the persuasion process (reception to evaluation to behavior—each with links to ad effectiveness—see Fig. 14.1). We end by providing recommendations to researchers and practitioners.

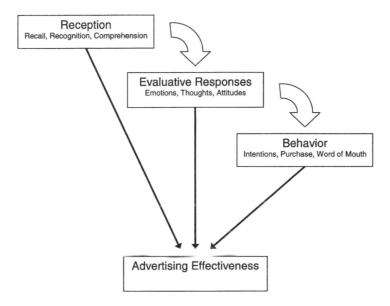

FIG. 14.1. Organizing framework for concepts covered in this chapter.

DEFINING ADVERTISING EFFECTIVENESS

Generally, specific definitions of advertising effectiveness can be organized around three psychological constructs: reception, evaluation, and behavior. Definitions of success, specific advertising aims, and common tactics exist for each of the constructs.

Reception

At the level of reception, success may be defined along a continuum. At one end of the continuum, an ad may be designed merely to slip into the recipient's mind (e.g., subliminal advertising); hence, consumers should have no conscious recollection of seeing a given presentation. More commonly (and legally) ads at the minimal end of the continuum may be designed to hold conscious attention only for a short period of time, such as ads designed to be processed in a peripheral fashion with little focal attention (e.g., to remind consumers that the product is out there). On the other end of the continuum, advertisers may intend that consumers deeply process an ad and form relevant long-term memory traces about a product (e.g., product attributes, price, special promotions, competitor weaknesses, purchase location, etc.) that can be recalled at will. Common measures of reception include measures of attention, recognition, recall, and comprehension. Tactics to increase reception may include catchy jingles, sex-appeals, repetition, vivid copy or imagery, and so forth.

Evaluation

In addition to teaching about the product and raising awareness, advertisers will typically aim to engender positive evaluative responses toward their brand, product, corporation, and so forth. Ideally, these positive evaluative responses will comprise a positive attitude that will influence both immediate and long-term product relevant responses accordingly. According to the tripartite model (e.g., Breckler, 1984), there are three different types of evaluative responses that can form the basis of attitudes: affective, behavioral, and cognitive. Measures of affective responses include affect ratings, open-ended responses, and physiological measures. Measures of behavioral responses include behavioral intent, facial electromyograph, and systematic observation. Measures of cognitive responses include thought listings, image listings, and rating scales. Typically, evaluative responses will be combined into a single evaluative judgment or attitude. Measures of attitudes include explicit attitude rating scales, ranking procedures, and, more recently, implicit measures of attitudes (Fitzsimons et al., 2002). Tactics designed to increase positive evaluative responses include celebrity endorsers, playing up the positive product qualities, and the use of humor, to name a few.

Behavior

Perhaps most obviously, advertisers may be interested in affecting consumer behaviors, such as buying and word-of-mouth endorsements. Measures of behavior include intentions, hypothetical choices, and actual decisions. Common tactics that target consumer behavior specifically include promotions and compliance techniques.

Overall Advertising Effectiveness

To justify advertising expenditures, advertisers will often conduct testing either to gauge the effects of their advertisements, or to aid in the construction of advertisements. In the former case, relative sales increases over a given period of time will be the definitive measurement. However, in both cases, advertisers will often want to gauge the effects of their advertisements on one or more of the three constructs just described. As noted, if all of the various measures of advertising effects were highly correlated, advertisers and researchers alike could focus on one or two simple measures and feel confident about making generalizations to other measures of ad effects, or even ad effectiveness more generally (ROI). However, research in the area of advertising effects has uncovered numerous factors that could lead to dissociations, or even negative association, between the various measures of ad effects. These factors are reviewed in this chapter.

ON MEASURING RECEPTION

Conscious reception of advertisements is often presumed to be an essential element in advertising success. This section tells, however, a much more complex story. We first discuss why the correlation between any two measures of reception can be questioned. We then discuss in detail reasons why discordance between measures of reception and evaluation, and hence behavior (see Fig. 14.1), might be expected or even predicted in certain situations.

Within Construct Divergence

Certainly, the reliability of any given measure of reception can be questioned. The less reliable a given measure, the less likely it is to be correlated with any other measure. A great deal of debate has centered on the reliability of measures of recall. For example, in a review of studies that measured ad recall, Gibson (1983) showed that recall data tend to be unreliable as they are influenced by exposure factors (e.g., viewing order, time of exposure, program liking), respondent factors (e.g., age, sex, education), and measurement factors (e.g., elapsed time, number of commercials, interviewer). The influence of these factors may be one reason for relatively moderate and variable test–retest correlations between measures of recall (between .67 and .87, in Gibson's, 1983, review).

Work in the area of memory bias and distortion also provides a compelling reason for the unreliability of recall measures. A large body of research has demonstrated pervasive biases and distortions in recall (Alvarez & Brown, 2002). For example, various processes can lead to the blending of actual memories with other information (Garry & Polaschek, 2000), or even the creation of completely false memories (Loftus, 1997). In the realm of advertising recall, it may be common that consumers blend information from two or more ads, or blend information that they themselves had generated during ad reception. Similar claims of potential unreliability can be made for almost any single measure of advertising effectiveness. Relevant to reception, for example, improperly constructed measures of recognition can be biased by guessing.

Although steps are continually being taken to create more reliable and valid measures of advertising effects, researchers and practitioners alike should keep issues of reliability and validity in mind at all times, especially when hoping to generalize specific measures of advertising effects to any of the other main psychological constructs, or to advertising effectiveness in general.

Reception and Evaluation

Low correlations between measures of reception (recall) and evaluation (attitudes) have typically been reported (e.g., Cacioppo & Petty, 1979), and passionate calls have been made against the practice of sole reliance on recall, or other measures of reception, to measure ad effectiveness (Gibson, 1983; Shavitt & Brock, 1986). Although the reliability of measures of reception has been forwarded as a reason for low reception–evaluation correlations (Gibson, 1983), theoretical concerns have also proven compelling. The practice of using measures of reception to make inferences about evaluation can be attributed in large part to the early message-learning theories of persuasion, which emphasized the connection between reception and persuasion (e.g., Hovland, Lumsdaine, & Sheffield, 1949; Mc-Guire, 1969). According to these theories, message learning sets an upper boundary for attitude change. Hence, the intuitive rationale: If they cannot even remember the ad, how could it possibly have persuaded them? As appealing as this rationale is, there are a number of reasons to expect low or even negative correlations between measures of reception and evaluation.

Reception Not Necessary for Attitude Change.   Advertisements need to impinge on consumers at some level; however, ads that are received below the level of consciousness (unlikely to be recalled or even recognized), may still have noticeable effects on measures of evaluation.

Attitude change has been shown to occur in the absence of communication recall via a variety of mechanisms. Nordhielm's (2002) work on ad repetition invoked a perceptual fluency model whereby repeated ad exposures may lead to more positive affective reactions due to increases in ease of processing (which can then be misattributed to increased liking). Nordhielm showed this misattribution is most likely to be observed under conditions of shallow levels of processing; that is, when recall should be most constrained.

Work on mere exposure is congenial with this perspective. For example, Zajonc (1968) demonstrated that merely being exposed to photographs resulted in increased liking for those photographs. Importantly, research has shown mere exposure effects are strongest under conditions of subliminal presentation (Bornstein & D'Agostino, 1992). Although subliminal persuasion in advertising is unethical, and largely thought to be impossible (e.g., Moore, 1988; Pratkanis & Greenwald, 1988), work examining preattentive processing has shown mere exposure-like effects on attitudes toward ads and brands (Janisewski, 1988, 1993; Shapiro, Heckler, & MacInnis, 1997). In these studies, participants view ads incidentally (ads are presented above the level of awareness, but participants are prevented from allocating focal attention to them). For example, Shapiro et al. (1997) had participants attend to a column of scrolling text on a monitor that was sandwiched in between two other columns of scrolling text. Occasionally, an ad would scroll by one of the unattended columns. Later, participants saw the target ads again and evaluated them. Despite chance recognition levels in the preattentive processing group (no difference with a control group who had not seen the ads before) attitude change relative to a control group was exhibited. While Shapiro et al. (1997) showed attitude change relevant only to ad attitudes, similar work by Janisewski (1993) showed changes in brand attitudes due to preattentive processing.

Finally, work based on Petty and Cacioppo's (1986) Elaboration Likelihood Model has shown that communication can influence attitudes through the transmission of peripheral cues such as putting participants in a positive mood (Petty, Schumann, Richman, & Strathman, 1993). When attitude change occurs via the peripheral route, attitude change would not necessarily be expected to correlate highly with ad recall or recognition because comprehension of the ad elements may be irrelevant (see also the Heuristic-Systematic Model; Chen & Chaiken, 1998).

In each case, the ads may have been expected to lead to increased sales despite seemingly low reception (in comparison to ads shown during neutral programming). These possibilities cannot be tested without measures of evaluation.

Reception Not Sufficient for Attitude Change. Even in cases where comprehension is high and, hence, recall and recognition are superior, the claim that superior reception equates to increased advertising effectiveness still cannot be made. Individual elaborations on the message, rather than recollections of message points, are typically more predictive of resulting attitudes and behavior (e.g., Brock, 1967; Greenwald, 1968; Wright, 1980). For example, an ad containing a disgusting scene may be highly memorable to participants, but personal reactions of disgust and disdain may be more likely to determine attitudes toward the ad and brand. To take another example, imagine an ad for a new medical product that touts being rated number one by most doctors. Although people may readily remember the strong endorsement, some individuals may reason, "Those doctors are all being paid off, so I do not trust this product."

Work by Padgett and Brock (1988) showed that attitude change can result even when people are given unintelligible messages. The rationale is that when messages arguments are unintelligible or absent, recipients will need to rely more heavily on the production of idiosyncratic cognitive responses. Unintelligibility can lead to increased attitude change when consumers take it upon themselves to imagine positive aspects of a given product or service. In these cases, unintelligibility might not only increase attitude change, but might also lead to attitudes that are more persistent, more resistant to change, and more predictive of behavior, as idiosyncratic thought generation may be associated with greater elaboration (attitude strength will be discussed more generally below). At the same time, reception will obviously suffer to the extent that messages are unintelligible.

Finally, Fishbein's (1967) expectancy-value model holds that the degree to which the valence of a product attribute will affect attitudes depends on the belief that the product actually has that attribute. In some cases, ads that can be easily recalled may seem too good to be true. In general, increasing the extremity of claims should simultaneously increase reception, while decreasing believability.

Work in the marketing domain has shown that ad repetition can, under some conditions, increase perceived validity of a given statement (Law & Hawkins, 1997). Increased perception of validity is especially likely when repetition of information from a single source is misattributed to a different source (see Arkes, Boehm, & Xu, 1991), but can occur more generally due to feelings of increased familiarity as already reviewed (Nordhielm, 2002). In these cases, reception and attitude change may be expected to correlate more highly; but even here, the much larger percentage of the variance in attitudes will be accounted for by evaluative responses to the information.

Recipient Characteristics and the Reception-Evaluation Link. There are a number of recipient based characteristics (intelligence, cognitive resources, persuasion knowledge, latent arousal, processing style, etc.) that can influence the association between reception and evaluation. One of the earliest such characteristics to be studied was recipient intelligence. McGuire's (1968) reception/yielding model proposed that individuals with high intelligence would be more likely to comprehend and successfully receive persuasive communications, but would be less likely to be persuaded by them due to superior resistance mechanisms. Since then, a number of factors and models have been proposed that predict similar discordance between evaluation and recall outcomes.

In particular, similar to McGuire's (1968) model, work on the resource matching model (Anand & Sternthal, 1989) suggested message processing will lead to optimal attitude change when the perceiver's allocation of message processing resources (resources available; RA) matches the amount of resources required (RR) to process the message. When RA is less than RR, insufficient resources will render persuasion generally ineffective. When RA is greater than RR, the resource-matching model proposes one of two likely outcomes: Either extra resources will be devoted to counterarguing, or extra resources will be devoted to cognitive elaboration. In the latter case, additional elaborations will typically be less compelling than the original message arguments and, hence, will tend to diminish persuasion (assuming that the original arguments and elaboration are averaged). Individuals who possess higher intelligence are more likely to have RA > RR, which, consistent with McGuire's work, would make them less susceptible to persuasion. Generally, then, the resource matching model would predict that increases in available resources should increase reception (higher recall, recognition), but decrease attitude change.

Other research has shown that recall for ads can be a good predictor of attitudes in situations when people are not forming an overall impression of the ad at the time of message exposure (on-line attitude formation) but are instead called upon to form attitudes from memory (memory-based attitude formation; see Beattie & Mitchell, 1985; Haugtvedt & Petty, 1992; Kardes, 1986; Mackie & Asuncion, 1990; Tormala & Petty, 2001). The rationale is as follows: When people form attitudes during ad exposure, the attitudes will be influenced by all available ad-related information. At some time in the future, when recall measures are administered, some portion of this initially available information will have decayed, and hence attitudes and recall will diverge. However, when attitudes are formed after message exposure (closer to the time when recall measures would be administered), both attitudes and recall are dependent on the reduced set of ad-relevant information. Hence, in situations where attitudes are formed online, divergence between attitudes and measures of reception would be expected. Even given memory-based processing, evaluative responses to recalled information would account for more variance in attitudes than the sheer number of ad elements recalled.

Friestad and Wright's (1994) model of persuasion knowledge also has implications for the correspondence between reception and evaluation. These authors discussed the role of consumers' naive theories about persuasion in reaction to persuasive communications. Ads that are very memorable may be perceived to have been associated with unfair persuasive tactics (the effects of which need to be debiased from one's judgments). In these cases, unfair persuasive tactics may be especially likely to be recalled, yet simultaneously, attitude change should be blunted (see also Petty & Wegener, 1993; Wilson & Brekke, 1994).

Finally, the latent arousal of ad recipients (unrelated to the ads themselves) can, in some situations, be misattributed to ads (also known as excitation transfer; Cantor, Zillmann, & Bryant, 1975). Latent arousal may come from anywhere (e.g., a rough day in traffic, a fight with a spouse, arousing entertainment). Regardless of the source, when consumers are responding to ads, this latent arousal may influence responses (especially when consumers are unaware of this potential bias). Participants in Bushman and Bonacci's (2002) study exhibited decreased memory for ads shown during violent or sexually oriented programming. It seems plausible that the latent positive arousal created by the violent and sexual programs may have been misattributed to the ads themselves, causing increased liking.

Conclusion

In the preceding section, we discussed numerous reasons to question the relationship between any given measure of reception, with any other measure of reception or evaluation. Hence, in selecting measures of advertising effects and effectiveness, it is important to match measures with advertising goals and definitions of advertising effectiveness. If a researcher or advertiser desires to make a conclusion about evaluation or behavior, more than measures of reception are needed. We conclude by noting that to the extent that attitudes often do predict behavior, it is also fair to question the reception/behavior link for all of the reasons listed (see Fig. 14.1). We now move on to examine the link between evaluations and behaviors.

ON MEASURING EVALUATION

Because we have already covered the relationship between reception and evaluation, we focus in this section on within-construct divergence (relevant to evaluation), and the evaluation–behavior link.

Within Construct Divergence

To begin, many of the same criticisms that can be made about measures of reception in terms of reliability can also apply to certain evaluative measures, most obviously thought listings. In addition, there is a voluminous literature relating to the many potential biasing factors of attitudinal rating scales, or any rating scale for that matter (for a review, see Schwarz, Groves, & Schuman, 1998; Wicker, 1969). Hence, issues of reliability and validity continue to be a concern with measures of evaluation. However, as with reception, there are more intriguing reasons to question researchers or practitioners who attempt to generalize a given measure of evaluation to any other measure.

For example, research has shown that ads may influence beliefs indirectly (for a review, see Yi, 1997). Hence, an ad may affect beliefs not explicitly discussed in the ad. Yi (1990) primed participants to interpret information about a computer's numerous features in one of two ways: (a) numerous features entail high versatility, or (b) numerous features entails difficulty of use. Importantly, neither versatility nor difficulty of use was actually mentioned in the ad. Results indicated higher brand attitudes and purchase intent when versatility (a positive characteristic) was primed as opposed to when less ease of use was primed (a negative characteristic). This study demonstrated that ads can affect attitude and belief change relative to product characteristics not even mentioned in the ad. Further, these indirectly affected evaluative dimensions can mediate changes in brand attitudes. Hence, obtaining null effects on evaluative dimensions directly attacked by an ad does not necessarily indicate total ad failure.

Early work by McGuire (1964) showed attitudes that tend to be highly stable over time (persistent) could nevertheless be amenable to change (not resistant), presumably because such attitudes are not buttressed by an underlying cognitive structure. Haugtvedt, Schumann, Schneier, and Warren (1994) extended this work into the realm of advertising. In this research, participants experienced repeated ad exposure. In one group, the substantive messages of the ads were varied from exposure to exposure. In a second group, cosmetic elements of the ads were varied, but the substantive message was held constant. After a week, both groups showed the same amount of attitude change relative to a control group (equal persistence), but those in the substantive-variation group showed less yielding to a subsequent attack (greater resistance). Hence, equally extreme attitudes are not always interchangeable, a point now discussed in greater depth.

In general, cognitive responses, even when coded only for valence (i.e., negativity/positivity), will be related to attitudes. In particular, both the valence of the thought and the number of valenced thoughts influences attitudes. The association between thoughts and attitudes is not perfect, however. A fundamental assumption of dual process models of persuasion, such as the Elaboration Likelihood Model, is that given peripheral route processing, thoughts will be more weakly associated with attitudes (Chen & Chaiken, 1998; Petty & Cacioppo, 1986). That is, thoughts are most likely to influence attitudes when elaboration or amount of thinking is high. More recent research has begun to examine properties of the thoughts themselves to better understand when thoughts influence attitudes. Specifically, Petty, Briñol, and Tormala, 2002 have suggested that the utility of cognitive responses or thoughts for predicting attitudes can be enhanced by measuring thought confidence (see also Briñol, Petty, & Tormala, 2004). That is, not only is it useful to measure the amount and valence of thoughts, but it is also informative to measure how confident individuals are about their thoughts. Petty and colleagues have suggested that thoughts are most likely to influence attitudes when the thoughts are held with a high degree of confidence; when individuals believe their thoughts are correct and appropriate. This perspective is congenial with models of consumer thought processing such as the accessibility–diagnosticity model (Feldman & Lynch, 1988), which proposes that for information to influence persuasion, it must be both accessible and perceived to be diagnostic.

Empirical research has demonstrated that predicting attitudes from thoughts can indeed be improved by measuring thought confidence (Briñol et al., 2004; Petty et al., 2002). For example, Briñol and colleagues (2004) measured participants' thoughts about a consumer product as well as their confidence in their thoughts. In this experiment, participants received either a message containing strong or weak arguments in favor of a consumer product. Not surprisingly, individuals generated more positive thoughts and less negative thoughts in response to the strong compared to the weak advertisement. However, with respect to individuals' attitudes, individuals only showed a differentiation between the strong and weak ads when they had confidence in their thoughts. Put differently, attitudes were only a reflection of participants' underlying thoughts when those thoughts were held with confidence.[1]

In short, in addition to factors such as elaboration, one reason thoughts may fail to predict subsequent attitudes is because the thoughts are not held with a high degree of confidence. In such situations, individuals may be forced to rely on factors besides their thoughts when ascertaining their attitudes (e.g., contextual cues). By knowing whether individuals are likely to have confidence in their

---

[1]Note that confidence moderated the thought–attitude relationship only under high-elaboration conditions (Petty et al., 2002) or for individuals high in need for cognition (Briñol et al., 2004). This finding follows logically from research showing individuals tend to consult their thoughts only under high-elaboration conditions (Petty & Cacioppo, 1986). Individuals' must be relying on their thoughts to determine their attitude for variance in thought confidence to matter.

thoughts research can better predict when thoughts are likely to influence attitudes.

Evaluation and Behavior

The Work of Ajzen and Fishbein. The link between evaluation (specifically attitudes) and behavior has a controversial past, with some suggesting no association whatsoever (Wicker, 1969). However, subsequent research has determined that attitudes can be very good predictors of behaviors under specific conditions. According to Fishbein's (1980) Theory of Reasoned Action, attitudes and behaviors will tend to be less correlated given differences in the level of specificity of each. The question, "Do you like to eat Beluga caviar?" is unlikely to predict purchase behavior (due in part to the expensiveness of the product). A much better question is, "What is your opinion about buying Beluga caviar?"

Ajzen's (1991) Theory of Planned Behavior also has implications for the link between evaluations and behavior. Behaviors are influenced not just by relevant attitudes, but also by prevailing social norms, and by perceptions of behavioral control. Relative to social norms, consumers may be very interested in a buying a particular product, but fail to do so because they feel they may be ridiculed if they do. With respect to perceptions of control, consumers may desire to buy a particular product, but may also feel a 3-hour car trip to the nearest retailer is not worth the bother. Hence, there are many conditions in which a simple report of attitudes would not be predictive of actual purchasing behaviors.

Attitude Strength. The point of Ajzen and Fishbein's work was to show that attitudes can indeed be useful for predicting behavior at some unknown point in time given that nonattitudinal sources of variance have been controlled. Furthermore, the higher the correspondence between attitudes and behavior, the more informative the attitude measure is for subsequent behavior. Likewise, the more stable the attitude is over time (i.e., persistent, resistant) the more informative the attitude at initial measurement is. In response to the question, "When are attitudes most likely to guide behavior and endure over time?," Krosnick and Petty (1995) offered the proposition that attitudes could vary in their strength, with some attitudes being relatively strong and others being relatively weak. Krosnick and Petty suggested that strong attitudes, relative to weak attitudes, had the properties of being more likely to be persistent over time, more resistant to attempts to change them, and more likely to influence behaviors.

Whereas attitudes are typically thought of as evaluations with some degree of positivity or negativity (Eagly & Chaiken, 1993), attitude strength is a more multifaceted construct (Krosnick & Petty, 1995). Aspects of attitude strength include both structural properties of the attitude (e.g., accessibility, attitude-relevant knowledge), and subjective properties of the attitude (e.g., certainty, intensity, importance). For example, attitudes are more likely to be strong when they are easily accessible, based on a large amount of knowledge, are held with a high degree of certainty and intensity, and are perceived to be important to the individual. Of course, because these features are independent, attitudes might be identical on all of the features except one (e.g., certainty), but a singular difference in strength may still have observable consequences.[2]

An accumulating body of research has begun to examine factors that lead to strong attitudes. For example, research has shown that elaboration, or the amount of thinking individuals' place into forming an attitude or evaluating attitude-relevant information, can influence the strength of the attitude (Petty, Haugtvedt, & Smith, 1995). To take one pertinent study, Petty, Cacioppo, and Schumann (1983) manipulated participants' elaboration to a consumer product by manipulating the product's relevance (for a discussion of relevance and elaboration see Petty & Cacioppo, 1979; Petty & Wegener, 1999). Specifically, in the high-relevance condition participants were told the product would soon be available in their area and they would have to make a judgment about the product category, whereas in the low relevance condition, participants were told that the product would not be available in their area and they would have to make a judgment about another product category. Petty and colleagues found that attitudes were more predictive of purchase intentions under high relevance/elaboration conditions as compared to low relevance/elaboration conditions. Additional research supports the view that greater elaboration is associated with attitudes that are more predictive of behavior (Shavitt & Brock, 1986; Sivacek & Crano, 1982), more persistent over time (Haugtvedt & Strathman, 1990; Petty, Haugtvedt, Heesacker, & Cacioppo, 1995, Experiment 1), and more resistant to change (Haugtvedt & Petty, 1992; Haugtvedt & Wegener, 1994; Petty et al., 1995, Experiment 2).

Along with elaboration, one of the most studied aspects of strong attitudes is attitude certainty. For example, Rucker and Petty (2004) examined attitudes that were formed as a result of considering mainly the positives (positive attributes) of a product or considering both the negatives (negative attributes) and the positives of a product. Because the products used by Rucker and Petty were designed to be strong and contain few negatives, individuals reported equally positive attitudes regardless of whether they had considered only the positives or both the positives and the negatives of the product. However, individuals reported feeling more certain of their attitude when they had considered both the potential negatives and the positives of the product. Furthermore, the increased certainty led attitudes to be more predictive of subsequent behavior (i.e., stronger). In general, research on attitude certainty has shown that attitudes held with greater certainty tend to yield a greater influence on behavior (Fazio & Zanna, 1978; Krishnan & Smith, 1998; Tormala & Petty, 2002),

---

[2]Attitude extremity has also been discussed by some as a component of strength (Abelson, 1995). However, we limit our discussion of strength to factors that lie beyond the extremity (evaluation) itself.

persist over time (Bassili, 1996), and be resistant to attempts to change them (Swann, Pelham, & Chidester, 1988; Tormala & Petty, 2002).

Elaboration and attitude certainty are only two aspects of strong attitudes. Although these can be useful in helping a researcher decide whether attitudes might correspond to behavior, it is important to note that other strength-related features, such as the accessibility of the attitude, are also likely to have an influence (see Fazio, 1995). The particular type of attitude strength feature of interest to researchers will likely depend on the specific goals and context of their current research. Nonetheless, being cognizant of attitude strength-related features at a general level might provide insight into situations where attitudes appear not to predict behavior (i.e., the attitude is weak). For a more detailed treatment of attitude strength, the reader is referred to Petty and Krosnick (1995).

Finally, examining cognitive responses specifically, Shavitt and Brock (1986) conceptually and experimentally investigated the issue of cognitive responses in the consumer literature. According to the authors, cognitive responses (as measured by thought-listing techniques) can be categorized into several distinct categories. Some will reflect mere "message playback" (recall of product or execution). Some will be modified message arguments (variations on self, product, or execution). Finally, some will be self-originating (relevant to self, product, or execution). The authors provided a rationale to suggest that self-relevant and self-originating thoughts would be better predictors of actual purchasing intentions and behaviors. In Study 1 of Shavitt and Brock (1986), self-thoughts were shown to be better predictors of purchase intentions than were message playbacks. In Study 2, when told to focus on self-thoughts (as opposed to message playbacks), higher attitude/behavior correlations were found.

In summary, attending to the strength-related features of attitudes and thoughts can be useful in furthering our understanding of when attitudes will be predictive of behavior, and when they are likely to be stable over time. For example, when attitudes are expected to be strong, there should be a strong correspondence between attitudes and behavior; when attitudes are expected to be weak, there could be a disconnect between attitudes and behavior. Thus, especially when the goal is to make inferences about behavior, the measurement of attitudes can benefit by taking into account whether the attitudes were formed in situations conducive of strong attitudes and/or by measuring the strength of the attitude directly.

Influence of Implicit Versus Explicit Attitudes.   Consumer researchers have begun to examine the role of nonconscious influences on consumer behavior. For example, Fitzsimons and colleagues (2002) recently commented on the influence of nonconscious processes on consumer attention and perception, goal activation and pursuit, learning and memory, attitudes and preferences, affect, and choice. One type of nonconscious phenomenon of particular interest to the present chapter is the notion that individuals have implicit attitudes. Although classic research on attitudes focused primarily on attitudes that individuals explicitly reported (i.e., explicit attitudes), recent work has suggested that individuals can form and hold implicit attitudes as well (e.g., Greenwald & Banaji, 1995). These are attitudes that individuals may not be aware of and may not have access to at the conscious level.

Importantly, the existence of implicit attitudes might, in some instances, account for low correlations between explicit attitudes and behavior. Specifically, research has demonstrated that implicit and explicit attitudes can diverge, and that each can have distinctive influences on different kinds of behavior. Much of this initial work has been conducted in the domain of stereotypes and prejudice. For example, studies have shown that the majority of White people have a negative implicit association towards Blacks despite the fact that the majority of this group report very low levels of explicit prejudice (Devine, 1989; Dovidio, Kawakami, K. Johnson, D. Johnson, & Howard, 1997). Dovidio and colleagues (1997; see also Dovidio, Kawakami, & Gaertner, 2002) had White subjects interact with Blacks, and found that implicit prejudice predicted less consciously controlled behaviors (such as eye contact) whereas explicit prejudice predicted more consciously controlled behaviors (such as the content of dialogue).

The Dovidio et al. (1997) prejudice study may have relevance for advertising and consumer behavior. In contexts where individuals have no strong explicit evaluations on which to rely, implicit evaluations might jump to the forefront and influence responses. Similarly, when conscious control is likely to be low (e.g., "I am in a hurry, and I need a bottle of ketchup—any bottle"), implicit attitudes might be more predictive of behavior (see Fazio & Olson, 2003). And, as the preceding example with direct and indirect advertising was meant to demonstrate, in many cases, and for many products and services, explicit attitudes may not form because ads were not consciously processed. In these cases, implicit attitudes are likely to influence evaluative responses and behavior.

Conclusion

We have reviewed numerous factors that could lead to low correlations between any given measure of evaluation and any other measure of evaluation or behavior. Our review indicates that if a researcher or advertiser desires to make an inference about behavior, measures aside from evaluation will often be useful.

ON MEASURING BEHAVIOR

We have already discussed possible causes for the dissociation between reception and evaluation, on one hand, and behavior, on the other hand. Hence, this section concerns itself only with reasons to suspect that any two measures of behavior might not be correlated. In general, whenever measures of behavioral intent are administered, or even when actual behavior is merely observed, there is always the possibility of demand effects. Those being observed may make choices or judgments that they feel are desirable in a given situation or context.

In addition, there is a large literature on the relationship between behavioral intentions (often measured in laboratory studies and in ad pretesting) and actual behaviors (e.g., Carver & Scheier, 1990). A theme of this literature is that behavioral intent is just one of many determinants of actual behavior. For example, behavior intentions that are accompanied by implementation intentions are more likely to be realized than behaviors that are not (e.g., Brandstatter, Lengfelder, & Gollwitzer, 2001)

One relatively recent and intriguing development in the study of behavioral intentions concerns the *mere measurement effect* (e.g., Morwitz & Fitzsimons, 2004). Research in this area has shown that merely administering measures of behavioral intent makes the actual behaviors much more likely than if behavior intent had not been assessed. This research has straightforward implications for the measurement of advertising effectiveness; generalizations based on measures of behavioral intent may be unduly rosy. Research on the mere measurement effect presents another argument for the continued measurement of nonbehavioral ad effects (reception, and evaluation) that may be less likely to influence actual purchase behaviors.

We end this section by returning to a previously discussed study. Dovidio et al. (2002) found that for White participants, implicit prejudice was a better predictor of less consciously controlled behaviors (nonverbal behaviors during an interaction with a Black person), whereas explicit prejudice was a better predictor of more consciously controlled behaviors (verbal speech). Although we discussed the obvious implications that this and similar studies would have for the relationship between evaluations and behaviors, it is also interesting to note that the correlation between the more and less consciously controlled behaviors (as indicators of prejudice) was only .08, and not statistically significant. Hence, it should not be assumed that any controlled behavior will be a good predictor of a corresponding uncontrolled behavior. For example, when consumers are actively thinking about a brand of ketchup to choose, they may choose brand X. However, in situations where the decisions will be influenced more heavily by uncontrolled processes (e.g., "I'm late to pick up the kids, and I have two seconds to grab a bottle of ketchup"), brand Y may end up in the cart.

The main point of this section is that even measures of advertising effectiveness that may appear to be very direct and pure (behavioral intentions and observed behaviors in a given context) can be questioned in terms of generalizability to other types of measurements or contexts.

IMPLICATIONS AND SUGGESTIONS

We do not claim to have conducted an exhaustive review of the way that any two measures of ad effects might diverge. Instead, we intended to survey some of the more common, or at least commonly researched reasons, for divergence. In doing so, we feel confident in urging practitioners and researchers to match measurement of ad effects with the corresponding definition of ad effectiveness. That is, what is the goal of the advertising campaign: simply to create brand recognition (reception-focused), to foster positive thoughts and attitudes (evaluation-focused), or to produce a particular behavior (behavior-focused)? Although there may be situations where only one of these factors is important, the net effects of an advertising campaign or advertising effectiveness may be best understood by measuring different aspects of each factor. Thus, practitioners who are interested in the general effects of an ad on consumers would be well advised to take measures of reception, evaluation, and behavior. Relying on measures from any one of these constructs to make generalizations about any other can lead to erroneous decisions. Researchers are also encouraged to include measures from each of the three main constructs in any given program of research. We emphasize the word "program" because it may not be clearly justifiable or practical to include measures of implicit and explicit attitudes, attitude strength, attitude persistence and resistance, perceptions of validity, recall, recognition, comprehension, behavioral intent, hypothetical choice, and so forth, in each and every study. However, when a researcher does not or cannot include a particular measurement, caution should accompany the generalizability of the results (i.e., reception should not be assumed to yield positive attitudes; positive attitude should not be assumed to yield positive behavior).

Especially in the consumer behavior and marketing domains, academics often intend for their work to be used by practitioners. When practitioners turn to academics for guidance in real-life situations, they will find the work much more useful to the extent that we can make confident statements about the likely effects of our manipulations at all levels of consumer response, from reception to behavior.

REFERENCES

Abelson, R. P. (1995). Attitude extremity. In R. E. Petty & J. A. Krosnick (Eds.), *Attitude strength: Antecedents and consequences* (pp. 215–246). Mahwah, NJ: Lawrence Erlbaum Associates.

Ajzen, I. (1991). The theory of planned behavior. *Organizational Behavior and Human Decision Processes, 50,* 179–211.

Alvarez, C. X., & Brown, S. W. (2002). What people believe about memory despite the research evidence. *The General Psychologist, 37,* 1–10.

Anand, P., & Sternthal, B. (1989). Strategies for designing persuasive messages: Deductions from the resource matching hypothesis. In P. Cafferata & A. M. Tybout (Eds.), *Cognitive and affective responses to advertising* (pp. 135–157). Lexington, MA: Lexington.

Arkes, H. R., Boehm, L., & Xu, G. (1991). Determinants of judged validity. *Journal of Experimental Social Psychology, 27,* 576–605.

Bassili, J. N. (1996). Meta-judgmental versus operative indexes of psychological attributes: The case of measures of attitude strength. *Journal of Personality and Social Psychology, 71,* 637–653.

Beattie, A. E., & Mitchell, A. A. (1985). The relationship between advertising recall and persuasion: An experimental investigation. In L. F. Alwitt & A. A. Mitchell (Eds.), *Psychological processes and advertising effects: Theory, research, and applications* (pp. 129–155). Hillsdale, NJ: Lawrence Erlbaum Associates.

Biel, A. L. (1996). Do you really want to know? *Journal of Advertising: Research Currents, March/April*, RC2–RC7.

Bornstein, R. F., & D'Agostino, P. R. (1992). Stimulus recognition and the mere exposure effect. *Journal of Personality and Social Psychology, 63*, 545–552.

Brandstatter, V., Lengfelder, A., & Gollwitzer, P. M. (2001). Implementation intentions and efficient action initiation. *Journal of Personality and Social Psychology, 81*, 946–960.

Breckler, S. J. (1984). Empirical validation of affect, behavior, and cognition as distinct components of attitudes. *Journal of Personality and Social Psychology, 47*, 1191–1205.

Briñol, P., & Petty, R. E., & Tormala, Z. L. (2004). Self-validation of cognitive responses to advertisements. *Journal of Consumer Research, 30*, 559–573.

Brock, T. C. (1967). Communication discrepancy and intent to persuade as determinants of counterargument production. *Journal of Experimental Social Psychology, 3*, 296–309.

Bushman, B. J. (1998). Effects of television violence on memory for commercial messages. *Journal of Experimental Psychology: Applied, 4*, 291–307.

Bushman, B. J., & Bonacci, A. M. (2002). Violence and sex impair memory for television ads. *Journal of Applied Psychology, 87*, 557–564.

Bushman, B. J., & Phillips, C. M. (2001). If the television bleeds, memory for the advertisement recedes. *Current Directions in Psychological Science, 10*, 44–47.

Cacioppo, J. T., & Petty, R. E. (1979). Effects of message repetition and position on cognitive responses, recall, and persuasion. *Journal of Personality and Social Psychology, 37*, 97–109.

Cantor, J. R., Zillmann, D., & Bryant, J. (1975). Enhancement of experienced sexual arousal in response to erotic stimuli through misattribution of unrelated residual excitation. *Journal of Personality and Social Psychology, 32*, 69–75.

Carver, C. S., & Scheier, M. F. (1990). Principles of self-regulation: Action and emotion. In E. T. Higgins & R. M. Sorrentino (Eds.), *Handbook of motivation and cognition* (Vol. 2, pp. 3–52). New York: Guilford Press.

Chen, S., & Chaiken, S. (1998). The heuristic-systematic model in its broader context. In S. Chaiken & Y. Trope (Eds.), *Dual-process theories in social psychology* (pp. 73–96). New York: Guilford.

Devine, P. G. (1989. Stereotypes and prejudice: Their automatic and controlled components. *Journal of Personality and Social Psychology, 56*, 5–18.

Dovidio, J. F., Kawakami, K., & Gaertner, S. L. (2002). Implicit and explicit prejudice and interracial interaction. *Journal of Personality and Social Psychology, 82*, 62–68.

Dovidio, J. F., Kawakami, K., Johnson, C., Johnson, B., & Howard, A. (1997). On the nature of prejudice: Automatic and controlled processes. *Journal of Experimental Social Psychology, 33*, 510–540.

Eagly, A. H., & Chaiken, S. (1993). *The psychology of attitudes*. Fort Worth, TX: Harcourt, Brace, Jovanovich.

Fazio, R. H. (1995). Attitudes as object-evaluation associations: Determinants, consequences, and correlates of attitude accessibility. In R. E. Petty & J. A. Krosnick (Eds.), *Attitude strength: Antecedents and consequences* (pp. 247–282). Mahwah, NJ: Lawrence Erlbaum Associates.

Fazio, R. H., & Olson, M. A. (2003). Implicit measures in social cognition research: Their meaning and use. *Annual Review of Psychology, 54*, 297–327.

Fazio, R. H., & Zanna, M. P. (1978). Attitudinal qualities relating to the strength of the attitude-behavior relationship. *Journal of Experimental Social Psychology, 14*, 398–408.

Feldman, J. M., & Lynch, J. G. (1988). Self-generated validity and other effects of measurement on belief, attitude, intention, and behavior. *Journal of Applied Psychology, 73*, 421–435.

Fishbein, M. (1967). A behavior theory approach to the relations between beliefs about an object and the attitude toward the object. In M. Fishbein (Ed.), *Readings in attitude theory and measurement* (pp. 389–400). New York: Wiley.

Fishbein, M. (1980). A theory of reasoned action: Some applications and implications. In H. E. Howe & M. M. Page (Eds.), *Nebraska symposium on motivation* (Vol. 27, pp. 65–116). Lincoln: University of Nebraska Press.

Fitzsimons, G. J., Hutchinson, J. W., Williams, P., Alba, J. W., Chartrand, T. L., Huber, J., Kardes, F. R., Menon, G., Raghubir, P., Russo, J. E., Shiv, B., & Tavassoli, N. T. (2002). Non-conscious influences on consumer choice. *Marketing Letters, 13*, 269–279.

Friestad, M., & Wright, P. (1994). The persuasion knowledge model: How people cope with persuasion attempts. *Journal of Consumer Research, 21*, 1–31.

Garry, M., & Polaschek, D. L. L. (2000). Imagination and memory. *Current Directions in Psychological Science, 9*, 6–10.

Gibson, L. D. (1983). If the question is copy testing, the answer is . . . not recall. *Journal of Advertising Research, 23*, 39–46.

Greenwald, A. G. (1968). Cognitive learning, cognitive responses to persuasion, and attitude change. In A. G. Greenwald, T. C. Brock, & T. M. Ostrom (Eds.), *Psychological foundations of attitudes* (pp. 147–170). New York: Academic Press.

Greenwald, A. G., & Banaji, M. R. (1995). Implicit social cognition: Attitudes, self-esteem, and stereotypes. *Psychological Review, 102*, 4–27.

Haugtvedt, C. P., & Petty, R. E. (1992). Personality and persuasion: Need for cognition moderates the persistence and resistance of attitude changes. *Journal of Personality and Social Psychology, 63*, 308–319.

Haugtvedt, C. P., Schumann, D. W., Schneier, W. L., & Warren, W. L. (1994). Advertising repetition and variation strategies: Implications for understanding attitude strength. *Journal of Consumer Research, 21*, 176–189.

Haugtvedt, C. P., & Strathman, A. (1990). Situational personal relevance and attitude persistence. *Advances in Consumer Research, 17*, 766–769.

Haugtvedt, C. P., & Wegener, D. T. (1994). Message order effects in persuasion: An attitude strength perspective. *Journal of Consumer Research, 21*, 205–218.

Hovland, C. I., Lumsdaine, A. A., & Sheffield, F. D. (1949). *Experiments on mass communication.* Princeton, NJ: Princeton University Press.

Janisewski, C. (1988). Preconscious processing effects: The independence of attitude formation and conscious thought. *Journal of Consumer Research, 15*, 199–209.

Janisewski, C. (1993). Preattentive mere exposure effects. *Journal of Consumer Research, 20*, 367–392.

Kardes, F. R. (1986). Effects of initial product judgments on subsequent memory-based judgments. *Journal of Consumer Research, 13*, 1–11.

Krishnan, S. H., & Smith, R. E. (1998). The relative endurance of attitudes, confidence and attitude-behavior consistency: The role of information source and delay. *Journal of Consumer Psychology, 7*, 273–298.

Krosnick, J. A., & Petty, R. E. (1995). Attitude strength: An overview. In R. E. Petty & J. A. Krosnick (Eds.), *Attitude strength: Antecedents and consequences* (pp. 1–24). Mahwah, NJ: Lawrence Erlbaum Associates.

Law, S., & Hawkins, S. A. (1997). Advertising repetition and consumer beliefs: The role of source memory. In W. D. Wells (Ed.), *Measuring advertising effectiveness* (pp. 67–75). Mahwah, NJ: Lawrence Erlbaum Associates.

Loftus, E. F. (1997). Creating false memories. *Scientific American, 277*, 70–75.

Mackie, D. M., & Asuncion, A. G. (1990). On-line and memory-based modification of attitudes: Determinants of message recall-attitude change correspondence. *Journal of Personality and Social Psychology, 59*, 5–16.

McGuire, W. J. (1964). Inducing resistance to persuasion. In L. Berkowitz (Ed.), *Advances in experimental social psychology* (Vol. 1, pp. 192–229). New York: Academic Press.

McGuire, W. J. (1968). Personality and susceptibility to social influence. In E. F. Borgatta & W. W. Lambert (Eds.), *Handbook of personality theory and research* (pp. 1130–1187). Chicago: Rand McNally.

McGuire, W. J. (1969). The nature of attitudes and attitude change. In G. Lindzey & E. Aronson (Eds.), *Handbook of social psychology* (2nd ed., Vol. 3, pp. 136–314). Reading, MA: Addison-Wesley.

Moore, T. E. (1988). The case against subliminal manipulation. *Psychology and Marketing, 5,* 297–316.

Morwitz, V. G., & Fitzsimons, G. J. (2004). The mere-measurement effect: Why does measuring intentions change actual behavior? *Journal of Consumer Psychology, 14,* 64–74.

Nordhielm, C. L. (2002). The influence of level of processing on advertising repetition effects. *Journal of Consumer Research, 29,* 371–382.

Padgett, V. R., & Brock, T. C. (1988). Do advertising messages require intelligible content?: A cognitive response analysis of unintelligible persuasive messages. In S. Hecker & D. W. Stewart (Eds.), *Nonverbal communication in advertising* (pp. 185–203). Lexington, MA: Lexington Books.

Petty, R. E., Briñol, P., & Tormala, Z. L. (2002). Thought confidence as a determinant of persuasion: The self-validation hypothesis. *Journal of Personality and Social Psychology, 82,* 722–741.

Petty, R. E., & Cacioppo, J. T. (1979). Issue involvement can increase or decrease persuasion by enhancing message-relevant cognitive responses. *Journal of Personality and Social Psychology, 37,* 1915–1926.

Petty, R. E., & Cacioppo, J. T. (1986). The elaboration likelihood model of persuasion. In L. Berkowitz (Ed.), *Advances in experimental social psychology* (Vol. 19, pp. 123–205). New York: Academic Press.

Petty, R. E., Cacioppo, J. T., & Schumann, D. (1983). Central and peripheral routes to advertising effectiveness: The moderating role of involvement. *Journal of Consumer Research, 10,* 135–146.

Petty, R. E., Haugtvedt, C., Heesacker, M., & Cacioppo, J. T. (1995). *Message elaboration as a determinant of attitude strength: Persistence and resistance of persuasion.* Unpublished manuscript, Ohio State University, Columbus.

Petty, R. E., Haugtvedt, C., & Smith, S. M. (1995). Elaboration as a determinant of attitude strength: Creating attitudes that are persistent, resistant, and predictive of behavior. In R. E. Petty & J. A. Krosnick (Eds.), *Attitude strength: Antecedents and consequences* (pp. 93–130). Mahwah, NJ: Lawrence Erlbaum Associates.

Petty, R. E., & Krosnick, J. A. (Eds.). (1995). *Attitude strength: Antecedents and consequences.* Mahwah, NJ: Lawrence Erlbaum Associates.

Petty, R. E., Schumann, D. W., Richman, S. A., & Strathman, A. J. (1993). Positive mood and persuasion: Different roles for affect under high- and low-elaboration conditions. *Journal of Personality and Social Psychology, 64,* 5–20.

Petty, R. E., & Wegener, D. T. (1993). Flexible correction processes in social judgment: Correcting for context induced contrast. *Journal of Experimental Social Psychology, 29,* 137–165.

Petty, R. E., & Wegener, D. T. (1999). The elaboration likelihood model: Current status and controversies. In S. Chaiken & Y. Trope (Eds.), *Dual process theories in social psychology* (pp. 41–72). New York: Guilford Press.

Pratkanis, A. R., & Greenwald, A. G. (1988). Recent perspectives on unconscious processing: Still no marketing applications. *Psychology and Marketing, 5,* 337–353.

Rucker, D. D., & Petty, R. E. (2004). When resistance is futile: Consequences of failed counterarguing for attitude certainty. *Journal of Personality and Social Psychology, 86,* 219–235.

Schwarz, N., Groves, R. M., & Schuman, H. (1998). Survey methods. In D. T. Gilbert, S. T. Fiske, & G. Lindzey (Eds.), *The handbook of social psychology* (4th ed., Vol. 1, pp. 151–192). New York: McGraw Hill.

Shapiro, S., Heckler, S. E., & MacInnis, D. J. (1997). Measuring and assessing the impact of preattentive processing on ad and brand attitudes. In W. D. Wells (Ed.), *Measuring advertising effectiveness* (pp. 27–44). Mahwah, NJ: Lawrence Erlbaum Associates.

Shavitt, S., & Brock, T. C. (1986). Self-relevant responses in commercial persuasion: Field and experimental tests. In J. C. Olson & K. Sentis (Eds.), *Advertising and consumer psychology* (Vol. 3, pp. 149–171). New York: Praeger Publishers.

Sivacek, J., & Crano, W. D. (1982). Vested interest as a moderator of attitude-behavior consistency. *Journal of Personality and Social Psychology, 43,* 210–221.

Swann, W. B., Pelham, B. W., & Chidester, T. R. (1988). Change through paradox: Using self-verification to alter beliefs. *Journal of Personality and Social Psychology, 54,* 268–273.

Tormala, Z. L., & Petty, R. E. (2002). What doesn't kill me makes me stronger: The effects of resisting persuasion on attitude certainty. *Journal of Personality and Social Psychology, 83,* 1298–1313.

Wicker, A. W. (1969). Attitudes versus actions: The relationship of verbal and overt behavioral responses to attitude objects. *Journal of Social Issues, 25,* 41–78.

Wilson, T. D., & Brekke, N. (1994). Mental contamination and mental correction: Unwanted influences on judgments and evaluations. *Psychological Bulletin, 116,* 117–142.

Wright, P. (1980). Message-evoked thoughts: Persuasion research using thought verbalizations. *Journal of Consumer Research, 7,* 151–175.

Wright-Isak, C., Faber, R. J., & Homer, L. R. (1997). Comprehensive measurement of advertising effectiveness: Notes from the marketplace. In W. D. Wells (Ed.), *Measuring advertising effectiveness* (pp. 3–12). Mahwah, NJ: Lawrence Erlbaum Associates.

Yi, Y. (1990). Contextual priming effects in print advertisements. *Journal of Consumer Research, 17,* 215–222.

Yi, Y. (1997). Advertising effectiveness and indirect effect of advertisements. In W. D. Wells (Ed.), *Measuring advertising effectiveness* (pp. 47–63). Mahwah, NJ: Lawrence Erlbaum Associates.

Zajonc, R. B. (1968). Attitudinal effects of mere exposure. *Journal of Personality and Social Psychology, 9,* 1–27.

CHAPTER FIFTEEN

The Positive Effects of Negative Advertising: It's a Matter of Time

Ronald C. Goodstein
Georgetown University

Deborah A. Cours
California State University at Northridge

Brian K. Jorgensen
Westminster College

Jaideep Sengupta
Hong Kong University of Science and Technology

Negative advertising, once found almost exclusively in the domain of political advertising, has become increasingly prevalent in the marketing of goods and services. Although many marketing executives and consumers disavow the suitability or effectiveness of negative advertising, the deployment of this weapon is common across both political and product domains (e.g., Neff, 1999). Definitionally, negative comparative advertising (hereafter called *negative advertising*) is a form of comparative advertising. The purpose of negative advertising is to degrade perceptions of an opponent by identifying a competitor for the purpose of imputing inferiority (Merritt, 1984). For instance, a new ad for the Lincoln Towncar states, "If our car had 20% less leg room and cost $2000 more, it would be a Cadillac Eldorado." By imputing inferiority of a competitor's brand, sponsors believe their own brand will seem more attractive (Merritt, 1984). In contrast, positive comparative advertising identifies a competitor for the purpose of claiming superiority, or at least equality versus a well-established opponent (e.g., Kalra & Goodstein, 1998; Merritt, 1984).

One of the prevailing reasons for the frequent use of negative political advertising is that it has high impact under conditions of low involvement (Ansolabehere & Iyengar, 1995; Garramone, 1984). Although contingencies exist to this generalization (Faber, Tims, & Schmitt, 1993), within the realm of print ads, this finding is robust. Interestingly, product advertising has also been described as being inherently noninvolving (Krugman, 1972). Then why has it taken so long for negative comparisons to become popular in the product domain and why is there a dearth of research in this arena? (See Sorescu & Gelb, 2000, for a notable exception in the product domain.)

Merritt (1984) suggested that negative comparisons are not appropriate for products because, unlike political races, product competition involves more than two alternatives and moving consumers away from one product does not guarantee the advertiser a move toward his brand. Further, negative advertising may have adverse effects or no effects when party or brand loyalty is strong (Merritt, 1984; Sorescu & Gelb, 2000). This logic implies that negative product ads may backfire for lower share brands, but may be an effective tactic in categories dominated by two brands. Interestingly, many product categories are dominated by two brands (e.g., colas—Coke™ and Pepsi™), word processing (Microsoft™ and WordPerfect™), fast food restaurants (McDonalds™ and Burger King™), perhaps explaining the recent move by close competitors to adopt this tactic. The question remains, however, as to when and how negative comparisons offer benefits over the more traditional, positive form of comparative advertising.

BACKGROUND

Negative Political Advertising

In recent years, the tone of political advertising has become increasingly negative and hostile. In these ads, the sponsoring candidates usually sharply criticize or question their opponent's credentials, abilities, or past record (e.g., see Pinkleton, Um, & Austin, 2002). Political experts in the popular press are very succinct in their explanation of why this tactic has grown so rapidly, namely, because it works (Devlin, 1989). Academic research, however, has been equivocal with respect to the effectiveness of negative advertising in the political arena. Although some researchers support that negative ads have positive outcomes for its sponsor (e.g., Garramone, 1985), others have found that the tactic actually hurts the sponsor (Faber, Tims, & Schmitt, 1993; Hill, 1989). Those supporting the effects of negative advertising base their hypotheses on research in psychology and consumer behavior indicating that information supportive of existing beliefs is easily assimilated and stored in memory (Markus & Zajonc, 1985). Because people's schemas of politicians are generally negative, negative advertising is more effective (Ansolabehere & Iyengar, 1995). Further, negative information may be more salient to viewers who are used to seeing predominantly positive ads, and therefore, better remembered (Lau, 1985). Alternately, those disconfirming the effectiveness of negative advertising point to its backlash effects or its noneffects (e.g., Faber et al., 1993). These authors do not deny that negative advertising may be better remembered, but that the tactic can influence voting behavior in either direction. In fact, viewers are three times more likely to remember comparative political advertising than comparative product advertising (Johnson-Cartee & Copeland, 1991).

One critique directed toward much of the aforementioned research is that its effects are confined to the lab and not to the "real world" of politics. This argument is centered on two major shortcomings. First, many of the studies rely on the use of fictitious candidates and thus shed little evidence on the interplay between voters' existing information and preferences and the effectiveness of negative advertising campaigns (e.g., Pinkleton et al., 2002). Second, many of the earlier studies measured attitudes and voting intentions immediately after ad exposure, when ad salience is high although actual voting behavior is unlikely to occur immediately after ad exposure. Therefore, it is more realistic to study whether the outcomes due to ad exposure remain intact over time (Chattopadhyay & Nedungadi, 1992).

Negative Product and Services Advertising

Although comparative advertising has been a common practice since the Federal Trade Commission approved its use in 1971, negative comparisons are a more recent phenomenon. Although politicians have used this technique since the 1960s (Ansolabehere & Iyengar, 1995), its use was discouraged for product advertising. The recent growth trend may reflect the belief that the tactic is successful in the political domain although academic research on the effectiveness of negative product advertising is scarce relative to other issues in comparative advertising (e.g., Jain, 1993; James & Hensel, 1991; Shiv, Edell, & Payne, 1997).

In terms of product advertising, James and Hensel (1991) developed an elaborate conceptual model of how negative product advertising will affect consumers' processing of ad information and how it will influence the effectiveness of the advertisement. These authors attempt to extend the definition of negative advertising proposed by Merritt (1984; imputing inferiority) to the product domain. They define as negative ads which (a) employ a differentiating technique, (b) identify a single competitor, (c) are perceived as malicious by consumers, or (d) violate consumers' perceptions of fair play. In other words, not only must negative ads impute inferiority, they must also be perceived as onerous or unethical by consumers. This latter criterion does not help to narrow the concept because different consumers will have different perceptions of what is "fair" in the marketplace (Campbell, 1995) and because the Federal Trade Commission (FTC; 1987) considered disparaging advertising to be fair as long as it is truthful. Both James and Hensel (1991) and Merritt (1984) agreed, however, that the primary goal of negative advertising is to impute inferiority about a competitor's brand. Therefore, for the purposes of this chapter, we define negative advertising as product advertisements that imply that a competitive brand is inferior to the sponsor's brand.

In addition to defining negative advertising, James and Hensel (1991) developed a series of propositions related to the effects of this tactic based on a review of marketing and political studies. Included among these propositions is that negative advertising will be effective as long as it appears to be a novel technique. Additionally, they hypothesize that relative to positive comparative ads, negative ads will increase recall, elicit stronger brand evaluations, and be more effective for new brands to the market. In total, the authors develop 13 propositions to be tested in future research, but do not empirically test any of their hypotheses.

Some of these propositions are addressed in an experimental study by Jain (1993). In his research, negative comparisons are those framed as "Brand X is not OK while I am OK" and positive comparisons are framed as "You're OK, I'm more OK" (p. 310). The key dependent variable in his studies is consumers' level of counterargumentation, because it is viewed as the most important process variable affecting message acceptance (e.g., Gorn & Weinberg, 1984; Jain, 1993). Jain operationalized level of counterargumentation as the percentage of negative thoughts to total thoughts evoked in response to either ad. In the first of two scenarios, Jain investigates the effects of comparative frame, sponsor and competitor market share, and brand reputation on claim acceptance and counterargumentation. He finds that negative ads lead to lower claim acceptance and greater counterargumentation than do positive comparisons. Additionally, he finds that counterargumentation is less and claim acceptance is greater when the sponsor has a high share, regardless of the ad's frame or the comparison brand's share. Finally, neither brand's reputation influences counterargumentation or claim acceptance.

In a more recent study, Sorescu and Gelb (2000) proposed that negative ads will work better when they attack specific ad claims rather than the ad's corporate sponsor. They supported this proposition using real brands, but only when the negativity in the ad was seen as minor, versus extreme. Further, the negative ads seemed to work only for nonusers of the comparative brand, although mildly negative ads were perceived to be more believable than were positive comparisons. They offer caution in applying these results, however, as respondents felt the negative ads to be unfair and manipulative and that affected their ratings.

Finally, in the services domain, Shiv et al. (1997) examined the effects of positive versus negative message framing on ad and brand attitudes, claim beliefs, and choice. They develop different comparative ads for airlines, one positively and one negatively framed. They predict that the effectiveness of negatively framed messages will depend on the manner in which the ad is processed. When scrutinized carefully, they find that subjects are persuaded by the arguments, but that this persuasion is offset by their dislike of the negative advertising persuasion tactic. When information is reviewed in a more cursory manner, however, subjects are persuaded by the negative ad without the backlash due to the tactic. Thus they suggest that negative advertising maybe be better used in low involvement scenarios.

Although each of the studies described furthers our understanding of comparative advertising, several aspects of these studies deserve further inquiry. For example, Jain's (1993) study might be criticized for the same reasons leveled against much of the political research. Namely, he relies on the use of fictitious brands and he measures his dependent variables immediately after exposure when ad salience is unusually high. These same two issues are found in the Shiv et al. (1997) chapter. Similarly, Sorescu and Gelb (2000) did not address whether the negative perceptions of the tactic affect attitudes over time, although their study does use real brands. The issue of longer term effects is an important one because ad tactic reactions tend to fade over time, whereas brand-based cognitions do not (Chattopadhyay & Nedungadi, 1992). Thus, negative advertising might work under both processing conditions if measured at a point beyond immediate reactions.

Ad Effects Over Time

Although ad exposure and brand purchase are rarely contemporaneous, only recently have marketing researchers began to investigate systematically how delay affects the relationship between ad and brand attitudes. Chattopadhyay and Nedungadi (1992) proposed that attitude persistence is a function of the delay between exposure and attitude measurement. They find that over time memory for ad-related cognitions fade and corresponding ad attitudes dissipate as well. Memory for brand cognitions, however, remains intact over time. In terms of the present investigation, this suggests that although reactions to negative ads are initially unfavorable (Jain, 1993), these attitudes are likely to fade with time. What remains is a memory for *what* the ad said rather than *how* it was said.

Much of the political research supports that ad-related memory abates with time and brand-related memory endures. For example, Sabato (1981) suggested that the backlash from negative advertising is short-lived. That is, although negative advertising may have adverse immediate effects on the sponsor, these negative effects usually disappear within a few days (Johnson-Cartee & Copeland, 1991). People claim to hate negative techniques, and this may be reflected in immediate measurement (cf. Jain, 1993). But the negative techniques appear to work. The negative reactions to the advertising technique diminish and memory for the advertising information is remembered (e.g., Pinkleton, Um, & Austin, 2002). This data is perfectly consistent with Chattopadhyay and Nedungadi's (1992) predictions, although political researchers do not attempt a psychological explanation for their findings.

RESEARCH QUESTION

The extent to which studies involving negative political advertising can be extended to the realm of negative product advertising remains unclear. Parallels can be found for most of the relevant variables: candidates and products, incumbency and market leadership, candidate image and brand image, and so forth. Yet, political and product advertising may have important differences that prevent extension, for example, such as that political races usually involve two candidates whereas brands usually have multiple competitors (Merritt, 1984). Jaben (1992), however, stated that links between the two domains can be made directly, in that negative product advertisements are most effective in markets dominated by two brands.

Research cited earlier indicates that negative comparative advertisements for fictitious brands elicit more negative cognitive responses than do positive comparisons for these brands, thereby rendering negative product advertising a potentially ineffective technique (Jain, 1993). Yet, immediately measuring reactions to negative ads for real brands may obscure their effectiveness at changing cognitive reactions and subsequent attitudes. We believe that given the growing popularity of negative advertising in product markets, more research is warranted before dismissing this technique. This study attempts to extend prior research by examining both immediate and delayed reactions to negative product advertising for real brands. Additionally, this study tests the robustness of Chattopadhyay and Nedungadi's (1992) model by applying their theory to both positive and negative comparative ads.

Based on the background literature, we hypothesize an interaction between the effects of ad frame (positive vs. negative) and measurement condition (immediate vs. delay) on the amount of negative cognitive responses that subjects evoke in response to the ads. Specifically, we believe that under immediate conditions, subjects exposed to negative ads will elicit more negative thoughts than those exposed to positive ads, as this may seem unfair to viewers (cf. Campbell, 1995; Jain, 1993). We also expect that the amount of negative thoughts evoked in response to negative ads will decrease significantly over time (cf. Chattopadhyay & Nedungadi, 1992).

METHODOLOGY

The study employed a 2×2 between-subjects factorial design. The two factors were (1) valence of the comparison (positive or negative) and (2) delay (no delay or 1-week delay). Subjects were first-year MBA students at a major Southwestern university. At the end of a core section, the authors came to class and asked students to participate in a marketing research study. Those participating in the 20-minute study ($n = 52$) were promised a chance to win a cash prize. Telephone answering machines were used as the stimulus category because they are very pertinent to the MBA audience. The ads were sponsored by Phonemate™ and featured a comparison to Panasonic™.

Pilot Study

The pilot study was used to identify which product advertisements to include in the study. Positive and negative comparative ads were developed for each of seven different product categories (graduate admission test educators, athletic shoes, telephone answering machines, computer disks, automobiles, long-distance companies, laser printers). For each category, one of the two dominant brands compared itself to the major competitor, either claiming superiority or imputing inferiority.

Thirty-six, first-year MBA students were asked to review a set of seven ads, one from each of the product categories. (These subjects were not included in the main experiment.) They saw either a positive or a negative ad for each category. After perusing an ad, subjects were asked to complete a scale that included 8 items intended to measure the ad's frame (positive or negative). The 7-point semantic differential scales measured the extent to which the ad (a) derogated/did not derogate another brand, (b) criticized/did not criticize another brand, (c) tried to damage/enhance the reputation of another brand, (d) praised/insulted another brand, (e) claimed superiority/imputed inferiority versus another brand, (f) was positive/negative about another brand, (g) violated/did not violate a sense of fair play, (h) maliciously/mildly attacked another brand. After reverse scoring where necessary, a confirmatory factor analysis indicated that these measures successful tapped into the construct of positive versus negative framing (alpha = .89). An index was formed by adding together these measures into an overall negativity scale (range: 8 = most negative, 56 = most positive).

A simple ANOVA then identified which product advertisements were differentiated using this scale. Although none of the comparative ads were rated as positive, per se, the scale values were most significantly different for the positive and negative answering-machine ads (Positive = 29.69, Negative = 15.39; $F(15, 17) = 3.71$, $p < .01$). Therefore, these ads served as the stimuli for the main study.

Independent Variables

The two independent factors were valence of the comparison and delay. The ads were designed to look like they would appear in a magazine. The positive Phonemate ad included the following copy and follows the framing development used by Shiv et al. (1997):

> Some people don't get important calls. But, you DO get important calls, and that is why you need a PHONEMATE 4000, which is much more reliable than some of the other machines out there, like the Panasonic 850. Consumer Reports consistently rates the PHONEMATE 4000 *better* than the Panasonic 850 on features such as clarity, ease of use, number of options and durability. Why risk missing that call? PHONEMATE 4000 (Available at The Good Guys and Circuit City.)

The negative Phonemate ad included the following copy:

> Some people don't get important calls. But, you DO get important calls, and that is why you need a PHONEMATE 4000, which is much more reliable than some of the other machines out there, like the Panasonic 850. Consumer Reports consistently

rates the Panasonic 850 *worse* than the PHONEMATE 4000 on features such as clarity, ease of use, number of options and durability. Why risk missing that call? PHONEMATE 4000 (Available at The Good Guys and Circuit City.)

To manipulate delay, half of the subjects completed the dependent measures immediately after ad exposure, and half completed them 1 week after viewing the ad (cf. Chattopadhyay & Nedungadi, 1992).

Dependent Measures and Covariates

Following Jain (1993), the major dependent measure was the amount of negative thoughts generated in response to the ad. This measure was operationalized using both the number of negative thoughts and the percentage of negative thoughts. The results were identical, so only the percentage of negative thoughts is presented in this chapter. Thought coding was done using the scheme developed by Wright (1973). Because subjects were in a high-involvement situation, both counterarguments and source derogations were likely to impact attitudes (Wright, 1973) and the two were summed to form the final "negative responses" measure. Two judges (blind to condition) worked independently to determine which thoughts were negative responses. Interjudge reliability was 83% and disagreements were resolved by a third judge.

Attitudes toward the ad (A_{ad}), sponsoring brand (A_s), and comparison brand (A_c) were also measured. Finally, subjects' prior attitudes toward Phonemate answering machines (Prior A_s) and toward Panasonic answering machines (Prior A_c) were included as covariates in the study (cf. Edell & Burke, 1987). All attitudes were measured by summing responses on three 7-point scales directed toward the respective attitude and were anchored by favorable and unfavorable, likable and dislikable, good and bad (alpha > .96 in all cases).

Procedure

In each classroom, subjects were asked to review a mock-up advertisement for use in a marketing research study. For participating, they would be included in a $20 lottery. Before reviewing the ad, subjects completed a set of questions pertaining to their prior attitudes toward eight products (embedded in this set were the two brands mentioned in the ad). Next, subjects read the ad carefully and then answered questions pertaining to the ad. These questions were a guise that evaluated the ad's layout and appropriateness for the school newspaper. Then participants wrote their name on the questionnaire, handed it in, and awaited the lottery. The lottery was drawn for subjects in the "1-week delay" classes and they were thanked and dismissed. Before the drawing for subjects in the "no delay" classes, however, a second questionnaire containing the dependent measures was distributed. These subjects were given 2 minutes to list all of the thoughts and feelings they had while reviewing the ad, even those that might have appeared irrelevant (cf. Goodstein, 1993). Finally, they indicated their A_{ad}, A_s, and A_c, respectively. At this point, they placed their name on the second questionnaire, turned it in, and participated in two lotteries for $20. Subjects in the delay condition completed the dependent measures 1 week after they saw the ads. Afterward, they were included in a second $20 lottery. All subjects were debriefed before being dismissed, and none suspected the hypotheses being tested.

RESULTS

The two hypotheses were tested using an analysis of covariance model that included the independent factors and the prior attitude measures. We first predicted that under immediate conditions, more negative responses would be associated with negative ads than with positive ads. A planned comparison analysis revealed that subjects elicited a significantly lower percentage of negative responses when exposed to the negative ad than to the positive ad (Negative = .401, Positive = .738; $F(1, 51) = 4.39$, $p < .05$). This result provides strong evidence disconfirming the hypothesis and contradicts Jain's earlier finding.

Further, we predicted that the amount of negative responses evoked in response to the negative ad would decrease over time. The analysis revealed a significant valence by delay interaction ($F(1, 51) = 8.75$, $p < .005$), and planned comparisons were used to compare the cell means. The contrast indicated that subjects elicited a significantly greater percentage of negative responses to the negative ad over time (No delay = .401, One-week delay = .787; $F(1, 51) = 4.64$, $p < .05$). Again, this result is in the exact opposite direction as predicted, disconfirming the hypothesis. Interestingly, planned comparison analysis reveals that the percentage of negative responses to the positive ad decreases significantly over time (No delay = .738, One-week delay = .477; $F(1, 51) = 4.19$, $p < .05$).

Finally, we proposed that, in the case of negative comparisons, brand attitudes would increase significantly over time. First, for subjects exposed to negative ads, attitude toward the brand improved significantly over time (No delay = 3.88, One-week delay = 4.58; $F(1, 51) = 4.11$, $p < .05$). Thus the findings support the hypothesis. Hypothesis 2b stated that, after one week, the brand attitude based on the negative ad would be no different than the attitude based on the positive ad. Our analyses revealed that the two attitudes were statistically equivalent (Negative = 4.55, Positive = 3.82; $F = 1.22$, n.s.). Therefore, our hypothesis was supported by the data indicating that negative and positive ads performed equally well in terms of overall brand attitudes, though negative ads may start out at a disadvantage. No other effects were significant.

Though the initial study was encouraging, there are several limitations that are to be addressed in a second study. First, the positioning of the ads was rather subtle in their differences. Namely, the "better/worse" position may have been viewed as innocuous versus some of the more blatantly negative advertising appearing in the press. Further, hypotheses 1 was not supported in this study. Is it the case that consumers have become less reactive against negative advertising or would a stronger manipulation have replicated these earlier findings? Finally, our results were in support of attitudinal changes but not so much in terms of cognitive responses.

DISCUSSION

Negative advertising is becoming more and more popular in the marketing domain, drawing its impetus from the effectiveness of negative political advertising. Although marketing researchers have cautioned that negative advertising is limited by consumers' adverse reactions to the tactic itself (e.g., Jain, 1993; Shiv et al., 1997), our study suggests that these concerns may be an artifact of the way ad reactions are measured. We exposed subjects to either a positive or negative comparative ad for a telephone answering machine and gathered their cognitive responses and attitudes either immediately or after a 1-week delay. The results indicate that, under immediate conditions, negative versus positive comparisons evoked marginally fewer negative cognitive responses and equivalent brand attitudes. We also established that brand attitudes evoked by negative comparisons improve over time and are no different than those evoked by positive comparisons after the delay. In particular, we find that the harmful effect of negative advertising on cognitions abates over time, rendering the tactic as effective as positive comparisons. Further, because negative advertising is rather novel compared to all other ads, the tactic itself may engender greater processing due to its atypicality (Goodstein, 1993). Thus, we conclude that negative and positive comparisons appear to be equally successful in terms of ad effectiveness and this may be positive for negative advertising.

With increasing competition in the marketplace and the tightening of disposable income, more advertisers are converting to negative ad tactics to differentiate their brands from competitors' (Jaben, 1992). Several researchers have questioned the viability of this strategy, suggesting that severe backlash effects might accrue to those using negative ads (e.g., Jain, 1993; Merritt, 1984). The current investigation implies that the detrimental effects of negative advertising on sponsors dissipate over time. That is, negative comparison advertising for products appears to be as effective as positive product comparisons in terms of brand attitudes.

Before accepting this conclusion, however, it is important to point out the limitations of our study. For example, our study utilized a relatively small sample of MBA students and included only a single product. The use of MBA students viewing one ad may have encouraged high-involvement ad processing. Recent evidence, however, suggests that level of ad involvement significantly impacts the effectiveness of positive-versus-negative comparative ads (Shiv et al., 1997).

Future research should address the impact of involvement on the effects of negative comparisons over time.

Before accepting this conclusion without caveats, however, we suggest a return to the political literature in which the tactic evolved. In addition to the issue of whether negative political advertising is effective for a particular candidate, it is also important to review the effects of negative advertising on voting behavior generally. Much conjecture in the political rhetoric suggests, based on anecdotal evidence, that negative advertising leads to lower voter turnout (Pinkleton et al., 2002) and some data support this conjecture (Ansolabehere & Iyengar, 1995). Conversely, Garramone, Atkin, Pinkleton, and Cole (1990) found that although negative ads increase image discrimination and attitude polarization, they have no effect on involvement in the election, information search, or voter turnout. Experts have speculated that whether or not a negative ad harms the ad sponsor, the resulting negative affect will spread to the entire product category. In this case, although the sponsor's product may be preferred, the consumer may choose to avoid the product category altogether. Thus, the issue of whether or not negative advertising affects the market size for products and services is an interest issue that warrants additional research.

REFERENCES

Ansolabehere, S., & Iyengar, S. (1995). *Going negative: How political advertisements shrink & polarize the electorate.* New York: The Free Press.

Campbell, M. C. (1995). When attention-getting tactics elicit consumer inferences of manipulative intent: The importance of balancing benefits and investments. *Journal of Consumer Psychology, 4*(3), 225–254.

Chattopadhyay, A., & Nedungadi, P. (1992) Does attitude towards the ad endure? The moderating effects of attention and delay. *Journal of Consumer Research, 19*, 26–33.

Devlin, L. P. (1989). Contrasts in presidential campaign commercials of 1988. *American Behavioral Scientist, 32*, 407.

Edell, J. A., & Chapman Burke, M. (1987). The power of feelings in understanding advertising effects. *Journal of Consumer Research, 14*, 421–433.

Faber, R. J., Tims, A. R., & Schmitt, K. G. (1993). Negative political advertising and voting intent: The role of involvement and alternative information sources. *Journal of Advertising, 22*(4), 67–77.

Garramone, G. M. (1984). Voter responses to negative political ads. *Journalism Quarterly, 61*(2), 250–259.

Garramone, G. M. (1985). Effects of negative political advertising: The roles of sponsor and rebuttal. *Journal of Broadcasting and Electronic Media, 29*(2), 147–159.

Garramone, G. M., Atkin, C. K., Pinkleton, B. E., & Cole, R. T. (1990). Effects of negative political advertising on the political process. *Journal of Broadcasting & Electronic Media, 34*, 299–311.

Goodstein, R. C. (1993). Category-based applications and extensions in advertising: Motivating more extensive processing. *Journal of Consumer Research, 20*, 87–99.

Gorn, G. J., & Weinberg, C. B. (1984). The impact of comparative advertising on perception and attitude: Some positive findings. *Journal of Consumer Research, 11*, 719–727.

Hill, R. P. (1989). An exploration of voter responses to political advertisements. *Journal of Advertising, 18*(4), 14–22.

Jaben, J. (1992). Mud wrestling: Microsoft's ads highlight new prominence of negative marketing in business. *Business Marketing, 77*, 28–32.

Jain, S. P. (1993). Positive versus negative comparative advertising. *Marketing Letters, 4*(4), 309–320.

James, K. E., & Hensel, P. J. (1991). Negative advertising: The malicious strain of comparative advertising. *Journal of Advertising, 20*, 53–69.

Johnson-Cartee, K. S., & Copeland, G. A. (1991). *Negative political advertising: Coming of age.* Hillsdale, NJ: Lawrence Erlbaum Associates.

Kalra, A., & Goodstein, R. C. (1998). The impact of advertising positioning strategies on consumer price sensitivity. *Journal of Marketing Research, 35*, 210–224.

Krugman, H. E. (1972). Why three exposures may be enough. *Journal of Advertising, Research, 12*, 11–14.

Lau, R. R. (1985). Two explanations for negativity effects in political behavior. *American Journal of Political Science, 29*, 119–138.

Markus, H., & Zajonc, R. (1985). The cognitive perspective in social psychology. In G. Linzey & E. Aronson (Eds.), *Handbook of social psychology* (3rd ed., pp. 137–214). New York: Random House.

Merritt, S. (1984). Negative political advertising: Some empirical findings. *Journal of Advertising, 13*(3), 27–38.

Neff, J. (1999, November). Household brands counterpunch. *Advertising Age*, 26.

Pinkleton, B. E., Um, N.-H., & Austin, W. E. (2002). An exploration of the effects of negative political advertising on political decision making. *Journal of Advertising, 31*, 13–25.

Sabato, L. J. (1981). *The rise of political consultants.* New York: Basic Books.

Shiv, B., Edell, J. A., & Payne, J. W. (1997). Factors affecting the impact of negatively and positively framed ad messages. *Journal of Consumer Research, 24*, 285–294.

Sorescu, A. B., & Gelb, B. D. (2000). Negative comparative advertising: Evidence favoring fine-tuning. *Journal of Advertising, 29*, 25–40.

Wright, P. L. (1973). The cognitive processes mediating the acceptance of advertising. *Journal of Marketing Research, 10*, 52–63.

CHAPTER SIXTEEN

When "What Might Have Been" Leads to What Isn't Best: Dysfunctional Counterfactual Thinking in Consumer Affect and Cognition

Sukki Yoon
Patrick T. Vargas
University of Illinois at Urbana-Champaign

Imagine two consumers, Mary and Kathy, filling up their respective gas tanks at a gas station in Chicago. Mary is delighted to learn that she pays $1.40 per gallon. On the other hand, Kathy feels upset when she learns that she has to pay $1.40 per gallon. What causes this emotional imbalance between these two people? Mary lives in Chicago where gas prices are usually higher, whereas Kathy happens to stop at this gas station while traveling from a small town, where gasoline costs less. One explanation for Mary's happiness and Kathy's disappointment derives from two types of thoughts that are likely to run through their minds. First, neither expected this price. Second, Mary and Kathy used different standards when evaluating the price: Mary compared the price with the average price in Chicago, which is normally higher than $1.40, whereas Kathy compared the price with the one in her hometown, which is normally lower than $1.40. That is, Kathy's unhappy feeling, instigated by the unexpected high price of gas, may have been intensified by her imagining an alternative counterfactual situation (i.e., "What if I had filled up back at home?"). Conversely, Mary's happy feeling may have been heightened by her imagining an alternative counterfactual situation (i.e., "What if I had filled up yesterday?"). This kind of "what if" thinking—the process of imagining alternatives to reality, or of comparing "what is" with "what might have been"—is what social psychologists refer to as *counterfactual thinking*.

Counterfactual thinking, along with reality, impacts consumers' behaviors, thoughts, and feelings. Previous research has demonstrated that both the presence and the direction of counterfactual thinking amplify satisfaction and regret (Medvec, Madey, & Gilovich, 1995; Medvec & Savitsky, 1997; Roese, 1994). As seen in the aforementioned scenario, for example, a consumer's counterfactual thinking, often initiated by a negative emotional experience (Roese, 1997), can magnify the individual's emotional status (Kahneman & Miller, 1986); it can exacerbate negative feelings or it can boost happy feelings. Like Mary in the example, downward counterfactual thinking (i.e., thinking about how a purchase outcome could have been worse) may help consumers feel better, whereas Kathy's upward counterfactual thinking (i.e., thinking about how a purchase outcome could have been better) can lead to negative affective consequences. Furthermore, evidence in social cognition research suggests that counterfactual thinking also plays a central role in judgment formation (e.g., Miller, Turnbull, & McFarland, 1989) and behavior (Roese, 1994).

People tend to make judgments on the basis of the ease with which they can imagine or mentally simulate an event rather than on the basis of its a priori probability. For example, people believe that the selection of a chocolate chip cookie from a jar containing one chocolate chip cookie and 19 oatmeal cookies is less likely than selecting a chocolate chip cookie from a jar holding 10 chocolate chip cookies and 190 oatmeal cookies (Miller et al., 1989). Of course, the objective likelihood of selecting a chocolate chip cookie by chance is identical in both conditions (5.3%). In terms of behavioral consequences, Roese (1994) found that the generation of upward counterfactual thoughts (i.e., imagining a better alternative counterfactual situation) following a failure in an anagram task led to intentions to perform success-facilitating behaviors and, indeed, to actual behavioral improvement in a subsequent task.

Regardless of the close connection between counterfactual thinking and affect, cognition, and behavior, all of which are considered important variables in consumer research, few have looked into the role of counterfactual thinking in the context of consumer-focused strategy. The main thesis of this chapter can be summarized in one question: How does counterfactual thinking influence consumers' perceptions and assessments of various promotional activities such as pricing and advertising? To answer this question, we begin by reviewing social psychological research on counterfactual thinking. Then we describe four experiments that look into the role of counterfactual thinking in a consumer-behavior context. Finally, we speculate on how the notion of counterfactual thinking aids our understanding of consumer cognition and action.

COUNTERFACTUAL THINKING IN CONSUMER RESEARCH

Counterfactual thinking is the mental process of thinking about the unrealized alternative version of a past or present outcome, which typically takes the form of a conditional statement (e.g., "If I had bought Brand B instead of Brand A, I would have paid less"). By engaging in counterfactual thinking, an individual mutates, or alters, the actual outcome (Kahneman & Miller, 1986). During the process of counterfactual thinking, an individual first considers what could have been the alternative outcome (e.g., paying less), and assesses how the alternative counter-factual outcome could have been achieved by mutating the factual outcome (e.g., "If only I had known Brand B was on sale"). The two-stage nature of this process facilitates comparisons with causal attribution; in counterfactual thinking, the perceived antecedents are mentally altered to undo the given outcome and achieve the counterfactual outcome.

One critical variable that influences counterfactual generation is the perceived closeness of an outcome to a more or less desired, alternative outcome. "Near misses" make counterfactual thinking highly available, and the availability of close counterfactual thinking is known to influence affect dramatically. For example, Kahneman and Tversky (1982) showed that having missed one's plane by 5 minutes is more disappointing than having missed it by 30 minutes.

Counterfactual thinking has its own structure and direction. Although a variety of terms have been used to describe its structure (e.g., action/inaction, Kahneman & Miller, 1986; commission/omission, Kahneman & Tversky, 1982; and addition/subtraction, Roese & Olson, 1993), counterfactual thinking either alters a previous action or a previous inaction. A person may engage in the fundamentally same, but superficially different, counterfactual thinking. For example, having only two alternatives of store choices, Store A and Store B, one might think, "If I had not shopped at Store A yesterday, I would have saved 10 dollars," or equivalently, "If I had shopped at Store B yesterday, I would have saved 10 dollars." The former is an example of subtractive counterfactual thinking (i.e., altering action), whereas the latter is an example of additive counterfactual thinking (i.e., altering inaction). Although both successful and unsuccessful outcomes can be undone either subtractively or additively, people tend to generate additive counterfactuals after failure but subtractive counterfactuals after success. That is, people typically remove a successful action to undo a success, but add an action to undo a failure (Roese & Olson, 1993). Similarly, consumers may mentally alter inaction more often than action following a poor consumption experience.

One may imagine a better alternative (upward counterfactuals) after failure or a worse alternative after success (downward counterfactuals). In upward counterfactual thinking, a consumer might think, "If I had shopped at Store B yesterday, I would have saved 10 dollars," but in downward counterfactual thinking, she or he might think, "If I had shopped at Store A yesterday, I would have wasted 10 dollars." Although the structure of counterfactual thinking is directly tied to the antecedent of the counterfactual statements ("if . . . had done/undone . . ."), the direction of counterfactual thinking is deeply linked to the outcome of the counterfactuals ("then . . . would have been better/worse . . .").

Previous literature in marketing has addressed the issue of counterfactual thinking in terms of the *expectancy disconfirmation model*, which suggests that marketers can satisfy their customers by improving the perceived performance of their products and by keeping consumers from setting unreasonably high levels of expectation (Iacobucci, Grayson, & Ostrom, 1994; Phillips, 2002; Yi, 1990).

Within the framework of counterfactual thinking, a large discrepancy between a high level of expectation and a low level of perceived performance evoke the abnormality of one's consumption outcome and subsequent counterfactual thinking.

While the expectancy-consistency model exclusively deals with the confirmation of one's expectations about the chosen item, Taylor (1997) included the expectations about unchosen options as an additional variable that affects consumer satisfaction. Prediction of consumer satisfaction was enhanced when participants reported both prior expectations about the last movie they saw as well as expectations about other alternatives they considered. Specifically, expectations about the forgone alternative were inversely related to satisfaction when the choice failed to meet expectations, but had no impact when the choice met expectations. In addition, Houston, Sherman, and Baker (1991) varied the type of choice sets and showed that the greatest satisfaction came when the chosen brand contained good features not shared by the rejected brand, suggesting that expectations about unchosen alternatives are an important component of consumer satisfaction.

In a similar vein, Inman, Dyer, and Jia (1997) asked participants to make choices between successive lottery pairs, gave them outcome feedback on the chosen and unchosen alternative in each lottery pair, and asked them to evaluate their decisions. Participants evaluated their decisions more harshly when the forgone alternative's outcome was better than their decision. Inman et al. (1997) further showed the asymmetric effects of disappointment (i.e., "the psychological state induced by comparing an outcome to an expected outcome"; p. 99) and regret (i.e., "the psychological state induced by comparing an outcome to the outcome of a forgone alternative"; p. 99): negative effects of disappointment and regret were greater than the positive effects of elation and rejoicing. Tsiros (1998) expanded Inman et al.'s (1997) findings to choice sets with more than two alternatives, and showed that when the outcome is positive, people choose the best-performing forgone alternative as a reference point for comparison, but when the outcome is negative, people choose the worst-performing forgone alternative as a reference point for comparison. Thus, just as people tend to compare themselves against similar others in social comparison (Festinger, 1954; Zanna, Goethals, & Hill, 1975), consumers base their comparison on the unchosen alternative that is most similar to their chosen alternative.

Along with counterfactual thinking, the role of *prefactual thinking* (i.e., imagining future or before-the-act possible states) and anticipated regret in advertising messages has been examined in various contexts (Hetts, Boninger, Armor, Gleicher, & Nathanson, 2000; McConnell et al., 2000). McConnell et al. (2000) had participants make a comparison between the satisfaction level of a protagonist who learned that the store would refund the price difference if a customer finds the same product advertised for less money within 30 days of purchase, and the satisfaction level of another protagonist who did not learn about the price guarantee. McConnell et al. (2000) concluded that the awareness of the price guarantee resulted in reduced anticipated regret, reduced anxiety, and greater satisfaction than not having a price guarantee available. Hetts et al. (2000) explored the impact of anticipated counter-factual regret on insurance decisions. Participants played a computer game, the object of which was to move a treasure along a path laden with obstacles. Participants initially given a $10 treasure had the opportunity to spend part of their treasure to buy insurance. Anticipated counterfactual regret was manipulated: Participants read either "If you don't get insurance and you lose all of your money, you will end up really wishing you had gotten the insurance"; or, "If you spend money to get insurance and then never use it, you will end up really wishing you had never gotten insurance." It was found that participants in the former condition were on average willing to pay higher premiums than participants in the latter condition. McConnell et al. (2000) and Hetts et al.'s (2000) findings together suggested that the study of counterfactual thinking is important for understanding how consumers evaluate advertising messages.

In the studies of counterfactual thinking in the marketing literature, anticipated outcome, not actual outcome, was normally viewed as the anchor for evaluation. The underlying assumption appears to be that consumers form initial evaluations based on the discrepancy between anticipated and actual outcomes and subsequently make adjustments based on the discrepancy between chosen and forgone outcomes. However, these models do not account for counterfactual thinking simply caused by the perceived closeness of an outcome. For example, a swimmer who has virtually no expectation of winning any kind of medal, but ends up winning the silver medal by a .001 second difference from the gold medalist, may still generate thoughts of almost winning the gold medal, and consequently suffer from feelings of disappointment and regret. In this case, it is not that the anticipated outcome was adjusted, but that the anchor (factual outcome) was constructed ad hoc. Thus, a full treatment of counterfactual thinking cannot be completely subsumed within extant theories of expectancy disconfirmation and regret. In addition, the influence of forgone alternatives has been limited to choice-behavior in previous consumer research, leaving open the issue of the generalizability of the results to other domains of consumer behaviors such as pricing and advertising. Lastly, we know of no studies that have compared the condition in which there is an anchor (i.e., forgone outcomes) and the one in which there is no such an anchor (i.e., no forgone outcome). Consumers are likely to use different types of decision-making frameworks in each condition as suggested in this chapter. Before addressing these issues, we first consider how and why consumers generate counterfactual thoughts, and what psychological and behavioral consequences it brings to consumers.

MECHANISMS AND CONSEQUENCES
OF COUNTERFACTUAL THINKING

Roese (1997) suggested that all counterfactual consequences are rooted in either of two underlying mechanisms: *contrast effects* or *causal inferences*. Contrast effects occur when the counterfactual alternative is salient, and therefore becomes more accessible. When a better alternative counterfactual outcome is salient (i.e., upward counterfactual thinking), a factual outcome is judged to be worse. But if a worse alternative outcome is more salient (i.e., downward counterfactual thinking), then a given outcome is likely to be judged to be better. In the gas station example used to open this chapter, the gasoline price is perceived to be more expensive by contrast if one has traveled from a town where gasoline is cheaper.

Norm theory provides a theoretical framework for this contrast effect. Kahneman and Miller (1986) proposed that the outcome is viewed as normal if it is close to one's norm or standard, but abnormal if the factual outcome differs from a given norm. The greater the perceived difference that exists between the factual outcome and the norm, the more abnormality is noticed, and the more counterfactual thinking is available to the individual. Because the main driving force of contrast effects is the salience or abnormality of the event, contrast-driven counterfactual thinking may be viewed as an automatic process with little emphasis on causality between a counterfactual antecedent (e.g., "If I had . . .") and a counterfactual outcome (e.g., "I would have . . ."). The salience of the alternative outcome via closeness or surprise is a sufficient condition for a contrast effect to occur.[1]

Causal inferences may also entail more effortful processing, in which causal linkage between the antecedent and the outcome within the counterfactual statement is crucial.[2] Unlike contrast effects, it is necessary for both the counterfactual antecedent and the counterfactual outcome to be salient in order for the causal inference mechanism to operate. The central notion of causal inferences is that a counterfactual statement is closely connected to the true state of an event. That is, an individual thinking, "If A had not happened, then B would not have happened," is a reference to the causal linkage between A and B (i.e., "A causes B"). For example, a consumer's counterfactual statement, "If I had not bought an extended warranty for the digital camera I bought last year, I would have spent more money to fix it today" essentially reflects his or her thinking, "Buying an extended warranty leads to saving money." In terms of the various effects demonstrated in the counterfactual literature, adverse affective consequences are often produced by the contrast-effect mechanism, whereas the causal-inference mechanism brings beneficial effects (Roese, 1997).

Why do people engage in counterfactual thinking? What is its behavioral consequence? Counterfactual thinking is frequently initiated by people's needs to predict and control future events (Roese & Olson, 1995). As attribution theorists and functionalists alike may argue, counterfactual thinking may play a significant

---

[1]This may appear to be contradictory, in that the near miss causes more affect than the distant miss in Kahneman and Tversky's (1982) findings presented in the previous section. However, the default norm under such circumstances is missing or attaining counterfactual alternatives by distance, not by closeness. Thus, missing the plane by 5 minutes is more abnormal than by missing it by 30 minutes.

[2]Causal attribution can also be automatic with little or no effortful processing (e.g., Gilbert & Malone, 1995).

role in helping an individual to understand what factors give rise to a certain outcome, to predict how and when the event will happen again, and to avoid (replicate) negative (positive) outcomes next time. Thus, counterfactual thinking is important preparation for the future. Evidence suggests that counterfactual thinking brings largely positive behavioral consequences to individuals.[3] For example, counterfactual thinking can serve the function of preparing for future improvement. Roese (1994) found that generation of upward counterfactual thoughts following a failure led to behavioral improvement in a subsequent task. A preparative function served by upward counterfactual thinking may be analogous to the one served by upward comparison in the social comparison literature (Taylor & Lobel, 1989). As an individual makes a comparison with someone who is better off than oneself for an improvement, a consumer may imagine a counterfactual situation that is better than the factual one for the same reason.

A number of studies have looked at positive and negative consequences of counterfactual thinking. Markman, Gavanski, Sherman, and McMullen (1993) found that in a gambling study, subjects who lost their money or expected to play the game again made more upward and fewer downward counterfactuals than those who won or who did not expect to play again, suggesting that upward counterfactuals provide superior alternate realities that allow for future improvement, whereas downward counterfactuals provide inferior alternate realities that offer compensatory affective reactions. In general, a downward counterfactual may bring about immediate feelings of satisfaction at the expense of preparation for the future, but upward and downward counterfactuals trade off immediate affect and preparation for the future. This trade-off is sensible, however, since the net effect of counterfactual thinking is beneficial (Roese, 1997). In sum, studies done in this area indicate that counterfactual thinking generally serves positive behavioral functions, although it is sometimes accompanied by negative affective consequences.

Of course, the causal inference process is not error-free because in some situations there are too many or too few counterfactual alternatives available. In order to establish valid causation, one needs to satisfy three necessary conditions: temporal precedence, covariation, and internal validity (Rosnow & Rosenthal, 1999). When a counterfactual simulation is run in one's head, the temporal precedence is obviously established because counterfactual thinking, by definition, is a post-hoc process. However, it is sometimes difficult to detect the other two necessary conditions. A *counterfactual antecedent* is nothing but an imagined cause of an alternative outcome, which is not necessarily the real cause. This limited capability of identifying the real cause of the outcome—whether factual or counterfactual—places a restriction on the practical utility of counterfactual thinking; one's imagi-

---

[3]Some negative effects may occur, also. Davis, Lehman, Wortman, Silver, and Thompson (1995) showed, for example, that counterfactual thinking is known to have detrimental consequences with nonrepetitive traumatic life events such as the unexpected death of an infant.

nation of undoing of the factual outcome may not lead to behavioral improvement in the future. It is not only difficult for an individual to come up with a counterfactual that "truly" undoes the factual outcome, but also, in some cases, there is no counterfactual alternative available that undoes the factual outcome. For example, a high-school graduate who failed to be admitted by the university she wished to attend might engage in counterfactual thinking such as "If only I had studied harder" that may not undo the factual outcome. Regardless of its imperfection, however, behavioral consequences of counterfactual thinking overall brings more gains than losses through the causal inference mechanism in the long run—counterfactual thinking generally helps us to be better off.

Some evidence indirectly and directly supports the claim that, in terms of behavioral improvement, what we gain through counterfactual thinking is far greater than what we lose. As already discussed, negative outcomes are more likely to generate more counterfactuals than positive outcomes (e.g., Gavanski & Wells, 1989). A higher frequency of upward counterfactuals represents a higher frequency of the preparative function of upward counterfactual thinking. Roese (1994) further demonstrated the beneficial consequences of counterfactual thinking by showing that people strategically use downward counterfactual thinking to make themselves feel better and upward counterfactual thinking to improve future performance; when people expect to perform a similar task in the near future, they deliberately engage in upward counterfactual thinking to prepare for the future even if they had a positive outcome.

The present section reviewed previous research suggesting that counterfactual thinking helps consumers think about how negative outcomes could have been avoided in the past and how future outcomes might be improved. Now that we have compared the two mechanisms underlying counterfactual thinking, both of which play important roles in consumer satisfaction, we turn to a discussion of some research relevant to the contrast effect and the causal inference mechanism. We first look at the contrast effect in the next section by presenting research that demonstrates that consumer satisfaction varies depending on whether advertising messages evoke counterfactual thinking.

THE FURNITURE SHOPPING STUDY

Consumers attempt to gather all the relevant information to arrive at the most logical conclusion, but at the same time, they also want to be efficient thinkers due to their limited capacity to process information. This basic human characteristic requires consumers to rely on the frequent use of heuristic cues that generally help reduce their cognitive loads in a given market environment. Nevertheless, heuristic processing sometimes leads to erroneous conclusions because consumers often face a trade-off between efficiency and accuracy. For example, deals with restrictions (e.g., "limit three per customer") are found to increase product sales more than the same deals without such restrictions (Inman, Peter, & Raghubir, 1997).

The pricing tactic used in Inman et al.'s (1997) study can be termed the *maximum purchase limit*, in which customers are not allowed to purchase or spend more than a given maximum amount to receive a discount. Effects of maximum purchase limits on sales have been found to be robust (Lessne & Notarantonio, 1988; Wansink, Kent, & Hoch, 1998), yet scholars provide different theoretical explanations for the effect. Although Inman et al. (1997) attributed the effect to perceived scarcity (see also Brannon & Brock, 2001; Lynn, 1992; Verhallen & Robben, 1994), Lessne and Notarantonio (1988) adopted *reactance theory*, which suggests that when a consumer's freedom to engage in a specific purchasing behavior is threatened, the threatened behavior becomes more attractive. Somewhat different from the motivational stance taken by Inman et al. (1997) and Lessne and Notarantonio (1988), Wansink et al. (1998) took on a more cognitive approach: Wansink et al. (1988) argued that an anchoring and adjustment model adequately describes the effect of the maximum purchase limit on increased purchase quantity. In a field study, Wansink et al. (1998) compared three different levels of maximum purchase limits ("no limit per person," "limit of four per person," or "limit of 12 per person") and observed increased sales volume of the product (Campbell's™ soups) with higher limits. Wansink et al. (1998) explained that maximum purchase limits provide consumers with an anchor from which they insufficiently adjust downward.

Conversely, another common type of message framing is the *minimum purchase requirement*, which requires customers to purchase more than a certain minimum amount of products, or to spend more than a proposed dollar amount, as a qualification for a discount (e.g., "Buy two, get one free" or "Spend $100, get 20% off"). Although conventional wisdom suggests that the use of minimum purchase requirement facilitates sales, few have closely looked into this variable in controlled lab settings. In the research described in the present section, the minimum purchase requirement is regarded as a marketing tool that potentially induces the generation of counterfactual thoughts, producing polarized consumer satisfaction and biased assessments of consumers' buying decisions.

One common objective of the retailers offering a minimum purchase requirement is to increase sales volume. Consumers buy a greater amount, but in return, they obtain a superior value. This deal-seeking behavior (i.e., getting more for the same price or paying less for the same amount) is apparently a rational choice. However, the presence of a minimum purchase requirement in a promotional message may draw a consumer's attention to the requirement itself to a great extent, compelling an individual to use the minimum purchase requirement as a reference point for evaluating one's purchase outcome; when faced with the minimum purchase requirement, consumers' assessment about their shopping performance is likely to be based on whether they attain the requirement. That is, individuals exposed to a minimum purchase requirement promotions are likely to rely on a success–failure framework (i.e., extremely positive and negative reaction for success and failure, respectively), whereas those who view a promotion without such a requirement are likely to use a continuous framework (i.e., the greater the discount, the more positive the reaction). Therefore, the presence or absence of a minimum purchase requirement may bring about a situation where consumers who receive a smaller discount and thus pay more exhibit a higher level of satisfaction than those who receive a greater discount and thus pay less. Of course, not having a minimum purchase requirement (e.g., "30% off all purchases") rather than having one (e.g., "Spend $100, get 30% off") is objectively a better deal for consumers because there is no restriction in the former case.

In order to observe such effects, we created two slightly different versions of a shopping scenario. Participants in both conditions first read an introduction that instructed them to imagine a person who goes shopping for some furniture with a shopping list. Next, in the minimum purchase requirement version, the protagonist encounters the promotional message with a requirement ("25% off all purchases if you spend at least $200"); in the no-minimum purchase requirement version, the protagonist encounters the promotional message without a requirement ("30% off all purchases"). As the scenario unfolds, the protagonist adheres to the shopping list, picks up only those items that appear on the shopping list, and later learns at the checkout counter that the amount he or she has spent turns out to be $201.86. The protagonist in the minimum-purchase-requirement scenario pays $151.39 after taking off 25%, whereas the protagonist in the no-minimum purchase requirement scenario pays $141.30 after taking off 30%. The scenario was created such that the protagonist in the requirement condition pays more ($151.39) than the one in the no-requirement condition ($141.30). If consumers were wholly rational, they should feel happier when they pay less for the same set of products. However, we hypothesized that the presence of the minimum purchase requirement prompts them to generate downward counterfactual thinking (e.g., "I could have paid more, but I did not"), boosting their affective and attitudinal reactions. As expected, participants in the minimum purchase requirement condition indeed significantly felt happier, although they paid more ($151.39), than those in the no-minimum purchase requirement condition ($141.30), but, contrary to our expectation, their attitudes toward the deal did not significantly differ. We explain this affective-attitudinal discrepancy shortly.

In another experiment, we examined whether upward counterfactual thinking has a similar effect in the opposite direction. Participants read the same scenario from the first experiment except that they were exposed to a different advertising message. In the minimum purchase requirement version, the message is framed as "30% off all purchases if you spend below $2,000, but 40% off if you spend $2,000 or more"; in the no-minimum purchase requirement version it is framed as "20% off all purchases." Contrary to the first experiment, in the present scenario the protagonist in the requirement condition objectively pays less ($1,398.79 after 30% off) than the one in the no-requirement condition ($1,598.62 after 20% off).

However, the presence of upward counterfactual thinking (e.g., "I could have received a greater discount, but I did not") was hypothesized to increase their negative affective and attitudinal reactions. Consistent with our prediction, participants in the minimum purchase requirement condition reported feeling worse, although they paid less ($1,398.79), than their counterparts in the no-minimum purchase requirement condition ($1,598.62). Participants in the minimum purchase requirement condition also displayed a more negative attitude toward the deal.

Why did only upward (Study 2), but not downward (Study 1), counterfactual thinking have a significant influence on attitude toward the deal, even though affect was influenced by both types of counterfactual thoughts? This is perhaps in part because the impact of downward counterfactuals is not sufficiently strong to generate observable effects on attitude measures. It is often suggested in the literature that the psychological impact of loss is greater than that of an equivalent gain (Kahneman & Tversky, 1979). Compared to positive outcomes, negative outcomes may recruit more directed cognition. As functionalists argue, negative outcomes are acute, signifying a problematic state of affairs that must be rectified instantly, thereby producing behavioral changes to improve future performance, whereas acquisition of gratifying stimuli is chronic, thus occupying the bulk of the consumer's time against a backdrop of essentially neutral outcomes (Roese & Olson, 1995). Further evidence indirectly supports this claim: Negative outcomes produce quicker decision making (Isen & Means, 1983), more complex, systematic information processing (Schwarz, 1990), and more intense thinking (Bohner, Bless, Schwarz, & Strack, 1988; Hastie, 1984; Weiner, 1985). Consistent with this reasoning, some theorists argue that counterfactual thinking is more likely to follow negative outcomes than positive outcomes (e.g., Gavanski & Wells, 1989; Landman, 1987), providing a partial explanation for our findings of the imbalanced impact of upward and downward counterfactual thinking on participants' attitudes.

THE ONLINE SHOPPING STUDY

We believed that the satisfaction reversal found in the furniture shopping study was mainly caused by perceived closeness to counterfactual alternatives. That is, the quantitative dollar amount landing in close proximity to the given minimum purchase requirement compelled participants to think about better or worse worlds, which in turn led to the exaggerated feeling of pleasure or disappointment. However, the contrast between factual and counterfactual alternatives should be perceived less vividly if one's factual outcomes are distanced from a given cutoff point. For example, Medvec and Savitsky (1997) demonstrated that those who just missed a higher letter grade on an exam with a marginal difference (e.g., receiving a B with a score of 89) expressed stronger dissatisfaction than those who completely missed it (e.g., receiving a B with a score of 86), whereas barely making a particular category (e.g., receiving an A with a score of 91) is associated with more heightened satisfaction than entirely making it (e.g., receiving an A with a score 97).

Following Medvec and Savitsky's (1997) findings, we attempted to demonstrate that the strength of counterfactual effects on consumer affect would deteriorate as one's purchase outcome moves away from a given minimum purchase requirement. That is, barely making it to the minimum purchase requirement or just missing it was anticipated to yield more dramatic affective effects than completely making it or entirely missing it.

In order to capture a realistic shopping environment and to extend previous findings to online-shopping contexts, we created a mock Web site that resembles an actual Internet retailer (Fig. 16.1). Participants were asked to behave as if they were shopping at the Web site of a Christmas gift store that was offering a special promotion. Participants first read the rules about the gamelike promotion that was given in detail throughout the Web page: Participants were told that they would (a) consecutively see four separate categories of Christmas gifts: books, electronics, apparel, and shoes; (b) see three items in each category without price information; (c) have to guess the prices of those items in each category and select only

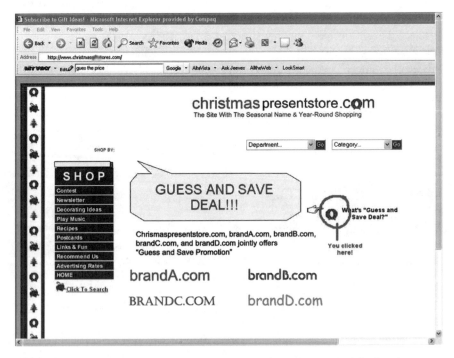

FIG. 16.1.   The Web site used in the online shopping study. Note: existing brands were used in the original experiment.

one item they intend to purchase; and finally (d) receive a certain amount of discount only if they made it to the proposed minimum purchase requirement.

Two variables were manipulated: counterfactual direction and outcome closeness to the minimum purchase requirement. First, the outcome was described as either success for downward counterfactuals (meeting the requirement and receiving a discount) or a failure for upward counterfactuals (not meeting the requirement so a smaller amount of discount). Second, the minimum purchase requirements for the discounts were altered so that participants were led to believe that they either nearly or entirely missed or made the minimum purchase requirement either for the higher or lower level of discount (the examples of the nearly-missing condition and the nearly-making condition are given in Fig. 16.2).

In addition, in order to show that the impact of downward counterfactual thinking is sufficiently stronger than upward counterfactual thinking to make a satisfaction reversal (i.e., the more money paid, the happier feelings felt), we deliberately altered the amount paid. As can be seen in Table 16.1, (a) the amounts paid

Total amount of $ for the 4 items you purchased is as follows

Congratulations!

brandA.com
brandB.com
BRANDC.COM
brandD.com

- Item 1: $17.89
- Item 2: $86.32
- Item 3: $78.42
- Item 4: $67.46

- You spent more than $250 dollars, so you get 25% off!

- You spent: $250.09

christmas presentstore.com
The Site With The Seasonal Name & Year-Round Shopping

- Total: $ 250.09

- You pay: $187.57

Nearly-making-it condition followed by a close downward counterfactual thinking

Total amount of $ for the 4 items you purchased is as follows

We are sorry!

brandA.com
brandB.com
BRANDC.COM
brandD.com

- Item 1: $17.89
- Item 2: $86.32
- Item 3: $78.42
- Item 4: $67.28

- You spent less than $250 dollars, so you don't get 45% off!
  (but, you still get 35% off)

- You spent: $249.02

christmas presentstore.com
The Site With The Seasonal Name & Year-Round Shopping

- Total: $ 249.91

- You pay: $162.44

Nearly-missing-it condition followed by a close upward counterfactual thinking

FIG. 16.2. Nearly-making/missing-it conditions followed by a close downward/upward counterfactual thinking.

TABLE 16.1
Experimental Conditions

	Upward (Missed it)	Downward (Made it)
Close (Nearly)	If $250 or more, 45%, otherwise 35% off $249.97 ($162.44)	If $250 or more, 25% off $250.09 ($187.57)
Far (Entirely)	If $270 or more, 40%, otherwise 30% off $249.97 ($174.94)	If $230 or more, 30% off $250.09 ($175.06)

Note. The amount spent (the actual amount paid after receiving a discount).

in the downward (made-it) conditions were manipulated to be greater than those in the upward (missed-it) conditions; (b) the amount paid in the close-upward (nearly-missed-it) condition is less than the amount paid in the far-upward (entirely missed-it) condition; and (c) the amount paid in the close-downward condition (nearly made-it) is greater than the amount paid in the far-downward (entirely made-it) condition. Accordingly, we hypothesized that upward counterfactual thinking participants were expected to feel worse than downward counterfactual thinking participants, but this effect should be moderated by distance such that near participants should have more intense feelings than far participants.

This is what we found: (a) participants who paid more in downward counterfactual thinking felt happier than their counterparts in upward counterfactual thinking; (b) downward counterfactual-thinking participants nearly attaining the minimum purchase requirement displayed higher satisfaction, although paying more ($174.44 vs. $162.44) than those who had entirely made the requirement; and (c) upward counterfactual thinking participants nearly missing the requirement displayed lower satisfaction, although paying less ($175.96 vs. $187.57) than those who entirely missed the requirement. That is, participants who paid most ($187.57) exhibited the most satisfaction, whereas those who paid least ($162.44) displayed the least satisfaction.

THE TEXTBOOK SHOPPING STUDY

The research described in the previous two sections shows how promotional framings can cause counterfactual thinking to inflate and deflate consumers' feelings and attitudes. In this section, we present research that examines whether counterfactual thinking in a shopping context influences another type of cognition: the attribution style, and the perceived likelihood of the same event happening in the future.

The influence of counterfactual thinking on causal judgment has been demonstrated by Wells and Gavanski (1989); people attribute greater causal significance to an event if its counterfactual default alternative would have yielded a different outcome than if the default alternative yielded the same outcome. In Wells and Gavnaski's (1989) first experiment, participants read a scenario in which a woman died from an allergic reaction to a meal ordered by her boss. When the boss was described as having considered another meal without the allergic ingredient, people were more likely to mutate his decision, and his causal role in the death was judged to be greater than when the alternative meal was also said to have the allergic ingredient. In conceptually similar work, Branscombe and Weir (1992) found that too much resistance on the part of a victim increases sympathy for the rapist, decreases observers' confidence that the assault actually was rape, and decreases the sentence advocated for the rapist. Branscombe and Weir (1992) claimed that victim's stereotype-inconsistent behavior (e.g., too much resistance as a female) would be construed as abnormal and unexpected, so counterfactual alternatives become more accessible. When simulating alternative actions of the victim (e.g., "If she had done something other than what she did") results in a new outcome (e.g., no rape), what the victim did would be perceived as causally contributing to the original outcome. Learning of some negative outcome evokes thoughts of how that negative outcome could have been avoided, and what kinds of counterfactual alternatives are momentarily available affects causal attributions.

Given this close linkage between counterfactual thinking and causal attribution, how do upward and downward counterfactual thinking influence causal attribution in the context of consumer behavior? As discussed earlier, counterfactual thinking is known to serve two major functions: downward counterfactual thinking boosts one's positive feelings, whereas upward counterfactual thinking helps an individual prepare for the future (Roese, 1994). In addition, counterfactual generation is asymmetric in that it is more likely to follow negative outcomes than positive outcomes in an automatic fashion (Gavanski & Wells, 1989; Landman, 1987; Roese, 1997).

As previously discussed, the automatic generation of upward counterfactual thinking following a negative outcome is a natural phenomenon because it helps an individual to identify the cause of the outcome. When an individual is confronted with a negative outcome, he or she makes a variety of attempts to comprehend how that event took place, and upward counterfactual thinking is one such attempt that assists one in assessing the situation in an efficient manner. Yet, the functional utility of such counterfactual thinking is not guaranteed a priori, because one does not know in advance whether one would be successful in identifying the actual cause of the event before engaging in a counterfactual reasoning process. Consequently, it is possible that an individual, seeking a solution that can help her avoid a similar negative incident in the future, may generate causally irrelevant counterfactual thoughts simply because a given outcome is negative. Furthermore, because such mutation can result in a different, better counterfactual outcome even though it is causally independent of the factual outcome, one may misconstrue the feature that is counterfactually mutated as the cause of the negative outcome.

The generation of upward counterfactual thinking as a defense mechanism may come into operation even when there is no clear solution for the negative outcome. Consumers may spontaneously alter whatever features that are salient at the moment, wishing to mitigate such negative experiences. Causal attribution under such circumstances is likely to be biased toward contextually salient features. When there are no salient external features that can be altered, however, consumers may turn to internal features that are chronically accessible, resulting in internally biased mutation.

On the contrary, as Roese and Olson (1995) suggested, an individual who enjoys a positive outcome has less need to prepare for the future; hence the exploration of better possibilities via upward counterfactual thinking is of less utility. Therefore, compared to those who suffer from negative outcomes, consumers satisfied with their purchases are less motivated to understand how their positive outcome occurred; downward counterfactual thoughts are not as useful as upward counterfactual thoughts in terms of future improvement. One end result of this asymmetry in their preparative functions may be that people engaging in downward counterfactual thinking after a success are less motivated to make a causal attribution, being more optimistic about their future, than those engaging in upward counterfactual thinking. Because the affective reward from downward counterfactual thinking tends to be spontaneous and immediate, people experiencing downward counterfactual thinking tend to enjoy current reality rather than to focus on causal attribution.

To illustrate the points made, consider yourself in the scenario used in the present study: As a college student, you go shopping for textbooks on the first day of a new semester. After finding a big crowd of students lining up to buy textbooks in two adjacent bookstores in campus town, Bookstore A and Bookstore B, you ask yourself at which store you should choose to shop. Of course you want to check and compare the prices in both stores, but it seems impossible because you might have to wait for an hour to get into either store. You suddenly recall that you shopped at Bookstore A last semester and received a good deal. So you decided to shop at Bookstore A again this time. After waiting for a while in the line, you walk into Bookstore A and buy the textbooks, and receive a 10% discount. On the way back home, however, you run into one of your classmates and learn that he shopped at the other bookstore and received a 30% discount for the same set of textbooks. You think to yourself, "It's my unlucky day! If I had shopped at Bookstore B, I would have received a 30% discount."

What would be your next thoughts? Would you blame yourself for not knowing that Bookstore B offers a better deal, or consider yourself just being unlucky as explicitly described in the scenario, thus attributing the poor outcome (i.e., paying more money by shopping at Bookstore A) to external factors? On the other hand, how would your reaction differ if you are the one who received a 30% discount while your classmate received only a 10% discount?

Among numerous factors that might affect your causal attribution in this regard, we propose that the sheer direction of counterfactual thinking (i.e., upward vs. downward) can influence a consumer's attribution type. We hypothesized that those who are in a happy mood caused by downward counterfactual thinking tend to correctly make an external attribution of the event and they are more optimistic about their chances of having the same luck again in the future. Conversely, consistent with the functional approach, the negative outcomes may compel one to search, in a counterfactual manner, for whatever solution is available even though there is no such solution, eventually leading them to pessimistic internal attributions, so the same cause of the event is less likely to be present again in the future. Why should participants make internal attributions? When making an internal attribution, the event appears to be more controllable because changing internal features is easier than changing external features. A person in a failure situation may have a high need for the feeling of controllability because something must be done, or undone, to change, possibly improve, the current status.[4]

As predicted, when participants were asked to report whether the cause of what happened in the scenario was due to something about themselves (internal attribution) or something about other people or circumstances (external attribution), participants in the upward counterfactual-thinking condition (receiving a 30% discount) tended to make internal attributions more often than those in the downward counterfactual-thinking condition (receiving a 10% discount). This was the case although the scenario made clear that (a) it was merely the unavoidable external factors (e.g., time restriction) that determined protagonist's choice of the store; and (b) he or she made a fairly rational decision based on what was given (e.g., past experience). What is more, participants in the upward counterfactual-thinking condition tended to think that the same cause of the event in the scenario (internal characteristics) would be less likely to be present in the future, suggesting that they view the event as more controllable, and therefore they are more capable of rectifying the cause of negative events in the future. Consistent with functionalist' views, upward counterfactual thinking as a defense mechanism may help consumers prepare for the future, yet as shown in the present study, a preparative effort as a consequence of upward counterfactual thinking does not necessarily have to be functional. Upward counterfactual thinking sometimes facilitates consumers' misattribution processes (e.g., blaming oneself for the negative outcomes when they are caused by external factors), which may lead them to make unnecessary changes in their behaviors, likely resulting in no improvements in future performances.

In addition, findings in the present section shed lights on Schindler's (1998) investigation on the role of perceived responsibility in consumer satisfaction. Schindler (1998) manipulated perceived responsibility and showed that when consumers view themselves as responsible for having obtained the discount, consumers not only felt better but also exhibited a higher likelihood of repurchase and

---

[4]Some scholars maintained that individuals with control over negative outcomes experience less stress than individuals who do not have control (e.g., Glass & Singer, 1972; Wortman & Brehm, 1975).

world-of-mouth communication about the product. As the perception of responsibility influences consumer satisfaction in Schindler's (1998) study, in the present study an affective state caused by counterfactual thinking can influence perceived responsibility in the opposite direction.

SUMMARY AND IMPLICATIONS

In the furniture-shopping study, we compared the effect of a minimum purchase requirement in promotional framing of prices on consumers affect and attitudes. Consumers evaluated promotional messages differently when the promotional message included a minimum purchase requirement (e.g., "Spend $100, get 30% off") than when it did not (e.g., "30% off all purchases"). When a minimum-purchase requirement was present, the purchase outcome swayed consumers' feelings and judgment to a greater extent than when it was absent. In such circumstances where a promotional message includes a minimum-purchase requirement, the role of counterfactual thinking is rather dysfunctional. Such restrictions often direct a consumer's attention to whether they qualify for the discount rather than the actual amount of the discount, leading to the biased assessment of the purchase outcome: (a) by attaining the minimum purchase requirement, consumers feel better, although paying more, than those who obtain a better deal without such minimum purchase requirements; but (b) when consumers fail to attain the minimum purchase requirement, their affective and attitudinal reactions are more negative, even though they pay less, than those who receive a smaller discount. As previous research demonstrates, about one third of unplanned purchases are made on the basis of in-store need recognition (Iyer, 1989) and more than half of all purchases are spontaneous (Block & Morwitz, 1999). Under such conditions, this type of artificially generated counterfactual thinking may have more long-term detrimental effects. Consumers' overly satisfied feelings boosted by close downward counterfactuals may mislead their future behaviors because they misjudge their poor purchase decision (i.e., buying and spending more) as a wise choice.

The online shopping study further confirmed our belief that the effects of the minimum purchase requirement become more extreme when consumers nearly miss or attain the minimum purchase requirement than when they remotely miss or attain it. Regardless of the fact that the absolute amount of money paid is greater, in our studies, downward counterfactual thinking always induced happier feelings than did upward counterfactual thinking. When consumers engage in the same directional counterfactual thoughts, whether upward or downward, the close counterfactuals generate more intense affective reactions than distant counterfactuals, such that (a) those who pay more for the same products in the close downward counterfactuals feel better than those who pay less in the distant downward counterfactuals, and (b) those who pay less for the close upward counterfactuals feel worse than those who pay more in the distant upward counter-factuals. Findings from the furniture shopping study and the online-shopping study together suggest that, when exposed to conditional price-cut deals, consumers pay more attention to what they achieve rather than how much they save.

The textbook shopping study revealed that momentarily boosted feelings rooted in counterfactual thinking can have a significant impact on one's causal explanation of a purchase outcome. It was shown that, compared to downward counterfactual thinking, upward counterfactual thinking following a failure tends to lead to internal attributions for the past event. Consumers thus tend to perceive the same negative outcome in the future as more avoidable. Counterfactual thinking sometimes distorts consumers' feelings, imparting a false understanding of the situation, finally leading them to make a pessimistic internal attribution, which is unlikely to help improve future performance.

The first two studies (i.e., the furniture shopping study and the online shopping study) in this chapter focused on contrast effects, and the last study (i.e., the textbook shopping study) examined the causal inference mechanism. Both contrast effects and causal inferences are of theoretical importance in consumer research, because consumers repeatedly generate both types of counterfactual thoughts in the marketplace. Under those circumstances where a purchase decision is made online (e.g., impulse buying), counterfactual thinking may take place automatically via heuristic processing, which is likely to be driven by the contrast effect mechanism. On the other hand, the causal inference mechanism may benefit consumers for the most part particularly when they invest a great amount of cognitive resources in their consumption decisions (e.g., high-involvement buying situations).

For example, imagine your shopping cart in Store A that holds two items—one DVD player and one pack of batteries. When your buying is done you learn from your neighbor that you could have saved a dollar on the battery pack if you had shopped at Store B. This information may activate various types of counterfactuals. For example, it could be subtractive (e.g., "What if I had not bought the battery today?"), additive (e.g., "What if I had checked out both stores before buying?"), upward (e.g., "What if I had shopped at Store B?"), or downward (e.g., "What if I had gone to Store B only to discover that the battery is out of stock?"). Following the contrast-effect mechanism, the most natural reaction appears to be an upward counterfactual, which in turn may worsen your feelings. The counterfactual alternative here is used as a heuristic that simply influences the momentary assessment of your purchase. This type of heuristic-focused counterfactual thinking is not likely to be stored in long-term memory, so it is not very useful for future improvement.

On the other hand, the causal inference mechanism is more likely to come into play and to wield more influence, particularly when one's focus is on a high-involvement product. One may become convinced that his or her shopping at Store A was a wise decision if, for example, mutating the counterfactual antecedent leads to no change in the factual outcome, or to an even more negative outcome (e.g., "If I had shopped at Store B, I would have bought a low-quality DVD player). In such situations, this counterfactual causal attribution will enhance one's preexisting loyalty to Store A. At other times, however, counterfactual thinking can mutate the negative aspects of the factual outcome (e.g., "If I had shopped at Store B, I would have had more choices). In either case, this type of counterfactual causal attribution is more likely to result in a long-term effect. The relation between the dual mechanisms of counterfactual thinking (i.e., contrast and causal effect) and dual-processing models of persuasion (e.g., the Elaboration Likelihood Model; Petty & Cacioppo, 1986) is one question that requires further exploration in consumer research.

The research presented in this chapter provides insights for consumer advocacy groups. First, it is suggested that, via counterfactual thinking, restrictions such as the minimum purchase requirement in promotional messages can misguide consumers' judgment. When a minimum purchase requirement is present, consumers may purchase more than intended, but feel overly satisfied. Counterfactual thinking generated by such restrictions may help simplify consumers' decision-making process or postevaluation of their purchase performance, but it does not help them arrive at optimal conclusions. In addition, findings in this chapter suggest that upward counterfactual thinking followed by a poor consumption experience may prevent one from viewing the world as it is; consumers may end up blaming themselves for what they are not responsible. Consumers' imagining about what might have been better or worse can be dysfunctional.

REFERENCES

Bohner, G., Bless, H., Schwarz, N., & Strack, F. (1988). What triggers causal attributions?: The impact of valence and subjective probability. *European Journal of Social Psychology, 18*, 335–345.

Block, L. G., & Morwitz, V. G. (1999). Shopping lists as an external memory aid for grocery shopping: Influences on list writing and list fulfillment, *Journal of Consumer Psychology, 8*, 343–375.

Brannon, L. A., & Brock, T. C. (2001). Limiting time for responding enhances behavior corresponding to the merits of compliance appeals: Refutations of heuristic-cue theory in service and consumer settings. *Journal of Consumer Psychology, 10*, 135–246.

Branscombe, N. R., & Weir, J. A. (1992). Resistance as stereotype-inconsistency: Consequences for judgments of rape victims. *Journal of Social and Clinical Psychology, 11*, 80–102.

Davis, C. G., Lehman, D. R., Wortman, C. B., Silver, R. C., & Thompson, S. C. (1995). The undoing of traumatic life events. *Personality and Social Psychology Bulletin, 21*, 109–204.

Festinger, L. (1954). A theory of social comparison processes. *Human Relations, 7*, 117–140.

Gavanski, I., & Wells, G. L. (1989). Counterfactual processing of normal and exceptional events. *Journal of Experimental Social Psychology, 25*, 314–325.

Gilbert, D. T., & Malone, P. S. (1995). The correspondence bias. *Psychological Bulletin, 17*, 21–38.

Glass, D. C., & Singer, J. E. (1972). *Urban stress: Experiments on noise and social stressors.* New York: Academic Press.

Hastie, R. (1984). Causes and effects of causal attributions. *Journal of Personality and Social Psychology, 46*, 44–56.

Hetts, J. J., Boninger, D. S., Armor, D. A., Gleicher, F., & Nathanson, A. (2000). The influence of anticipated counterfactual regret on behavior. *Psychology and Marketing, 17*, 345–368.

Houston, D. A., Sherman, S. J., & Baker, S. A. (1991). Feature matching, unique features, and the dynamics of choice process: Predecision conflict and postdecision satisfaction. *Journal of Experimental Social Psychology, 27*, 411–430.

Iacobucci, D, Grayson, K, & Ostrom, A. (1994). Customer satisfaction fables. *Sloan Management Review, 35*(4), 93–96.

Inman, J. J., Dyer, J., & Jia, J (1997). A generalized utility model of disappointment and regret effects on post-choice evaluation. *Marketing Science, 16*(2), 97–101.

Inman, J. J., Peter, A., & Raghubir, P. (1997), Framing the deal: The role of restrictions in accentuating deal value. *Journal of Consumer Research, 24*(1), 68–79.

Isen, A. M., & Means, B. (1983). The influence of positive affect on decision-making strategy. *Social Cognition, 2*, 18–31.

Iyer, E. S. (1989). Unplanned purchasing: Knowledge of shopping environment and time pressure, *Journal of Retailing, 65*, 40–57

Kahneman, D., & Miller, D. T. (1986). Norm theory: Comparing reality to its alternatives. *Psychological Review, 93*, 136–153.

Kahneman, D., & Tversky, A. (1979). Prospect theory: An analysis of decision under risk, *Econometrica, 47*, 263–291.

Kahneman, D., & Tversky, A. (1982). The simulation heuristic. In D. Kahneman, P. Slovic, & A. Tversky (Eds.), *Judgment under uncertainty: Heuristic and biases* (pp. 201–208). New York: Cambridge University Press.

Landman, J. (1987). Regret and elation following action and inaction: Affective responses to positive versus negative outcomes. *Personality and Social Psychology Bulletin, 13*, 524–536.

Lessne, G. J., & Notarantonio, E. M. (1988). The effects of limits in retail advertisements: A reactance theory perspective. *Psychology and Marketing, 5*, 34–44.

Lynn, M. (1992). Scarcity's enhancement of desirability: The role of naive economic theories. *Basic and Applied Social Psychology, 13*, 67–78.

Markman, K. D., Gavanski, I., Sherman, S. J., & McMullen, M. N. (1993). The mental simulation of better and worse possible worlds. *Journal of Experimental Social Psychology, 29*, 87–109.

McConnell, A. R., Niedermerier, K. E., Leibold, J. M., El-Alayli, A. G., Chin, P. P., & Kuiper, N. M. (2000) What if I find it cheaper someplace else?: The role of prefactual thinking and anticipated regret in consumer behavior. *Psychology and Marketing, 17*, 281–198.

Medvec, V. H., Madey, S. F., & Gilovich, T. (1995). When less is more: Counterfactual thinking and satisfaction among Olympic athletes. *Journal of Personality and Social Psychology, 69*, 603–610.

Medvec, V. H., & Savitsky, K. (1997). When doing better means feeling worse: The effects of categorical cutoff points on counterfactual thinking and satisfaction. *Journal of Personality and Social Psychology, 72*(6), 1284–1296.

Miller, D. T., Turnbull, & W., & McFarland, C. (1989). When a coincidence is suspicious: The role of mental simulation. *Journal of Personality and Social Psychology, 57*, 581–589.

Petty, R. E., & Cacioppo, J. T. (1986). *Communication and persuasion: Central and peripheral routes to attitude change.* New York: Springer-Verlag.

Phillips, D. M. (2002). The role of consumption emotions in the satisfaction response. *Journal of Consumer Psychology, 12*, 243–252.

Roese, N. J. (1994). The functional basis of counterfactual thinking. *Journal of Personality and Social Psychology, 66*, 805–818.

Roese, N. J. (1997). Counterfactual thinking. *Journal of Personality and Social Psychology, 121*, 133–148.

Roese, N. J., & Olson, J. M. (1993). The structure of counterfactual thought. *Personality and Social Psychology Bulletin, 19*, 312–319.

Roese, N. J., & Olson, J. M. (1995). Functions of counterfactual thinking. In N. J. Roese & J. M. Olson (Eds.), *What might have been: The social psychology of counterfactual thinking* (pp. 169–197). Mahwah, NJ: Lawrence Erlbaum Associates.

Rosnow, R. L., & Rosenthal, R. (1999). *Beginning behavioral research.* Englewood Cliffs, NJ: Prentice-Hall.

Schindler, R. M. (1998). Consequences of perceiving oneself as responsible for obtaining a discount: Evidence for smart-shopper feelings. *Journal of Consumer Psychology, 7*, 371–392.

Schwarz, N. (1990). Feelings as information: Information and motivational functions of affective states. In E. T. Higgins & R. M. Sorrentino (Eds.), *Handbook of motivation and cognition: Foundations of social behavior* (Vol. 2, pp. 527–561). New York: Guilford.

Taylor, K. (1997). A regret theory approach to assessing consumer satisfaction. *Marketing Letters, 8*, 229–238.

Taylor, S. E., & Lobel, M. (1989). Social comparison activity under threat: Downward evaluation and upward contacts. *Psychological Review, 96*, 569–575.

Tsiros, M. (1998). Effect of regret on post-choice valuation: The case of more than two alternatives. *Organizational Behavior & Human Decision Processes, 76*(1), 48–69.

Verhallen, T. M., & Robben, H. S. J. (1994). Scarcity and preference: An experiment on unavailability and product evaluation. *Journal of Economic Psychology, 15*, 315–331.

Wansink, B., Kent, R. J., & Hoch, S. J. (1998). An anchoring and adjustment model of purchase quantity decisions. *Journal of Marketing Research, 71*, 71–81.

Weiner, G. (1985). "Spontaneous" causal thinking. *Psychological Bulletin, 97*, 74–84.

Wells, G. L., & Gavanski, I. (1989). Mental simulation of causality. *Journal of Personality and Social Psychology, 56*, 161–169.

Wortman, C. B., & Brehm, J. W. (1975). Responses to uncontrollable outcomes: An integration of reactance theory and the learned helplessness model. In L. Berkowitz (Ed.), *Advances in experimental social psychology* (Vol. 8, pp. 377–389). New York: Academic Press.

Yi, Y. (1990). A critical review of consumer satisfaction. In V. A. Zeithaml (Ed.), *Review of marketing* (pp. 68–123). Chicago: American Marketing Association.

Zanna, M. P., & Goethals, G. P., & Hill, J. F. (1975). Evaluating a sex-related ability: Social comparison with similar others and standard setters. *Journal of Experimental Social Psychology, 11*, 86–93.

CHAPTER SEVENTEEN

Complementary Roles of Dual-Process Models, Theory of Reasoned Action, Media Priming, and the Concept of Consideration in the Development of Advertising Message Strategies: A Case Study Concerning Youth Views of Military Service Amidst September 11, 2001

John Eighmey
Wanda Siu
University of Minnesota

The identification of the strategic content of a specific message argument is a well-established and important step in the development of effective advertising campaigns to promote the purchasing of products or other forms of behavior (such as health care practices, political participation, person perception, etc.). The strategic quality of advertising messages is promoted by considered contrasting of a range of possible message arguments that have the capacity to associate the action to be advocated in the advertising (such as a product purchase, a heath-related behavior, or a view about a politician) with specific audience member beliefs concerning the outcome or benefit to be obtained from the action. In this way, the content of advertising campaigns can be productively focused on the issues and concerns that are of greatest relevance to the members of the intended audiences.

To assist in this development and evaluation process, consumer surveys are commonly used to acquire information about the related interests of the target population. During such surveys, members of the target market serving as study participants are often asked to think about specific questions concerning the importance of a range of goals (or desired outcomes) that are important to them, and this information is studied in relation to specific attitudes and intentions concerning product use. This chapter examined a case study demonstrating how a dramatic series of events can affect consumer viewpoints related to a product category and the value of employing several theoretical perspectives to provide a more complete analysis of the case at hand.

ADVERTISING MESSAGE STRATEGY

The purpose of an advertising *message strategy* is to direct the attention of those who write and produce advertising messages to the value system of the intended audience in order to increase the effectiveness of the communication process (Overholser & Kline, 1975). The message strategy outlines the message argument that is to provide the desired structure for the message. The *message argument* is essentially a statement identifying what is believed to be the most leverageable outcome (or benefit) of product use from the standpoint of consumers of the product and the attribute of the advertised product that delivers that outcome. *Leverage* comes from the identification and selection of an outcome that is extensive (widely known to potential consumers), important (highly valued by potential consumers), and closely associated with a key performance attribute of the advertised product. In the most favorable circumstances, the key attribute of the advertised product is superior to its competition with respect to the capacity to provide consumers with the desired benefit.

INTEGRATIVE APPLICATION OF THEORETICAL APPROACHES

The continuing advancements in attitude research and more generally in social psychology are providing conceptual structures for understanding target populations that are improving the process of advertising message strategy development (Norins, 1990). However, given the wide range of theories about cognitive processes, attitude formation, and change, and mass media effects there is a need for integrative approaches that identify the key underlying assumptions and concepts (Fishbein & Yzer, 2003; Smith & DeCoster, 2000). In addition to advancing understanding of the alternative conceptual structures or theories, such integrative approaches also offer the promise of better informing the process of selecting the audience member beliefs and attitudes most appropriate as the "target beliefs" during the development of specific advertising campaigns. In the present case study, four theoretical perspectives were applied: (a) The Theory of Reasoned Action, (b) dual-process approaches, (c) media priming, and (d) the concept of *consideration*.

The Theory of Reasoned Action

A key portion of *Theory of Reasoned Action* (TRA) involves a model of how beliefs about a desired outcome (called *outcome evaluations*) and beliefs about the extent to which an attitude object is likely to deliver the desired outcome (called *behavioral beliefs*) combine to affect a person's attitude toward the object (Ajzen & Fishbein, 1980). In the formation of an attitude toward an object (such as a brand), the TRA posits that attitudes are predicted by combining outcome evaluation and behavioral belief measures in a multiplicative manner (in essence, weighting the outcome evaluation according to the degree of the behavioral belief). Other important factors, such as normative beliefs about perceived expectations of relevant other people are considered in the TRA and are combined with attitude toward the object to predict a person's intention to engage in the behavior being examined. In the analysis for this case study, our focus is only on the portion of the TRA that depicts attitude toward an object as a function of a set of outcome evaluations and their respective behavioral beliefs.

The TRA concepts of outcome evaluations and behavioral beliefs have been widely employed as the underlying conceptual approach in surveys designed to reveal the relationships among consumers, or target audience members, or beliefs and attitudes about products and brands. It is not uncommon to encounter market-segmentation studies containing banks of questions about a range of relevant outcome evaluations and a set of corresponding behavioral beliefs for each product or brand of interest. In this approach, the TRA posits that the attitudinal impact of a range of beliefs concerning specific outcomes can be systematically assessed in terms of the mean value of each specific outcome evaluation, the mean value of the corresponding behavioral belief, and in an overall manner by a third variable created by the product of each outcome evaluation and behavioral belief (Fishbein & Yzer, 2003). This approach presents a potential knowledge base for identifying specific beliefs to be targeted with message strategies designed to reinforce these beliefs or to change them, depending on the communication objectives.

Dual-Process Models

The *dual-process models* generally posit two realms of cognition: a more quickly accessible realm (or mode) in which individuals quickly and seemingly intuitively respond to stimuli and a more formalistic realm (or mode) in which individuals apply considered thought in order to elaborate the content of their beliefs, attitudes, and intentions. Differences in the manner of cognition, or "elaboration" in the case of the Elaboration Likelihood Model (ELM), are either inferred by means of observing and assessing cognitive responses to persuasive information, or by means of manipulating the qualities of persuasive messages in experimental designs (Petty, Cacioppo, & Schumann, 1983). Importantly, one means of assessing the nature of elaboration is to examine the strength and extensiveness of the relationships of relevant information (such as beliefs about desired outcomes) and target audience attitudes about the product or issue in question (Petty & Cacioppo, 1986). This approach to assessing elaboration has particular application in the interpretation of surveys of consumer beliefs and attitudes used in the development of possible advertising message strategies. The notion that there are differing levels of elaboration leads to the possibility that the strength of the associations of beliefs with attitudes or intentions can reveal the beliefs that are most relevant to the elaboration process and, therefore, to attitude change.

A related approach presents the duality as simultaneous use of *heuristic* and *systematic* processing (Chen & Chaiken, 1999). In this approach, the heuristic form of processing is seen as guided by an assortment of highly accessible decision rules such as "popular products are a safe choice." Systematic processing, such as considered evaluation of a new product or reevaluation of an existing belief, can take place simultaneously when triggered by circumstances or specific communications that either invite or enable more circumspect analysis of information.

A more broadly based dual-process model of memory parallels the ELM and heuristic–systematic models of attitude formation and change by positing two underlying memory systems (Smith & DeCoster, 2000). This approach is based on the need for a "rapid response" capability as well as a more ordered and complete organizational structure providing an accessible knowledge base based on accumulated experiences. In this approach, which is somewhat similar to the heuristic–systematic model, the rapid response capability provides immediate access to "associations" (decision rules in the heuristic–systematic model) whereas use of the deeper level of memory points to more systematic use of conceptual knowledge about facts and perceived relationships such as causal attributions.

Media Priming

Media priming (MP) is viewed as an effect of mass media exposure given to a message or event that results in the temporary activation or saliency of a construct that affects the evaluative judgments of media audience members. This effect can be seen as the activation of relevant portions of a person's established store of knowledge as well as the incorporation new information (see Price & Tewksbury, 1997). For example, the content of television programming can be seen as a priming influence that increases the accessibility of the ideas, issues, and themes to the extent they are included in television programs (Shrum, Wyer, & O'Guinn, 1998). Experimental research has shown that heavy viewers of television use television-based information to construct their estimates of the prevalence of certain behaviors in society (Shrum et al., 1998).

The activation or accessibility of an idea, issue, or theme for audience members is seen as a function of the recency, intensity and frequency of exposure to the construct. Media priming research has primarily examined priming effects on related attitudes and intentions as opposed to the process of mental elaboration or the resultant changes in patterns among related beliefs (Shah, Kwak, Schmierbach, & Zubric, 2004). It is, however, this intervening structure of the associations among related product-related beliefs that is an essential part of the knowledge base for more effective design of communication strategies.

Consideration

In the field of buyer behavior, the process known as *consideration* includes information search and evaluative behavior leading to a purchase decision. Howard and Sheth (1969) described *buying behavior* as an active process of seeking information from commercial and social environments leading to the narrowing of choice alternatives and an eventual choice from what they called and "evoked set" of alternative brands. Howard and Sheth (1969) posited that attitudes and intentions about choice alternatives are formed during this process. More recently, the term *consideration set* has been employed to designate the brands consumers would consider purchasing and consumer research interest has focused on the process of consideration whereby information is acquired and used in some fashion to arrive at a consumer choice (Roberts & Lattin, 1991).

Brands with more favorable attitudes have been shown to be more likely to be considered for purchase, and it has been shown that consideration can be promoted by advertising messages that invite elaboration (Priester, Dhananjay, Fleming, & Godek, 2004). Brand choice can also be affected by brand accessibility in memory, absent any change in brand evaluations (Nedungadi, 1990). In this connection, media priming of brand-related information can be seen as playing a role in the relative saliency of specific brands during the consideration process. Moreover, it has been shown in an experimental design setting that the process of brand retrieval and consideration can have effects on brand choice that are independent of brand evaluations (Kardes, Kalyanaram, Chandrashekaran, & Dornoff, 1993). For example, pioneering brands can have a saliency advantage in simple-choice situations that appears to bypass the consideration process.

Indeed, consideration can be seen as a continuum somewhat paralleling the concept of *depth of elaboration*. While advertising, and other forms of media content, can be seen as sources of *priming* information affecting such factors as the salience of specific choice criteria and the association of brand names with various choice criteria. Consumers for whom a product has potential relevancy may engage in various combinations of systematic and heuristic thinking as they form their attitudes and intentions. Consumers for whom a product has little or no relevancy may engage in the least amounts of systematic or heuristic thinking with respect to the product.

The concept of consideration is also central to planning advertising message strategies. Potential buyers are usefully segmented into those who have never considered a product, considered but not yet purchased, and nonusers of the product in order to determine whether there are unique information needs associated with these groupings. It is likely that consideration groups may differ in the extent of the beliefs associated with a product category and that discovery of such distinctions could point to message strategies to promote more complete consideration.

COMPLEMENTARY ROLES OF TRA, DUAL-PROCESS MODELS, MP, AND CONSIDERATION

Each of the four conceptual models provides important perspectives for understanding the persuasion process and developing more effective message strategies for advertising and other intervention campaigns. Importantly, the concept of the *associa-*

tion of specific beliefs about valued outcomes with intentions to use specified attitude objects, such as brands to be purchased or health-related behaviors to be adopted, provides a bridging idea (or intersection) among the four conceptual models. The manner and extent of associations can be examined by contrasting the intercorrelations among a group of relevant beliefs along with the correlation of each belief item with intentions relating to an object, product, or person of interest.

1. In the TRA, attitudes toward an object are seen as a function of the importance of specified outcomes (called *outcome evaluations*) and the extent to which each outcome is seen as being associated with the attitude object (called *behavioral beliefs*). However, the concept of *belief saliency* introduces the idea that the materiality of a particular belief to a specific attitude may not accord with the relative magnitude of the importance of the belief (see Fishbein & Ajzen, 1975). The TRA posits a systematic approach in which each of the outcome evaluations is weighted by its respective behavioral belief. But, in specific applications of the TRA, questions remain about the actual extent of systematic thinking and, therefore, the salience or materiality of each outcome as it relates to attitude and intention. Accordingly, it would appear that the correlations of specific outcome evaluations with an attitude or intention can provide an indication of the saliency of the individual outcome evaluations. Moreover, this view could also be applied to the respective behavioral beliefs.

2. In the dual-process models, the correlation of a belief (such as an outcome evaluation or behavioral belief) with an attitude object can provide an indication of the degree of elaboration involving that belief and the action recommended in a persuasive message. The size of the correlations of beliefs relating to an attitude object are revealing of the manner and extent of elaboration and accessibility of rules or associations that may guide immediate or intuitive action or promote elaboration. Such information points the way to the beliefs that invoke central processing by message recipients (the most complete form of evaluation). This is useful information in the development of more effective advertising message strategies.

3. In *media priming*, the correlation of the importance of specific belief with a corresponding attitude indicates the effects of the priming construct (or frame) on attitude strength or saliency. Patterns in the intercorrelations among the related beliefs and the correlations of the individual beliefs with an attitude or intention toward an object or action can provide a model of the mental context in which a behavior of interest takes place. Fishbein and Yzer (2003) contrasted the TRA with MP by stating that the effects of MP can be seen in terms of changes in the association between a predictor and its outcome, even when the mean value of the predictor remains unchanged. In other words, a construct or framework used in a message in the mass media or a news story might raise the saliency of one or more beliefs concerning an attitude object. Fishbein and Yzer (2003) viewed the likely effects of priming as increasing the correlation of a related belief to an attitude ob-

ject without necessarily affecting the mean value of the corresponding outcome evaluation or behavioral belief. However, as our results suggest, it would seem possible that media priming might affect the mean value of a belief as well as the correlation of that belief with other beliefs, as well as attitudes and intentions.

4. With respect to consideration process leading to the purchase of a product or adoption of an idea, the size of the correlation of a specific belief (outcome evaluation or behavioral belief) with the attitude toward the brand is reflective of the prominence of that belief in the evolving elaboration of information about the product or brand. Comparison of such correlations across levels or possible stages in the consideration process could indicate possible target belief areas for the development of message strategies targeted specifically to the unique interests of audiences at various stages in the consideration process. In particular, the beliefs of greatest prominence in the early stages of consideration point to the readiness to accept specific message arguments.

A Case Study

Two recent national surveys measured a variety of youth beliefs and provided an opportunity for a case study exploration of the role of association as a linking concept among the four models: saliency of beliefs in the theory of reasoned action, spreading associations in the dual-process approach, media priming to affect the saliency and association of relevant beliefs, and contrasting of the saliency of beliefs across levels of consideration. The youth beliefs in this case study involve a grouping of career-related goals that relate to consideration of military service. One survey was conducted in 1999, the other one month following the events of September 11, 2001.

Study Design.   The national surveys of youth beliefs and attitudes conducted by the United States Department of Defense (DOD) provided an opportunity for secondary analysis of questionnaire items that operationalized the variables in the four research issue areas just discussed. The DOD conducts an annual telephone survey of youth ages 16 to 21 in the United States who are not currently serving in the military, have not previously served in the military, and have not enlisted to serve at a future date. The two surveys employed in this article were administered in October and November of 1999 and 2001.

Sample.   The 1999 DOD survey was based on a random sample totaling 10,000. The 2001 sample was limited to 2,000 survey participants. Quotas were established so as to reflect the gender, education, race, ethnicity, and regional profile of the youth population in the United States. The sample frame for 1999 included youth, age 16 to 24, while the frame for 2001 focused on youth, age 16 to 21. To account for the differences in sample frame, the present study utilized only the participants in the age 16 to 21 range. The interviews were conducted during the evening and weekend hours. The callback procedures involved an initial call and a maximum of nine callbacks before substitution of another randomly selected household.

It should be noted that this survey was in the field one month after the tragic events of September 11, 2001, and during the height of media coverage of the aftermath. The survey included a specific question inquiring about youth interest in the military as a result of those events.

Measures.   Of particular interest to the current investigation were questionnaire items about the importance of a grouping of 24 youth goals (measures of outcome evaluations) and the extent to which each goal was seen as associated with military service (measures of behavioral belief). In addition to the questions concerning the 24 youth goals, the survey questionnaire included questions about youth attitudes toward the military, extent of consideration of military service, intention to enlist, and media priming in connection with the events of September 11, 2001.

Outcome evaluations for the 24 youth goals were rated on a 4-point scale from (*1*) *not important* to (*4*) *extremely important*. Survey participants were asked, "How important is it to you to _____?" The eight items of interest in this study reflect major youth goals associated with career choices. The order of the items was randomized for each survey participant.

To examine *behavioral beliefs*, survey participants were asked, "Would you be more likely to (insert belief item) in the military, a civilian job, or equally in both?" The responses were ordered for analytical purposes in this study by coding the civilian response as a *1*, equally in both as a *2*, and the military response as a *3*.

Intention to enlist in the military was measured with the question, "How likely is it that you will be serving in the military in the next few years?" Four response categories were provided in rotated order: *definitely not, probably not, probably,* and *definitely*.

Consideration of military service was measured with the question, "Before we talked today, had you ever considered the possibility of joining the military?" *Never thought about it* was coded as a *1, gave it some consideration* was coded as a *2*, and *gave it serious consideration* was coded as a *3*.

The presence of *media priming* was examined with the question, "Does the situation related to the World Trade Center and the Pentagon make you more likely or does it make you less likely to consider joining the U.S. military as an option?" For the analysis in this case study, "makes you less likely" was re-coded as a *1*, "neither" as a *2*, and "makes you more likely" as a *3*.

Results and Discussion

Previous studies of youth interest in military service have considered a range of material job-related benefits (or *occupational benefits*) as well as values and norms that differentiate military service from civilian work (or *institutional* benefits) (Moskos & Wood, 1988). To provide a conceptual structure for the analysis, eight of the 24 youth goals were selected as most representative of the occupational–institutional dichotomy. Occupational considerations were seen as exemplified by goals such as good pay, getting money for education, learning work-related skills, and preparing for a future career. Institutional considerations were seen as exemplified by value-oriented goals that involve fulfilling responsibilities to others such as leadership skills, self-discipline, duty to country, and working as a team member.

Theory of Reasoned Action Perspective. Table 17.1 shows the mean values of the outcome evaluations and behavioral beliefs for the 1999 Youth Poll. As a group, the highest rated outcome evaluations are for the occupational goals. However, the ratings for the behavioral beliefs indicate that none of the eight can be said to favor military employment. Indeed, six of the behavioral beliefs signifi-

TABLE 17.1

1999 Survey: Outcome Evaluations, Behavioral Beliefs,
and Correlations With Intention to Enlist

Outcome Evaluations	Mean Values		Correlation With Intention to Enlist
Institutional Goals			
Develop leadership skills	3.1	*	.09
Develop self-discipline	3.1		.11
Do something for your country	2.7		.30
Work as part of a team	3.1		.07
Occupational Goals			
Have a good paying job	3.4		.06
Get money for education	3.1		.05
Learn a valuable trade or skill	3.1		.09
Get experiences that prepare you for a future career	3.2		.04
Behavioral Beliefs			
Institutional Goals			
Develop leadership skills	1.7	**	.19
Develop self-discipline	2.0		.16
Do something for your country	1.8	**	.03
Work as part of a team	1.6	**	.00
Occupational Goals			
Have a good paying job	1.6	**	.11
Get money for education	2.0		.04
Learn a valuable trade or skill	1.4	**	.07
Get experiences that prepare you for a future career	1.5	**	.07
	N = 1,400		N = 1,400

*Means significantly different at the .001 level.

**Means significantly less than 2.0 (midpoint of scale) at less than the .001 level.

cantly favor civilian employment. These results, taken alone, would point to the importance of the occupational goals in the development of recruitment campaigns and the additional need to focus on the related behavioral beliefs as the target of message strategies to advance the standing of military employment.

Elaboration Perspective. The second column in Table 17.1 shows the correlations for each of the outcome evaluations and behavioral beliefs with intention to enlist in the military. The significant correlations point to the relative salience of certain specific beliefs with intention to enlist in the military. From this perspective, it is the institutional goals that show the greatest "readiness" in terms of the belief structure of the youth population in 1999. In terms of "latitude of acceptance," it is information concerning institutional goals that would seem to connect most readily with the view of the youth population at that point in time.

Media Priming Perspective. Based on the extensive public concern and media coverage following the events of September 11, 2001, one would expect media priming effects involving attention to constructs such as personal safety, national security, heroism, and feelings of patriotism. Indeed, in response to the question concerning media priming, 51% of the survey respondents reported that the events of September 11, 2001, made them more likely to consider joining the military, and there was a correlation of .36 (significant beyond the .001 level) between the priming question and intention to enlist in the military.

As shown in Table 17.2 and Table 17.3, the effects of media priming were revealed by changes both in the means for certain outcome evaluations and behavioral beliefs as well as by changes in the correlations of these variables with attitude toward the military. Most of the ratings of the importance of outcome evaluations in Table 17.2 remained stable from 1999 to 2001. However, the mean importance of "doing something for your country" increased from 2.7 to 2.9 while the importance of "work as part of a team" decreased from 3.1 to 2.8. It appears that the events of September 11, 2001 heightened a sense of personal duty toward country. The decline in the importance of teamwork suggests the possibility that youth, in the context of the time period, may see increasing value in individual initiative rather than teamwork.

Turning to Table 17.3, comparison of the correlations of outcome evaluations and behavioral beliefs with attitude toward the military reveals patterns consistent with the *spreading association* concept associated with media priming as well the possibility of *halo effects*. Halo effects with respect to ratings (such as traits, or goal items as in this case) are seen as a form of bias arising from an overall impression of the rated object (Guilford, 1954). In the 1999 and 2001 Youth Polls, the ratings of the outcome evaluations were not placed in the context of military service, therefore these ratings in the Youth Polls would seem to be less susceptible to halo effects arising from overall views of the military. However, behavioral beliefs are generally measured in a manner that specifically places these belief rat-

TABLE 17.2

Comparison of Outcome Evaluations and Behavioral Beliefs in 1999 and 2001

	Mean Values	
Outcome Evaluations	*1999*	*2001*
Institutional Goals		
Develop leadership skills	3.1	3.0
Develop self-discipline	3.1	3.1
Do something for your country	2.7	2.9 *
Work as part of a team	3.1	2.8
Occupational Goals		
Have a good paying job	3.4	3.4
Get money for education	3.1	3.1
Learn a valuable trade or skill	3.1	3.0
Get experiences that prepare you for a future career	3.2	3.3
Behavioral Beliefs		
Institutional Goals		
Develop leadership skills	1.7	2.2 **
Develop self-discipline	2.0	2.4
Do something for your country	1.8	2.3
Work as part of a team	1.6	2.1
Occupational Goals		
Have a good paying job	1.6	1.7
Get money for education	2.0	2.3 **
Learn a valuable trade or skill	1.4	2.0
Get experiences that prepare you for a future career	1.5	1.9
	$N = 1,400$	$N = 2,000$

*Mean values of outcome evaluations significantly different at the .01 level.
**Mean values of behavioral beliefs significantly greater than 2.0 at the .01 level.

ings in terms of relevance to a specific attitude object. In the case of the Youth Polls, behavioral beliefs were measured in terms of the extent of their association with either civilian or military work. Therefore, this specific priming of a civilian versus military comparison during the administration of these question items could lead to a halo effect. Halo effects can also arise from item order in a questionnaire. However, in the Youth Polls, the specific items concerning outcome evaluations and behavioral beliefs were randomized during the administration process to eliminate halo effects arising from item order.

In 1999, outcome evaluations for only three of the institutional goals and one of the occupational goals were associated with intention to enlist in the military. In 2001, immediately following the events of September 11, all four of the outcome evaluations for institutional goals and none of the occupational goals were significantly associated with intention to enlist in the military suggesting differentiation among goals with respect to the possibility of the spreading activation perspective.

TABLE 17.3

Comparison of Correlations With Intention to Enlist in 1999 and 2001

	Correlation With Intention to Enlist	
Outcome Evaluations	1999	2001
Institutional Goals		
Develop leadership skills	**.09**	**.06**
Develop self-discipline	**.11**	**.08**
Do something for your country	**.30**	**.23**
Work as part of a team	.07	**.16**
Occupational Goals		
Have a good paying job	.06	.04
Get money for education	.05	.05
Learn a valuable trade or skill	**.09**	.05
Get experiences that prepare you for a future career	.04	.01
Behavioral Beliefs		
Institutional Goals		
Develop leadership skills	**.19**	**.22**
Develop self-discipline	**.16**	**.18**
Do something for your country	.03	**.20**
Work as part of a team	.00	**.16**
Occupational Goals		
Have a good paying job	**.11**	**.24**
Get money for education	.04	**.18**
Learn a valuable trade or skill	.07	**.21**
Get experiences that prepare you for a future career	.07	**.29**
	$N = 1,400$	$N = 2,000$

Correlations in bold significantly greater than .0 at the .01 level.

Returning to Table 17.2, changes in the mean values for five of the eight behavioral beliefs indicate these goal items have an increased relevance to military service as opposed to civilian work. Interestingly, the pattern of the changes among these eight goals points to a differential saliency associated with the institutional goals as opposed to the occupational goals. As with the results for the outcome evaluation correlations in Table 17.3, the changes in ratings of the behavioral beliefs center on the institutional goals. It appears there is no indication of a general halo effect associated with increased media coverage of the military that generalizes to both institutional and occupational goals. Indeed, the occupational goal, "get money for education," has been an ongoing theme in recruitment advertising for the U.S. Army and during the time period from 1999 to 2001 became a major feature in advertising for the U.S. Navy. Accordingly, the increased rating for that goal shown in 2001 could be related to media priming, increases in advertising message exposure, or some combination of both factors.

TABLE 17.4

Correlations Among Outcome Evaluations
for Institutional Goals: 1999 Versus 2001

Institutional Goals	For Country	Part of Team	Leadership	Self-Discipline
1999				
Do something for your country	1.000			
Work as part of a team	.268	1.000		
Develop leadership skills	.265	.420	1.000	
Develop self-discipline	.244	.456	.378	1.000
2001				
Do something for your country	1.000			
Work as part of a team	.360	1.000		
Develop leadership skills	.343	.346	1.000	
Develop self-discipline	.345	.360	.393	1.000

Correlations in bold significantly greater than .0 at the .01 level. In 1999, sample sizes for correlations ranged from 156 to 210, while in 2001, $N = 2,000$ for all correlations.

Table 17.4 details the correlations among the outcome evaluations for the institutional goals in 1999 and 2001. Along with the increased rating for "doing something for your country" and the decreased rating for "work as part of a team," there is a strengthening of association with "doing something for your country" and a weakening of the associations with "work as part of a team." Once again, we see the divergent effects of priming with respect to the importance of specific goals and the relative strengths of the associations among these goals.

Consideration Perspective. Another perspective on elaboration and the possibility of spreading activation is offered by contrasting groups based on the extent of their reported extent of consideration of the topic. Table 17.5 contrasts the mean values of the outcome evaluations and behavioral beliefs across the three levels of consideration of military service. As shown in the top portion of Table 17.5, all four of the outcome evaluations in the institutional group showed significant differences across all three levels of consideration. Whereas among the outcome evaluations associated with occupational goals, only "learn a valuable trade or skill" showed significant differences associated with the three levels of consideration.

The consistent and significant differences among the means of the institutional goals across the levels of consideration points to the relative importance of this goal area as youth consider the possibility of military service. Interestingly, "do something for your country" was among the lowest rated outcome evaluation in terms of its grand mean (2.92) across the three levels of consideration, yet it showed consistent and significant increases across all three levels of consideration and conceptually appears to exemplify the values associated with the institutional concept. Indeed, based on the variations across levels of consideration, the institutional concepts appear to have priority, whereas based on the overall mean values of importance ratings, priority would appear to go to the occupational goals.

The lower portion of Table 17.5 contrasts the mean values of the behavioral beliefs across the three levels of consideration of military service. As might be expected, when contrasting consideration levels, all eight of the behavioral beliefs showed significant increases across the three levels of consideration. With grand means of 2.14 for "work as part of a team" to 2.38 for "self-discipline," the institutional goals were seen as more closely associated with military service than the occupational goals, with grand means ranging from 1.68 for "have a good paying job" to 2.27 for "get money for education."

TABLE 17.5

2001—Means for Outcome Evaluations and Behavioral
Beliefs Across Level of Consideration

		Level of Consideration		
Outcome Evaluations		*Never*	*Some*	*Serious*
Institutional Goals				
Develop leadership skills	1	3.00	3.02	**3.19**
Develop self-discipline	1	3.07	3.08	**3.22**
Do something for your country	1	**2.78**	**2.92**	**3.13**
Work as part of a team	2	2.71	2.78	**2.89**
Occupational Goals				
Have a good paying job		3.39	3.36	3.43
Get money for education		3.09	3.10	3.07
Learn a valuable trade or skill	3	**2.82**	**3.01**	**3.19**
Get experiences that prepare you for a				
future career		3.31	3.29	3.35
Behavioral Beliefs				
Institutional Goals				
Develop leadership skills	4	2.01	2.18	2.33
Develop self-discipline	4	2.23	2.40	2.56
Do something for your country	4	2.11	2.29	2.39
Work as part of a team	4	2.06	2.12	2.30
Occupational Goals				
Have a good paying job	4	1.56	1.69	1.84
Get money for education	4	2.09	2.29	2.49
Learn a valuable trade or skill	4	1.88	1.98	2.12
Get experiences that prepare you for a				
future career	4	1.69	1.88	2.16
		(N = 582)	(N = 1,023)	(N = 395)

1—Means across row significantly different at the .01 level.
2—Means across row significantly different at the .02 level.
3—Means across row significantly different at the .05 level.
4—Means across row significantly different at the .001 level.

TABLE 17.6

2001—Outcome Evaluation and Behavioral Belief Correlations
With Intention to Enlist in the Military Across Level of Consideration

	Level of Consideration		
Outcome Evaluations	*Never*	*Some*	*Serious*
Institutional Goals			
Develop leadership skills	−.01	−.02	**.16**
Develop self-discipline	.00	−.01	**.22**
Do something for your country	**.15**	**.17**	**.26**
Work as part of a team	**.12**	**.15**	**.18**
Occupational Goals			
Have a good paying job	.01	.02	09
Get money for education	.01	−.03	**.14**
Learn a valuable trade or skill	.02	.06	.08
Get experiences that prepare you for			
a future career	−.07	−.06	.09
Behavioral Beliefs			
Institutional Goals			
Develop leadership skills	.08	**.14**	**.28**
Develop self-discipline	.06	**.13**	**.16**
Do something for your country	**.11**	**.13**	**.28**
Work as part of a team	.06	**.10**	**.21**
Occupational Goals			
Have a good paying job	**.15**	**.15**	**.28**
Get money for education	.04	.07	**.24**
Learn a valuable trade or skill	**.12**	**.16**	**.23**
Get experiences that prepare you for			
a future career	.09	**.22**	**.30**
	(*N* = 582)	(*N* = 1,023)	(*N* = 395)

Correlations in bold significantly greater than .0 at the .01 level.

Table 17.6 focuses on 2001 and contrasts the correlations of the outcome evaluations and behavioral beliefs with attitude toward the military across the three levels of consideration of military service. Interestingly, it is the outcome evaluations and behavioral beliefs associated with the institutional goals that once again show the strongest correlations with a favorable view of the military. In particular, the goal of "do something for your country" shows the strongest correlation with attitude toward the military at all three levels of consideration. The pattern of increasing association for the behavioral beliefs once again reflects what might be expected when contrasting groups, based on how seriously they have considered a possible action.

Message Strategy Development.   Developers of advertising message strategies could draw a variety of conclusions from the information in Table 17.1 through Table 17.6. Occupational concerns such as acquisition of job skills and career preparation have been common advertising themes in military advertising since the inception of the All Volunteer Force in 1975 (Sackett & Mavor, 2003). In 1999, as shown in Table 17.1, the value of the occupational approach to message strategy development is indicated by the greater importance of the occupational goals, with a grand mean of 3.2, versus the institutional goals, with a grand mean of 3.0. However, the correlations for both outcome evaluations and behavioral beliefs with attitude toward military service point to the "institutional" goals as the area with the greatest potential for "associational readiness" concerning information about military service. This is a different message strategy than those employed by the military at that time. However, as shown in Table 17.3, the media priming following the events of September 2001 established a more widespread set of goals that were seen as associated with military service. This evolution in the information context presented a greater potential for developing a variety of options for message strategies. Similarly, the pattern of the results for behavioral beliefs shown in the lower portion of Table 17.5 also indicate the relative strength of the institutional goals when contrasted with occupational goals.

The pattern of correlations shown in Table 17.6 leads one to consider institutional goals as possibly the most productive belief area for the development of advertising message strategies in support of military recruitment. Indeed, the relative size of the correlations for "do something for your country" indicate that this is the belief area with the strongest potential for elaboration (or central processing). Coupled with the lower mean for the outcome evaluation for "do something for your country" (see Table 17.2), there appears to be high potential for such a message strategy direction as a means of increasing youth interest in the possibility of military service.

CONCLUSIONS

In this chapter, four theoretical perspectives were used to explore the interrelationships among a grouping of beliefs related to youth interest in military service and their implications in the development of advertising message strategies. The availability of a complete set of the variables of interest in two national surveys provided for a broader view of the relationships among the theoretical perspectives, and the results demonstrated the importance of triangulating theoretical perspectives in the development of more effective advertising message strategies. For example, the data analyzed for this article showed that it would be a mistake to rely solely on mean belief values from the TRA model of attitude change to develop advertising message strategies. The mean values of the outcome evaluations and behavioral beliefs must be viewed in the light of the correlations of these variables with the attitude object in question. These correlations appear to be reflective of the salience of the beliefs in a "mental network" of belief and intention associations that point to the areas of greatest potential for elaboration or central processing on the part of message recipients who are at differing stages in a consideration process. It is the concept of association (correlation) between beliefs and attitudes that appears to be the linkage among the four theoretical perspectives and the area in which each theory might be productively developed. Moreover, the timing of the two national surveys demonstrate how dramatic events can reshape the critical information environment of the audiences of interest and underscore the value of systematic yearly assessment of the relationships among beliefs and intentions.

REFERENCES

Ajzen, I., & Fishbein, M. (1980). *Understanding attitudes and predicting social behavior.* Englewood Cliffs, NJ: Prentice-Hall.

Chen, S., & Chaiken, S. (1999). The heuristic-systematic model in its broader context. In S. Chaiken & Y. Trope (Eds.), *Dual-process theories in social psychology* (pp. 73–96). New York: Guilford.

Fishbein, M., & Ajzen, I. (1975). *Belief, attitude, intention, and behavior: An introduction to theory and research.* Reading, MA: Addison-Wesley.

Fishbein, M., & Yzer, M. C. (2003). Using theory to design effective health behavior interventions. *Communication Theory, 13*(2), 164–181.

Guilford, J. P. (1954). *Psychometric methods.* New York: McGraw-Hill.

Howard, J. R., & Sheth, J. N. (1969). *The theory of buyer behavior.* New York: Wiley.

Kardes, F. R., Kalyanaram, G., Chandrashekaran, M., & Dornoff, R. J. (1993). Brand retrieval, consideration set composition, consumer choice, and the pioneering advantage. *Journal of Consumer Research, 20*, 62–75.

Moskos, C. C., & Wood, F. R. (1988). *The military: More than just a job?* New York: Pergamon-Brassey's.

Nedungadi, P. (1990). Recall and consumer consideration sets: Influencing choice without altering brand evaluations. *Journal of Consumer Research, 17*, 263–276.

Norins, H. (1990). *The Young & Rubicam traveling creative workshop.* Englewood Cliffs, NJ: Prentice-Hall.

Overholser, C. E., & Kline, J. M. (1975). Advertising strategy from consumer research. In D. A. Aaker (Ed.), *Advertising management: Practical perspectives* (pp. 80–88). Englewood Cliffs, NJ: Prentice-Hall.

Petty, R. E., & Cacioppo, J. T. (1986). The Elaboration Likelihood Model of persuasion. In L. Berkowitz (Ed.), *Advances in experimental psychology* (pp. 123–205). San Diego, CA: Academic Press.

Petty, R. E., Cacioppo, J. T., & Schumann, D. (1983). Central and peripheral routes to advertising effectiveness: The moderating role of involvement. *Journal of Consumer Research, 10*, 135–146.

Price, V., & Tewksbury, D. (1997). New values and public opinion: A theoretical account of media priming and framing. In G. A. Barnett & F. J. Boster (Eds.), *Progress in communication sciences* (pp. 173–212). Greenwich, CT: Ablex.

Priester, J. R., Dhananjay, N., Fleming, M. A., & Godek, J. (2004). The A^{2}SC^2 model: The influences of attitudes and attitude strength on consideration and choice. *Journal of Consumer Research, 30*, 574–587.

Roberts, J. H., & Lattin, J. M. (1991). Development and testing of a model of consideration set composition. *Journal of Marketing Research, 28*, 429–440.

Sackett, P. R., & Mavor, A. S. (2003). *Attitudes, aptitudes, and aspirations of American youth: Implications for military recruitment.* Washington, DC: The National Academy Press.

Shah, D. V., Kwak, N., Schmierbach, M., & Zubric, J. (2004). The interplay of news frames on cognitive complexity. *Human Communication Research, 30*(1), 102–120.

Shrum, L. J., Wyer, R. S., & O'Guinn, T. C. (1998). The effects of television consumption on social perceptions: The use of priming procedures to investigate social processes. *Journal of Consumer Research, 24*, 447–458.

Smith, E. R., & DeCoster, J. (2000). Dual-process models in social and cognitive psychology: Conceptual integration and links to underlying memory systems. *Personality and Social Psychology Review, 4*(2), 108–113.

CHAPTER EIGHTEEN

The Promise of Sociocognitive Consumer Psychology

Paul M. Herr
University of Colorado

Jacques Nantel
HEC Montréal

Frank R. Kardes
University of Cincinnati

As this volume illustrates, the field of social cognition has contributed a great deal to the field of consumer psychology. Sociocognitive psychological theories, paradigms, and methodologies are used routinely by consumer psychologists to the benefit of their field. Furthermore, the field of sociocognitive consumer psychology contributes to social cognition by investigating new mediating and moderating variables that influence the processing of information about products and services, and by testing the influence of these variables in a critically important context: the consumer judgment and decision-making context. This everyday context is important because it is frequently encountered by nearly all individuals and because decisions made in this context are consequential: Billions of dollars are at stake and decisions made in this context have a major impact on the global economy.

Most of the chapters in this volume build on Wyer's pathbreaking work on social information processing (Wyer, 1974, 2004; Wyer & Carlston, 1979; Wyer & Srull, 1989). In chapter 1 of this volume, Wyer summarizes his most recent work on this topic and integrates sociocognitive psychological research and behavioral decision research in a unified consumer information-processing model. Historically, researchers in the former camp pursued a theory-driven research agenda, whereas researchers in the latter camp pursued a phenomenon-driven research agenda. Although researchers in both camps studied similar topics, most researchers in one camp ignored research conducted in the other camp to the detriment of both camps. Wyer reviews evidence demonstrating that both camps study similar psychological processes and phenomena, and that the sociocognitive camp tends to focus on early stages of information processing (i.e., attention, comprehension, memory, judgment) and that the behavioral decision-research camp tends to focus on the last stage of information processing (i.e., choice). Wyer also shows that different psychological processes are involved when consumers focus on a single alternative (e.g., noncomparative judgment involving one brand or one product) as opposed to multiple alternatives (e.g., comparative judgment involving many brands or products).

The importance of single-alternative versus multiple-alternative decisions is also emphasized by Posavac et al. (chap. 2), who show that selective information processing is more likely for single- than for multiple-alternative decisions. One important consequence of selective information processing is the *brand positivity effect*, or the tendency to overvalue a focal brand. Another consequence is the tendency to overestimate the strength of the relationship between price and quality. Yet another consequence is the tendency of managers to overestimate the effectiveness of a focal marketing strategy. All of these consequences are reduced when consumers or managers compare multiple alternatives. However, noncomparative, single-alternative decisions are surprisingly common. In fact, heavy-handed experimental instructions telling people to compare multiple alternatives are often needed to induce comparative judgment processes (Wang & Wyer, 2002).

Silvera and Laufer (chap. 3) review several attribution theories (Heider, Jones, Kelley, and Weiner) from social cognition and show how they have been applied to consumer psychology. The most extensively used model in consumer psychology is Weiner's model, and Silvera and Laufer extend Weiner's model by integrating this model with Gilbert's work on *correspondence bias*, or the tendency to overestimate the causal role of dispositional influences on behavior. Specifically, they show how the lack of awareness of situational constraints, unrealistic expectations, overly broad behavioral categories, and insufficient adjustment influence judgments of the locus of causality. They also show how inferences about stability influence expectations of success or failure and feelings of hope or fear, whereas inferences about controllability influence judgments of responsibility and blame and feelings of anger toward the manufacturer of a substandard product.

Machin and Fitzsimons (chap. 4) show how asking questions leads consumers to create opinions that would not have occurred to them otherwise (the *mere measurement effect*). These opinions then take on a life of their own and influence other related judgments and responses. The mere measurement effect has been observed in a wide variety of settings, including studies of volunteering, voting, name generation, automobile shopping, and financial services shopping. When a focal alternative is moderately favorable, the mere measurement effect often inflates evaluations and intentions, and this encourages consumers to buy products that they normally would not buy. Moreover, consumers are often unaware of the presence or the consequences of the mere measurement effect.

Chandrashekaran et al. (chap. 5) review research on their JUMP (Judgment Uncertainty and Magnitude Parameters) model that simultaneously captures and isolates the independent effects of judgmental uncertainty and extremity on behavior. They also present the results of a new study of consumer trust, loyalty, and word-of-mouth communications, and show that the JUMP model effectively separates the determinants of judgmental uncertainty and extremity both across and within individual consumers.

Tietje and Brunel (chap. 6) summarize recent developments concerning the Implicit Association Test (IAT) and their implications for branding strategy. They also develop a unified theory of branding that integrates sociocognitive psychological research on associative networks, implicit attitudes, stereotypes, self-esteem, and the self-concept with consumer psychological research on brand associations, brand evaluations, brand awareness, brand image, brand equity, brand personality, brand relationships, brand extensions, and brand alliances.

March and Woodside (chap. 7) review research on planned and unplanned purchases, and show that unplanned purchases are surprisingly common. They explore the nexus between planned and actual behaviors by examining the variables that influence intentions and behavior, whether they are planned or unplanned and whether the behavior is performed or not performed. March and Woodside also provide strategic insights into how marketing strategists can segment their market more efficiently and communicate information more effectively to their intended customers.

Markman and Brendl (chap. 8) review research on the *devaluation effect*, or the tendency to devalue objects unrelated to focal goals. Hungry consumers devalue nonfood products and objects, and nicotine-deprived consumers devalue noncigarette products and objects. Surprisingly, both groups of consumers devalue money even though money can be used to buy food and cigarettes. Markman and Brendl also show there is a continuum of object-relatedness to a focal goal, and devaluation increases as relatedness decreases. These results are interpreted as consistent with the implication of Kruglanski et al.'s (2002) theory of goal systems.

Chun and Kruglanski (chap. 9) also build on Kruglanski et al.'s (2002) theory of *goal systems*. Consumers who are high in the need for cognitive closure wish to reach solutions to cognitive problems as quickly as possible ("seizing") and to continue to use these solutions as long as possible ("freezing") because seizing and freezing facilitate closure (Kruglanski & Webster, 1996). One way to reach closure quickly and to avoid spending a lot of time making many purchase decisions is to buy one multipurpose product. Consistent with this hypothesis, Chun and Kruglanski show that multipurpose products (in several domains) are preferred more strongly by consumers who are high (vs. low) in the need for cognitive closure.

Kardes et al. (chap. 10) show how implementation intentions can be used to increase new product consumption. Implementation intentions link intentions to perform a behavior (e.g., to use a new product) to the contexts in which the behavior is expected to be performed (e.g., when, where, and how the new product will be used) and to preplanned sequences of responses needed to implement the behavior. When these associations in memory are sufficiently strong, encountering a relevant context automatically primes the appropriate response and increases intention-behavior correspondence.

Florack et al. (chap. 11) show how promotion versus prevention regulatory focus influences consumer preferences. Higgins' (1998, 2002) *regulatory focus theory* suggests that a promotion focus emphasizes hopes and aspirations and heightens concerns about approaching desired end states, whereas a *prevention focus* emphasizes duties and responsibilities and heightens concerns about avoiding undesired end states. This sociocognitive psychological model has been applied to many topics in consumer psychology (e.g., persuasion, tastes and preferences, cross-cultural consumer research). Florack et al. show that promotion priming increases the influence of promotion-oriented claims in noncelebrity advertising, whereas prevention priming increases the influence of prevention-oriented claims in celebrity advertising. Their results highlight the importance of matching persuasive messages to the regulatory goals of consumers.

Strahan et al. (chap. 12) show that subliminal priming procedures enhance persuasion when primed goals match currently accessible goals. Dimofte and Yalch (chap. 13) demonstrate that advertising can be effective even when consumers do not believe advertised claims. As noted, this yields profound public-policy implications that a traditional analysis (devoid of social cognition) would miss. Mazzocco et al. (chap. 14) review evidence demonstrating that advertising can be effective even when consumers are unable to remember critical details conveyed in advertised messages. The authors' analysis provides a much-needed critical questioning of what ought to be measured in assessing advertising effects and effectiveness. In work reminiscent of the "sleeper effect," Goodstein et al. (chap. 15) show that negative comparative advertising can backfire initially but can have more desirable consequences later with the passage of time. The basis for the effect appears to be a faster decay of the negative cognitions linked to the sponsor of the negative ads than the negative attitude toward the target engendered by the ad.

Yoon and Vargas (chap. 16) show how counterfactual reasoning can alter the way consumers interpret the prices of products. A specific price can seem high or low depending on the price one usually pays for a product or service. When a price is higher than expected (e.g., the price of gas), consumers experience anger or regret and these feelings are intensified by *counterfactual thinking* or "what if" thinking (e.g., "What if I filled up yesterday?"). When a price is lower than expected, consumers experience relief or satisfaction and these feelings can also be intensified by counterfactual thinking. Yoon and Vargas applied Kahneman and Miller's (1986) norm theory to studies of furniture shopping and online shopping and developed a causal inference model of the effects of counterfactual thinking in low- and in high-involvement situations.

In the preceding chapter, Eighmey and Siu (chap. 17) show how several socio-cognitive psychological models—including dual-process models, the theory of reasoned action, media priming, and consideration set processes—influence a highly consequential decision. Namely, the decision to devote years of one's life to the service of one's country.

Collectively, the chapters demonstrate the power of the social cognition paradigm in consumer psychology. With its focus on process rather than simply end states, we not only may determine the existence of a particular phenomenon, but may provide an answer to "how" the phenomenon occurs as well. This answer fuels both theoretical and practical fires. We now turn to the promise of social cognition: What interesting unanswered questions may the paradigm be uniquely capable of answering? We admit the answer may be highly subjective. Nonetheless, we devote the remainder of this chapter to briefly identifying areas that we believe would benefit from the application of the social cognition paradigm.

Given the broad waterfront covered by marketing in general and consumer psychology in particular, it should not be surprising for us to claim that the potential for social cognition advances in these domains is vast. Space constraints prohibit us from describing the advances already made by this approach; it is sufficient here to note that all traditional areas of marketing have been touched by work that addresses how consumers and decision makers process information. We suggest that each traditional division of marketing may benefit from further work that addresses the following:

CHANNELS

Because much of the channels literature deals with understanding and structuring the supply chain, a better knowledge of how decision makers mentally represent power relations, and the influence of different mental representations on subsequent negotiations and behavior may lead to better informed supply chain decisions. Moreover, by examining the mental representations and behavior of consumers, more efficient channels may be created, and the overall evolution of channels may be better predicted.

PROMOTION

Social cognition has perhaps been most applied to the area of promotion. Additional work is needed, however, to more fully understand consumer responses to advertising, sales promotions, direct marketing, and other communication strategies, as well as to better understand the communication strategies employed by consumers in their response to marketer's efforts. As work in the present volume notes, a simple focus on the end state of persuasion misses the point. By identifying the intervening processes (both implicit and explicit) between exposure to communication and consumer behavior we are in a much stronger position to understand exactly what it means to be persuaded.

PRODUCT

A social cognitive approach can lead to a much richer understanding of product design, branding, consumer use and nonuse of package labels, and a host of other product-related issues. Much of what academics have told branding practitioners, for example, rests on the belief that brand-associations are important, and help determine the value of a brand. Although this is an unarguable truism, it lacks power in informing good brand management (aside from the injunction to avoid negative associations and foster positive associations). Of considerably more use is a science that tells managers how such associations come into being, may be strengthened and weakened in a coherent memory and perceptual system, and are used by consumers in their product choice decisions. Although parts of this work exist, and the beginning of such a theory is described in this volume, a coherent sociocognitive theory of branding is sorely lacking. Such a theory has implications both for the management and consumption of brands.

PRICE

Much of the work in pricing stems from the older adaptation level and social judgment literatures (e.g., Helson, 1964; M. Sherif & C. W. Sherif, 1967). Although this work is clearly informative and important, it too lacks the power that is reflected in the work in this volume, and a more general theory of consumer response to and use of prices.

CODA

In their Society for Consumer Psychology presidential addresses, two of the three authors of this chapter called for a more scientifically rigorous field of consumer psychology that is responsive to the concerns of practitioners (Herr, 2003; Kardes, 1996). In our opinion, this volume contributes to this agenda, to the benefit of both scientists and practitioners. The chapters in this volume demonstrate that rigorous consumer information-processing models can be applied to consumer-focused strategy.

However, we recognize that many practitioners will be unable to fully appreciate the contributions of this volume because many practitioners prefer to think in concrete terms and, consequently, prefer to avoid thinking about abstract concepts

(Kardes, 1996). Everyday time pressures and deadlines heighten the need for closure and increase the preference for concrete thought. This is unfortunate because recent research shows that concrete thinking impedes creativity (Forster, Friedman, & Liberman, 2004). For misguided reasons, many practitioners also choose to ignore scientific research involving undergraduate participants (Kardes, 1996). This, too, is unfortunate because recent research shows that studies involving undergraduates are highly generalizable to other samples (Anderson, Lindsay, & Bushman, 1999). Specifically, the effect sizes of laboratory studies involving undergraduate participants and field studies involving a wide range of nonundergraduate participants and a wide range of manipulations and measures were highly correlated ($r = .73$).

Although this chapter has all the earmarks of a call for a grand unified theory of sociocognitive consumer behavior, such is not our intent. We believe the odds of such a theory being "successful" fall somewhere between slim and none. That said, the pursuit of a grand theory would not be without benefit, as the individual pieces that emerge (as in this volume) would likely contribute significantly both to a better understanding of consumer psychology and marketing, as well as to the boundaries of our knowledge of consumer responses to marketing efforts. Perhaps more importantly, the pursuit of a grand theory may well lead to the reduction of what appear to be arbitrary boundaries between investigations of individual marketing mix variables, and fostering work that addresses the impact of the entire marketing mix on consumer psychology and that provides a foundation for the designing and building effective consumer-focused strategies.

REFERENCES

Anderson, C. A., Lindsay, J. J., & Bushman, B. J. (1999). Research in the psychological laboratory: Truth or triviality? *Current Directions in Psychological Science, 8*, 3–9.

Forster, J., Friedman, R. S., & Liberman, N. (2004). Temporal construal effects on abstract and concrete thinking: Consequences for insight and creative cognition. *Journal of Personality and Social Psychology, 87*, 177–189.

Helson, H. (1964). *Adaptation-level theory: An experimental and systematic approach to behavior*. New York: McGraw-Hill.

Herr, P. M. (2003). On avoiding the fate of the league of semi-superheroes: Consumer psychology and heroic research. *Journal of Consumer Psychology, 13*, 362–365.

Higgins, E. T. (1998). Promotion and prevention: Regulatory focus as a motivational principle. In M. P. Zanna (Ed.), *Advances in experimental social psychology* (Vol. 30, pp. 1–46). San Diego, CA: Academic Press.

Higgins, E. T. (2002). How self-regulation creates distinct values: The case of promotion and prevention decision making. *Journal of Consumer Psychology, 12*, 177–191.

Kahneman, D., & Miller, D. (1986). Norm theory: Comparing reality to its alternatives. *Psychological Review, 93*, 136–153.

Kardes, F. R. (1996). In defense of experimental consumer psychology. *Journal of Consumer Psychology, 5*, 279–296.

Kruglanski, A. W., Shah, J. Y., Fishbach, A., Friedman, R., Chun, W. Y., & Keppler, D. S. (2002). A theory of goal system. In M. P. Zanna (Ed.), *Advances in experimental social psychology* (Vol. 34, pp. 331–376). New York: Academic Press.

Kruglanski, A. W., & Webster, D. M. (1996). Motivated closing of the mind: "Seizing" and "freezing." *Psychological Review, 103,* 263–283.

Sherif, M., & Sherif, C. W. (Eds.). (1967). *Attitude, ego-involvement, and change.* New York: Wiley.

Wang, J., & Wyer, R. S. (2002). Comparative judgment processes: The effects of task objectives and time delay on product evaluations. *Journal of Consumer Psychology, 12,* 327–340.

Wyer, R. S. (1974). *Cognitive organization and change: An information processing approach.* Hillsdale, NJ: Lawrence Erlbaum Associates.

Wyer, R. S. (2004). *Social comprehension and judgment: The role of situation models, narratives, and implicit theories.* Mahwah, NJ: Lawrence Erlbaum Associates.

Wyer, R. S., & Carlston, D. E. (1979). *Social cognition, inference, and attribution.* Hillsdale, NJ: Lawrence Erlbaum Associates.

Wyer, R. S., & Srull, T. K. (1989). *Memory and cognition in its social context.* Hillsdale, NJ: Lawrence Erlbaum Associates.

Author Index

Subject Index

A

Advertisements
 consumer behavior and, 300, 302–305, 308–312
 evaluation of, 300–311
 reception of, 299, 301–305
Advertising, *see also* Persuasion
 ad repetition, 304
 comparative, 47
 consumer selective processing and, 47
 false positive information and, 284–288
 implementation intentions and, 231
 issue of lying in, 294–295
 negative, 319–329
 product information and, 282–283
 regulatory focus theory and, 242–245, 256–257, 258–259
 unintelligible messages, 303
Advertising effectiveness
 advertising effects and, 297–298, 300
 defining, 299–300
 implications of divergence between measures of, 312–313
 measuring behavior, 311–312
 measuring evaluative responses, 306–311
 measuring reception, 301–305
 as return on investment, 297
Advertising effects
 advertising effectiveness and, 297–298, 300
 behavioral responses, 300, 311–312
 evaluative responses, 300, 306–311

general constructs, 298
 implications of divergence between constructs, 312–313
 reception, 299, 301–305
Advertising messages, 357
Advertising message strategies
 complementary roles of conceptual models in, 357–368
 consumer surveys and, 353
 importance of linking theoretical perspectives in, 368–369
 for military advertising, 367–368
 overview of, 354
 theoretical approaches to, 354–357
 youth interest in military service case study, 359–368
Affect
 categorization and, 17–19
 confirmation processes, 19–20
 consumer judgment and, 15–22
 spontaneous appraisals of products and, 20–21
Affect transfer, 149
American Marketing Association, 91
Anchoring, 85
Appreciation, 28
Asian cultures, 12–13, 15
Associations, 357–358, 359, 369
Association strength, 137
Attitude(s), 138, *see also* Brand attitudes
 certainty, 309–310
 change, 302–305